A Life of Alexander Campbell

Douglas A. Foster

WILLIAM B. EERDMANS PUBLISHING COMPANY
GRAND RAPIDS, MICHIGAN

Wm. B. Eerdmans Publishing Co.
4035 Park East Court SE, Grand Rapids, Michigan 49546
www.eerdmans.com

26 25 24 23 22 21 20   1 2 3 4 5 6 7

ISBN 978-0-8028-7633-1

Library of Congress Cataloging-in-Publication Data

Names: Foster, Douglas A. (Douglas Allen), 1952– author.
Title: A life of Alexander Campbell / Douglas A. Foster.
Description: Grand Rapids, Michigan : William B. Eerdmans Publishing Company,
    2020. | Series: Library of religious biography | Includes bibliographical references and
    index. | Summary: "A biography of Alexander Campbell, one of the founders of the
    Stone-Campbell Movement"—Provided by publisher.
Identifiers: LCCN 2019042743 | ISBN 9780802876331 (paperback)
Subjects: LCSH: Campbell, Alexander, 1788-1866.
Classification: LCC BX7343.C2 F67 2020 | DDC 286.6092 [B]—dc23
LC record available at https://lccn.loc.gov/2019042743

"Douglas Foster successfully illuminates the real and seeming contradictions of this complex nineteenth-century leader's inflexible teaching of baptism and the Holy Spirit, recognition of the genuine Christianity of persons who did not share his views, and relationships with persons whom he viewed as opponents or threats to his program to advance God's coming reign of peace and justice that was to begin in the United States."

— D. NEWELL WILLIAMS
Brite Divinity School

"Foster's monumental biography of Alexander Campbell presents students of the Stone-Campbell Movement with the distilled judgments of an eminent and prolific historian of the tradition. The book teems with fresh insights into Campbell's stormy Scots-Irish background, his shaping as a charismatic controversialist on the American frontier, his interpretation of the 'American Dream' and of the labor of restoring the 'ancient order of things' therein, and the curious chemistry of liberalism and legalism in his agenda for Christian unity. Foster contextualizes Campbell without simply reducing him to a 'product of his times' and reveals his complex character as a religious reformer in interactions with friends and nemeses alike. Furthermore, Foster brilliantly reveals the heights scaled by Campbell in American Protestant culture while also exposing the epic failure of his response to chattel slavery in his program to reform American society along Christian lines. This will doubtless be the definitive biography of Alexander Campbell for many years to come."

— PAUL M. BLOWERS
Emmanuel Christian Seminary at Milligan College

"What a debt of gratitude we owe to Doug Foster for providing students of American Religion with such a clear, concise, and comprehensive biography of Alexander Campbell. What a blessing!"

— EDWARD ROBINSON
Texas College

LIBRARY OF RELIGIOUS BIOGRAPHY

Mark A. Noll, Kathryn Gin Lum, and Heath W. Carter, series editors

Long overlooked by historians, religion has emerged in recent years as a key factor in understanding the past. From politics to popular culture, from social struggles to the rhythms of family life, religion shapes every story. Religious biographies open a window to the sometimes surprising influence of religion on the lives of influential people and the worlds they inhabited.

The Library of Religious Biography is a series that brings to life important figures in United States history and beyond. Grounded in careful research, these volumes link the lives of their subjects to the broader cultural contexts and religious issues that surrounded them. The authors are respected historians and recognized authorities in the historical period in which their subject lived and worked.

Marked by careful scholarship yet free of academic jargon, the books in this series are well-written narratives meant to be read and enjoyed as well as studied.

Titles include:

*The Miracle Lady: **Katherine Kuhlman** and the Transformation of Charismatic Christianity* by Amy Collier Artman

***George Whitefield**: Evangelist for God and Empire* by Peter Y. Choi

***Abraham Lincoln**: Redeemer President* by Allen C. Guelzo

*One Soul at a Time: The Story of **Billy Graham*** by Grant Wacker

For a complete list of published volumes, see the back of this volume.

To my wife, Linda.
Thank you for your constant love,
encouragement, patience, and support.

Alexander Campbell (1788–1866) in the hexagonal brick study where he did most of his writing. He wanted the study, built in 1832, near but separate from the house so his work would not be disturbed. This photo was taken in 1858. Used with permission from Bethany College, T. W. Phillips Memorial Library, Archives and Special Collections, Bethany, West Virginia.

Few can enter into the feelings and labors of one who has to write. By the time we have got ourselves up to the writing point upon any subject, and have got the oil melted on the wheels of the mind, the fastidious taste of the times whispers in our ear, "This is as much as we can bear, in one sitting, on this subject: let us have something else." One says, "This is too long;" another, "It is too short;" and a third, "It is out of place." Thus is the mind impeded in its career, and half the time lost in taking off one set of harnesses and in gearing it anew for another car. However, none but authors know the pangs of our travails, and therefore we can expect no sympathy from readers. All we ask is forgiveness when they think we sin against their wishes and taste.

—Alexander Campbell, "A Dozen of Apologies in One," 1832

CONTENTS

Section One: Formation

Section Two: Creation

Section Three: Defense and Conflict

Section Four: Surrender

Section Five: Legacy

Scotch-Irish reformer Alexander Campbell has always had a problematic reputation in American Christian history. In his own day, many Christian leaders condemned him for heresy and exclusivist attacks on the legitimacy of their Christian traditions. "Campbellism" became the derisive label for his ideas and movement. His own religious descendants in bodies known as Churches of Christ, Disciples of Christ, and Christian Churches have been ambiguous about his significance in the creation of their theologies and practices. Very few members of churches in the Campbell heritage today know much about him or think he has significance for their beliefs and practices. True, some always saw him as an important pioneer who recaptured vital Christian truths that had been obscured or ignored. But most who cited his work at all did so selectively to promote their own agendas—whether embracing his rationalistic restoration principles that seemed to justify religious exclusivism or his ecumenical and progressive statements that challenged that very attitude.

A prime example is his doctrine of baptism. The teaching that immersion of believers for remission of sin was the only true Christian baptism was at the core of his reform. Out of that conviction he advocated closed membership in the congregations of his movement. Yet he stated forcefully and unequivocally during a crisis in his reform in the 1830s that it was the height of sectarianism to claim that only the immersed were Christians. Few in the history of the Stone-Campbell Movement were stronger advocates of believers' immersion than Alexander Campbell. Yet he did not make it the invariable act of Christian identity—a failure that has led to consternation in many of his theological descendants then and now.

Campbell possessed an impressive intellect. He was a curious and voracious reader, an incisive thinker, and a person of significant organizational and communication skills. He was also indefatigable. He maintained an unrelenting schedule of work—writing, publishing, preaching, teaching, debating, running a large agricultural operation, as well as founding and leading an institution of higher learning. His travel was nothing short of extraordinary, given the modes of transportation of the day. He traveled widely every year from the 1810s to the 1860s, often for months at a time. In 1847, when almost sixty, he made a six-month tour of Britain and France, his only "foreign" trip (except to Canada) after arriving in America. While he increasingly complained of fatigue and "dyspepsia" in letters home, he kept on the move, right up to the outbreak of the Civil War.

An underlying conviction contributing to this relentless drive was his millennial faith that God had prepared America for a special work—one he believed included his reform agenda. His worldview involved a specific understanding of how that reform would progress—starting with what he labeled "a restoration of the ancient gospel and order of things." His program depended on the rise of America's power and influence, something he believed was part of God's providential working. Though this positive view of his adopted country waxed and waned during his life, he became very protective of that vision, especially when threatened by challenges from enemies and colleagues alike, and by the menace of slavery and national disunion. The elitist attitudes he brought with him from Ireland led easily to his full embrace of American white supremacist ideology and his conviction that whites and blacks could never live together as equals.

Many popular interpretations of Campbell during his lifetime and afterward painted him as a cold rationalist, intent only on ferreting out the "facts" of Scripture in order to reconstruct the "Christian System." This he understood as a list of propositions to be believed and commands to be obeyed.[1] There is no question that Alexander Campbell was thoroughly rational and often systematic. Constant pressure to produce huge amounts of text for his papers, debates, and books, however, sometimes resulted in writing that was not very succinct or sharp. Nevertheless, at his best he was capable of assessing tremendous amounts of data, then developing and communicating his ideas persuasively.

Yet the accusation that he believed intellectual assent to facts was the

---

1. The reputation was widespread even in his day. The eastern Christians strongly rejected the union of Barton W. Stone's Christian movement with the Campbell reformers. See Barton W. Stone's defense of Campbell against accusations made by the editor of the *Christian Palladium* in "Brother Badger," *Christian Messenger*, May 1835, 106–11.

essence of Christianity is a misreading of Campbell and his theology. Though his Lunenburg letter articles of 1837 were not a systematic treatment of his views of salvation and were arguably a departure from his main doctrinal focus, they provide one of the most moving expressions of Campbell's core beliefs.

While he insisted that immersion of believers was the baptism of the New Testament, he rejected the idea that one's submission to baptism—or to any other commandment—achieved salvation. Anyone who intentionally disregarded an ordinance of Christ like immersion could not be a Christian, he insisted. Yet he expressed his conviction that it was wrong to claim that if someone "mistook the meaning of any institution, while in his soul he desired to know the whole will of God, he must perish forever." Something else was key. "It is the image of Christ the Christian looks for and loves; and this does not consist in being exact in a few items, but in general devotion to the whole truth as far as known."[2]

While he readily admitted that the name Christian was first given only to immersed believers, "we do not think that it was given to them because they were immersed, but because they had put on Christ." Just as Paul said in Romans 2 that there were "*inward*" and "*outward*" Jews, he believed it was just as possible to have the same with Christians. "Can a person who simply, not perversely, *mistakes* the outward baptism, have the inward? I answer that, in my opinion, *it is possible*."[3]

For Campbell, inward transformation manifested by the image of Christ in the believer's life was the confirmation of one's Christian identity. He never budged from urging "faith, repentance and baptism upon all, as essential to their constitutional citizenship in the Messiah's kingdom, and to their sanctification and comfort as Christians."[4] Yet he believed that a person whose life was shaped like Christ was the true Christian.

These themes remained consistent throughout Campbell's life, though his focus was almost always on believers' immersion for the remission of sins as the embodiment of the gospel. Even in his classic work *Christian Baptism* published in 1851, Campbell insisted that anyone trying to be justified by works was not in a state of mind to be justified by the blood of Christ or the grace of God. "To justify a man for any work of which he is capable, would be

2. Alexander Campbell, "Any Christians among Protestant Parties," *Millennial Harbinger*, September 1837, 412, 414.

3. Alexander Campbell, "Christians among the Sects," *Millennial Harbinger*, November 1837, 507.

4. Campbell, "Christians among the Sects," 508.

to confirm him in carnality, selfishness and pride. But convinced, humbled, emptied of himself, and learning, through faith in the gospel, that God has provided a ransom for the ruined, the wretched, and the undone, he gladly accepts pardon through sovereign mercy, and humbles himself to a state of absolute dependence on the merits and mercy of another."[5]

At the end of the book he reiterated that being buried in baptism does not "make void either law or gospel, but establish[es] and confirm[s] both."[6] This central theme held in tension the pieces of his theology of salvation and the church, a tension that would be played out during his entire life.

Campbell, like all human beings, was complex. Though his core commitments appeared early and continued to influence the development of his theology, his thought grew and evolved in response to life experiences. At times he appeared clearly self-contradictory, even on key theological matters. Figuring out how to understand these apparent contradictions makes the task of the biographer and interpreter a daunting but very interesting one.

Since Campbell's death in 1866, many from within his movement have written accounts that provide details of his career that I will not duplicate here. Two previous biographies in particular chronicle specifics of his life.

The first appeared immediately following Campbell's death in 1866 when his close friend and colleague Robert Richardson published the two-volume *Memoirs of Alexander Campbell*. Richardson's work has significant historical value despite its hagiographical tendency because of his access to documents no longer extant and his detailing of Campbell's life. Eva Jean Wrather, an independent scholar from Nashville, Tennessee, began writing a biography of Campbell in the 1940s that was published after her death in three volumes by Texas Christian University Press between 2005 and 2009. Wrather largely followed Richardson, a characteristic of most other treatments of Campbell. A number of reminiscences or memoirs, many with an apologetic or inspirational purpose, appeared in the late 1800s and 1900s. A renaissance of Campbell studies began in the 1960s as the centennial of his death approached, resulting in specialized studies on specific aspects of Campbell's work.

This volume is neither a chronicle of Campbell's life nor an amassing of data from previous specialized studies. It humbly claims to be a critical biography that assesses principal parts of Campbell's life and thought to

5. Alexander Campbell, *Christian Baptism: With Its Antecedents and Consequents* (Bethany, VA: Alexander Campbell, 1851), 283.

6. Campbell, *Christian Baptism*, 285.

discover something of his significance for American Christianity and the worldwide movement that emerged from his work. The book is organized in five sections, with the second and third the most extensive. The first examines formative influences in Ireland, Scotland, and America that would shape and drive Campbell's career. The second focuses on the creation of his reform agenda, including his convictions on baptism, Scripture, and the millennium. The third and most extensive section details the rise of opposition to his agenda—real or imagined—and his defense of it in conflicts with both enemies and colleagues. Section 4 examines his "surrender" in the final years of his life as he reassessed his vision of America as the God-prepared land. Finally, a brief appraisal of Campbell's legacy closes the study.

This material attempts to reveal, admittedly imperfectly, the core identity of a gifted and determined reformer to whom millions of Christians around the globe today owe much of their identity—whether they know it or not. I pray that this study will open Campbell's life and thought to many who know nothing of him and give those who already know him well something to think about.

DOUGLAS A. FOSTER
July 15, 2019

ACKNOWLEDGMENTS

A project that has gone on as long as this one owes much to many people.

The support and encouragement of Eerdmans Publishing extended the entire length of the project, through the initial possibility of such a volume raised by Reinder Van Til, to the kindness, patience, and professionalism of religious biography series editor David Bratt, and the support of my friend and esteemed fellow scholar, New Testament editor Trevor Thompson. Thank you all.

To my dear cousins Robbie and Hank Davis, who graciously offered two weeks of solitude and writing in their secluded lake house on the beautiful Tennessee River in north Alabama at a crucial time in the evolution of the project, I am deeply grateful.

For the constant backing of my colleagues at Abilene Christian University: fellow teachers who were genuinely interested in the progress of the project and in what I was learning. To College of Biblical Studies Dean Ken Cukrowski and Graduate School of Theology Dean Tim Sensing for willingly allowing me time and space to focus on this task. To Library Dean John Weaver for the constant encouragement and support of this and other historical pursuits and for providing a forum for testing the ideas of several chapters in faculty presentations over the past few years. And to the weekly prayer group that listened to reports for many years—thank you David, John, Jeff, and Kilnam.

To a long line of graduate assistants over the past decade, most recently Mitch East and Austin McCoy, I owe very much. As my GA during the last years of the project's completion, Austin has done extensive and invaluable work to advance the project, from gathering materials and creating bibliographies for specific topics and chapters to doing one of the most crucial and tedious tasks—the checking of footnotes for style and content.

To my friend, brother, and collaborator on many projects through the years, President Newell Williams of Brite Divinity School, I give my heartfelt gratitude. His intimate knowledge of the life of Barton Stone saved me from perpetuating inaccuracies about this important player in the life of Alexander Campbell.

For invaluable insights over many years of research, infectious excitement about the project, and continued friendship well beyond retirement, I am forever grateful to Jeanne Cobb, former archivist at Bethany College. No one alive today knows the details of Alexander Campbell's life as she does. I hope she is not too disappointed with my efforts. In addition, the vital help of two essential collaborators was more of a boost to the completion of the project than they will ever know. Shelley Jacobs, Archivist for the Disciples of Christ Historical Society (now located in Bethany, West Virginia, on the campus of Bethany College), and Sharon Monigold, Archives Librarian for the T. W. Phillips Library of Bethany College, showed themselves to be expert professionals in locating and providing access to many of the photos and illustrations for the book. But beyond their invaluable expertise and assistance, I found them to be genuine friends whom I missed when I left the village of Bethany.

And to my colleague in the Center for Restoration Studies, Mac Ice, for his "last minute" assistance in locating and scanning difficult-to-obtain images for the book I am deeply grateful.

SECTION ONE

Formation

FAREWELL! My dear, my much-lov'd native land!
    For ether scenes on a far distant shore,
Where kind Columbian callies wide expand,
    I now will dare the boist'rous ocean's roar!

Ye freeborn souls, who feel—and feel aright!
    Come, cross with me, the wide, Atlantic main,
With Heaven's aid we'll to the land of light,
    And leave these ravagers th' unpeopl'd plain.

There, far-extending, boundless prospects lie—
    Sweet peace and liberty await us there;
Then why, my friends! My dear companions, why
    Remain in voluntary fetters here?

                —Samuel Thomson, "The Bard's Farewell," 1793

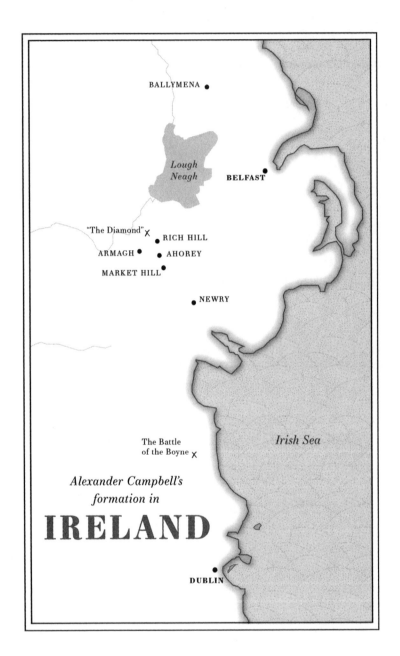

Map of locations in Ireland relating to Alexander Campbell's formation.

CHAPTER 1

The Formation
of Alexander Campbell's Ireland

Alexander Campbell was born September 12, 1788, near Ballymena, County Antrim, in what is today Northern Ireland. His parents were Thomas Campbell, a rising Scotch-Irish Seceder Presbyterian minister, and Jane Corneigle, of Huguenot Reformed descent. Though Alexander would leave Ireland in 1808 at age twenty, returning briefly only once in 1847, what he went through in those early years profoundly shaped him temperamentally, spiritually, and intellectually. These experiences contributed to his commitment to religious reform and formed the basis for his certainty—shared with many before him—that God had prepared America for just such a reform.

Much of what young Alexander experienced was mediated through the life of his minister father, including the church into which Thomas was ordained: the Anti-Burgher Seceder Synod of Ulster. The very name embodied two of the rancorous divisions among Scotch-Irish Presbyterians. Yet the fights that fractured the Church of Scotland and its Irish affiliates were only one set of hostilities wracking his homeland. Clashes—theological and sometimes physical—flared between Protestants and Catholics, between Anglican Protestants and Presbyterian Protestants, and between the fissiparous factions of Presbyterians. While these conflicts may seem at first to be strictly religious, each one was linked to competing political loyalties. The Campbell family faced these realities every day. To begin to make sense of these conflicts and how they shaped the Ireland of Alexander Campbell's youth, we must start with the Protestant Reformation in Scotland.

The Scottish Reformation

The Protestant Reformation came relatively late to Scotland and was a long and violent affair. England and Scotland were distinct kingdoms on the island of Great Britain when Protestantism began. In England the Reformation was under way as early as the 1510s, mainly in the universities through the work of leaders like William Tyndale. Henry VIII's concerns for a male heir played a large part in the progress of the Reformation in England, but true Protestant gains began under his young son Edward VI and his protectors between 1547 and 1553. These gains were partially reversed by Mary Tudor (Bloody Mary) in the mid-1550s but finally came to fruition under Elizabeth I. She oversaw the establishment by 1563 of a Protestant Church of England with the monarch as its "Supreme Governor."[1]

The Reformation in Scotland was a different matter. In England and almost everywhere else, rulers imposed Protestantism on the people. In Scotland, the people and Protestant nobles tried to impose the new religion on the nation against the will of their rulers. The conflict erupted into a bloody civil war that continued for at least four decades, between the 1540s and the 1570s, with all the horrors and deprivations of such conflicts.[2]

The monarchs of Scotland were from the Stuart line, related by blood to the staunchly Roman Catholic French. When James V of Scotland died in 1542, his daughter Mary (Mary Queen of Scots) was crowned queen. But Mary was an infant, so a series of regents actually ran the nation until she was able to do so herself. In 1546, by order of the powerful Catholic leader Cardinal David Beaton, Scottish officials captured Reformation preacher George Wishart and burned him at the stake at Saint Andrews castle.

Later that year, however, Protestants ambushed and murdered Beaton in his room at the castle and took over the fortress. A colleague of Wishart's named John Knox became chief spokesperson for the movement. When French forces arrived in June 1547, they overpowered the Protestants and forced the leaders, including Knox, into galley slavery in the French fleet. When freed nineteen months later, Knox went to England, where Henry VIII's son Edward VI and his Protestant ministers were in control. When

---

1. Felicity Heal, *Reformation in Britain and Ireland* (Oxford: Oxford University Press, 2003); Derek Wilson, *A Brief History of the English Reformation: Religion, Politics, and Fear; How England Was Transformed by the Tudors* (Philadelphia: Running Press, 2012).

2. J. H. S. Burleigh, *A Church History of Scotland* (Oxford: Oxford University Press, 1960); Clare Kellar, *Scotland, England & the Reformation: 1534–61* (Oxford: Oxford University Press, 2003).

Catholic Mary Tudor (Bloody Mary) succeeded Edward in 1553, however, Knox fled to Geneva, where he encountered John Calvin's theology and views of church.

Meanwhile, Protestant sentiment continued to grow in Scotland, despite the anti-Protestant policy of Mary of Guise, the mother of Mary Queen of Scots, who had become regent in 1554. A group of nobles calling themselves the Lords of the Congregation of Christ signed a covenant in 1557 pledging to "establish the most precious Word of God and His congregation" and to support and defend ministers who would "truly and purely minister Christ's Gospel and Sacraments to his people." They vowed to do whatever it took to defend the Congregation of Christ (Protestants) against the Congregation of Satan (the Roman Catholic Church), which they renounced "with all the superstitious abomination and idolatry thereof."[3]

With Protestantism on the rise, Knox returned to Scotland in 1559, openly advocating resistance to Catholic rulers. The Scottish Protestant nobles forced Mary of Guise to flee to France that same year. When French troops arrived once again to help secure Scotland for Catholicism in 1560, Protestant Queen Elizabeth of England could not allow such foreign interference on her doorstep and sent English armies to drive the French out. Although French and English troops had been drawn into the conflict, it was still essentially a bitter and bloody civil war—Scottish Catholics against Scottish Protestants.

After the defeat of the French and the death of Mary of Guise in 1560, the Scottish Parliament met to address the issues facing the nation. The Protestant nobles petitioned for a total cleansing of "papism" from the Church of Scotland, and the Parliament directed them to draw up a national statement of doctrine. John Knox and five other Protestant ministers composed the Scottish Confession of Faith, approved by Parliament on August 17, 1560. This was the first Scottish statement of religious belief—written by Scots for the new Scottish Reformed (Calvinist) Protestant church.

Eighteen-year-old Mary Queen of Scots, who had been living in France, returned to assume her throne as the legitimate ruler of Scotland in 1561. For six years she and John Knox waged a constant war of words. Weakened by opposition from the nobles and imprisoned on the island of Loch Leven,

---

3. See full text at True Covenanter, "The First Covenant of Scotland. At Edinburgh, 1557," http://www.truecovenanter.com/covenants/knox_history_covenant_1557.html; Henry Cowen, *John Knox: The Hero of the Scottish Reformation* (New York: Putnam's Sons, 1905), 178.

Mary abdicated and fled to England in 1567—but not before giving birth to a son by her husband Henry Stewart, Lord Darnley, the year before. The baby was crowned James VI of Scotland (he would also become James I of England in 1603) and was raised as a Protestant while Protestant regents ran the country.[4]

James was definitely not a fan of the Reformed Church of Scotland, however. He supported a church ruled by divinely appointed bishops—the episcopal system—that went hand in hand with belief in the divine right of kings. The Scottish church's structure was Presbyterian—rule by elders and ministers. James saw the Church of England where the monarch ruled the church through bishops as the ideal model. After becoming king of England and Ireland, he tried to restore rule by bishops in the Church of Scotland, but Presbyterian leaders strongly opposed him. When he died in 1625, he left a very conflicted Scottish church.

James's son Charles followed him as king of Scotland, England, and Ireland and continued the policy of pushing the Church of Scotland to conform to the church structure and theology of the Church of England. Charles appointed William Laud as archbishop of Canterbury, who proceeded to replace John Knox's *Book of Discipline* in the Scottish church with a new book more like the Anglican Book of Common Prayer. In 1638, Scottish Presbyterians who considered this new book "popish" banded together to sign yet another pact known as the Scottish National Covenant, based on the 1581 "King's Confession." The signers affirmed their dogged commitment to "abhor and detest . . . all kind of papistry . . . damned and confuted by the Word of God and Kirk of Scotland," and solemnly pledged that they would adhere to and defend the true Reformed religion.[5]

Many English Protestants shared the Scots' antagonism toward Charles and his "Catholic leanings" (he was married to French Catholic princess Henrietta Maria). In 1642, Calvinist "Puritans" in the English Parliament led a rebellion against Charles that began the English Civil War. Scottish Protestants sent representatives to support the move, and the two groups signed still another pact—the Solemn League and Covenant of 1643. In it leaders pledged to preserve the Reformed religion in Scotland and to work

---

4. Mary was executed in 1587 after being convicted of conspiring against her Protestant cousin Queen Elizabeth I. Since Elizabeth died with no heir, this opened the way for James, a great-great-grandson of Henry VII, to become king of England upon her death.

5. "The Scottish National Covenant," Constitution Society, http://www.constitution .org/eng/conpur023.htm; James King Hewison, *The Covenanters: A History of the Church of Scotland from the Reformation to the Revolution* (Glasgow: John Smith and Son, 1913).

for its full introduction in England and Ireland. Between 1643 and 1649, an assembly of theologians met in Westminster to formulate a statement of Reformed doctrine. This gathering produced the Westminster Confession of Faith, the classic declaration of Presbyterian theology and polity in the English language.[6]

The Scottish Parliament's ratification of the Westminster Confession of Faith in 1647 worried many Scots. Ever since the merger of the English and Scottish crowns in 1603 under James I, they had feared they were in danger of losing their distinct Scottish identity. They regarded the Westminster Confession as a foreign English document. Fights arose over which covenant they should honor, many insisting on the Scottish Confession of 1560 instead of the "English" Solemn League and Covenant and Westminster Confession.

Despite the opposition of monarchs who viewed Presbyterianism as incompatible with their notion of divine right monarchy, after decades of conflict the Church of Scotland would become a distinctly Reformed (Calvinist) church theologically and a Presbyterian body structurally. In 1690, after the Glorious Revolution of 1688 overthrew Catholic James II of England and brought in Protestant rulers William and Mary, Scotland officially established a full-blown Presbyterian church.

The Glorious Revolution of 1688

So far this story has barely mentioned Ireland—the supposed subject of the chapter. Yet everything described thus far is relevant to Ireland's history. The Glorious Revolution played a direct role in shaping the Irish politics and religion Alexander Campbell experienced. This event was rooted in the English Civil War of the 1640s when Puritan leaders in the British House of Commons challenged the absolute authority of King Charles I. Though the Church of England of which Charles was head was Protestant, it included both those with conservative "high church" convictions—including that monarchs and bishops held power directly from God and did not answer to any earthly power—and others who held less traditional "low church" views of governance and worship. Charles was decidedly "high church," and his marriage to a French Catholic made matters worse for the Puritan leaders of Parliament, fueling fears of a possible Catholic comeback.

6. John D. Brewer and Gareth I. Higgins, *Anti-Catholicism in Northern Ireland, 1600–1998: The Mote and the Beam* (New York: St. Martin's, 1998), 25.

In the end the parliamentary forces won the English Civil War, executed Charles, and in 1653 established a Puritan-led protectorate under Oliver Cromwell to govern the nation. After a decade of virtual Puritan dictatorship, however, a majority of English leaders decided that a restoration of the monarchy was preferable to a continuation of Cromwell's repressive policies under his son Richard. In 1660 Parliament brought the son of the executed Charles I back from France and crowned him Charles II. When he died in 1685 without a legitimate heir, his brother became King James II.

The problem was that James had become a Roman Catholic in 1670. He was also a strong defender of the divine right of monarchs. James was old, however, and his daughters Mary and Anne were raised as Protestants, making it almost certain that when he died Protestant rule would continue. But in 1688 Protestant England got a surprise that reignited fears of a return to Catholicism. James had a son and had him baptized as a Catholic.

A group of leaders in Parliament took matters into their own hands and called on William of Orange of the Netherlands—James's nephew who was also married to his Protestant daughter Mary—to invade. William did so in November, and James soon fled to France. Parliament then deposed James and crowned William and Mary monarchs the following year. The event was labeled the Glorious Revolution because of the relative ease and lack of bloodshed with which it accomplished the ouster of James and the preservation of a Protestant England.

But the Glorious Revolution was far from bloodless in Ireland. There the Catholic majority continued to recognize James as king. The next year James landed in Ireland with a largely French force believing he could gain a foothold there from which to reclaim the crown of England. Two years of hard fighting in Ireland ended in James's defeat by William at the Battle of the Boyne on July 1, 1690.

A significant number of people living in Ireland were ethnically English and Anglican, or Scottish and Presbyterian, and had supported William in the war. The Catholic majority, however, had supported James, reinforcing the idea that Ireland was a second-class kingdom of questionable loyalty. The Scotch-Irish Presbyterians were bitterly disappointed that their loyalty to William was not rewarded by removal of the "disabilities" they suffered because they were regarded as "dissenters," that is, not members of the Anglican Church. Even Irish Anglicans were frustrated that English officials still refused to allow them to run their own affairs. Something of the history of these two "non-Irish" groups and how they came to be in Ireland is important to the story at this point.

The Irish Plantation

The Protestant Reformation never happened in Ireland—the island remained almost entirely Roman Catholic and therefore different from the rest of Britain. As early as 1586 Elizabeth had begun "planting" Protestant English settlers in the province of Munster in an effort to gain a foothold in Catholic Ireland. In 1609 under James I, the so-called plantation of Ulster—the northernmost of the four traditional provinces of Ireland—began in earnest; it was designed to root out resistance to British rule. The new arrivals were English Anglicans and Scottish Presbyterians loyal to the king.[7]

Unlike earlier immigrants from Britain who came before the Protestant Reformation and in many ways became part of Catholic Irish culture and society (identified as the "Old English"), these new settlers did not. The Reformation virtually assured this. Theology became an essential part of the division of Irish society into two groups: the Catholics, consisting of the Gaelic-Irish and the Old English, portrayed as savage, uncivilized, and poor; and the economically privileged Protestants—mostly English and Scottish planters—who saw themselves as culturally superior to the ignorant and superstitious Catholics.[8]

While Ireland was different from the rest of Britain, Ulster was different from the rest of Ireland. The O'Neills and their followers, who fought the English in what is called the Nine-Years War from 1595 to 1604, had retreated there to continue attacks on the hated Protestant settlers before fleeing to Europe. Protestant immigrants from Scotland, who were often in the majority in Ulster, lived in constant fear of violent attacks by those they viewed as uncivilized and ruthless Catholics. The aggressive hostility between Catholics and Protestants that pervaded the province was reflected in the prediction by one Irish Presbyterian minister in 1634 that "the dead bodies of many thousands, who this day despise the glorious gospel, shall lie upon the earth as dung unburied."[9]

While Scottish Presbyterians in Ulster definitely feared and distrusted their Irish Catholic neighbors, they had no love for members of the established Church of Ireland either. Just as in England, any Protestants not members of the Anglican Church were dissenters and suffered "disabilities" like

---

7. Jane H. Ohlmeyer, *Making Ireland English: The Irish Aristocracy in the Seventeenth Century* (New Haven: Yale University Press, 2012).

8. Brewer and Higgins, *Anti-Catholicism in Northern Ireland*, 20–21.

9. Brewer and Higgins, *Anti-Catholicism in Northern Ireland*, 22–23.

being denied the right to hold public office, gain access to higher education, and have their marriages recognized by the state. The Ascendancy, the name for the Anglican English in Ireland, owned most of the land and controlled politics, even though by 1640 the Scotch-Irish Presbyterians outnumbered them five to one in the north.

The constant hostility between Scotch-Irish Presbyterians and their Catholic and Anglican neighbors in the seventeenth century created a distinct culture in the northern Irish counties. These "Ulster Scots" formed self-contained communities distinct from the rest of Irish society, politics, and religion, including a fully developed Presbyterian church tied to the Church of Scotland. That religious bond with their Scottish homeland included reproducing all the divisions that had arisen in the preceding two centuries.[10]

As already seen, Scottish Presbyterians had a tradition of signing covenants. This distinguished them not only from Anglicans and Catholics but also from other Presbyterians. Since the covenants had both theological and political dimensions, covenantal disputes were more than simply theological debates. Scottish conflicts over subscription to the "English" Westminster Confession, for example, led to division between its supporters and enemies who saw it as eroding Scottish identity.

Scottish Presbyterians had accepted the 1638 Scottish National Covenant in resistance to Charles I and Archbishop William Laud before the English Civil War. However, when the Puritan theologians wrote the Westminster Confession during the war with the help of Scottish representatives, there was strong pressure to support that document. The Reformed theology of the Church of Scotland clearly lined up with the beliefs of the English Puritans fighting Charles. The Assembly's pledge to make the Church of England truly Reformed and free from the rule of bishops led many Scottish Presbyterians to support the new confession.

While the Scottish church did accept the Westminster Confession in 1647, as mentioned, many still feared it was too English. At first, neither the Scottish Parliament nor the General Assembly of the Church of Scotland required subscription to the confession. But by the time the Church of Scotland was firmly in place in 1690, both bodies declared it to be the church's official doctrine and structure and made subscription a requirement. En-

10. See the discussion of this in Kevin L. Yeager, "The Power of Ethnicity: The Preservation of Scots-Irish Culture in the Eighteenth-Century American Backcountry" (PhD diss., Louisiana State University and Agricultural and Mechanical College, 2000), 1:16–17.

forcement was not always strict, however, and a number of church officials voiced various "scruples" against subscription and refused to comply.[11]

Since Church of Scotland controversies always made their way into Irish Presbyterian circles, subscription became a heated topic there too. The Irish Presbyterian Church insisted in 1698 that a license to preach required subscription to the Westminster Confession. Presbyteries in Ireland, however, were even more lax about enforcing the rule than were those in Scotland.

In 1705 a group of nonsubscribers formed the Belfast Society to coordinate the work of church leaders in County Antrim who objected to making subscription to any "man-made confession" a test of orthodoxy. Known as "New Lights," this group felt that interpretation of Scripture should be left to individual conscience and that religious obedience should be founded on personal persuasion, not loyalty to human covenants. New Light theology clearly represented the more enlightened and unorthodox wing of Presbyterianism. "Old Lights," on the other hand, were traditional Calvinists committed to the covenantal tradition. Yet even they could not agree among themselves whether to be loyal to the Scottish or English covenants.[12]

The Seceders

Still another layer of religious complexity entered Ireland in the early 1700s when zealous Scottish Seceders arrived in Ulster. This faction in the Church of Scotland came out of a dispute over "patronage," the long-established custom that gave the hereditary owner of property donated to build a parish church the right to select and install the minister. Because many Scottish landowners had remained loyal to the Roman Catholic King James II after the Glorious Revolution (who became known as Jacobites, after the Latin word for James, *Jacobus*), the General Assembly of the Church of Scotland rejected the practice of patronage in 1690 to make sure Catholics weren't appointed to these churches. However, some unsettling changes in the British royal line led to the reestablishment of patronage, sparking one more division among Scottish Presbyterians.

Anne, the second daughter of James II, was Protestant. She had become

11. Charles Scott Sealy, "Church Authority and Non-Subscription Controversies in Early 18th Century Presbyterianism" (PhD diss., University of Glasgow, 2010), 66–103.

12. Sealy, "Church Authority," 104–30. The terms "new light" and "old light" signify progressive and conservative attitudes, respectively, and mean something different in each context in which they are used.

queen after the death of King William in 1702 (William's wife, Queen Mary, died in 1694). Anne died without heirs only two years after being crowned, however, ending the Protestant Stuart line. Since Parliament had passed the Act of Settlement of 1701 that restricted the monarchy to Protestants, they had to locate the Stuarts' nearest Protestant relatives. They found them in the German House of Hanover, and King George I began the new Hanoverian line. However, Anne had a Catholic half brother, another James, living in France, who claimed hereditary right to the throne. British leaders were doing everything they could to keep James out of the picture and strengthen the new dynasty. One tactic was to restore the right of patronage to landowners who would pledge loyalty to the Protestant line of succession.

The General Assembly of the Church of Scotland still opposed patronage in theory, but they opposed a Catholic monarch coming to the throne even more. They accepted the reintroduction of patronage with the understanding that local presbyteries had the right to overrule any patron's appointment of a minister. In 1730, however, the British Parliament took that right away, and a number of presbyteries protested strongly. When the General Assembly of the Church of Scotland overruled the protesters and continued to sanction patronage, the dissident presbyteries seceded to form their own Associate Presbytery in 1733. By 1745 the Seceders had grown large enough to form the Associate Synod. These staunch Scottish Presbyterians saw themselves as the true church, in contrast to the compromisers in the main body of the Church of Scotland.

It was not long, however, before the Seceders themselves divided into two groups labeled Burghers and Anti-Burghers, over another issue rooted in anti-Catholicism. In 1745, the grandson of James II, Charles Stuart (known as Bonnie Prince Charlie) backed by his cousin Louis XV of France, tried one last time to take back the throne of England for the Catholic Stuarts. The attempt failed, but a significant number of Scots had supported the uprising, raising fears that there might be yet another rebellion.

To stop that from happening, burgesses (city officials) in Glasgow, Edinburgh, and Perth, cities where support for Charles Stuart had been high, were required to take a loyalty oath.[13] In addition to swearing allegiance to the monarch George II and a list of other British authorities, they were required to declare that they held to "the true religion presently professed within this realm, and authorized by the laws thereof," and that they would

13. Callum G. Brown, *Religion and Society in Scotland Since 1707* (Edinburgh: Edinburgh University Press, 1997), 23.

abide in and defend that faith to their life's end, "renouncing the Roman Religion called Papistry."[14]

The controversy was over whether or not Seceders could legitimately take this "Burgess Oath." Some interpreted the words "the true religion" to mean the corrupt patronage-supporting Church of Scotland from which they had separated. Others understood it simply to mean a renunciation of Catholicism and had no problems with the oath. When a slight majority of the Seceder Associate Synod condemned the oath and anyone who had taken it in 1746, those who thought the oath was acceptable separated, keeping the name Associate Synod. Those who opposed the oath were called Anti-Burghers and called themselves the General Associate Synod. Two years later the Anti-Burghers deposed and excommunicated all Burgher ministers. This controversy became one of the most heated in the Scottish church, leading to mutual condemnation and mutual forbidding of intermingling.[15]

Astoundingly the story becomes even more complicated with yet another dispute about loyalty to covenants. This controversy was over the section of the Westminster Confession of Faith that gave civil magistrates the authority to suppress "all blasphemies and heresies," to prevent or reform "all corruptions and abuses in worship," and to call and preside over synods.[16] Some supported this traditional role for civil rulers as a safeguard for orthodox Calvinist doctrine and the covenants. Others, however, believed that such authority should never be in the hands of laypeople. This second group also tended toward easing strict adherence to Calvinist doctrine, stressing the offer of salvation to all and eventually advocating disestablishment of the state church. In the end, both the Burgher and Anti-Burgher synods of the Secession Church divided into "Old Lights," who supported this role for civil rulers as described by the Westminster Confession, and "New Lights," who opposed it—the Burghers in 1799 and the Anti-Burghers in 1806.[17]

The Ireland into which Alexander Campbell was born in 1788 was rife with religious, social, and political strife—each strand inseparable from the others. His father, Thomas, was an ordained minister in the Anti-Burgher Seceder Presbyterian Synod of Ulster, a body reflecting all the internal

14. Thomas Sommers, *Observations on the Meaning and Extent of the Oath Taken at the Admission of Every Burgess in the City of Edinburgh* (Edinburgh: William Turnbull, 1794), 7–8.

15. William Stephen, *History of the Scottish Church*, vol. 2 (Edinburgh: David Douglas, 1896), 521.

16. Westminster Confession of Faith, chapter XXIII, "Of the Civil Magistrate."

17. Brewer and Higgins, *Anti-Catholicism in Northern Ireland*, 24.

Presbyterian divisions. Campbell's family lived in the midst of Catholics and Anglicans who viewed each other with suspicion and animosity. In addition, resentment was steadily growing among many Irish—Catholics and Protestants alike—toward their hated British overlords. Furthermore, the persistent "liberal" New Light sentiment challenged, though still feebly, the rampant intolerance and disposition to conflict. All these circumstances were at work in the formation of Alexander's father, Thomas, who would initiate the religious reform Alexander would lead for over half a century.

CHAPTER 2

The Formation
of Alexander Campbell's Father

The previous chapter provided an overview of the nearly incomprehensible Irish religious and political context into which Alexander Campbell was born. Precisely how Campbell's family fit into that story is not easy to determine. There are gaps in the account and at least two versions. Eva Jean Wrather explained that Alexander's great-grandfather, another Thomas Campbell, migrated from Argyle Shire, Scotland, to County Down, Ireland, in 1710. However, Robert Richardson, Campbell's first biographer, believed that this Thomas was born in Ireland.[1]

Alexander Campbell agreed with Richardson that his grandfather Archibald had been a Roman Catholic early in life.[2] This seems to throw doubt on the account that the older Thomas Campbell emigrated from Scotland since Catholicism was not typical of Scottish emigrants to Ulster. If he had come from Scotland, either that branch of the Campbell family had remained Catholic in a Presbyterian Scotland, which was possible, or Archibald had converted to Catholicism after moving to Ireland, conceivable but not common. While the records are simply not clear, the consensus that Archibald was Catholic lends weight to the version that he was born in Ireland, where Catholicism was the majority faith.[3]

---

1. Eva Jean Wrather, *Alexander Campbell: Adventurer in Freedom; A Literary Biography*, 3 vols. (Fort Worth: Texas Christian University Press, 2005–2009), 1:5; Robert Richardson, *Memoirs of Alexander Campbell*, 2 vols. (Philadelphia: J. B. Lippincott & Co., 1868–1870), 1:21.

2. Alexander Campbell, *Memoirs of Elder Thomas Campbell* (Cincinnati: H. S. Bosworth, 1861), 8.

3. A fire in the Public Records Office in Dublin during the Irish Civil War in 1922 destroyed many government and Church of Ireland records. While a few survived, specifics regarding Alexander's family are missing, including any record of Archibald's conversion from Catholicism to Anglicanism in the Catholic Qualification and Convert Rolls or other

In Alexander Campbell's brief biography of his father published in 1861, he explained that Archibald converted from Catholicism to the established Church of Ireland after serving in the British military in America during the Seven Years' War. Conversion would have provided him privileges available to neither Catholics nor Presbyterians. When his sons were old enough to make their own decision, however, Thomas, the oldest, and two of his three brothers became Seceder Presbyterians—part of the Anti-Burgher Synod of Ulster. While Archibald was not happy about the choice, the brothers had become part of the majority religious group in their section of Northern Ireland.[4]

A strong sense of independence, self-sufficiency, and isolationism characterized these Irish Seceder Presbyterians. They saw themselves as the elect, in a covenant with God and each other to maintain the pure (Reformed) faith. Catholics and Anglicans were outside of the covenant.[5] Their Anglican rulers, in turn, labeled them dissenters and never fully trusted their political loyalty.

Significant economic changes in Ireland in the mid-1700s aggravated the religious and political tensions already present. In response to the British Parliament's tariffs on Irish wool designed to protect the English wool industry, Ireland began producing linen. To encourage Irish growers, the British allowed duty-free exports of linen to England and its colonies in the early 1700s. This sparked a rise in Irish linen production in the north that brought increasing prosperity to Catholic mill workers. As a result, these workers were able to pay more for rent to the mostly Anglican landowners, who happily accepted the higher rents.

By the 1780s many laboring-class Protestants in County Armagh were becoming increasingly angry over the increased rents and the surge in the number of Catholic tenants and workers in the linen industry. Some of these laborers formed a secret organization called the Peep O'Day Boys (named after their practice of attacking Catholic homes just before sunrise) designed to terrorize Catholics and their Protestant collaborators. In response, the Defenders, formerly a group dedicated to land reform for all Irish, became

---

available records. Wrather's information is largely based on speculation concerning possible connections with other Campbell families in Scotland and Ireland. Wrather, *Alexander Campbell*, 1:xv, 4–6.

4. Alexander Campbell, *Memoirs of Elder Thomas Campbell*, 1:7–8; David Stewart, *The Seceders in Ireland, with Annals of Their Congregations* (Belfast: Presbyterian Historical Society, 1950).

5. John D. Brewer and Gareth I. Higgins, *Anti-Catholicism in Northern Ireland, 1600–1998: The Moat and the Beam* (New York: St. Martin's, 1998), 23–24.

Arthur Acheson, Lord Gosford (1744–1807), was governor of County Armagh during intense sectarian violence. Impressed by Thomas Campbell's education and refusal to become involved in the strife, Acheson asked Campbell to become tutor to his family, an offer Campbell refused. Used by license from National Trust Images, www.nationaltrust.org.uk.

a Catholic defense organization to meet the Peep O'Day Boys with their own tactics.[6]

For almost two decades in the late 1700s, the two groups carried out constant raids on each other. The governor of County Armagh, Arthur Acheson, first earl of Gosford, described the Protestant Peep O'Day Boys

6. Brewer and Higgins, *Anti-Catholicism in Northern Ireland*, 45.

as "a low set of fellows . . . who with guns and bayonets, and other weapons break open the houses of the Roman Catholics, and as I am informed treat many of them with cruelty."[7] The Catholic Defenders matched the brutality. Edward Hudson, Presbyterian minister at Jonesborough, described an incident that occurred in January 1791.

> In rushed a Body of Hellhounds—not content with cutting & stabbing [their Protestant victim] in several places, they drew a cord round his neck until his Tongue was forced out—It they cut off and three fingers of his right hand—Then they cut out his wife's tongue and . . . with a case knife cut off her Thumb and four of her fingers one after another . . . she I fear cannot recover—there was in the house a Brother of hers about fourteen years old . . . his Tongue those merciless Villains cut out and cut the calf of his leg with a sword.[8]

Alexander Campbell had just turned seven when a Protestant-Catholic clash known as the Battle of the Diamond took place about ten miles from his family's home at Market Hill. On Thursday, September 17, 1795, Catholic Defenders began gathering just southwest of a crossroads known as the Diamond, near Loughgall in County Armagh. On the opposite hill just northeast of the crossroads a group of Protestant Peep O'Day Boys also began to gather. Attempts to stop a violent confrontation, including bringing three Catholic priests to help negotiate, seemed to be working until Sunday night. The Defenders, as many as three hundred by then, decided to attack. The Peep O'Day Boys, though outnumbered, had the better position and weapons and killed seventeen Catholics without suffering any fatalities.[9] The "battle" was short, yet it became a symbol of the bitter conflict between Catholics and Protestants in Ulster. On the night after the clash, a small group of Peep O'Day Boys met nearby and founded the Orange Order.[10]

The Orange Order was named after Protestant king William of Orange, who, in July 1690, had defeated the deposed Catholic James II at the Battle of the Boyne, ending the threat to British Protestantism. The order carried

7. David W. Miller, *Peep O'Day Boys and Defenders: Selected Documents on the Disturbances in County Armagh, 1784–1796* (Belfast: Public Records Office of Northern Ireland, 1990), 49.

8. Miller, *Peep O'Day Boys and Defenders*, 103–4.

9. W. E. C. Fleming, *The Diamond: A North Armagh Parish* (W. E. C. Fleming, 2009), 124–25. Different accounts give larger numbers of Catholic fatalities.

10. *The Formation of the Orange Order, 1795–1798* (Belfast: Grand Orange Lodge of Ireland, 1994).

out a campaign of violence and intimidation against Catholics with the intention of driving them out of Northern Ireland. The governor of County Armagh, Lord Gosford, lamented that Orangemen killed many Catholics and destroyed their property with little done to protect them by local magistrates. Instead of uniting Protestants against Catholics, however, the group's violence polarized Protestants against Protestants, especially Protestant landlords who opposed the Orange Order for the disruption it brought to commerce and civil order.[11]

Alexander Campbell was ten in May 1798 when one of the most significant events in modern Irish history began—the United Irishmen's rebellion. The Society of United Irishmen had formed in 1791 on the basis of a shared hatred of British rule and included Catholics, Anglicans, and Presbyterians. The group called for Irish home rule and full political rights for Catholics, alarming many Irish Protestants who feared what a Catholic citizen majority might do to them.[12] With the help of troops from the new revolutionary government of France, thousands of Irish rose up against their British overlords in a concerted effort to drive them from the island.

The rebellion lasted from May to September, but in the end the British fought back with a vengeance and the rebellion collapsed. During the months of fighting, several major battles took place within miles of the Campbells' house. After the rebellion's failure, the British carried out widespread and brutal reprisals against suspected rebels in the area.

Because many Presbyterians were part of the United Irishmen, Thomas Campbell's church came under suspicion of sympathizing with the rebellion. During a church service in late June or early July 1798, probably at his rural church at Ahorey, eight miles from Armagh, a group of Welsh cavalry stationed at Newry surrounded the building. This group was notorious for its brutality toward anyone suspected of sympathizing with the rebels, a brutality that included indiscriminate execution of old men, boys, and women.

According to the story, the captain of the unit dismounted and marched menacingly into the church. As he stalked up the aisle, fiercely looking back and forth at the worshipers, one of Campbell's elders sitting nearby told Campbell to start praying. Campbell did so. "In a deep, unfaltering voice he began in the language of the forty-sixth Psalm: 'Thou, O God, art our

11. Brewer and Higgins, *Anti-Catholicism in Northern Ireland*, 45–46.
12. John Ranelagh, *A Short History of Ireland* (New York: Cambridge University Press, 1983), 41, 47–48; *Records of the General Synod of Ulster from 1691 to 1820*, vol. 3, 1778–1820 (Belfast: John Reid and Co., 1898), 157.

Thomas Campbell (1763–1854), though part of one of the most exclusivist Presbyterian sects in Ireland, worked for unity among the divided bodies there and in America for the sake of evangelism. Photo used with permission from the Disciples of Christ Historical Society, Bethany, West Virginia.

refuge and strength, a very present help in trouble. Therefore will not we fear, though the earth be removed and though the mountains be carried into the midst of the sea.'" When Campbell started praying, the captain stopped and bowed his head. The prayer, which likely lasted for some time, was apparently designed to assure the cavalryman that no one there was guilty of treason. When the prayer finally ended, the captain turned, walked out of the building, and rode off with his troops to look for rebels elsewhere.[13]

Though the story sounds suspiciously hagiographical, numerous written reports by officials and ordinary citizens alike of acts of violence in Campbell's part of Ireland make it plausible. Together the accounts construct a picture of constant unrest permeating Alexander Campbell's growing-up years. The passion produced by religious and political discord was a major part of

13. Richardson, *Memoirs of Alexander Campbell*, 1:44. On the Welsh Guard, see Richard Gott, *Britain's Empire: Resistance, Repression, and Revolt* (London: Verso Books, 2011), 490n10.

Campbell's early thought world. Its memory would be an important factor in the shaping of his reform movement in the "promised land" of America.

Licensed to preach in 1791 by the Anti-Burgher Seceder Synod of Ulster, Thomas Campbell was ordained and became minister of the newly established church in the village of Ahorey in 1798, the year of the United Irishmen rebellion. The minutes from 1799 explained that the synod had "been prevented from meeting according to adjournment, at Ahogill last year; by the ever memorable and melancholy disturbances of the country, particularly in the place of meeting." Members of the Associate Presbytery of Markethill "having reported the ordination of the Rev. Thomas Campble [*sic*] in Ahorey by Presbytery since last meeting of Synod, in due form—Mr. Campble was added to the list and took his seat accordingly."[14]

When the New Light–Old Light schism occurred in the Anti-Burgher Synod in 1806, Campbell found himself part of the Old Lights—apparently not so much because of strong convictions about the role of civil rulers in religion but because of personal relationships. In fact, his attitudes tended more toward "liberal" New Light sentiments than the strict and exclusive stance of his group. This tendency would show up in his commitments to peace and unity in both Ireland and America.

The failed United Irishmen rebellion of 1798 must have emboldened Thomas Campbell to do something to lessen the division and strife rampant in his country. In October that year, ten-year-old Alexander surely overheard discussion surrounding his father's role in forming the Evangelical Society of Ulster (ESU). The founding leaders used the General Evangelical Society formed in Dublin eleven years earlier as a model.[15] Thomas Campbell had consistently spoken against membership in any society that might encourage rebellion and violence, which included the United Irishmen and the Orange Order—themselves at opposite ends of the political spectrum.[16] The ESU, in contrast, had the potential to decrease the antagonisms wracking Ireland and his church.

The new body's evangelistic goals included the support of Reformed missionaries regardless of their denomination. From its beginning, the ESU had ties to the London Missionary Society, established in 1795 by English Congregationalists and Secession Presbyterians. The ESU quickly asked that

14. "Minute Book Associate Synod of Ireland (Anti-Burgher Seceder) Years 1788, 1797–1808," Public Records Office of Northern Ireland, Belfast, 110–11.

15. David Hempton and Myrtle Hill, *Evangelical Protestantism in Ulster Society, 1740–1890* (London: Routledge, 1992), 15–16.

16. Richardson, *Memoirs of Alexander Campbell*, 1:41–45.

body to send two itinerant preachers to Ireland, which they did in 1799. Over the next year the ESU gained members and support.[17]

However, at the same July 30–August 1, 1799, meeting of the Anti-Burgher Synod that formally admitted Thomas Campbell to its ministry, that body challenged the legitimacy of his participation in the ESU. The assembly posed the question, "Is the Evangelical Society of Ulster constituted on principles consistent with the Secession Testimony?" In other words, would a member of the Associate Synod violate its doctrinal and polity standards by being a member of the ESU. After considerable discussion, the synod voted that the ESU's principles were not compatible with the Associate Synod's. Three elders then met with Campbell to determine if he would submit to the decision. He agreed to "try to see eye to eye" with the synod, promising to withdraw from any leadership role in the ESU, though he would remain a member.[18] Campbell apparently left the ESU in 1800—his name disappears from the society's records that year—and by 1803 his synod had prohibited anyone under its authority from having any connection at all with the society.[19]

A significant factor in the synod's ruling against Campbell was the internal struggles among Irish Anti-Burghers. The oath that had caused the division between Burghers and Anti-Burghers in the first place had never been required in Ireland—it was actually applicable only in three Scottish cities. Yet the two factions condemned and excluded one another in Ireland just as they did in Scotland. In 1790 Seceder Presbyterians in Northern Ireland consisted of twenty-five congregations in the Anti-Burgher Synod of Ulster and forty-two in the Burgher Synod.[20]

A problem arose within Anti-Burgher ranks when some leaders, including Thomas Campbell, came to believe that since the Burgher oath was irrelevant in Ireland, there was no reason to remain separated from the Burghers there. In October 1804 Campbell participated in a consultation meeting at Rich Hill that wrote a formal proposal for the union of the Burghers and Anti-Burghers

17. See the extensive discussion of the Evangelical Society of Ulster in James L. Gorman, *Among the Early Evangelicals: The Transatlantic Origins of the Campbell Movement* (Abilene, TX: Abilene Christian University Press, 2017), 95–124.

18. "Minute Book Associate Synod of Ireland (Anti-Burgher Seceder) Years 1788, 1797–1808," 116–18.

19. Gorman, *Among the Early Evangelicals*, 112.

20. Peter Brooke, "Controversies in Ulster Presbyterianism, 1790–1836" (PhD diss., University of Cambridge, 1980), ix. Numbers extracted from Stewart, *The Seceders in Ireland, with Annals of Their Congregations.*

Independent Church at Rich Hill where Thomas and Alexander Campbell heard reformers like the Haldanes and John Walker. This photo was taken August 27, 1910, by Errett Gates. Used with permission from the Disciples of Christ Historical Society, Bethany, West Virginia.

in the country. Later that year, when the drafters presented the proposal to the Synod of Ulster meeting in Belfast, that body "favorably received" it.[21]

However, when the General Associate Synod—the body in Scotland that was over all the Anti-Burgher churches—got word of these meetings, it moved to block the union proposal from being introduced at its assembly. Despite the opposition, the Irish Synod sent Thomas Campbell to the General Associate Synod meeting in Glasgow with a formal request to allow the Irish churches to make their own decision about this matter. The synod allowed him to argue his case but refused to allow the proposition to come to a vote, effectively ending the union effort for a while.[22]

Alexander, now a young man of eighteen, witnessed his father's enthu-

21. Richardson, *Memoirs of Alexander Campbell*, 1:57. He also mentions another gathering at Lurgan in March 1805 that unanimously passed the union resolution.

22. Alexander Campbell, *Memoirs of Elder Thomas Campbell*, 8–9; Richardson, *Memoirs of Alexander Campbell*, 1:57–58.

siasm about the union proposal and his deep disappointment at its failure. He saw Thomas's demanding work schedule of teaching, ministering to his Ahorey congregation, and helping lead his Anti-Burgher Synod. He accompanied his father to services of independents on Sunday evenings in Rich Hill when the Ahorey church did not meet, which provided opportunities for conversations about the state of religion in Ireland and beyond.[23]

Alexander also watched his father develop a debilitating illness caused by the cumulative stress of his situation. Thomas's physician told him that the only remedy was to remove himself from the relentless strain. The doctor advised a sea voyage; so Campbell did what tens of thousands of people from Ulster had already done—he sailed to America. He left Ireland on April 8, 1807, placing his oldest son, Alexander, in charge of the family and his school until he either sent for them to join him or returned to Ireland.

Sailing from Londonderry on the American ship *Brutus*, Campbell arrived in Philadelphia after a thirty-five-day voyage. Though the synods in Scotland continued to oppose union, the Associate Synod of North America had already combined the Burgher and Anti-Burgher Seceders in the United States.[24] This body just happened to be meeting when Campbell arrived. After resting briefly, Campbell appeared before the synod and presented letters from the Market Hill Presbytery and his church at Ahorey. The body welcomed him and assigned him to the Chartiers Presbytery in western Pennsylvania—an area where several of Campbell's acquaintances from Ireland already lived. He quickly headed west and settled near the town of Washington, Pennsylvania.

If Campbell thought he was going to escape religious stresses in this new land, he soon found that he was mistaken. Though the physical violence over doctrinal disputes he had experienced in Ireland was largely absent in America, there was plenty of theological conflict. His troubles started in August 1807 when he traveled to conduct a sacramental service at the Associate Synod church at Cannamaugh (today Conemaugh), seventy miles east of Pittsburgh. William Wilson, a younger minister assigned to assist Campbell, was upset by some of the religious views Campbell had formed in Ireland,

23. Richardson, *Memoirs of Alexander Campbell*, 1:60.

24. William L. Fisk, "The Seceders: The Scottish High Church Tradition in America," *Journal of Presbyterian History* 62, no. 4 (Winter 1984): 295–98. New Light Burghers and Anti-Burghers united in Scotland in 1820, followed by other unions and divisions. See Archibald MacWhirter, "The Last Anti-Burghers: A Footnote to Secession History," *Records of the Scottish Church History Society*, 1944, 254–91.

particularly his opposition to subscription to creeds and his openness to fellowship with Christians not part of his Presbyterian body.

To make matters worse, Campbell invited non-Seceder Presbyterians attending his service that Sunday to participate in communion—a practice strictly forbidden by the Anti-Burgher Seceder Synod. After the trip, Wilson complained about Campbell's beliefs and actions to several other ministers from the Chartiers Presbytery. One of them, John Anderson, had been assigned to accompany Campbell on a preaching trip soon afterward, but he refused to go because he believed Campbell was teaching doctrines "inconsistent with some articles of our testimony."[25]

When the assembly at the October presbytery meeting asked Anderson to explain his refusal to fulfill his assignment with Campbell, he accused Campbell of unfaithfulness to Seceder teachings. Though Campbell had supporters and the accusation sparked a long discussion, a majority of the presbytery sided with Anderson.[26] When Campbell challenged Anderson's accusations, the body ruled against him, and Campbell stormed out of the meeting. The presbytery appointed a committee of five, including Anderson and three of Anderson's former pupils, to investigate Campbell's heresy. It also suspended all of Campbell's preaching appointments.

At the presbytery meeting in January 1808, Anderson and the committee brought a list of seven formal charges against Campbell. In addition to accusing him of heresies concerning the Lord's Supper and confessions of faith, they charged him with teaching that it was acceptable to hear ministers not part of the Secession church. They also accused him of preaching in a church that already had a minister without being assigned to do so by the presbytery.[27]

When Campbell responded to the charges the next month, the presbytery accepted two of his answers on doctrinal matters but said the remainder of his answers were evasive or actually admitted the charge. The presbytery then voted to censure Campbell and suspend his ministerial standing.[28]

In May Campbell appealed his case to the Associate Synod of North America in Philadelphia. The synod reprimanded the presbytery for allow-

25. Lester G. McAllister, *Thomas Campbell: Man of the Book* (St. Louis: Bethany, 1954), 72–75.

26. "Minutes of the Chartiers Presbytery," 124, quoted in William Herbert Hannah, *Thomas Campbell, Seceder and Christian Union Advocate* (Cincinnati: Standard Publishing, 1935), 33.

27. Hannah, *Thomas Campbell*, 39–43.

28. McAllister, *Thomas Campbell*, 78–84.

ing Anderson to renege on his appointment with Campbell and removed their suspension of Campbell's ministerial standing. Still, it voted to censure Campbell with a rebuke and an admonition. Though disappointed and angry, Campbell submitted to the synod and spent two months ministering in Philadelphia under the synod's supervision. When he returned home in August, however, he discovered that the Chartiers Presbytery still refused to give him any preaching assignments. In September, Campbell presented a paper denouncing the actions of the Chartiers Presbytery and the Associate Synod. Then at the synod meeting in May 1809, he submitted a document titled "Declaration and Address to the Associate Synod" in which he removed himself from their authority.

Campbell had no ministerial appointment and no source of income, but supporters in western Pennsylvania stepped forward to help. He continued to preach in the vicinity of Washington, Pennsylvania, to people who sympathized with his ideas. By early summer, however, many felt they needed a more organized way of proceeding. Abraham Altars, in whose home Campbell was living, hosted a meeting to discuss possibilities. Campbell laid out his ideas concerning the unity of the church as the basis for evangelism based on what he believed were the clear teachings of Scripture. These concepts were essentially the same as the ones that had driven the work of the Evangelical Society of Ulster several years earlier.

Those who had gathered to discuss a way forward were excited to hear Thomas Campbell's proposals. However, when he recommended that the group's operating principle be "where the Scriptures speak, we speak; and where the Scriptures are silent, we are silent," some objected because it seemed to cast doubt on the practice of infant baptism. Baptism was already a controversial topic in the group, so Campbell assured them that he did not believe that adopting this "Scripture principle" would lead to a rejection of infant baptism.

When the group met again in August, Campbell proposed that they form themselves into a society for the spread of the gospel to be called the Christian Association of Washington. This moved the group even closer to an imitation of the Evangelical Society of Ulster he had helped found eleven years earlier. The group accepted his proposal and commissioned Campbell to write an explanation of what they were about and how they would be organized.

By September he had completed his second "Declaration and Address" of the year. This one, though, was not a document of separation but a call for Christians of all denominations to come together to "promote simple evan-

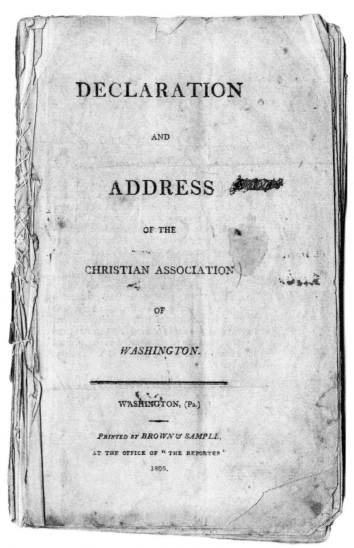

The front cover of Thomas Campbell's *Declaration and Address* of 1809. The document reflected many of the unity ideals of the Evangelical Society of Ulster and became one of the founding documents of the Stone-Campbell Movement. Used with permission from Bethany College, T. W. Phillips Memorial Library, Archives and Special Collections, Bethany, West Virginia.

gelical Christianity." The *Declaration and Address of the Christian Association of Washington, Pennsylvania* committed the body to support ministers from any denomination who would preach only those things that conformed to the "original standard"—Scripture—and who practiced simple New Testament Christianity.[29]

Just as in the ESU's founding document, cooperation across denominational lines was a central part of the Christian Association's agenda. Why would any Christian think it incredible that the church's original unity, peace, and purity should resume "in this highly favored country"? Campbell asked. If everyone took Scripture at its plain, simple meaning, all would agree on the great central truths of Christianity. Actually, he asserted, Christians already agreed on those things; inferences and opinions, especially when made obligatory in church confessions, were what divided Christians. He pledged to abandon any of his opinions not explicitly taught in Scripture so that he could return "to the original constitutional unity of the Christian Church; and, in this happy unity, enjoy full communion with all our brethren, in peace and charity."[30]

Thomas Campbell had sent word for his family to join him in America in January 1808. Twenty-year-old Alexander began the journey to America as leader of the family later that year. An unexpected ten-month delay, however, provided him with important experiences that would further prepare him to deal with his father's religious shifts and the American religious scene, as well as to begin the creation of his own religious reform.

29. Thomas Campbell, *Declaration and Address* (Washington, PA: Brown & Sample, 1809), 35. Full text available at https://webfiles.acu.edu/departments/Library/HR/rest mov_nov11/www.mun.ca/rels/restmov/texts/tcampbell/da/DA-1ST.HTM.

30. Thomas Campbell, *Declaration and Address*, 6, 20.

CHAPTER 3

The Formation of the Mind
of Alexander Campbell

Alexander Campbell and the rest of the family began preparation for the voyage to America as soon as they received Thomas's letter in spring 1808. But a smallpox outbreak put everything on hold until late August. Nine-year-old Jane, Alexander's sister, was the first to become sick, and before the rest of the family could be inoculated, some of the younger children were also infected. Before inoculation and vaccination became widely available, smallpox was fatal for a high percentage of children, and when not fatal, it often resulted in blindness.[1] Fortunately, the cases among the Campbell children were mild except for Jane's. She survived but was significantly scarred for the rest of her life. After her recovery, Alexander traveled to Londonderry and booked passage for the family on the ship *Hibernia*.[2]

The family, consisting of Alexander's mother, Jane, and seven children ranging from twenty-one-year-old Alexander to Alicia, who was two, departed Ireland on Saturday, October 1, 1808. The ship sailed out into the North Atlantic and up the west coast of Scotland for three or four days. Then strong winds forced the captain to anchor in Loch Indaal next to the Isle of Islay to wait for better weather.

In what seems like an offhand description of what Campbell did while waiting for the storm to pass, Robert Richardson actually provides a revealing glimpse into Campbell's attitude toward people he considered beneath him in status and intelligence. Recalling Campbell's description of the event,

---

1. Stefan Riedel, "Edward Jenner and the History of Smallpox and Vaccination," *Baylor University Medical Center Proceedings* 18 (January 2005): 21–25.

2. Robert Richardson provides a detailed account of the preparation for and events of the journey in *Memoirs of Alexander Campbell*, 2 vols. (Philadelphia: J. B. Lippincott & Co., 1868–1870), 1:90–106.

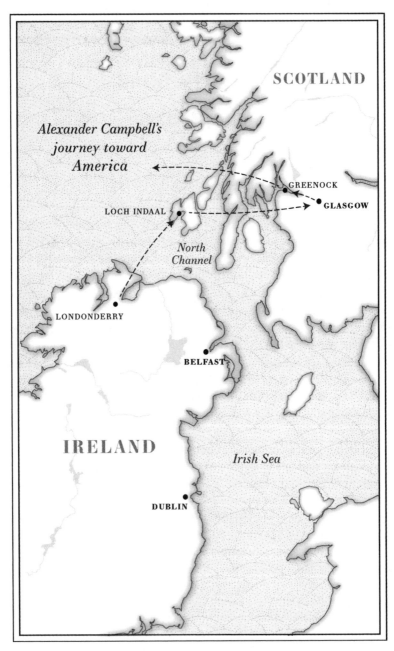

Map of Northern Ireland with Derry and the west coast of Scotland.

Richardson explained that the young man had busied himself "observing the motley crowd of passengers" and "conversing occasionally with the more intelligent." When some of the Catholic passengers who had observed his daily family prayers contemptuously asked him to pray for them, Campbell "paid no attention, knowing well the ignorance and bigotry by which they were dictated."[3]

Neither his anti-Catholicism nor his condescension toward less-educated people should be surprising. These attitudes had been forming during his whole life. Eva Jean Wrather attributed Campbell's "spirit"—some would say arrogance—to his proud and combative Scots Highlander ancestry. Most Irish Catholics had very limited education because the penal laws outlawed Catholic schools, and they generally had no money to send their children abroad to be educated. This reinforced the Protestant stereotype that Catholics were inherently ignorant and superstitious. Furthermore, the sense of religious superiority characteristic of the Seceder Presbyterians surely contributed to Campbell's elitist views. His tendency to disdain anyone who did not share his heritage, education, or faith would manifest itself often throughout his long and influential career, including in his attitudes toward African Americans held in slavery in the United States.

After they had waited three days for the weather to improve, on Friday evening, October 7, the wind dragged the ship onto a rock that smashed its hull. Rescued by residents from the nearby island, the ship's passengers salvaged what they could from the wreckage. Alexander was especially concerned to save his books and spent considerable time drying and caring for them over the next several days. He would later have a number of these volumes rebound, some of which became treasured parts of his extensive library in America.[4]

Though the shipwreck delayed the family's trip to America for ten months, the time proved extremely important for Alexander's intellectual and spiritual formation. With help from distant relatives on the island of Islay, the family was able to move to Glasgow, where they lived until it was safe to try the voyage again. While there, Alexander took advantage of the opportunity to attend classes at the University of Glasgow as well as form relationships with several prominent religious reformers.

3. Richardson, *Memoirs of Alexander Campbell*, 1:99.
4. Selina Huntington Campbell, *Home Life and Reminiscences of Alexander Campbell* (St. Louis: John Burns, 1882), 55–56. See Charles Penrose, *Short Title List of Alexander Campbell's Library Now in Bethany College Library* (n.p., 1947), https://digitalcommons.acu.edu/sc_teaching_series/1/.

Alexander Campbell's Early Education

Before Thomas Campbell left for America, he made sure his son had a strong classical education. Alexander's first formal training had been at an elementary school in Market Hill, followed by a couple of years in an academy at Newry run by his uncles Archibald and Enos Campbell. When Alexander returned from Newry at age eight or nine, Thomas intended to tutor him at home, but Alexander was not particularly interested in studying. Thomas was worried about his son's lack of desire for learning but didn't push the matter. Instead, he put Alexander to work with the laborers on the farm he leased to provide extra income for the family. Whether or not Thomas was trying to shock his son into realizing that academic pursuits were preferable to strenuous physical labor, after several months the teenager informed his father he was ready to study and to become, as recounted later by Richardson, "one of the best scholars in the kingdom."[5]

Campbell became a voracious reader, interacting with some of the most important philosophical and theological writers in the English language. Thomas made sure that Alexander read John Locke. Richardson specifically mentioned his study of the "Letters on Toleration" (part of which Alexander would reprint in January 1844 in his journal the *Millennial Harbinger*, referring to Locke as "the great Christian philosopher") and the "Essay concerning Human Understanding." Clearly Thomas was preparing his son for study at the university level and included in his program Latin and Greek. This groundwork would serve Alexander well when the unexpected opportunity came to study for a term at his father's alma mater, the University of Glasgow.

In the meantime, however, the farm was not providing enough extra income for the family, so Thomas decided to stop farming and move to the nearby town of Rich Hill to open a school. This change served several purposes. It provided Thomas the opportunity to continue schooling his own children while also taking in students as a source of income. And it gave Alexander, now seventeen and already relatively well educated, the opportunity to help his father teach the younger pupils, thereby strengthening his academic competence even as his father continued tutoring him.

Sometime during this period Alexander had what can only be described as a "conversion experience." His father had been urging him to become part of the church, but Reformed theology taught that a person must first have a

5. Richardson, *Memoirs of Alexander Campbell*, 1:31–32.

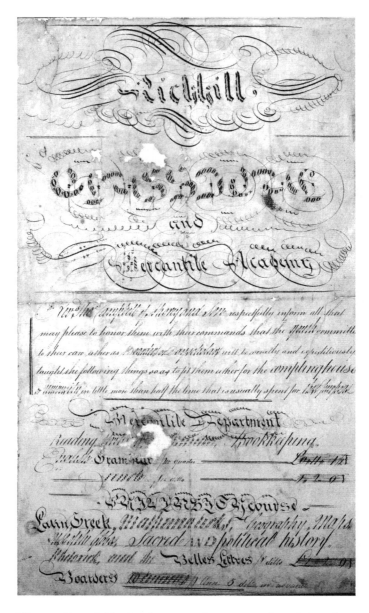

Thomas Campbell gained a reputation as a good teacher and attracted students to his schools in Ireland and America. He operated this school in his home in Rich Hill before emigrating in 1807. Used by license from the Armagh County Museum, Armagh, Northern Ireland, United Kingdom.

personal experience confirming his or her "election" to salvation. Campbell spent some time brooding over this until he became convinced that he did in fact have saving faith. Richardson recorded Campbell's later description of the event.

> From the time that I could read the Scriptures, I became convinced that Jesus was the Son of God. I was also fully persuaded that I was a sinner, and must obtain pardon through the merits of Christ or be lost forever. This caused me great distress of soul, and I had much exercise of mind under the awakenings of a guilty conscience. Finally, after many strugglings, I was enabled to put my trust in the Saviour, and to feel my reliance on him as the only Saviour of sinners. From the moment I was able to feel this reliance on the Lord Jesus Christ, I obtained and enjoyed peace of mind.[6]

Interestingly, this account does not figure prominently in his faith story. Later, as he constructed his new religious movement in America, Campbell would talk extensively about how one obtains true assurance of Christ's salvation, but not in terms of an experience like this. Richardson, whose view of religion was definitely more experiential than Campbell's, must have thought it was important to record Campbell's account of this event as somehow significant to Campbell's theology of salvation. Campbell and Richardson would later clash strongly on matters of spiritual experience. Campbell himself largely seems to have ignored the incident, and the vast majority of his followers would likely have found it puzzling.[7]

After Thomas left for America in April 1807, Alexander continued operating his father's school until the end of the term, at which time he went to Newry to teach classes for his uncle Archibald. He was there when Thomas's letter calling the family to America arrived in March 1808. And so, by the time Alexander arrived in Glasgow, he not only had a solid classical education that included philosophy, theology, and church history but also had considerable teaching experience. During the months in Glasgow, two major influences shaped young Alexander: his interaction with Scottish Independents and his studies at the University of Glasgow.

---

6. Richardson, *Memoirs of Alexander Campbell*, 1:49.

7. See Cloyd Goodnight and Dwight E. Stevenson, *Home to Bethphage: A Biography of Robert Richardson* (St. Louis: Christian Board of Publication, 1949), 168–94, and C. Leonard Allen and Danny Gray Swick, *Participating in God's Life: Two Crossroads for Churches of Christ* (Orange, CA: New Leaf Books, 2001), 37–53.

Alexander Campbell and the Scottish Independents

Campbell's relationship with the Independents in Glasgow planted the seeds of many of his lifelong commitments. Among these were restoring the pure gospel and church, a strict view of the silence of Scripture, separation of church and state, congregational autonomy, weekly Lord's Supper, and simple worship.[8] James L. Gorman has shown that the Campbell movement in America began as part of the transatlantic evangelical mission movement championed by Independents that combined restorationism, millennialism, and Christian unity—convictions that would always be at the core of Campbell's vision.[9]

Through his father's contacts Campbell had come to know several Independents who had separated from the Presbyterian Church to form networks of congregations with a vision to re-create the first-century church. A small group of Haldane Independents actually met in Rich Hill under the leadership of John Gibson, a member of the Evangelical Society of Ulster who had left his Burgher synod.[10] Thomas Campbell and Gibson were friends, and Thomas and Alexander visited his services occasionally when Thomas was not ministering at his own church at Ahorey.[11] This familiarity paved the way for Alexander to form relationships with Independent leaders in Glasgow, especially Greville Ewing, who became an important mentor and friend during his time in Scotland.

Ewing, ordained in the Church of Scotland, was a close associate of James Alexander and Robert Haldane. The Haldanes, disappointed in the Church of Scotland's lack of interest in evangelizing the country, formed the Society for the Propagation of the Gospel at Home in 1798 to send evangelists to preach throughout Scotland. When the Church of Scotland opposed them for their use of lay preachers, they withdrew and began forming independent Congregational churches. Ewing's support of the Haldanes' ideals led him to resign his ministry in the Church of Scotland and join their efforts.[12]

---

8. Lynn McMillon, *Restoration Roots* (Dallas: Gospel Teachers Publications, 1983).

9. James L. Gorman, *Among the Early Evangelicals: The Transatlantic Origins of the Stone-Campbell Movement* (Abilene, TX: Abilene Christian University Press, 2017).

10. Gorman, *Among the Early Evangelicals*, 108–10.

11. Richardson, *Memoirs of Alexander Campbell*, 1:59–61. Presbyterian discipline sometimes allowed "occasional hearing" at services of other Christian bodies, though some synods prohibited it. See "Occasional Hearing," Reformed Presbyterian Church (Covenanted), http://www.covenanter.org/reformed/2015/8/18/an-article-from-the-covenanter-magazine-on-occasional-hearing?rq=Occasional%20Hearing.

12. Alexander Haldane, *Memoirs of the Lives of Robert Haldane of Airthrey and of His Brother James Alexander Haldane* (New York: Robert Carter & Brothers, 1853), 214–24.

One of the letters of introduction Campbell carried to Glasgow was from George Fulton, a family friend in Rich Hill who knew Ewing. As soon as Alexander arrived in the city, he took Fulton's letter to Ewing.[13] Ewing kindly helped the family find a place to live and, over the next few days, introduced Alexander to several professors at the University of Glasgow. For the next nine months Ewing and the other Independents who were a significant part of Glasgow religion had a profound influence on Campbell, who became close friends with many.[14]

In Ewing's home Campbell heard discussions on topics ranging from weekly Lord's Supper to church structure and baptism.[15] Ewing strongly supported infant baptism. This subject had divided the Independents, however, especially after the Haldane brothers received immersion—though they never made it a term of communion. This topic would become a dominant issue in the Christian Association of Washington, Pennsylvania, and arguably the principal issue of Alexander Campbell's religious reform.

Alexander Campbell at the University of Glasgow

With Ewing's help, Campbell began taking classes at the university on November 8, 1808. This was exhilarating for Campbell and fulfilled an ambition he had largely abandoned because of the responsibility to help provide income for his large family. He was determined to take full advantage of this heaven-sent opportunity. One of his most formative courses was on the Scottish commonsense philosophy of Thomas Reid taught by Professor George Jardine, a pupil of Reid's and one of Campbell's favorite teachers. Central to this philosophy was the belief that the data collected by the human senses, when confirmed by the testimony of others, was a reliable source of knowledge. Against the skeptical philosophy of David Hume, Reid insisted that the things humans perceive are the real external objects themselves, not images created by the mind. Through a careful, slow, painstaking process of

---

13. Alexander Campbell, "Journal of a Voyage from Ireland towards America, 1808," Manuscript D, Disciples of Christ Historical Society, Bethany, West Virginia, 33.

14. Campbell included at least six ministers in his list of close friends in Glasgow, including Greville Ewing and Rev. Dr. Balford—most likely Robert Balfour. Alexander Campbell, "Journal of a Voyage from Ireland towards America, 1808," 40–41. See discussion in Gorman, *Among the Early Evangelicals*, 147–50.

15. Richardson, *Memoirs of Alexander Campbell*, 1:149.

Greville Ewing (1767–1841) left the Church of Scotland in 1798 and became a major leader in Scottish Congregationalism. He befriended and mentored Alexander Campbell during his months in Glasgow in 1808–1809. Used by license. © National Portrait Gallery, London.

experimentation and observation, of collecting data and inducing patterns, one could arrive at the facts—theoretically about anything.[16]

Crucial to the Scottish commonsense philosophy was the thought of

16. Ryan Nichols and Gideon Yaffe, "Thomas Reid," in *Stanford Encyclopedia of Philosophy*, last substantive revision September 23, 2014, https://plato.stanford.edu/archives/win2016/entries/reid/; Theodore Dwight Bozeman, *Protestants in an Age of Science: The Baconian Ideal and Antebellum American Religious Thought* (Chapel Hill: University of North Carolina Press, 1977), 3–21.

Francis Bacon—a set of ideas that became extremely important to Campbell's philosophy. Jardine introduced Campbell to Bacon's concepts through the study of his *Novum Organum*, in which Bacon articulated an early form of the "scientific method." He insisted that one comes to knowledge through a meticulous process of observation, gathering of sense data, and drawing conclusions from careful analysis of the data—the inductive method. Campbell would come to rely entirely on the Baconian method to arrive at Christian doctrine, as described by Richardson:

> As, before the time of Bacon, the facts of nature were explained or perverted to suit the theories of philosophers, so now the facts and teachings of the Bible were applied and interpreted to suit the various systems of theology. Lifting himself above all human theories and speculations, Mr. Campbell strictly applied the inductive method to the Bible, and made its facts and revelations the great basis of religious thought and the sure foundation of all religious trust. His method of discoursing was hence totally unlike that of other preachers.[17]

The Baconian method also fit well with John Locke's philosophical assumptions, which rejected the notion that humans are born with innate ideas. The mind, Locke would famously insist, was like a blank slate on which students write lessons. The only way humans got ideas was through experiencing things. Those sense perceptions would write, so to speak, on the blank slate. Campbell also agreed with Locke's assertion that while certain ideas received through divine revelation are "above reason," they are not contrary to reason. To accept the truths of revelation was not to go against reason.[18]

In 1952, a remarkable group of essays handwritten by Campbell for a philosophy class at Glasgow was mailed from Australia to Bethany College. It was one of a number of original Campbell items taken to Australia in 1920 by family members who immigrated there. "Manuscript B"—the name given it by Campbell—provides insight into the formation of young Campbell's thought while taking classes at the university between December 1808 and June 1809.[19]

---

17. Richardson, *Memoirs of Alexander Campbell*, 2:106.

18. See the discussion of the sources and major contours of Campbell's philosophical premises in Caleb Clanton, *The Philosophy of Religion of Alexander Campbell* (Knoxville: University of Tennessee Press, 2013), 13–19, and S. Morris Eames, *The Philosophy of Alexander Campbell* (Bethany, WV: Bethany College, 1966).

19. Lester G. McAllister, *Alexander Campbell at Glasgow University, 1808–1809* (Nashville: Disciples of Christ Historical Society, 1971), 1; Carisse Mickey Berryhill, "A Descriptive

In the first essay, "Genius," Campbell pinpointed a set of necessary abilities for anyone to be called a person of genius. These included a quick and clear perception, the ability to focus one's attention, the capacity to abstract and generalize, a strong memory, and "above all, a strength of and warmth of Imagination, with a soundness of Judgement and depth of Reason." While he highlighted imagination as the faculty on which genius most depended, this was no endorsement of indiscriminate speculation. Speaking of the genius of Homer's *Iliad*, for example, Campbell described Homer's process of collecting and combining in his mind "all the circumstances, characters, events, battles, etc.," using his reason to analyze and employ the data for his purposes.[20] "The end and intention of all our reasoning is to discover things unknown: if we knew and could understand all things intuitively Reason would not be requisite to our existence—but in our present existence this faculty is that which distinguishes us from the brutal Creation: all our discoveries depend on it."[21]

As he closed the essay, Campbell provided a description of youthful genius to which he must have aspired and perhaps already saw in himself, a description that would ring true as he developed his career as a religious reformer in America. "Genius: 1st an ardent desire of improvement expressed by an inquisitive curiosity, attention to instruction, patience and pleasure of improvement. An early fondness for Reading, a Distinctness and tenacity of memory, sensibilities of our nature; as well as Intellectual turn; a love of fame, with a keenness and activity in juvenile Recreation—these are all strong indications of Genius in Youth."[22]

Other essays on the Socratic method, syllogisms, and the difference between judgments and propositions further reflected his intellectual training and the development of his attitudes about truth and falsehood.[23]

The few months Campbell spent in Scotland between the shipwreck off the Isle of Islay and the resumption of the trip to America were massively

---

Guide to Eight Early Alexander Campbell Manuscripts," December 2000, http://webfiles .acu.edu/departments/Library/HR/restmov_nov11/www.mun.ca/rels/restmov/texts /acampbell/acm/ACM00A.HTM, 1.

20. Alexander Campbell, "Manuscript B. Juvenile Essays on Various Subjects by Alex'r. Campbell in the University of Glasgow 1808–1809," 6–10, in McAllister, *Alexander Campbell*, 9–12.

21. Alexander Campbell, "Manuscript B," 14, in McAllister, *Alexander Campbell*, 14.

22. Alexander Campbell, "Manuscript B," 17, in McAllister, *Alexander Campbell*, 16.

23. Another Campbell item returned from Australia, titled Manuscript L, contains Campbell's notes on George Jardan's (Jardine's) lectures on logic and some class exercises.

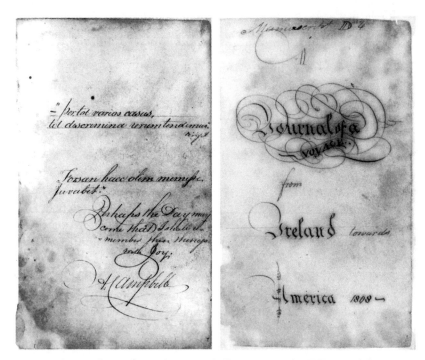

Two leaves from Alexander Campbell's "Manuscript D," one of Campbell's journals taken to Australia by descendants in 1921. In it he gives an account of the shipwreck in 1808 and the family's stay in Glasgow. The Latin is from Virgil's *Aeneid*, book 1, lines 204 and 203. "Through varied fortunes, through countless hazards, we journey." "Perhaps even this distress it will some day be a joy to recall." Used with permission from the Disciples of Christ Historical Society, Bethany, West Virginia.

important for shaping his thought and self-perception. The philosophical grounding he received at the University of Glasgow would guide his attitudes and work for religious reformation for the rest of his life. The religious concepts he learned from both Independents and Seceder Presbyterians provided inspiration for the commitments that would guide his new movement in America. He was now about to start the final leg of the journey to that new life.

When the university term ended in May, the Campbell family got ready to travel again, though it took three months to book passage on a ship. During that time the semiannual "communion season" observed by the Seceder church arrived. Though John Calvin had recommended "frequent communion" for the Reformed churches, the Church of Scotland had the

Presbyterian communion tokens like this, given by church elders to members judged worthy to partake, were required for entrance to sacramental services. Though Alexander Campbell received the token and was allowed entrance to the 1809 service in Glasgow, he refused to partake. Photo courtesy of Mac Ice, Abilene, Texas.

custom of taking it only twice a year.[24] In preparation for this important event, congregational elders examined the spiritual state of each member. Members the elders already knew usually had only to show up to receive the metal token necessary for entrance to the communion service. Since Alexander did not have a letter from the Irish Synod certifying his good standing, the elders asked him to appear before them for an oral examination. They had no problem with his answers and gave him the token.[25] But Campbell had changed during the previous months.

The Scottish tradition was to serve people at large tables in shifts. Campbell presented his token, entered the room, and took his seat. When the bread and wine came around, however, he passed them on without taking the elements.[26] Apparently no one noticed Campbell's refusal to partake, or at least it didn't cause a stir. This was not unheard of—Reformed sacramental literature warned against taking the Lord's Supper "in an unworthy manner," frightening especially sensitive members into abstaining.[27] Yet the reason

24. John Calvin, "Times of Using the Supper, Propriety of Frequent Communion," in *Tracts and Treatises of John Calvin*, 3 vols. (Eugene, OR: Wipf & Stock, 2002), 2:179–80.

25. See Leigh Eric Schmidt, *Holy Fairs: Scottish Communions and American Revivals in the Early Modern Period* (Princeton: Princeton University Press, 1989); W. R. Smith, "The Presbyterian Usages of 'Giving Tokens and Fencing the Communion Table,' Explained and Vindicated," *Literary & Evangelical Register* 1 (May 1830): 519–25.

26. Richardson, *Memoirs of Alexander Campbell*, 1:188–90.

27. Westminster Confession of Faith 29.8. John Calvin's "Short Treatise on the Supper of Our Lord" (1541) reflects a problem of Christians excluding themselves from partaking for fear of blasphemy. See sections 20–32. http://www.the-highway.com/supper1_Calvin.html.

for Campbell's act was not fear. He would later remember it symbolizing his rejection of the sectarianism he had experienced in Ireland and Scotland and a turn toward religious reform, setting the stage for what would happen when he joined his father in America.[28]

The family finally set sail from Greenock, Scotland, on August 3, 1809, on the ship *Latonia*. After almost two months at sea, they arrived in New York, on September 29, and spent a few days surveying the city. Alexander was very impressed, especially by the commercial enterprise. These powerful first impressions led him to embrace the idea that America was God's "Chosen Land" and also reinforced his belief in the myth of Anglo-Saxon Protestant superiority.

After New York they made their way to Philadelphia, where they hired a wagon and driver to take them the 350 miles across the mountains to meet Thomas in Washington, Pennsylvania. The first day they traveled about thirty miles, stopping at an inn for the night. Richardson described Alexander's thoughts that evening after returning from a long walk in the woods.

> Returning to the hotel, he found that all its inmates had retired to rest, a light having been left for him upon the table. Upon attempting to fasten the door, he was surprised to find it without lock or bolt, and with nothing but a latch, as he perceived was also the case with the door of his sleeping apartment. Coming direct from the Old World, where nocturnal outrages were frequent, and every house had its bolts and bars, he was much impressed with such a token of fearless security, and congratulated himself still more in having reached a country where the fabled golden age seemed to be restored, and where robbery and injustice appeared to be undreaded and unknown. In attempting to account for this, to him, unwonted security, his experience in the Old World led him to refer it, in a large measure, to the absence of Catholicism; and, after his devotions, he gradually fell into slumber amidst grateful reflections upon the goodness of Providence in bringing him to a land under the benign influence of the free institutions, the equal rights, the educational advantages, and the moral and religious elevation secured to all in a purely Protestant community.[29]

This experience, within days of his arrival in America, inseparably tied his anti-Catholicism with his growing conviction that God's providence had

---

28. Richardson, *Memoirs of Alexander Campbell*, 1:190.

29. Richardson, *Memoirs of Alexander Campbell*, 1:209–10.

prepared America for the religious reforms he and his father would undertake. In this land, free from the corruptions of Europe and the heathenism of the rest of the world, with God's help he would restore what he labeled "the ancient gospel and order of things." Campbell accepted the Puritan vision of a land created to bring about God's purposes, but he would form his own version of it.

Thomas got word of the family's arrival a few days after they landed and immediately left with a friend to meet them on the road. When the family was reunited on October 19, Thomas and Alexander began to fill each other in on the details of the past two years. The most intense exchange must have been about each other's religious journeys. Thomas told of his separation from the Associate Synod of North America and the creation of the Christian Association. Alexander must have talked about how his thought had evolved through his studies at the university and in the homes of Glasgow Independents—and his refusal to take communion with the Seceder church in Scotland.

Thomas had just written the *Declaration and Address*, the document explaining the purpose and structure of the Christian Association of Washington. It called Christians to unite on the plain teachings of Scripture and to take a nonsectarian gospel to the world. His handwritten draft was already at the printers, and as soon as the proof sheets came back, Alexander carefully read his father's proposals. After studying them intently, he told Thomas that he fully agreed with his plan and wanted to be part of it. Thomas urged Alexander to spend the next six months studying Scripture in preparation for the work ahead.

In many ways, those next months were a continuation of the private tutoring Thomas had given his oldest son in Ireland. It was basically an apprenticeship, a model common in frontier American ministerial training. Not only did Alexander study Scripture, he also read in theology and church history. On July 15, 1810, Alexander preached his first sermon to the Christian Association. He did well, and within a few weeks he was receiving calls to preach in other places. Thomas's encouragement of Alexander's preaching even though he was not ordained, however, was one reason the Synod of Pittsburgh of the Presbyterian Church in the United States of America (PCUSA) rejected Thomas's application for ministerial affiliation that October.[30]

Though the *Declaration and Address* was clear that the Christian As-

---

30. Richardson, *Memoirs of Alexander Campbell*, 1:328.

sociation of Washington was not a church, it certainly began to look like one. Most Sundays both Campbells preached to the group's members. A little over six months after Thomas's rejection by the PCUSA, the Christian Association organized itself into the "First Church of the Christian Association, meeting at Crossroads and Brush Run" on May 4, 1811. On New Year's Day the following year, Thomas Campbell ordained twenty-three-year-old Alexander to the Christian ministry.[31]

In the months ahead, Alexander would begin the process of assuming chief leadership of the reform movement. His quick mind, massive self-confidence, and unbounded energy would eventually propel him onto the national stage, where he would be hailed as both a great Christian reformer and a destructive heretic. He would construct over the next decade and a half a reform movement with a distinctive theology and appeal that would expand to become one of the largest Christian bodies in America by the mid-1800s. Part of the story of how he did that is the subject of the next section.

31. Eva Jean Wrather, *Alexander Campbell: Adventurer in Freedom; A Literary Biography*, 3 vols. (Fort Worth: Texas Christian University Press, 2005–2009), 1:165–70.

Creation

I say, the principles on which the church of Jesus Christ—all believers in Jesus as the Messiah—can be united with honor to themselves, and with blessings to the world; on which the gospel and its ordinances can be restored in all their primitive simplicity, excellency, and power, and the church shine as a lamp that burneth to the conviction and salvation of the world:—I say, the principles by which these things can be done are now developed, as well as the principles themselves, which together constitute the original gospel and order of things established by the Apostles.

—Alexander Campbell, *The Christian System*, 1835

CHAPTER 4

The Creation of a Career

Alexander Campbell quickly began to make a name for himself in the region around Washington, Pennsylvania. This included the panhandle of western Virginia and the Western Reserve that would become northeast Ohio. Campbell honed his theological and speaking skills under his father's coaching and began to share preaching responsibilities for the Christian Association congregation.

The texts Campbell used for his November 1, 1810, sermon reflected utter confidence in what he and his father were doing. Isaiah 57:14 and 62:10 in the King James Version read: "Cast ye up, cast ye up, prepare the way, take up the stumblingblock out of the way of my people. . . . Go through, go through the gates; prepare ye the way of the people; cast up, cast up the highway; gather out the stones; lift up a standard for the people." On nine tightly written pages, Campbell explained that the prophet's task was to remove anything that would obscure God's word to the people. He was issuing a call to everyone who truly wanted to follow God to leave the gates of Babylon—the corrupt Christian establishment—and travel the highway that was now to be cleared of the stumbling blocks of human doctrines. Under the second heading of his text he wrote, "Show that we have attempted to perform these duties."[1]

He and his father, along with the Christian Association, saw their task as removing human opinions as terms of communion, clearing away all obstacles on the path to truth and teaching only the New Testament as the perfect

---

1. Alexander Campbell, "Journal of a Voyage from Ireland towards America, 1808," Manuscript D, Disciples of Christ Historical Society, Bethany, West Virginia, 68–69. On page 163 Campbell recorded that he preached his very first sermon on July 15, 1810, on Matt 7:26–27, "And every one that heareth these sayings of mine, and doeth them not, shall be likened unto a foolish man."

Map of western Pennsylvania, western Virginia, and northeast Ohio.

constitution for the church.[2] Campbell then listed and answered objections some were making to their reform: the Christian Association was divisive, it undermined respect for properly trained ministers by endorsing lay preaching, and it had no clear doctrinal standard (it claimed to follow the New Testament alone), which would inevitably lead to lax discipline.

Next, he addressed the accusation that the association rejected infant baptism. Campbell replied that the critics were making infant baptism an essential practice when it was not a clear command. They were saying, in effect, "Except ye baptize your children, you cannot be saved!" Campbell insisted that infant baptism was not a term of communion for the Christian Association—it was a matter of forbearance. They would not exclude members for failing to have their children baptized. Neither would they ask church members who were baptized as infants to repudiate that baptism—to be "put out of" the church, immersed, and readmitted. This, they believed, would be as divisive and sectarian as requiring infant baptism. Their position was very much like the one taken by the Haldanes, who had deeply influenced the Campbells in Ireland and Scotland.[3]

2. Campbell, "Journal," 71–72.

3. Campbell, "Journal," 72–75; Robert Richardson, *Memoirs of Alexander Campbell*, 2 vols. (Philadelphia: J. B. Lippincott & Co., 1868–1870), 1:335–47, 349, 371–73.

This sermon was a clear statement of what Alexander Campbell believed he and his father were doing. They were clearing away whatever blocked the road to God—the human teachings that obstructed the pathway and obscured the gospel. It was a call to abandon those doctrines and practices and unite on the "clear teachings of the New Testament." Campbell's journal contains texts or outlines of fifty other sermons, and Richardson says he preached 106 times that year.[4]

As Campbell's reputation as a preacher grew, he began receiving invitations to preach to other Christian groups in the area, often in private homes. His father had taught him to preach in the classical Presbyterian way, writing out full manuscripts that he memorized and delivered. Within weeks, however, he began moving toward a more extemporaneous style. Many of his hearers on the American frontier did not relate well to what they considered an "aristocratic" style—they wanted something less stiff, more accessible.

Though Campbell's preaching continued to evolve over the next decade, he increasingly accommodated it to what his new American audience wanted, free from the stilted form, style, and elocution of aristocratic Europe.[5] Campbell's speaking also began to reflect the American fondness for plain speaking and confrontation. He seemed particularly attracted to this style, and it would come to characterize much of his speaking and writing for the next fifty years.

Clearly journalism attracted Campbell just as much as speaking. His elitist attitude toward many in frontier American society and his gift for biting sarcasm combined to create an especially provocative writing style. Campbell viewed many of his new neighbors as lacking the education and cultured sophistication he saw in himself and which he wanted in those he dealt with. In early 1810 he began publishing a series of anonymous essays written for the weekly *Washington Reporter* in which he attacked what he considered the uneducated and rude social behavior of the youth in the area.

Writing at first under the female name "Clarinda," he condemned the conduct that so offended him under the guise of offering corrective advice. Conversations at parties were at best frivolous, and at worst sexually promiscuous. The young women who attended were like a flock of geese that chattered simultaneously whenever one began. Based on such behavior, "Clar-

---

4. Richardson, *Memoirs of Alexander Campbell*, 1:317.
5. Michael W. Casey, "From British Ciceronianism to American Baconianism: Alexander Campbell as a Case Study of a Shift in Rhetorical Theory," *Southern Communication Journal* 66 (Winter 2001): 154–61.

inda" wrote, the females must have small minds and the young men lacked a rational soul. She continued that she was not at all opposed to parties or other social gatherings, with one condition—that they be occasions for learning and discussing important topics that would nourish one's eternal soul rather than for "giddy dissipation, in thoughtless mirth, in needless festivity."[6]

That fall he began another series of disparaging articles written over the name "Bonus Homo." These focused on a local Presbyterian school known as Washington College. His disdain for the developing American educational system (he pointed out "many defects" in it compared to the system at the University of Glasgow) came to a head with the closing exercises of the college's summer session on September 27. Bonus Homo mockingly praised the ceremonies as reflecting the high attainments of the students under the direction of the "sacred characters" who ran the school. He was happy to discover that the students' displays of fencing, boxing, "polite swearing," popular singing, fiddle music, and acting disproved the reports he had heard of the community's narrow-minded attitudes that had formed during recent religious revivals. He continued contemptuously that the student presentations were an "auspicious omen for the progressive amelioration of society" since these students would soon occupy the leadership positions in church and government. In a sarcastic PS, Bonus Homo reported hearing that after the school exercises, opposition to bringing horse racing to the community had diminished significantly.[7]

Angry responses to Bonus Homo accused him of insulting the reputation of the school and its faculty and pouring contempt on the community's religion. Bonus Homo shot back that the school exercises had exposed the gross defects in the American educational system. In October the *Reporter* printed a twenty-seven-stanza poem by Campbell that continued to ridicule the school's exercises and American education in general. The stanzas below give a sense of his disgust.

3) E'en here where savage wildness reigns,
And rudeness spreads her wide domains
    The arts a mansion found.

5) But how, their gentle visage foiled,
Their beauty and proportion spoiled,

6. Quoted in Richardson, *Memoirs of Alexander Campbell*, 1:279–94.
7. Quoted in Richardson, *Memoirs of Alexander Campbell*, 1:295–301.

How mangled and disgrac'd!
My muse declare; say how they're chang'd
How their fair features are derang'd
And all their charms defac'd!!

9) The virtuous matron with her pride,
Her sons and daughters by her side,
    The heart decoying maid;
The pining virgin, and the prude,
The foppish beaux of manners rude
    A brilliant audience made.

14) *This*, at our college is the mode
As the last exhibition show'd,
    To point out virtue fair:
First to be vicious as they can,
That others thence may wisely learn
    Of vices to beware.

25) Such then my friend in plain blunt truth,
Is the fair progress of our youth,
    In all these lib'ral arts;
Such is the science, such the skill,
which our wise seminary fill,
    In these rude western parts.[8]

The articles ended in December, but Campbell's 1810 entrance into journalism, as well as another set of bitingly critical articles in the same paper in 1820–1821, showed him the power of the press.[9] In the next decade he would harness that power with his own publishing operation, using his books and journals to propagate his reform ideas for over forty years.

8. Bonus Homo (Alexander Campbell), "The Genius of the West," *Reporter* 3, no. 10 (October 22, 1810): 2, https://news.google.com/newspapers?nid=gAJFiZdMcUIC&dat=18101022&printsec=frontpage&hl=en.

9. The second set of essays was written under the pseudonym "Candidus" and attacked the moral societies Campbell believed sought to exercise oppressive power over people's personal lives contrary to the ideals of American freedom and democracy. Eva Jean Wrather, *Alexander Campbell: Adventurer in Freedom; A Literary Biography*, 3 vols. (Fort Worth: Texas Christian University Press, 2005–2009), 1:234–45.

These early articles also revealed a deeply ingrained self-assurance, fearlessness, and elitism. Campbell's first biographer, Robert Richardson, who usually minimized Campbell's arrogance, could do so only a little in this case. Comparing him to Martin Luther, Richardson described the 1810 articles as revealing "that Alexander had, as has been well said of Luther, 'an inflexible reliance on the conclusions of his own understanding and on the energy of his own will,' which striking traits in his character, already thus developed, will be found constantly to display themselves in his future history."[10]

One of the most significant events in Campbell's life—both personally and in the development of his religious agenda—happened in October 1810 when he met his soon-to-be wife Margaret Brown. Her father, John, a devout Presbyterian and friend of Thomas Campbell, was a prosperous farmer who lived about twenty miles from Washington in Virginia. Alexander met Margaret when his father sent him on an errand to deliver some books to her father. Afterward Alexander was in the Brown home often, and on March 12, 1811, less than five months after their first meeting, he and Margaret were married. A couple of weeks after the marriage the new couple moved into the Brown home, where Campbell assisted his father-in-law in farming—work Campbell knew well from his days on the farm in Northern Ireland. Eventually this house would become Campbell's home, and the village that grew up around it would be named Bethany. Bethany became Campbell's base of operations for the rest of his life.[11]

In many ways it was the birth of their first child, Jane, one year and one day after their wedding, that marked the beginning of Campbell's unique Christian reform movement. Thomas and Alexander had listened to and participated in discussions about the legitimacy of infant baptism for several years. It had become a hotly debated subject among the Independents in Scotland and Ireland. Robert and James Haldane's acceptance of immersion in 1808 had intensified the controversy among Alexander's Independent friends during his year in Scotland.

Now, however, with a child about to be born, infant baptism became personal. Though Alexander and his father believed that infant baptism was not explicitly authorized in the New Testament, they, like the Haldanes, made it a matter of forbearance. Alexander threw himself into serious study of Scripture to determine whether he would have his baby baptized. Several

10. Richardson, *Memoirs of Alexander Campbell*, 1:308.
11. The village was originally called Buffalo. But when Campbell was granted a post office in 1827 with himself as postmaster, he chose the name Bethany, since Buffalo was already taken. He likely named it after the home of Mary, Martha, and Lazarus mentioned in the Gospels. Richardson, *Memoirs of Alexander Campbell*, 1:181.

years later he would claim that he studied every biblical issue by approaching the text with no preconceived notions, as if he had never seen the Scriptures before.[12] He must have seen himself doing that in this case. At any rate, after weeks of intense study, he concluded that he could accept only immersion of penitent believers as legitimate baptism. Whether he could continue to regard the issue as a matter of forbearance was growing more doubtful by the day. This matter would eventually become a significant controversy among the churches of his reform movement.

The implication of Campbell's decision was that his baptism as an infant was not scriptural, so he went to a Baptist minister he knew, Matthias Luce, to request immersion. This was not as easy as it might seem. Calvinist understandings held by most Baptists taught that a candidate for baptism must first relate a "conversion experience" confirming that he or she was saved—among the elect—and therefore eligible for baptism. Campbell told Luce that the procedure was a human rule unauthorized by Scripture, therefore he would not follow it. He would instead be baptized just as the first Christians were—on a simple profession of faith in Christ as the Son of God and Savior.

Though Luce objected at first because the procedure was not according to Baptist practice, he eventually agreed, and they set the date for June 12, 1812. When the day arrived, Campbell's wife, parents, sister Jane, and two other members of the Brush Run church had decided to be immersed with him.[13]

Thomas Campbell had already immersed three members of the Brush Run church who had never received baptism of any kind. Yet he had continued to oppose "rebaptizing" anyone who had been baptized as an infant and was living a faithful Christian life. Alexander's decisive move influenced Thomas and the others to accept believers' immersion as the only scriptural baptism. Alexander had initiated the contact with Luce and had persuaded him to baptize him and the others in the only way he believed consistent with the New Testament.

This set of events moved Alexander into the chief leadership role of the reform. Though twenty-five years younger than Thomas, Alexander had taken his father's movement in a new direction. His passion for a comprehensive reform of the church and for Christian unity would drive the creation of an American religious enterprise that over the next two centuries would become a global movement.

---

12. Alexander Campbell, "Reply," *Christian Baptist* 3 (April 1826): 229.
13. Richardson, *Memoirs of Alexander Campbell*, 1:394-98.

Matthias Luce was the Baptist minister who immersed Alexander Campbell and six other members of the Brush Run Church (formerly the Christian Association) in 1812. Luce was one of many Baptists who came to sympathize with Campbell's restoration ideas. Used with permission from the Disciples of Christ Historical Society, Bethany, West Virginia.

Campbell and the American Dream

Despite his contempt for things he judged to be defective in American society, Campbell deeply admired much about America. He was convinced that the nation's Protestant character, its democratic style of government, its freedom of religion, and its separation of church and state were exactly what was needed for a thorough reformation of both church and society. In a December 1815 letter to his uncle Archibald in Ireland, Campbell exclaimed:

I cannot speak too highly of the advantages that the people in this country enjoy in being delivered from a proud and lordly aristocracy; and here it becomes very easy to trace the common national evils of all European countries to their proper source, and chiefly to that first germ of oppression, of civil and religious tyranny. I have had my horse shod by a legislator, my horse saddled, my boots cleaned, my stirrup held by a senator. Here is no nobility but virtue; here there is no ascendance save that of genius, virtue and knowledge. The farmer here is lord of the soil, and the most independent man on earth. No consideration that I can conceive of would induce me to exchange all that I enjoy in this country, climate, soil and government, for any situation which your country can afford. I would not exchange the honor and privilege of being an American citizen for the position of your king.[14]

Campbell, like others before him, came to see "European" destructive attitudes of dominance and aristocracy inherent in American slavery. Because of this, he resisted the institution not as a moral evil but as a detriment to the advancement of white America. Furthermore, his hatred of aristocratic tyranny and his celebration of democracy did not make him at home with the white American populist vision of the "common person" as the source of all virtue. Despite his participation in the antiaristocratic rhetoric of the early republic, Campbell never embraced its democratized notion of equality. Campbell believed that the masses of people should defer to the people who were most gifted to lead—the educated, far-sighted "natural aristocrats"—such as himself. In this he reflected the attitude of American leaders like Thomas Jefferson, who stated in 1813,

The natural aristocracy I consider as the most precious gift of nature for the instruction, the trusts, and government of society. And indeed it would have been inconsistent in creation to have formed man for the social state, and not to have provided virtue and wisdom enough to manage the concerns of the society. May we not even say that that form of government is the best which provides the most effectually for a pure selection of these natural aristoi into the offices of government?[15]

14. Quoted in Richardson, *Memoirs of Alexander Campbell*, 1:465–66.
15. Jefferson to John Adams, October 23, 1813, in Lester J. Cappon, *The Adams-Jefferson Letters* (Chapel Hill: University of North Carolina Press, 1959), 388.

Campbell lived in the tension between his belief that many Americans were ignorant, crude, and incapable of leadership and the unavoidable need to appeal to ordinary people to support his reform.[16]

Campbell's acceptance of Scottish commonsense philosophy and the Baconian inductive method for learning the facts of Scripture seem right in line with American populist notions that the common person using common sense could arrive at those truths. Campbell's intellectual commitments certainly embraced the notion that everyone could come to the same biblical facts. However, he also believed that the meticulous use of the scientific method that was necessary to arrive at those facts was beyond the capacity of the masses of uneducated common people.

While theoretically Campbell agreed that all people of normal intelligence could be educated to discern the facts (central to his educational efforts), the reality was that many, perhaps most, Americans either did not have easy access to education or believed they did not need it. He also had to admit that not all human beings had the same capacity to be educated. While he prized common sense for its opposition to the corrupt sensibilities of European aristocrats, only an educated and virtuous common sense had value — the kind of sense that natural aristocrats like himself possessed "naturally."

Proper use of commonsense Baconianism was the foundation for Campbell's religious reform. However, despite the "scrupulous impericism" and rigorous accumulation of facts inherent in the Baconian method, in the words of C. Leonard Allen, "the invocation of Bacon or Baconianism easily became in practice simply a means of legitimizing whatever cause one wished to support and a tool for attacking the views one disliked. Baconian method, that is, sometimes had little to do with the actual theological or scientific method."[17]

Campbell's theological beliefs were certainly not mere creations of his will — his astounding work ethic, intellectual integrity, and solid education insured that. Yet his intellectual naïveté concerning the ability to approach Scripture without preconceived notions and his unwavering confidence in the irrefutable truth of his conclusions, along with his "natural aristocratic"

16. Nathan Hatch has described the tension between the radical populist vision of America and the view of most of the nation's founders that popular sovereignty was not to be understood literally. Nathan O. Hatch, *The Democratization of American Christianity* (New Haven: Yale University Press, 1989), 22–24. See also Sean Wilentz, *The Rise of American Democracy: From Jefferson to Lincoln* (New York: Norton, 2005).

17. C. Leonard Allen, "Baconianism and the Bible in the Disciples of Christ: James S. Lamar and the *Organon of Scripture*," *Church History* 55 (March 1986): 67.

leanings, would be the source of considerable frustration as others equally committed to the Baconian method came to different conclusions. Nevertheless, Campbell advanced his ideas through the use of "the true philosophy" of Baconianism rooted in Scottish commonsense philosophy throughout his long career.

Campbell and Millennialism

There was yet another element with massive importance for shaping Alexander Campbell's reform agenda and doctrinal conclusions—millennialism. Thomas and Alexander Campbell were no strangers to millennial ideas. Apocalyptic millennial beliefs were behind the campaigns for Irish independence and the evangelization of Catholics in eighteenth-century Ireland. On the other hand, Thomas's ministerial training at the University of Glasgow was filled with Scottish Enlightenment thought that insisted humans had the ability to bring change for good by the proper use of reason. This idea led many to believe the millennium would come through education, evangelism, and the removal of evils blocking the coming of that blessed age.[18]

Yet not everyone with a belief in human ability to carry out God's purpose was so optimistic. Many held that all human action could do was to get as many people as possible ready for the dreadful cataclysmic return of Christ.[19]

The Campbells could not have avoided the pervasive millennial thought of their day—neither in Ireland and Scotland nor in America. In Ireland, many held the expectation of wonderful things about to happen, including religious and political freedom for the Irish. Others lived in fear of imminent disaster and the wrath of God. Regardless of the attitude, evangelism often became the focus for hastening the millennial changes—particularly evangelism of Catholics. The Evangelical Society of Ulster (ESU), founded in October 1798 just after the United Irishmen uprising, was partly motivated by urgency to spread evangelical Christianity throughout Ireland.

The millennial ideas of the ESU's first secretary, George Hamilton, deeply influenced Thomas Campbell. In a sermon to the ESU in October

18. Crawford Gribben, "Antichrist in Ireland—Protestant Millennialism and Irish Studies," in *Protestant Millennialism, Evangelicalism, and Irish Society, 1790–2005*, ed. Crawford Gribben and Andrew R. Holmes (New York: Palgrave Macmillan, 2006), 9–10.

19. Gerhard Sauter, "Protestant Theology," in *The Oxford Handbook of Eschatology*, ed. Jerry L. Walls (New York: Oxford University Press, 2008), 253.

1798, Hamilton asserted that God was "shaking . . . the nations," reporting on evangelical missions to the South Seas and Africa and "a wonderful revolution in Italy," that is, Napoleon's taking of Rome—the seat of the pope—the previous January.[20] The underlying anti-Catholicism of all the evangelical missionary societies was clear. Hamilton viewed these events, as well as the work of evangelical societies like the newly formed ESU, as fulfillment of biblical prophecies regarding the end of time.[21]

The disastrous Irish rebellion of 1798 made the evangelism of Catholics and others outside of evangelical Christianity even more urgent. Thomas Campbell, though forced to leave the ESU by his Anti-Burgher Seceder Synod, shared the Society's sense of urgency to prepare for a great work of God as the end of time rapidly approached. In America, Thomas's *Declaration and Address* urged action partly because of the "signs of the times" that included allusions to European revolutionary events.[22]

Most historians have labeled Alexander Campbell's optimistic vision for his reformation "postmillennial." Literally, the term signifies that Christ's second coming would be after the millennium—the thousand years of blessed existence on earth. This view assumed that God had given human beings (Christians) the ability and responsibility to evangelize the world and move it toward a perfect society through elimination of evils like alcoholism, inhumane prisons, and slavery. Postmillennialism held a high view of what humans could do to bring in the millennium.

Others, with views labeled "premillennial," maintained that the world would get progressively worse until Christ returned, destroyed his enemies, and began the millennium. In other words, the only way the millennium could arrive was by Christ's violent return—not human action. Much of Alexander Campbell's writing does seem to reflect a postmillennial stance. The reality, however, especially when looking at his entire career, is more complex. While the differences between postmillennial and premillennial tenden-

---

20. George Hamilton, *The Great Necessity of Itinerant Preaching: A Sermon Delivered in Armagh at the Formation of the Evangelical Society of Ulster, on Wednesday, 10th of Oct. 1798. With a Short Introductory Memorial, Respecting the Establishment and First Attempt of the Society* (Armagh: Printed and Sold by T. Stevenson, and by each Member of the Committee, 1799), 27; quoted in James L. Gorman, "Transatlantic Evangelical Missions Culture and the Rise of the Campbell Movement" (PhD diss., Baylor University, 2015), 159.

21. See quotations and discussion in Gorman, "Transatlantic Evangelical Missions Culture," 159–60.

22. Thomas Campbell, *Declaration and Address of the Christian Association of Washington* (Washington, PA: Brown & Sample, 1809), 14.

cies were real, neither ordinary people nor Christian leaders in Campbell's day sharply defined and separated the theories. Even the Puritan confessions, including the Westminster Confession of Faith that profoundly shaped the Campbells' religious beliefs, cannot be pigeonholed into current millennial categories.[23] What at first glance might seem to be postmillennial views of progress toward the millennium were often mixed with views of imminent disaster and tribulation—what James W. Davidson calls the "afflictive model of progress."[24] And what appear to be premillennial descriptions of doom often included the belief that God's people were to assist God's work of fulfilling prophecy and bringing in the millennial age.[25] The larger story of Alexander Campbell's millennial views will appear in other parts of the biography, but a few glimpses now are important to see the direction he was about to take in his reform.

Even before Campbell arrived in the United States, he had a vision of a land free from the religious and political conflicts of his homeland, filled with unlimited opportunities for improvement.[26] After he landed in New York in late September 1809, his vision began to be confirmed. America, like Ireland, was rife with millennial ideas about the nation's role in Christ's second coming. Many Americans viewed the United States as God's fulfillment of prophecy that would soon lead to the establishment of the everlasting kingdom. Yet as stated, different versions of the story reflected either optimistic views (the advance of Christianity and the regeneration of the world) or pessimistic ones (the embattlement of the church and the destruction of the world).[27]

Campbell believed God had prepared the United States for the restoration and spread of what he came to call the "ancient gospel and order of things." As people heard the truth—the plain facts of the Bible uncorrupted by human philosophy—sectarianism would disappear. This would, in turn, unite all Christians, lead to the conversion of the world, and bring in the blessed millennium.[28]

23. Paul S. Boyer, *When Time Shall Be No More: Prophecy Belief in Modern American Culture* (Cambridge, MA: Belknap Press of Harvard University Press, 1992), 76–83. See also Ruth H. Bloch, *Visionary Republic: Millennial Themes in American Thought, 1756–1800* (Cambridge: Cambridge University Press, 1985), 131–35, and Crawford Gribben, "The Eschatology of the Puritan Confessions," *Scottish Bulletin of Evangelical Theology* 20 (Spring 2002): 53–54.

24. James W. Davidson, *The Logic of Millennial Thought: Eighteenth Century New England* (New Haven: Yale University Press, 1977), 260.

25. Boyer, *When Time Shall Be No More*, 82–83.

26. Richardson, *Memoirs of Alexander Campbell*, 1:79.

27. See, for example, Timothy P. Webber, "Millennialism," in Walls, *The Oxford Handbook of Eschatology*, 365–69.

28. See Anthony L. Dunnavant, "United Christians, Converted World: John 17:20–23

Yet Campbell often criticized the actions of American political leaders he believed were scuttling progress toward the millennium. In 1833 he lashed out at the "injustice, cupidity, ambition, oppression" of US political institutions. These vices signaled the doom of the nation "to the vials of vengeance" and would lead to its destruction "before the triumphant day of the Lord come."[29]

He could also describe God's destruction of corrupt governments and apostate churches in ways that rivaled the most pessimistic premillennialist. In the 1833 series of articles quoted above, Campbell spoke of the unremitting war against the rule of Christ waged by the world and the politicians of the United States. He described the joy followers of Christ would feel when the angel announced the hour of final judgment on all earthly powers. This judgment, he warned, would be worse than all God's previous judgments in the flood and in the destruction of Sodom and Gomorrah, Babylon, and Jerusalem.

Lumping Catholic, Anglican, and Presbyterian churches together as "Babylon the Great," he exclaimed: "But strong is the arm of the Lord who avenges her! When the hour of her judgment is come she shall be hurled into perdition as a millstone into the sea. The tares will be collected into bundles and given to the devouring flame, and she shall bewitch the nations no more."[30] In other words, he did not see human action consistently moving things "ever upward and onward," even in his beloved adopted country.

Campbell was now on the cusp of creating a concrete plan to restore the "ancient gospel and order of things" that would result in the unity of Christians and the conversion of the world. These events would begin the thousand years of peace and prosperity, after which Christ would return. Exactly how he thought that would happen is the next part of the story.

---

and the Interrelation of Themes in the Campbell-Stone Movement," *Discipliana* 46 (Fall 1986): 44–46; Anthony L. Dunnavant, *Restructure: Four Historical Ideals in the Campbell-Stone Movement and the Development of the Polity of the Christian Church (Disciples of Christ)* (New York: Lang, 1993), 19–24.

29. Alexander Campbell, "Everlasting Gospel. No. II," *Millennial Harbinger*, March 1833, 121.

30. Alexander Campbell, "Everlasting Gospel—No. 3," *Millennial Harbinger*, May 1833, 225; "Everlasting Gospel—No. 4," *Millennial Harbinger*, July 1833, 319.

CHAPTER 5

The Creation of the Ancient Gospel and Order of Things

The 1820s were crucial for the formation of Alexander Campbell's unique Christian movement. In that decade his vision of a reformed church and society took clear shape and became his lifelong agenda. The birth of his first child led him to make a decisive move on baptism—a move that propelled him into the chief leadership of the movement. His provocative writing further developed his self-confidence, elitism, and arrogance, all fueled by his sharp intellect and physical strength. His hatred of the tyranny of hereditary European aristocracy was paired with an equal disgust for the tyranny of the uneducated and coarse mobs of American "common people." Campbell now began a decade of advance and struggle in which he would create a system he believed was the answer for the world's ills and the best hope for bringing in the millennial age.

Central to these developments was his belief in the crucial importance of believers' immersion. Soon after Campbell's immersion by Baptist minister Matthias Luce, the church of the Christian Association (renamed the Brush Run church in 1811) became a congregation of immersed believers and in 1815 joined the Redstone Baptist Association. Campbell's encounter with Baptist leaders, however, reinforced his dislike of uneducated people. He explained in the 1848 history of his reform movement that the Baptist preachers he had known then were "narrow, contracted, illiberal, and uneducated men."[1] His opinion of many members of Baptist churches, however, was better, and he soon became the denomination's champion in advocating believers' immersion—though he was still at odds with other Baptist theological positions.

---

1. Alexander Campbell, "Anecdotes, Incidents, and Facts," *Millennial Harbinger*, June 1848, 345.

The evolution of Campbell's beliefs toward an insistence on immersion for the remission of sins moved significantly forward between 1820 and 1823 in two debates on baptism with Presbyterian ministers John Walker and William Maccalla. Yet it was a controversial sermon by Campbell at the September 1, 1816, Redstone Baptist Association meeting that laid the foundation for the two debates and the formulation of what would become a hallmark of his movement—the restoration of the ancient gospel.

Campbell's "Sermon on the Law"

Most attendees at the Redstone Baptist Association meeting that year expected to hear the widely popular Campbell preach. Instead, several of Campbell's opponents, led by Elder John Pritchard of the host congregation, insisted on asking a different preacher who was visiting from Ohio. When that preacher became ill, another leader favorable to Campbell informed him that he was the preferred substitute. Campbell knew that at this point they needed him to fill the position. He agreed to speak, but only if Pritchard asked him in person—which he did.[2]

According to Campbell's later account, he had only a couple of hours to prepare. He quickly jotted down a few notes and delivered what came to be known as his "Sermon on the Law."[3] His point was this: the old law had been transcended by the new law of Christ, and therefore the Old Testament, while true in all it said, did not regulate the lives of those under the new covenant of Christ. This was not a new topic for Campbell. He had been strongly influenced by a stream of Reformed theology that tended in this direction, and he had preached on it at least once before in 1813.[4]

He spent considerable time making sure his hearers understood the definition of "the law." The distinction made in Reformed theology between moral, ceremonial, and judicial law was an unscriptural human invention, he insisted. He, on the other hand, was using the term just as the Bible used it—"the law" was the entire law of Moses given to the Israelites.[5] His goal was to invalidate the use of the Old Testament as a justification for practices

2. Robert Richardson, *Memoirs of Alexander Campbell*, 2 vols. (Philadelphia: J. B. Lippincott & Co., 1868–1870), 1:469–71.

3. Alexander Campbell, "Sermon on the Law," *Millennial Harbinger*, September 1846, 494.

4. Everett Ferguson, "Alexander Campbell's 'Sermon on the Law': A Historical and Theological Examination," *Restoration Quarterly* 29, no. 2 (1987): 72n7.

5. Campbell, "Sermon on the Law," 497–500.

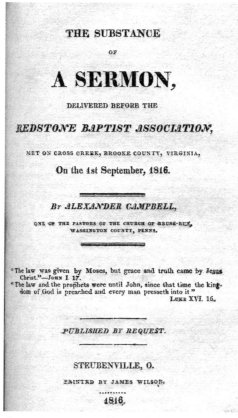

Soon after he delivered the controversial "Sermon on the Law," Campbell wrote out a more developed version from his hastily prepared notes and had it printed. He would later reprint the sermon in the *Millennial Harbinger* in 1846. Used with permission from the Disciples of Christ Historical Society, Bethany, West Virginia.

like infant baptism (by analogy to the practice of circumcision in the old covenant), tithing to pay preachers, fasting as preparation for the Lord's Supper, and other practices based on the old covenant.[6] While Baptist theology certainly rejected infant baptism, it did not make the sharp distinction Campbell advocated between the Old and New Testaments.

Anticipating the objection that if Christians were completely free from the law they would live immoral lives, Campbell quoted Paul's argument

6. Campbell, "Sermon on the Law," 520.

in Romans 6:15: we are not under the law but under grace; and we who are under grace are dead to sin and do not live in it any longer. That argument should be clear enough for most people, he asserted; but apparently it was not so clear to Baptist leaders whom he labeled "learned Rabbis and Doctors of the Law."[7] The old covenant, he insisted, had no power to motivate people to come to Christ or live a holy life, nor did it regulate the church.

Campbell's position directly contradicted the Baptist Philadelphia Confession of Faith, to which technically all churches in the Redstone Association were required to subscribe. The confession described the Ten Commandments as "a perfect rule of Righteousness" and stated that while Christ had taken away the ceremonial law, Christians were still obligated to follow the Old Testament's moral law embodied as a rule of life. Despite the requirement, there was so much antisubscription feeling in the association in 1815 when the Brush Run church was admitted that the congregation was not required to subscribe.

Campbell's views had a long history in Christian theology. The early church, Anabaptists, and Scottish Independents all believed in a radical distinction between law and grace. His father, Thomas, made the distinction in the *Declaration and Address* when he referred to the Old Testament as authoritative for God's people before the Christian age.[8] In some ways Campbell's position resembled Dutch Reformed covenant theology in its teaching of a sharp break between law and grace. However, the Dutch taught that God had begun the covenant of grace at the fall of humanity; Campbell insisted that it had not begun until the finished work of Christ.[9]

Characteristically, Campbell declared that his investigation into these matters was completely impartial and that his conclusions would be obvious "to every unbiased and reflecting mind" who had an ear for distinguishing truth from falsehood.[10] The sermon did gain him a hearing and persuaded several to take his position. However, traditional Baptist leaders who held strictly to the Calvinist ideas of the Philadelphia Confession of Faith viewed his teachings as heresy.

Campbell's sharp separation of old and new covenants in the "Sermon on the Law" became, by his own account, central to his reform. In the introduction to his 1846 reprinting of the sermon, he remarked, "the intelligent

---

7. Campbell, "Sermon on the Law," 509–10.

8. Ferguson, "Alexander Campbell's 'Sermon on the Law,'" 76–78.

9. Eva Jean Wrather, *Alexander Campbell: Adventurer in Freedom; A Literary Biography*, 3 vols. (Fort Worth: Texas Christian University Press, 2005–2009), 1:218.

10. Campbell, "Sermon on the Law," 512–13.

reader will discover in it the elements of things which have characterized all our writings on the subject of modern Christianity from that day to the present."[11] The distinction would be crucial to his arguments in the 1820 debate on baptism with Presbyterian minister William Walker.

The Campbell-Walker Debate

The events leading to the Campbell-Walker debate started with the success of Ohio Baptist minister John Birch in immersing a large number of people in eastern Ohio in 1819. To block further Baptist advances, Seceder Presbyterian minister John Walker began a series of sermons that fall attacking Baptist doctrine, especially their insistence on immersion. Birch, who heard at least one of Walker's sermons, contended that Walker was misrepresenting Baptist teaching. Walker in turn challenged Birch "or any other regular Baptist minister of good moral character and standing" to debate him on the subject of baptism.[12]

Birch, who admired Campbell and his work, immediately asked Campbell to be the Baptist representative. In his account of what happened next that appeared in the published debate, Campbell said simply, "I hesitated for a little." Other accounts, however, portray much more of a struggle. According to Robert Richardson, Thomas Campbell had always opposed "public oral debates" because he believed they provoked unchristian passions, made winning more important than finding the truth, and pushed Christians apart. Alexander's deference to his father's feelings, as well as his busy schedule running Buffaloe Academy, a school he had begun in January 1818, apparently contributed to his initial unwillingness to accept Birch's invitation.

According to Richardson, however, Alexander was by temperament a debater. Even as a boy he was known for debating his schoolmates and had become very self-confident in his "dialectical power." Birch kept urging Campbell to accept Walker's challenge, even recruiting others to put pressure on Campbell. In May 1820 Campbell accepted, after persuading his father that such a "public defense of revealed truth" was a good thing. Campbell also admitted that he didn't want anyone to think he was afraid of defending the truth.[13]

---

11. Campbell, "Sermon on the Law," 493.

12. Alexander Campbell, "Preface," in *Debate on Christian Baptism, Between Mr. John Walker, A Minister of the Secession, and Alexander Campbell*, 2nd ed., enlarged (Pittsburgh: Eichbaum & Johnston, 1822), 5.

13. Richardson, *Memoirs of Alexander Campbell*, 2:13–16; Campbell, "Preface," 5.

The substantial Quaker community in Mt. Pleasant treated Campbell kindly and most likely allowed the use of their recently constructed Yearly Meeting House for the debate between Campbell and John Walker, June 19–20, 1820. Photo courtesy of the *Times-Reporter*, New Philadelphia, Ohio.

The debate began on Monday, June 19, 1820, at Mount Pleasant, Ohio. John Walker was minister for four small Seceder Presbyterian churches in the area, including the one in Mount Pleasant. Quakers made up a large part of the town's population of around a thousand, and the area was a stronghold of abolitionist sentiment, serving as an important station on the Underground Railroad. Though accounts do not identify the building in which the debate took place, the Quakers had constructed a large meetinghouse in the village in 1814 that would hold two thousand people and was likely the location of the event.

The debaters settled on two topics: who should be baptized, and how to baptize—sprinkling, pouring, or immersion. They would, however, also address the purpose of the act. Both sides agreed that the debate would continue until the audience or the moderators were satisfied that enough had been said. In reality, however, it lasted only two days. Much to Campbell's surprise, Walker and his moderator called for final speeches Tuesday afternoon. Campbell accused Walker of simply not being prepared for the contest.

According to Campbell's published version of the debate, while the rules allowed forty minutes for each speech, Walker's first one lasted less than five. His sole point was that there had been one divine covenant of grace for God's people since the Fall, and that since baptism had taken the place of circumcision as the seal of that covenant for Christians, the infants of God's people had a right to baptism.[14]

Campbell had clearly rejected this reasoning in his 1816 "Sermon on the Law." He attacked the notion that there was only one covenant, drawing from Hebrews 8 to contrast the old covenant with the newer and better one of Christ. He then identified inconsistencies with making baptism analogous to circumcision: they had different administrators and prerequisites, as well as different forms and purposes. Circumcision conveyed earthly blessings for the Jews—the promise of inheriting the land of Canaan and becoming a great nation. Baptism, on the other hand, conveyed spiritual blessings, the promise of remission of sins and the gift of the Holy Spirit. Furthermore, circumcision was for males only and was done eight days after birth. Most importantly, Scripture gave absolutely no authorization for saying that baptism replaced circumcision as the sign of God's covenant.[15]

Clearly, Campbell was at odds with several basic beliefs of Baptist theology. Three years later he would tell a group of Kentucky Baptists during his second public debate that he had "as much against you Baptists as I have against the Presbyterians."[16] Yet in his final speech of the debate with Walker, Campbell asserted that using the principle of going to the Scriptures to think for himself and decide all doctrinal matters "made me a Baptist."[17] Although he did not have time to develop his theology of baptism fully in this brief debate, at this point it was clearly very Baptist.[18]

Like all Baptists, he rejected any continuity between circumcision and baptism. Baptism was, rather, a figure of the spiritual blessings conveyed by the sealing of the Holy Spirit that had already occurred in the life of those who believed in Christ. Using Paul's language of the renewing of the Holy Spirit, Campbell explained that spiritual renewal changed one's mind and led the renewed "to submit to 'be buried with Christ in Baptism.'" Immersion represented one's faith in the death, burial, and resurrection of

---

14. *Debate on Christian Baptism, Between Mr. John Walker, A Minister of the Secession, and Alexander Campbell*, 9.

15. *Debate on Christian Baptism, Between Mr. John Walker, A Minister of the Secession, and Alexander Campbell*, 12–21.

16. Richardson, *Memoirs of Alexander Campbell*, 2:88.

17. *Debate on Christian Baptism, Between Mr. John Walker, A Minister of the Secession, and Alexander Campbell*, 140.

18. I am indebted for this discussion to John Mark Hicks, "The Recovery of the Ancient Gospel: Alexander Campbell and the Design of Baptism," in *Baptism and the Remission of Sins: An Historical Perspective*, ed. David Fletcher (Joplin, MO: College Press, 1990), 111–70.

Christ and represented our obligations to a new life.[19] In the appendix to the printed debate, he was even more explicit: as soon as a person believed the gospel, he or she was sealed with the Holy Spirit. That seal was the utterly "sufficient guarantee and earnest, and requires not any external ordinance to perfect it."[20]

At the end of the debate Campbell appealed to the audience to go home, read their Bibles, and judge the matter for themselves—just as he said he had done. The clergy had prevented them from exercising that right, as if they were not capable of reasoning for themselves! Those blind guides insisted that everyone look to them for answers and consult human creeds rather than the Scriptures. He then challenged any minister of good standing in any denomination that practiced infant baptism to debate the issue with him in oral or written form.[21]

Further Developments of Campbell's Baptismal Theology

That new challenge would be accepted three years later by another Seceder Presbyterian minister, William L. Maccalla, in a much more substantial encounter in Washington, Kentucky. In the meantime, Campbell's ideas concerning the nature of baptism continued to develop in significant ways. While Campbell would later recall that he had first begun to connect baptism and remission of sins during the debate with Walker, another development actually provided an important resource for his continued development of the doctrine.[22]

While in Pittsburgh in late 1821, Campbell visited the home of the father of his future colleague and biographer Robert Richardson. While there he had an important conversation with the man who would become perhaps his closest colleague in the reformation, Walter Scott. A Scottish Presbyterian immigrant who had moved to Pittsburgh in 1819, Scott taught in a school run by a Haldane named George Forrester. After Forrester convinced Scott to submit to believers' immersion as the only biblical baptism, Scott began

19. *Debate on Christian Baptism, Between Mr. John Walker, A Minister of the Secession, and Alexander Campbell*, 138.

20. *Debate on Christian Baptism, Between Mr. John Walker, A Minister of the Secession, and Alexander Campbell*, 171.

21. *Debate on Christian Baptism, Between Mr. John Walker, A Minister of the Secession, and Alexander Campbell*, 140–41.

22. Alexander Campbell, "Events of 1823 and 1827," *Millennial Harbinger*, October 1838, 467.

helping lead the Haldane congregation. When Forrester accidently drowned in 1820, Scott assumed responsibility for both Forrester's school and the church.

In early 1821 Scott received a copy of a tract on immersion written by Henry Errett, a Scotch Baptist living in New York. The ideas in the booklet excited Scott so much that he spent three months with Errett's church examining its teaching on baptism. Though the church's narrow attitudes greatly disappointed Scott, the booklet drove him to pursue a deeper grasp of the nature and purpose of baptism. Several weeks before his conversation with Scott in Pittsburgh, Campbell also received a copy of Errett's pamphlet. The ideas in the booklet sparked considerable discussion between Alexander and his father.

For both Scott and the Campbells, Errett's list of effects explicitly connected with baptism in Scripture was one of the most stimulating aspects of the tract. These included remission of sins, escape from the wrath to come, spiritual birth, salvation, and regeneration. However, in line with Scotch Baptist understandings, Errett rejected the notion that these promises were actually tied to baptism—that they came to the believer as a result of being immersed. Such statements were not to be taken literally any more than statements about the Lord's Supper being Christ's body and blood were to be taken literally.

So for Errett, the act itself did not bring remission of sins nor was it required for salvation—notions contrary to Baptist understandings. Yet neither was it a superfluous action without real significance. It was the public profession of the believer's faith and salvation, the act that put the saved into Christ's visible church and allowed them to participate fully in the communion of the church.[23] But despite Errett's insistence that the promises connected with baptism could not be taken literally, his long list of Scriptures that seemed to connect baptism with salvation bore deeply into the minds of Scott and the Campbells. Errett himself had stated, "From these several passages we may learn how baptism was viewed in the beginning by those who were qualified to understand its meaning best. No one who has been in the habit of considering it merely as an ordinance, can read these passages with attention, without being surprised at the wonderful powers, and qualities, and effects, and uses, which are there apparently ascribed to it."[24]

---

23. Hicks, "The Recovery of the Ancient Gospel," 126–27.

24. Quoted in William Baxter, *Life of Elder Walter Scott* (Cincinnati: Bosworth, Chase & Hall, 1874), 51.

The meeting between Scott and Campbell in late 1821 was likely the first time the two had ever discussed the matter, but over the next months each continued to ponder the implications.

The Campbell-Maccalla Debate

Campbell's challenge at the end of the Walker debate went unaccepted for almost three years. In May 1823, Campbell received a letter from William Maccalla, Seceder Presbyterian minister at Augusta, Kentucky, forty miles southeast of Cincinnati. Maccalla was taking up the challenge.

Campbell was excited finally to have the opportunity to explain his new ideas on baptism. He believed Maccalla would be a more capable opponent than Walker. But as he was preparing for the contest, a problem arose. He had issued his challenge to "any Pedo-baptist minister of any denomination, of good standing in his party." The assumption was that he himself was also in "good standing" as a Baptist minister. However, his enemies were even then moving to charge him with heresy and excommunicate him from the Redstone Baptist Association. This would have discredited him as a legitimate Baptist representative and likely stopped the debate.

Campbell devised an ingenious plan to avoid having to cancel. He quickly petitioned the Brush Run church to allow him and about twenty other members to move their membership from the Brush Run church, which was in the Redstone Association, to a new church at Wellsburg, Virginia, a few miles away. Then the new Wellsburg congregation petitioned for admission and was accepted into the Mahoning Baptist Association, which was strongly supportive of the Campbell reform. Since Campbell was no longer in the Redstone Association, he was no longer subject to its jurisdiction. Campbell attended the association meeting as usual, where his opponents, assuming he was a messenger from the Brush Run church, were prepared to charge him with heresy. Before they could carry out their plan, however, they discovered he was there merely as an observer. They angrily realized they could not touch him.[25]

With the excommunication stopped, Campbell proceeded to finalize arrangements for the debate. Alexander and his father spent considerable time discussing immersion for the remission of sins as New Testament baptism but told almost no one of their thoughts. A few weeks before the debate,

---

25. Alexander Campbell, "Anecdotes, Incidents, and Facts—No. IV," *Millennial Harbinger*, October 1848, 553–56.

however, Walter Scott visited them in Bethany and they raised the "novel" idea with him. They all agreed that the debate with Maccalla would be the platform for examining the idea as the design and purpose of baptism.[26]

Though Maccalla was minister in Augusta, Kentucky, the debate took place in the larger town of Washington, Kentucky, twenty miles away. The opening session was on Wednesday morning, October 15, 1823. Maccalla took the same position that Walker had taken three years earlier—the seal of God's covenant of grace had been circumcision in the Old Testament church, and now, in the New Testament church, the seal was baptism. During most of the debate Maccalla read from manuscripts written earlier and often failed to respond directly to Campbell's arguments—much to Campbell's annoyance.[27] But by far the most significant part of the debate was Campbell's introduction on the second day of his "novel" teaching on immersion for the remission of sins.

After arguing that baptism was only for believing persons and only by immersion, he stated that since immersion was for the remission of sins, it made no sense to baptize infants, who did not need such remission. In the most explicit statement he had ever made in public, Campbell declared,

> The Lord saith, "He that believeth and is baptized shall be saved." He does not say, he that believeth, and keeps my commands, shall be saved: but he saith he that believeth and is baptized shall be saved. He placeth baptism on the right hand of faith. Again he tells Nicodemus, that "except a man be born of water and of the spirit, he cannot enter into the kingdom of God."—Peter, on the day of Pentecost, places baptism in the same "exalted place"—"Repent," says he, "and be baptized every one of you, FOR the remission of sin."—Ananias saith to Paul "Arise and be baptized and WASH AWAY your sins, calling upon the name of the Lord."—Paul saith of the Corinthians, "Ye were once fornicators, idolators, adulterers, effeminate, thieves, covetous, drunkards, rioters, extortioners, but ye were WASHED in the name of the Lord Jesus," doubtless referring to their baptism. He tells Titus, God our Saviour saved us by the washing of regeneration and renewing of the Holy Spirit.—See again its dignified importance! Peter finishes the grand climax, in praise of baptism—"Baptism doth also now save us, by the resurrection

---

26. Campbell, "Events of 1823 and 1827," 468.

27. Alexander Campbell, *A Debate on Christian Baptism Between the Rev. W. L. Maccalla, a Presbyterian Teacher, and Alexander Campbell* (Buffaloe, VA: Campbell & Sala, 1824), 82, 87–88. See https://books.google.com/books/about/A_Debate_on_Christian_Baptism.html?id=hr8MAAAAIAAJ.

of Jesus Christ from the dead." I have thus, in the naked import of those testimonies, shown, that it is of vast import, of glorious design.[28]

Yet, even after this unambiguous linking of baptism and remission of sins, he was still not willing to make baptism absolutely necessary for salvation. He continued to separate the actual forgiveness of sins that occurred at the time of one's belief in Christ and "formal" remission that took place in the act of baptism. "Paul's sins were really pardoned when he believed, yet he had no solemn pledge of the fact, no formal acquittal, no formal purgation of his sins, until he washed them away in the water of baptism." He insisted that nothing was "essential to salvation but the blood of Christ," but went on to say that God had made baptism "essential to their formal forgiveness in this life, to their admission into his kingdom on earth."[29] Interestingly, in 1828, at the beginning of a series on baptism, he would remember having said in the Maccalla debate that the immersion of believers "formally and in fact" conveyed remission of sins.[30]

In his debate with Maccalla, Campbell had definitely moved beyond traditional Baptist understandings in his connection of immersion with God's work of redemption. Instead of a human action in response to God's accomplishment, baptism was fundamentally God's work. It was the divine pledge that assured believers of their actual pardon—the remission of all their sins.[31]

Campbell's position would continue to develop over the next few years to an overt, unambiguous, and essential connection of believers' immersion with conversion and redemption. By 1828 Campbell would come to see real and formal remission of sins as simultaneous in the act of believers' immersion. "He that goeth down into the water to put on Christ, in the faith that the blood of Jesus cleanses from all sin, and that he has appointed immersion as the medium, and the act of ours, through and in which he actually and formally remits our sins, has, when immersed, the actual remission of his sins."[32]

---

28. Campbell, *A Debate on Christian Baptism Between the Rev. W. L. Maccalla, a Presbyterian Teacher, and Alexander Campbell*, 117.

29. Campbell, *A Debate on Christian Baptism Between the Rev. W. L. Maccalla, a Presbyterian Teacher, and Alexander Campbell*, 116, 125, 135.

30. Alexander Campbell, "Ancient Gospel—No. I. Baptism," *Christian Baptist* 6 (January 1828): 121.

31. Campbell, *A Debate on Christian Baptism Between the Rev. W. L. Maccalla, a Presbyterian Teacher, and Alexander Campbell*, 135, 144.

32. Alexander Campbell, "Ancient Gospel—No. IV. Immersion," *Christian Baptist* 5 (April 1828): 213.

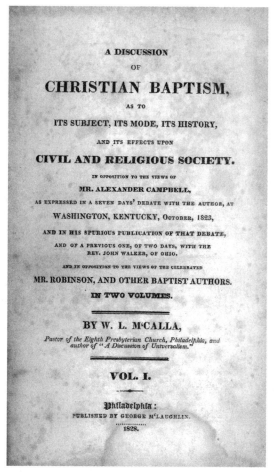

In 1828 W. L. Maccalla (here spelled M'Calla) published a two-volume refutation of Campbell's published accounts of the 1820 and 1823 debates among Campbell and John Walker and himself. Courtesy of the Center for Restoration Studies, Abilene Christian University, Abilene, Texas.

Several things happened between 1823 and 1828 to move Campbell toward this stronger position. First, in July 1823 he began a monthly journal to spread his reform ideas beyond what he could do through preaching and debating. The highly successful publication and sales of the Walker and Maccalla debates convinced Campbell that a publication of his own would be a powerful tool to disseminate his message. This journal, the *Christian Baptist*, served as the chief means for spreading his ideas until 1830, when he began a new paper, the *Millennial Harbinger.*

In the *Christian Baptist* Campbell continued the controversial style of writing he had used in his early articles in the *Washington Reporter.* Though his tone overall was not as strident and sarcastic in his second journal, the *Millennial Harbinger,* an aggressive, combative style remained a hallmark of his writing and could break out in furious strength if he were crossed by someone he felt was questioning his honesty or who differed with him on what he considered a plain scriptural truth.

In February 1824 Campbell began a pivotal series titled "A Restoration of the Ancient Order of Things." In these thirty-two articles he examined matters of theology, practice, and church order he believed needed scrutiny. Among these were creeds and confessions, the Lord's Supper, the office of bishop, use of scriptural terms in hymns, and discipline in the church. By the time he finished in September 1829, he had laid out core commitments of his reform movement, including simple worship, local congregational leadership, weekly Lord's Supper, insistence on Scripture alone, and strict adherence to biblical terminology in all aspects of life and church. Over the next decade Campbell developed these ideas in articles and sermons, publishing his "Christian System" in a more systematic form, first in 1835 and then in an expanded version in 1839.[33]

Campbell, Scott, and the Ancient Gospel

Perhaps even more crucial to the creation of Campbell's reform agenda, however, was a series on "the ancient gospel" he began in January 1828. A remarkable revival led by Walter Scott the previous year pressured Campbell to write the articles. In 1827 Campbell had visited Scott, who was operating a school in Steubenville, Ohio, and urged him to accompany him to the annual meeting of the Mahoning Baptist Association. Supporters of the Campbell reform dominated the association, and during the meeting it offered to support Scott

33. Alexander Campbell, *A Connected View of the Principles and Rules by Which the Living Oracles May be Intelligibly and Certainly Interpreted* (Bethany, VA: M'Vay and Ewing, 1835). The publisher placed the words "Christianity Restored" on the spine without Campbell's approval. Alexander Campbell, *The Christian System, In Reference to the Union of Christians, and a Restoration of Primitive Christianity, as Plead in the Current Reformation,* 2nd ed. (Pittsburgh: Forrester & Campbell, 1839).

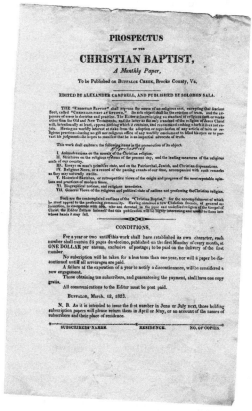

Prospectus for the *Christian Baptist*. Campbell announced and began soliciting pre-publication subscriptions for his forthcoming journal in early 1823. He actually published the first issue in August, eventually publishing seven complete volumes. He began the *Millennial Harbinger* in January 1830, publishing both papers through July. Used with permission from Bethany College, T. W. Phillips Memorial Library, Archives and Special Collections, Bethany, West Virginia.

as a traveling evangelist in the Western Reserve (what would become northeastern Ohio). Scott accepted the invitation and prepared to begin his work.

That appointment gave Scott just the platform he needed to begin teaching and actually practicing baptism for remission of sins. This was the doctrine with which he and the Campbells had been grappling since reading Henry Errett's tract in 1821, and to which Alexander Campbell had moved very close in his debate with W. L. Maccalla. Though working as an evangelist for a Baptist association, Scott began using a baptismal formula that was very different from the one used by Baptists. In it he explicitly stated at the time of each immersion that he baptized in the name of the Father, Son, and Holy Spirit for the remission of sins and the gift of the Holy Spirit.[34]

This baptismal formula reflected Scott's message that anyone who heard and believed the gospel could come to Christ and receive forgiveness and salvation through baptism. Though this was a new teaching for many, it was also a word of hope. The Calvinist understanding that one must wait for a conversion experience initiated by God implied that humans had nothing to do at all with their salvation. Scott, in contrast, told hearers that if they simply had faith in the facts of the gospel, they could decide to submit to immersion and receive salvation. This was in everyone's grasp—not just a small "elect" who had a mysterious conversion experience. Thousands responded to Scott's invitation.[35]

News of Scott's phenomenal success prompted Alexander to send his father to check up on Scott. He was afraid the large number of immersions might be the result of his colleague's having fallen into some kind of emotional excess. When Thomas arrived and heard what Scott was preaching, he endorsed it completely.[36] In an 1833 article published in Scott's journal the *Evangelist*, Scott quoted from a letter written by Thomas Campbell in April 1828 in which he enthusiastically endorsed Scott's preaching as the first time he had seen "the *direct exhibition* and *application*" of the ancient gospel. Scott preached that believing penitents should respond immediately to the gospel by being immersed for the remission of sins.

Alexander himself remarked in the October 1831 *Millennial Harbinger* that Scott had, in the "Fall of 1827, arranged the several items of Faith, Repentance, Baptism, Remission of Sins, the Holy Spirit and Eternal Life, restored them in this order to the church under the title of *Ancient Gospel*, and successfully preached it for the conversion of the world."[37] His phenomenal success moved Alexander to describe him as "the active agent of the most important revolutions and conversions in the present day, as far as has come to my ears."[38]

Scott was at the height of his remarkable success when Alexander began a series titled "Ancient Gospel. Immersion." Apparently Scott had given Campbell the idea for the title when he visited Campbell's home in 1827.

---

34. Campbell, "Events of 1823 and 1827," 469.

35. Baxter, *Life of Elder Walter Scott*, 103–10.

36. Baxter, *Life of Elder Walter Scott*, 158–59.

37. Alexander Campbell, "Brother Walter Scott," *Millennial Harbinger*, October 1831, 480.

38. Walter Scott, "Letters on the Events of 1823 and 1827," *Evangelist*, December 1838, 280. Scott was quoting Alexander Campbell, "The Beaver Anathema," *Christian Baptist* 7 (July 1830): 269.

Walter Scott became the most avid promoter of what Campbell labeled "the ancient gospel and order of things." His preaching and practice of immersion explicitly "for the remission of sins" on the Western Reserve in 1827 brought thousands into the Campbell reformation. Campbell regarded Scott's techniques with suspicion. Used with permission from the Disciples of Christ Historical Society, Bethany, West Virginia.

Campbell's continued nervousness that Scott may have employed inappropriate emotional means to induce people into being immersed, as well as his use of the "new formula," apparently motivated him to begin the series. Though Scott and Alexander Campbell were intimately united in the work of reform, subtle tensions began to form between them that would eventually erupt into an open feud that threatened the reform's advance.

*   *   *

The Campbell movement's agenda was essentially created in the days of the *Christian Baptist*. Campbell elaborated on these doctrines and practices for the rest of his career, especially in three important volumes. In 1826 he edited the first edition of a translation of the New Testament, followed by major revisions in 1828, 1832, and 1835. In 1835 and 1839 he published a kind of systematic theology for the movement popularly known as *The Christian System*. And in 1851 he produced the most thorough statement of his baptismal theology in his masterpiece, *Christian Baptism: With Its Antecedents and Consequents.* These books were designed to explain and convince readers of the truth of what Campbell called "the ancient gospel and order of things." Immersion for the remission of sins and salvation was, he believed, the missing key to everything else.

There was, of course, much more to Alexander Campbell's agenda. His speeches and writings covered topics from education to phrenology, gospel ordinances to the end of time, slavery to war, the church, and civil government. He also participated in the civic life of America at many levels as both religious leader and statesman. He served as a delegate from Brooke County to the Virginia Constitutional Convention in 1829–1830, where he was a vocal advocate of democratic reform and an opponent of slavery.[39] Yet, the hub of his reform was a set of doctrines and practices centered around immersion of penitent believers for the remission of sins.

Campbell's motives were as pure as any human being's could be—he did not do what he did simply for selfish ambition or to make a name for himself. His intelligence, arrogance, and tendency for confrontation could certainly make him seem that way to anyone who disagreed with him. But his political, intellectual, and religious experiences in Ireland and Scotland, shaped by the American context of unlimited opportunity for progress, fueled his desire for a reform of church and society and drove him to almost frenetic activity to promote his ideas. His confidence in his ability to discern and communicate the ancient gospel and order of things merged with his millennial optimism that saw America as the God-prepared place for true reform. He wanted to use the abilities God had given him to advance and bring that reform to fruition in his lifetime.

But something in Campbell's personality ironically worked against the very goal he so intensely pursued. This appeared clearly in Campbell's arguments in the debate with W. L. Maccalla. While his logic, clear speaking, and inductive approach to Scripture connected with his hearers and convinced many to join his quest for the "ancient gospel," a corrosive element was also at work.

In spring 1826, respected Virginia Baptist minister Robert Baylor Semple, a somewhat sympathetic follower of Campbell's work, wrote to Campbell about the Maccalla debate.[40] He started by saying that he had read

---

39. Dickson D. Bruce Jr., *The Rhetoric of Conservatism: The Virginia Convention of 1829–30 and the Conservative Tradition in the South* (San Marino, CA: Huntington Library, 1982), 37, 53–56.

40. Semple had converted from Anglicanism in 1787. Biographical sketch in James Taylor, *Virginia Baptist Ministers* (Philadelphia: J. B. Lippincott, 1859): 305–52; James B. Taylor, "Robert B. Semple," Baptist History Homepage, http://baptisthistoryhomepage .com/semple.robert.bio.html.

Robert Baylor Semple (1767–1831) was raised Anglican but became a Baptist at age twenty. He became the historian of early Baptist history with *A History of the Rise and Progress of the Baptists in Virginia* in 1810. He showed interest in Campbell's work but criticized him for his caustic manner of presenting his ideas. From *History of the Baptists in Virginia*, 1810, 1894.

the *Christian Baptist* since it began, and as far as he could tell, Campbell's views were largely the same as those of the Sandemanians and Haldanes, who were narrow and lacking in forbearance.[41] Semple complimented

41. The Sandemanians were named for Robert Sandeman, a follower (and son-in-law) of strict restorationist John Glas, who was expelled from the Church of Scotland for rejection of the legitimacy of the state church. Sandeman became the chief spokesperson for the group, which spread to England and America. They practiced closed communion and taught that saving faith was simple assent to the propositions of the gospel. John Howard Smith, *The Perfect Rule of the Christian Religion: A History of Sandemanianism in the Eighteenth Century* (Albany: SUNY Press, 2008). Robert and James A. Haldane were also Scottish Independents who promoted evangelism, baptized by immersion, and practiced weekly Lord's Supper. Alexander Haldane, *Memoirs of the Lives of Robert Haldane of Airthrey and of His Brother James Alexander Haldane* (New York: Robert Carter & Brothers, 1853).

Campbell on the eloquent preaching and pleasant manner he demonstrated in a recent visit to Semple's home church in King and Queen County, east of Richmond. Yet he warned Campbell that the attitude displayed in his writing was contrary to the spirit of the New Testament.

He then gave his evaluation of the 1823 *Debate on Baptism.* Though Campbell's arguments were clear and forceful enough "to convince every pedo-baptist that may ever read it, . . . the bitterness of the expressions unfortunately blind their minds with resentment, so as to stop up the entrance of truth." This, according to Semple, was Campbell's most serious flaw. While his arguments may have been logically sound and even biblically correct, his acrimonious approach turned people against him.[42]

Campbell's response was respectful to the older minister. He insisted that though he was indebted to the writings of Sandeman, the Haldanes, other independents, and even Luther, Calvin, and Wesley, none of them "had clear and consistent views of the Christian religion *as a whole.*" Their faulty systems of thinking prevented them from seeing some of the clearest teachings of Scripture—specifically baptism. Anyway, he had not looked at any of the works of those leaders in ten years—he had simply gone to Scripture.

Furthermore, he asserted, "there is not a man upon the earth whose authority can influence me, any farther than he comes with the authority of evidence, reason, and truth." He insisted that he read the Scriptures as if no one—including himself—had ever read them before! "I am as much on my guard against reading them today, through the medium of my own views yesterday, or a week ago, as I am against being influenced by any foreign name, authority, or system whatever." Campbell insisted that even if Semple's accusation that the *Christian Baptist* reflected the narrowness of the Sandemanians were true, the journal's tone was exactly what the apostles would use if they were to come back and see all the defects and apostasies in the church.[43]

Prophetically, Semple remarked that Campbell's views were so different from those of most Baptists, "that if a party was to go fully into the practice of your principles, I should say a new sect had sprung up, radically different from the Baptists, as they are now."[44] Within a few years that would become reality as many Baptist leaders condemned Campbell's positions and the churches affiliated with his reform withdrew or were excluded from Baptist associations.

42. R. B. S., "Brother Campbell," *Christian Baptist* 3 (April 1826): 197–200.
43. Alexander Campbell, "Reply," *Christian Baptist* 3 (April 1826): 202–6.
44. R. B. S., "Brother Campbell," 200.

CHAPTER 6

The Role of Christian Unity
in Alexander Campbell's Agenda

For Alexander Campbell, the restoration of the ancient gospel and order of things was the crucial starting place for his reformation. Yet anyone familiar with the history of the Stone-Campbell Movement knows that Christian unity was a major component of his agenda. The very title of his "systematic theology" highlighted unity's prominent role in his reform: *The Christian System, In Reference to the Union of Christians, and a Restoration of Primitive Christianity, as Plead in the Current Reformation.*[1] Unity and restoration were inseparable for Campbell. But why was unity of Christians so important to him, and how did it fit into his program?

Campbell's longing for Christian unity stemmed from the traumatic experiences of religious turmoil in Ireland and his father's failed efforts to bring unity to warring Presbyterian factions. These events created a hunger for a church free from what his father labeled in the *Declaration and Address* the "heinous and pernicious" animosity among followers of Christ; "tired and sick of the bitter jarrings and janglings of a party spirit, we would desire to be at rest."[2]

Alexander enthusiastically embraced his father's dedication to the pursuit of unity in both Ireland and America and made it a vital part of his reform vision. Yet Alexander added a component to the unity quest that, whether he recognized it or not, made it quite different from his father's. Thomas proposed only the core beliefs of the gospel on which all Christians

---

1. The terms "unity" and "union" were often used interchangeably in the Stone-Campbell Movement, though union especially signified the visible unity of the church, that is, the actual physical coming together of all followers of Christ in every locality. This was assumed to include the dissolution of denominational structures that divided Christians.

2. Thomas Campbell, *Declaration and Address of the Christian Association of Washington* (Washington, PA: Brown & Sample, 1809), 3.

THE
CHRISTIAN
SYSTEM

IN REFERENCE TO THE UNION OF
CHRISTIANS, AND A RESTORATION OF
PRIMITIVE CHRISTIANITY, AS PLEAD
IN THE CURRENT REFORMATION.

BY

ALEXANDER CAMPBELL

GOSPEL ADVOCATE COMPANY
NASHVILLE, TENN.
1980

The title of Campbell's "systematic theology" gave Christian unity priority over the restoration of primitive Christianity. In fact, his teaching on
the restoration of immersion for the remission of sins was the centerpiece of the study, which has remained continuously in print since the
second edition of 1839. Courtesy of the Center for Restoration Studies,
Abilene Christian University, Abilene, Texas.

already agreed as the basis for Christian union. Now Alexander insisted that acceptance of the ancient gospel and order of things—a very precise set of beliefs and practices that not all Christians accepted—was the prerequisite. In fact, in Alexander's mind this restoration was absolutely necessary for true unity, a unity that would trigger the conversion of the world and the beginning of the millennium. The goal of first importance, then, was restoration, not Christian unity.

The Campbells' Concept of Christian Unity

After Thomas Campbell's expulsion from the Associate Synod of North America and the beginning of his reform, he had been extremely uncomfortable at remaining separate from other Christians. In 1810 this anxiety led him to seek affiliation with the Synod of Pittsburgh in the Presbyterian Church USA. The synod rejected his appeal, but within three years—after the adoption of believers' immersion—the Campbells and their Brush Run church had become part of the Redstone Baptist Association. Thomas believed it was crucial to work for reform as part of an existing Christian body. Yet their belief in believers' immersion now convinced them to become part of a body with a view of baptism that separated them from most other Christians.

In 1823, eight years after uniting with the Baptists, Alexander Campbell began publishing the *Christian Baptist*, which became the most powerful influence on the thought of the Campbell movement in these formative years. In April 1824 he published his first article on the topic of unity titled "The Foundation of Hope and of Christian Union." After painting a dismal picture of religion in pre-Christian times, which he paralleled to his own day, he stated the conclusion to which he and his father had come over the past decade: a Christian is anyone who believes one fact and submits to one institution, and whose actions are in harmony with the system of morality and virtue taught by Jesus.

> The one fact is, that Jesus the Nazarene is the Messiah. The one institution is baptism [immersion] into the name of the Father, and of the Son and of the Holy Spirit. Every such person is a Christian in the fullest sense of the word, the moment he has believed this one fact, and has submitted to the above named institution; and whether he believes the five points condemned or the five points approved by the synod of Dort, is not so much as to be asked of him; whether he holds any of the views of the Calvinists or Arminians,

Presbyterians, Episcopalians, Methodists, Baptists, or Quakers, is never once to be asked of such a person, in order to admission into the Christian community, called the church.[3]

Alexander seemed to make the basis for Christian unity broad and inclusive. Differences over doctrinal details were not relevant to the achievement of unity. Immersion for the remission of sins, however, was an absolute nonnegotiable. It was not an opinion—it was the one absolutely required institution.

In his *Christian Baptist* series "A Restoration of the Ancient Order of Things," the terms "unity" and "union" almost never appeared. Although in the second article he expressed his conviction that the conversion of the world was dependent on the unity of all followers of Christ as well as "the apostles' testimony," this was practically the last mention of Christian unity in the *Christian Baptist*.[4] This makes sense when one understands that in these articles he was directing all his energies to the *means* of achieving unity—the restoration of the primitive church. Restoration began with immersion for remission of sins and included the destruction of human creeds, names, opinions, and practices and the reinstitution of what he believed were lost or obscured biblical forms of worship, discipline, and church.

Campbell's focus on restoring the church reflected Puritan ideas embedded in the Presbyterian theology that formed him. For the Puritans, as for virtually every movement to "restore" Christ's body throughout Christian history, the object was a pure and holy church. That inevitably meant that true Christians had to separate from the corrupt church that would not or could not reform. Purity, not unity, was the goal. Campbell's contribution to the concept of restoration was his insistence that restoring the primitive gospel and order was the only means of bringing back the "lost" unity of the church. Once all true followers of Christ saw the brilliance and clarity of these restored truths, they would naturally accept them and flow together.

At times Campbell clarified that he was not actually calling for a restoration of *the church* itself, as if it had ceased to exist. Instead, he sought to restore Christians to the standard of the New Testament. That, he believed, would lead naturally and organically to their unity with one another. Fur-

3. Alexander Campbell, "The Foundation of Hope and of Christian Union," *Christian Baptist* 1 (April 1824): 221–22.

4. Alexander Campbell, "The Restoration of the Ancient Order of Things. No. II," *Christian Baptist* 2 (March 1825): 157–58.

thermore, this process was a spiritual one—not an institutional union, or as he called it, a "union of sects." In 1825 he declared, "I have no idea of seeing, nor one wish to see the sects unite in one grand army. This would be dangerous to our liberties and laws. For this the Saviour did not pray. It is only the disciples of Christ dispersed among them, that reason and benevolence would call out of them. Let them unite who love the Lord, and then we shall soon see the hierling [*sic*] priesthood and their worldly establishments prostrate in the dust."[5]

Campbell's view of unity was of individual Christians in every locality leaving the sectarian organizations that separated them to join in worship and work. Attempting to bring denominational structures together would be nothing more than an armistice between warring nations. "Christian union is a more intimate, spiritual, celestial sort of thing, into which we can enter only in our individual capacity and upon our own individual responsibility."[6]

Despite his rejection of structural union of Christian denominations, in 1839 Campbell actually proposed a "congress" of official delegates from all Protestant groups as well as the Greek and Roman Catholic churches. If attendees would agree that the doctrines and practices accepted by all would be the basis of union, and all would "abandon whatever tenets, forms or usages they may have which are not admitted as of divine authority by all Christendom," such a meeting could do much good. He prefaced the discussion, however, reiterating his focus on the union of individual Christians. The union of sects would not be the union of Christians, he asserted, nor would most likely a union of Christians be a union of the sects, although an effort to unite the sects might tend to unite Christians.[7]

Campbell's goal was a doctrinal and structural restoration of the ancient church that people could see, not an invisible or interior one. America was where this could take place, because here for the first time since the great apostasy Christians suffered no persecution and therefore had no legitimate distractions to divert them from the full visible restoration of the ancient gospel and order.[8]

---

5. Alexander Campbell, "A Restoration of the Ancient Order of Things," *Christian Baptist* 2 (April 4, 1825): 173. See also "Christian Union—No. I," *Christian Baptist* 2 (July 1825): 234–39.

6. Alexander Campbell, "Elder William F. Broddus, of Lexington, and the Union Meeting," *Millennial Harbinger*, June 1841, 265.

7. Alexander Campbell, "Union of Christians—No. I," *Millennial Harbinger*, May 1839, 212.

8. Alexander Campbell, "Opinionisms," *Millennial Harbinger*, August 1859, 437; Rich-

Unity as the Outcome of Restoration

In the 1830s, as Campbell became more focused on spreading his reform, his thought turned to a more direct emphasis on Christian unity as the outcome of restoration. Although he did not specify unity as a goal in the proposal for his new *Millennial Harbinger*, he dedicated the paper to the "destruction of sectarianism" and "the development and introduction of the millennium."[9] Yet Campbell definitely saw Christian unity as a key step in bringing in the millennium. Only the restored church, or, as he began to call it, the "Millennial Church," could produce the unity in both church and society necessary for the millennial age.[10]

Reading selectively in Campbell's writings might lead to the conclusion that he sometimes forgot his insistence on restoration. Campbell, like his colleague Walter Scott, identified belief that "Jesus the Nazarene is the Messiah, the Son of God" as the bond of union among Christians.[11] Yet, taken as a whole, his writings clearly indicate he believed this proposition was shorthand for the whole Christian faith. Campbell's biographer and son-in-law, Robert Richardson, illustrated the idea in an 1852 article by describing a lofty, spreading oak that originated in an acorn. In the same way, God wrapped up in this simple confession of faith "that vast remedial system, which may overspread and shelter, in its full development, the whole assembled family of man."[12] Underlying all of Campbell's doctrinal statements was the assumption that immersion for the remission of sins and the full set of doctrines and practices embodied in the ancient gospel as he saw it were inherently part of this simple affirmation of faith.

On the other hand, Campbell did seem to allow for a wide diversity of religious views. "Amongst the peculiarities of our profession there is one

---

ard T. Hughes, "A Comparison of the Restitution Motifs of the Campbells (1809–1830) and the Anabaptists (1524–1560)," *Mennonite Quarterly Review* 45 (October 1971): 329.

9. Alexander Campbell, "Proposals," *Christian Baptist* 7 (October 5, 1829): 67.

10. Alexander Campbell, "Millennium—No. I," *Millennial Harbinger*, February 1830, 53–58; Ronald E. Osborn, *Experiment in Liberty: The Ideal of Freedom in the Experience of the Disciples of Christ*, Forrest F. Reed Lectures for 1976 (St. Louis: Bethany, 1978), 26–27. See H. Richard Niebuhr's assessment of the utilitarian nature of restorationism in the Campbells' thought in *Social Sources of Denominationalism* (New York: Holt, 1929), 180.

11. Alexander Campbell, "To Elder William Jones of London. Letter VIII," *Millennial Harbinger*, January 1836, 29; Alexander Campbell, "Union, Union, Union," *Millennial Harbinger*, February 1862, 49–50.

12. Robert Richardson, "Principles and Purposes of the Reformation," *Millennial Harbinger*, November 1852, 610.

prominent one—that we are not allowed to make our own private judgement, interpretation or opinion, a ground of admission into, or of exclusion from, the Christian Church."[13] In 1830 he had insisted that while opinions must be discarded as bonds of union, no one should ever be asked to give up opinions. "We ask them only not to impose them upon others."[14]

Yet he also maintained that there were bounds to opinion. This became clear in an 1846 exchange with J. J. Harvey of the Eastern Christian Connexion (the Smith/Jones, O'Kelly, and Stone churches that remained separate from the Campbell movement). As these Christian groups discussed union with the Unitarians, Campbell argued that while some opinions do not affect the foundation of the church, others do. "The Apostle . . . supposes that a man immersed into the true faith may hold opinions of such injurious tendency as to amount to the denial of the faith, and to make Christ of no effect [Paul's judgment of the Judaizing teachers in Galatians 5]. Any theory that degrades my redeemer to the rank of any mere creature, and his death to that of a distinguished martyr, expresses opinions more subversive of the Christian faith than those which Paul notices."[15]

Still, Campbell exhibited an antidogmatic spirit when he insisted that "Christianity consists infinitely more in good works than in sound opinions."[16] Furthermore, he maintained that if anyone were to cause division by insisting on private opinions or "private judgment," that person must be marked as a factionist and expelled from the church—not because of the doctrinal difference but because of making the "opinion an idol, and demand[ing] homage to it."[17] Yet behind all such statements was his firm conviction that believers' immersion for the remission of sins was not an opinion or private judgment but an unmistakably clear teaching of Scripture.

Alexander Campbell's unwavering emphasis on restoration eventually persuaded his father, Thomas, to shift his understanding of how to effect visible unity. In 1839, in Alexander's absence, Thomas printed several articles on Christian unity in the *Millennial Harbinger*, including two lengthy ones of his own. At the end of one article in which he described the primitive apostolic church in sixteen points, he stated: "We make this appeal to the un-

---

13. Alexander Campbell, "Our Position to American Slavery," *Millennial Harbinger*, May 1845, 233.

14. Alexander Campbell, "Millennium—No. II," *Millennial Harbinger*, April 1830, 145.

15. Alexander Campbell, "Christian Union—No. V," *Millennial Harbinger*, December 1846, 692.

16. Alexander Campbell, "The Foundation of Hope and of Christian Union," 177.

17. Alexander Campbell, "Remarks on the Above," *Christian Baptist* 7 (June 1830): 263.

derstanding and practice of the primitive churches, not to authorize our faith and practice, but merely to show, that we understand the apostolic writings upon these subjects, just as they were understood from the beginning. . . . And this we think all true Christian unionists are bound to do; because it is only upon the belief of the apostolic doctrine, that Christ has proposed and prayed for the unity of his people."[18] In other words, anyone who truly wanted the unity of all followers of Christ would accept the doctrinal conclusions he and Alexander had reached.

Alexander Campbell constantly reminded his hearers that the purpose of restoring the ancient gospel and order was the unity of Christians. That was in turn essential to the conversion of the world. "Neither truth alone, nor union alone is sufficient to subdue the unbelieving nations: but truth and union combined are omnipotent. . . . The union of Christians is essential to the conversion of the world."[19] For Campbell, restoration and unity were indispensable to each other, to global conversion, and to the introduction of the millennial age. Still, nothing else could happen until the ancient gospel and order were restored.

Historian Richard Hughes has argued that when his restoration agenda did not succeed as rapidly as he believed it should have, Campbell began looking more toward American evangelical Protestantism's "civil religion" as the hope for bringing in the millennium. He therefore shifted his focus away from restoration and toward the advance of Anglo-Saxon Protestant culture to usher in the golden age.[20] Hughes cites Campbell's willingness to represent Christianity in his debate with social reformer and skeptic Robert Owen in 1829, and to serve as spokesman for Protestants in a debate with Catholic bishop John Purcell of Cincinnati in 1837, as evidence of this shift.

That explanation, however, does not reflect Campbell's consistent vision of transforming church and society through the restoration of the ancient gospel and order. To the end of his life, Campbell linked his view of unity

---

18. Thomas Campbell, "Christian Union," *Millennial Harbinger*, April 1839, 164.

19. Alexander Campbell, *The Christian System, In Reference to the Union of Christians, and a Restoration of Primitive Christianity, as Plead in the Current Reformation*, 2nd ed. (Pittsburgh: Forrester & Campbell, 1839), 111.

20. Richard T. Hughes, "The Role of Theology in the Nineteenth-Century Division of Disciples of Christ," in *American Religion: 1974 Proceedings*, ed. Edwin S. Gaustad (Tallahassee, FL: American Academy of Religion, 1974), 56–78, and "From Primitive Church to Civil Religion: The Millennial Journey of Alexander Campbell," *Journal of the American Academy of Religion* 44 (March 1976): 87–103.

and the beginning of the millennium inseparably with the restoration of the ancient gospel and order. In 1832 he insisted that

> If the Christians in all sects could be drawn together, then would the only real, desireable, and permanent union, worthy of the name of the union of Christians, be achieved. . . . To us, it appears, the only practicable way to accomplish this desireable object, is to propound the ancient gospel and the ancient order of things in the words and sentences found in the apostolic writings—to abandon all traditions and usages not found in the Record, and to make no human terms of communion . . . a union amongst Christians can be obtained only upon scriptural grounds and not upon any sectarian platform in existence.[21]

In 1840 he emphatically reaffirmed that the ancient gospel's teaching on immersion for the remission of sins was the only stance that would allow for unity. It was, therefore, "the duty of all the true and loyal friends of Jesus to preach and teach immersion."[22] In his 1851 masterwork *Christian Baptism: With Its Antecedents and Consequents*, Campbell continued to hold up immersion of believers for the remission of sins as the center of his program and the key to Christian unity. And not long before his death, in an article titled "Christian Baptism a Basis for Christian Union," Campbell denied the validity of anything but adult immersion, asserting that it was that act alone that translates one into the kingdom of God's Son.[23]

Despite Campbell's consistent position on immersion, the members of his reformation reflected a spectrum of views. Some held that those baptized by a mode other than immersion but whose lives demonstrated their devotion to Christ were Christians, though perhaps imperfect ones. Others emphatically denied this. For them the logic was inescapable: if immersion into Christ is the means by which one receives remission of sins, salvation, and entrance into the church, then those who have not been immersed are not among the saved, not Christians, not members of the church. Followers on each side of the issue quoted Campbell to bolster their position.[24]

21. Alexander Campbell, "The Union," *Millennial Harbinger*, May 1832, 195.
22. Alexander Campbell, "Union," *Millennial Harbinger*, November 1840, 485–86.
23. Alexander Campbell, "Christian Baptism a Basis of Christian Union," *Millennial Harbinger*, May 1862, 207.
24. For Campbell's more inclusive statements, see his articles concerning the "unimmersed" in the 1837 and 1838 *Millennial Harbinger*, especially Alexander Campbell, "Any

Nevertheless, Campbell remained firm on immersion as the linchpin of his entire system.[25]

Christians in all the sects had to be convinced of the reasonableness of the ancient gospel and order. Since the truth of these ideas was self-evident, whenever reasonable people heard them they would unite on that truth. Christian union was an inevitable consequence of the restoration of the ancient order of things plainly seen in Scripture. So for Campbell restoration was not just a means to the immediate end of unity; it was the only means for accomplishing that end.[26]

The splintering of the Stone-Campbell Movement within a few decades of Campbell's death was evidence to some that the concepts of restoration and unity were ultimately incompatible and that restoration was inherently divisive.[27] Whether or not that is true, in Campbell's mind they were inseparable and indispensable to one another. The exigencies of life challenged his confidence in a swift restoration, unity, and millennium. Yet his vision for a pure church, restored to its primitive unity, with the power to convert the world, was the driving force for Campbell's work until his death.

Christians among Protestant Parties," *Millennial Harbinger*, September 1837, 411–14; Alexander Campbell, "Christians among the Sects," *Millennial Harbinger*, November 1837, 506–8.

25. In his *Christian System* of 1839, baptism is by far the most prominent topic.

26. Alexander Campbell, "The Union," 195.

27. A. T. DeGroot, "The Grounds of Divisions among the Disciples of Christ" (PhD diss., University of Chicago, 1939), 220, and A. T. DeGroot, *The Restoration Principle* (St. Louis: Bethany, 1960), 7–8.

CHAPTER 7

The Creation of a Better Bible

Alexander Campbell was steeped in the Protestant tradition of the supreme importance of the Bible. His father, Thomas, instilled this conviction in all his children, in part through daily family worship that included Scripture recitation and catechesis from the Westminster Confession. The Confession's first chapter established the Protestant Bible as the whole counsel of God and the supreme judge of all religious matters.[1]

As he assumed chief leadership of the reform movement, Alexander's devotion to Scripture became even stronger. Like his father, he was convinced that when freed from the shackles of human creeds and confessions, anyone could read, understand, and follow the teachings of the New Testament. This conviction was foundational to his reform. As a result, he believed that a clear, accurate translation of the Bible was crucial to the restoration of the primitive church. "We are assured that more depends on a perspicuous and correct translation of the New Testament, for the illumination of the christian community, and for the conversion of the world, than upon any other means in human power."[2]

---

1. Robert Richardson, *Memoirs of Alexander Campbell*, 2 vols. (Philadelphia: J. B. Lippincott & Co., 1868–1870), 1:232. Thomas Campbell stated in 1809, "We are by no means to be understood as at all wishing to deprive our fellow Christians of any necessary and possible assistance to understand the scriptures: . . . for which purpose the Westminster Confession and Catechisms, may with many other excellent performances, prove eminently useful." Thomas Campbell, *Declaration and Address of the Christian Association of Washington* (Washington, PA: Brown & Sample, 1809), 42. Though Alexander was later critical of having to learn the Westminster Confession, he clearly did learn it. Alexander Campbell, "Education—No. 2," *Millennial Harbinger*, June 1830, 252.

2. Alexander Campbell, "Historical Sketch of the Origin and Progress of the New Translation," *Millennial Harbinger*, June 1832, 271.

The King James Version maintained a virtual monopoly among English-speaking Protestants, and Campbell certainly held that anyone could learn the truth from that translation. He believed, however, that it had flaws that, if corrected, would aid the progress of his reform.[3] Campbell was just one of many calling for a better English version of the Bible. During the early nineteenth century, American religious leaders produced dozens of new translations or revisions, with at least thirty-five appearing by 1880.[4] Campbell was part of a growing group of religious leaders calling for a translation in contemporary English rather than the KJV's archaic Elizabethan language. The discovery of Greek and Hebrew manuscripts not available to the King James Version translators, and the production of a revolutionary new critical edition of the Greek text of the New Testament by Johann Griesbach, offered the prospect of translating from a more ancient and "uncorrupted" text of Scripture.[5]

Campbell's Version of the New Testament

Campbell was convinced that producing the best possible version of the New Testament would allow everyone to see the writers' meaning and therefore advance the restoration of the ancient gospel and order. This conviction led him to revise and publish a New Testament that had first appeared in London in 1818. That volume brought together translations by Scottish scholars George Campbell (the Gospels), James Macknight (the Epistles), and Philip Doddridge (Acts and Revelation). Soon after the London version's appearance, a New York bookseller proposed an American edition but failed to secure funding. Campbell, who had supported that venture and was now very much in the printing business, began considering publishing it himself.[6]

Campbell shared two key commitments with other nineteenth-century

3. For a summary of Campbell's problems with the KJV, see James L. Gorman, "The Sacred Writings and Alexander Campbell's Contentions with the KJV," *Restoration Quarterly* 53, no. 3 (2011): 159–69.

4. Paul C. Gutjahr, *An American Bible: A History of the Good Book in the United States, 1777–1880* (Stanford, CA: Stanford University Press, 1999), 91, appendix 5, 193–94.

5. Gutjahr, *An American Bible*, 92, 98, 102. On Griesbach's critical text, see G. D. Kirkpatrick, "Griesbach and the Development of Text Criticism," in *J. J. Griesbach, Synoptic and Text Critical Studies, 1776–1976*, ed. Bernard Orchard and Thomas R. W. Longstaff (New York: Cambridge University Press, 1978), 136–53, and Jerry Wayne Brown, *The Rise of Biblical Criticism in America, 1800–1870: The New England Scholars* (Middletown, CT: Wesleyan University Press, 1969), 23–25.

6. Alexander Campbell, "Historical Sketch," 268–69.

Bible revisers: to produce a version in contemporary English so the message would be clear to all, and to use a Greek text that was as close to the original as could be obtained.[7] He chose the Campbell, Macknight, Doddridge version because he believed its contemporary English was a major improvement over the antiquated language of the King James Version. Furthermore, the text was available for anyone to use since the proposed American edition never materialized. In his quest for the best Greek text, Campbell chose the groundbreaking critical text of Johann Griesbach, often changing the wording of Campbell, Macknight, and Doddridge when he felt Griesbach's text provided sufficient warrant. He also consulted other translations in the process of arriving at his own choices.[8]

Campbell's quest for a better translation, even as part of his agenda to advance his reform, mirrored the belief among Protestants that the Bible was the most important book in the world. It and it alone contained the message of God for salvation. Paul Gutjahr summarizes the attitude: "Textual accuracy was more than simply an issue of good craftsmanship; it could mean the difference between orthodoxy and heresy, a life that led to heaven or a life that led to hell. Accurate Bibles were a matter of spiritual life and death."[9]

Sometime before June 1825, Campbell issued a proposal for his new version and began soliciting subscriptions.[10] For the next ten months, he carefully compared the text of the London edition with the three scholars' original work, Griesbach's text, and other translations. He made corrections he deemed justified and compiled a list of variant readings for an appendix. When the first edition of Campbell's work appeared in 1826, the title page listed his contributions as *Prefaces to the Historical and Epistolary Books; and an Appendix, Containing Critical Notes and Various Translations of Difficult Passages.* Campbell published two major revisions in 1828 and 1832 (actually printed in 1833), with the third becoming the standard for subsequent printings.[11] The version became popularly known as *The Living Oracles.*

---

7. Gutjahr contends that Charles Thomson, who in 1808 produced the first of the nineteenth-century American Bible translations, set these twin concerns of "first texts" and "first readings" as major concerns for all subsequent translators. Gutjahr, *An American Bible*, 93–94.

8. Cecil K. Thomas, *Alexander Campbell and His New Version* (St. Louis: Bethany, 1958), 24–25.

9. Gutjahr, *An American Bible*, 90.

10. Alexander Campbell, "History of the English Bible. No. IV," *Christian Baptist* 2 (June 1825): 260.

11. Thomas, *Alexander Campbell*, 44–66. The numbering of the editions is some-

In Cecil K. Thomas's detailed study of Campbell's translation, he noted that many of Campbell's changes had already been made by others, especially updating words and phrases to modern English. Examples included revising the KJV's "The book of the generation of Jesus Christ" in Matthew 1:1 to "The History of Jesus Christ," and dropping "-eth" verb endings. At times, however, Campbell's wording seemed to obscure rather than aid meaning, as in his curious rendering of Luke 11:17, a passage with numerous manuscript variants. The KJV read, "Every kingdom divided against itself is brought to desolation; and a house divided against a house falleth." Campbell's translation read, "By intestine broils, any kingdom may be desolated, one family falling after another." Campbell's attempt to reflect difficulties in the Greek text was certainly not helpful in clarifying the verse's meaning.

In other cases he translated words that had only been transliterated in earlier English Bibles, like using "favor" instead of "grace," "messenger" instead of "angel," and "reform" in place of "repent." Using text-critical principles, Campbell omitted or marked as doubtful passages not in the earliest and best Greek manuscripts. For example, he omitted Acts 8:37 (Philip's response to the Ethiopian eunuch, "If thou believest with all of thine heart, thou mayest. And he answered and said, I believe that Jesus Christ is the Son of God") and part of Mark 13:14 ("spoken of by Daniel the prophet"). He relied on Griesbach; comments by Campbell, Macknight, and Doddridge; and the work of other scholars for these judgments—not on original critical work.[12]

Perhaps the most sensitive of Campbell's changes was his consistent translation of forms of the Greek *baptizo* as "immersion" and "immerse" instead of the KJV's transliteration as "baptism" and "baptize." In fact, Campbell's version was apparently the first English Bible to do this.[13] To be clear, Campbell's work was more than simply an immersionist version. His commitment to "first texts" and "first meanings," to accuracy, critical scholarship, and clear communication, gave his version a level of integrity and credibility despite its many critics. And on the immersion issue, even Presbyterian scholars George Campbell and James Macknight agreed that

---

times confusing, since a fourth edition with slight revisions appeared in 1833, the same year the third edition actually came from the press. The Online Computer Library Center's (OCLC) WorldCat database lists sixty-nine editions or reprints (though some appear to be duplicates), the most recent in 2016, with eleven more in digital or microform formats.

12. Thomas, *Alexander Campbell*, 28–43.

13. Gutjahr, *An American Bible*, 101–3.

the original meaning of *baptizo* was "to immerse," though they had not used the term in their translations.[14]

However, it is equally clear that Campbell's insistence on "immerse" rather than the ambiguous transliteration "baptize" went well beyond the theological commitments of even most who agreed that the rendering was accurate. Campbell's baptismal theology had developed to a form that even most other immersionists could not accept. Immersion, he said in an article in his 1828 series "The Ancient Gospel," was in fact "the gospel in water."[15] The articulation of these views culminated in 1851 with his last major publication, *Christian Baptism: With Its Antecedents and Consequents*. Here he collected and edited writings from the previous three decades in which he insisted that immersion was the point of conversion, remission of sins, salvation, and regeneration for penitent believers.

Campbell was solidifying his baptismal theology at the same time he was working on the new translation. Campbell's focus on baptism for remission of sins coincided with the debate with William Maccalla and the beginning of the *Christian Baptist* in 1823, fueling his commitment to publish the new translation. But his views of baptism also drove many Baptists who would otherwise have been attracted to an immersionist version of the Bible to oppose his efforts.

When the first edition of his new version appeared in 1826, Campbell's reform movement was still embedded in Baptist churches. Many Baptists sympathized with his ideas and praised the new translation. Within fifteen years Campbell reported that his New Testament had sold thirty-five thousand copies, with an additional five thousand having been distributed free. Even so, he complained that with a membership in the churches of his movement of two hundred thousand in 1842, many more copies should have been sold.[16] Though neither provides a source, both David Daniell and Paul Gutjahr claim that Campbell's version sold more copies in America than any other translation except the KJV until the American Standard Version of 1901.[17] Given the fact that the *Living Oracles* remained in print throughout his lifetime and well beyond, the claim is believable.

---

14. Thomas, *Alexander Campbell*, 33.

15. Alexander Campbell, "Ancient Gospel—No. II. Immersion," *Christian Baptist* 5 (February 1828): 158; *Christian Baptism: With Its Antecedents and Consequents* (Bethany, VA: Alexander Campbell, 1851). See especially 277–312 on justification and sanctification.

16. Alexander Campbell, "The Bible Society and the Reformation," *Millennial Harbinger*, November 1842, 521–22.

17. Gutjahr, *An American Bible*, 105; David Daniell, *The Bible in English* (New Haven: Yale University Press, 2003), 648.

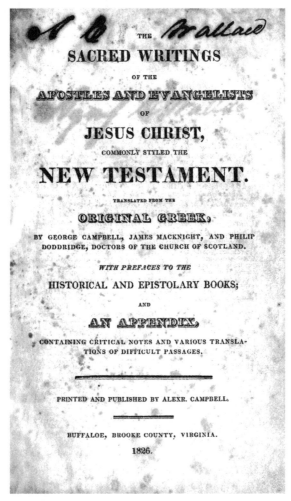

THE

SACRED WRITINGS

OF THE

APOSTLES AND EVANGELISTS

OF

JESUS CHRIST,

COMMONLY STYLED THE

NEW TESTAMENT.

TRANSLATED FROM THE

ORIGINAL GREEK,

BY GEORGE CAMPBELL, JAMES MACKNIGHT, AND PHILIP
DODDRIDGE, DOCTORS OF THE CHURCH OF SCOTLAND.

WITH PREFACES TO THE

HISTORICAL AND EPISTOLARY BOOKS;

AND

AN APPENDIX,

CONTAINING CRITICAL NOTES AND VARIOUS TRANSLA-
TIONS OF DIFFICULT PASSAGES,

PRINTED AND PUBLISHED BY ALEXR. CAMPBELL,

BUFFALOE, BROOKE COUNTY, VIRGINIA.
1826.

Title page to the 1826 first edition of Alexander Campbell's version of
the New Testament titled *The Sacred Writings*. The shorthand name
became *The Living Oracles*, usually printed on the spine. The revision
of 1835 became the standard that has been reprinted numerous times
in the nineteenth and twentieth centuries. Used with permission from
the Disciples of Christ Historical Society, Bethany, West Virginia.

Opposition to Campbell's Version

Opposition arose toward Campbell's new version immediately after its
release. Some of the strongest criticisms came from those who accused it

and him of being Unitarian. While Campbell was definitely not Unitarian,[18] several of his translation choices made it look to many like he was. He mirrored the dedication of Unitarian scholars to restoring the biblical text to its "primitive integrity." This meant freeing it from false ideas derived from human creeds that warped the ancient meaning of Scripture and resulted in tainted translations and tainted theology.[19] Also, he insisted on using only terms that actually appeared in Scripture in his teaching and writing and therefore rejected the word "Trinity."[20]

At roughly the same time Campbell was producing his new version, three other translators, all Unitarian in their theology—Abner Kneeland (1823), George R. Noyes (1827, 1833–1837), and John Gorham Palfrey (1828)—published translations with many of the same changes Campbell incorporated, including use of text-critical evidence to alter or exclude passages in the KJV. Some of the omitted passages had traditionally been used to support Trinitarian views, like the middle of 1 John 5:7–8 (omitting "in heaven, the Father, the Word, and the Holy Ghost: and these three are one").[21]

Furthermore, Campbell consistently denied being a "Trinitarian," even while denying he was Unitarian or Arian.

I have been asked a thousand times, "What do you think about the doctrine of the Trinity—what do you think about the *Trinity*?" Some, nay many,

18. For example, in contrasting his views with those of Unitarians, he stated, "In *our* Christian religion we have a '*divine nature,*' and we have *three persons*—the FATHER, the WORD, and the HOLY SPIRIT." Alexander Campbell, "Unitarianism as Connected with Christian Union. No. II," *Millennial Harbinger*, July 1846, 393. "The Holy Spirit is the Spirit of God in another personality, equally Divine, and equally co-operant with the Father and the word incarnate, who illuminates, sanctifies, and perfects." Alexander Campbell, "Millennium," *Millennial Harbinger*, December 1856, 700–701. For discussions of Campbell's de facto Trinitarianism, see Kelly D. Carter, *The Trinity in the Stone-Campbell Movement* (Abilene, TX: Abilene Christian University Press, 2015), 47–81, and John Mark Hicks, "Theological Orientation for Churches of Christ: Resourcing Alexander Campbell's Trinitarian *Christian System*," *Christian Studies* 28 (2016): 21–36.

19. See "Preface to the Epistles," in Alexander Campbell, *The Sacred Writings of the Apostles and Evangelists of Jesus Christ, Commonly Called the New Testament*, 6th ed. (Pittsburgh: Forrester & Campbell, 1839), 27–28.

20. See "Purity of Speech," in Alexander Campbell, *The Christian System, In Reference to the Union of Christians, and a Restoration of Primitive Christianity, As Plead in the Current Reformation*, 2nd ed. (Pittsburgh: Forrester & Campbell, 1839), 124–27. The "first edition" was his 1835 *A Connected View of the Principles and Rules by Which the Living Oracles May be Intelligibly and Certainly Interpreted*, popularly known as *Christianity Restored*. See chap. 5, n. 33.

21. Gutjahr, *An American Bible*, 96–99; Thomas, *Alexander Campbell*, 75–78.

think that to falter here is terrible; that to doubt here, or not to speak in the language of the schools, is the worst of all errors and heresies. I have not spent, perhaps, an hour in ten years in thinking about the *Trinity*. It is no term of mine. It is a word that belongs not to the Bible in any translation of it I ever saw. I teach nothing, I say nothing, I think nothing about it, save that it is not a scriptural term, and consequently can have no scriptural ideas attached to it. . . . The whole controversy is about scholastic distinctions and unprofitable speculations.[22]

His strong statement led even supporters to fear his position was heretical. When they confronted him, he replied that he leaned neither toward Unitarianism nor toward Trinitarianism but simply believed in God, in God's Son Jesus Christ, and in the Holy Spirit.[23] In an 1846 series criticizing Unitarian theology, Campbell repeated his opposition to "scholastic Trinitarianism" because of its unscriptural vocabulary, describing it as "learnedly obscure and unintelligible."[24] All of this gave Campbell's opponents a plausible basis for attacking him as a heretic in his beliefs about the nature of God.

One of the most virulent attacks on Campbell's translation came from Presbyterian leader Robert Wharton Landis. In 1839 Landis was minister of the Jeffersonville, Pennsylvania, Presbyterian church (New School) in the Presbytery of Philadelphia. That year he wrote a seventy-page exposé of "Campbellism" published in the January and April issues of the *American Biblical Repository* edited by Absalom Peters.

Landis proposed to examine both the Campbellite doctrinal system and "their adopted translation of the New Testament." Throughout the two articles, Landis attacked not only Campbell's theology and translation but also his personal integrity. He labeled Campbell an "opposer of the gospel," an "erroist," and a "pretender, whose popularity in some parts of our country has given him the power of destroying much good." He denounced Campbell's baptismal theology as "a ridiculous travesty of the gospel" and labeled Campbell's New Testament "a pretended translation" and "a dreadfully corrupt version of the inspired writings."[25]

Landis primarily condemned Campbell's teaching on immersion, which

22. Alexander Campbell, "The Trinity," *Christian Baptist* 7 (April 1830): 208–10.

23. Alexander Campbell, "Brother Semple," *Millennial Harbinger*, August 1830, 358.

24. Alexander Campbell, "Unitarianism as Connected with Christian Union—No. III," *Millennial Harbinger*, August 1846, 451.

25. R. W. Landis, "Campbellism," *American Biblical Repository*, 2nd ser., 1 (January 1839): 95–96, 98, 130; (April 1839): 327.

he saw embedded in the new translation. Over half of the second article branded Campbell and his movement as Unitarian, charging Campbell with filling his translation with errors and falsehoods. Campbell, he said, was intentionally vague about his true beliefs concerning the Godhead. The main evidence that Campbell was in fact Unitarian was that his movement had united with Barton Stone's beginning in 1832. Landis established the clear Unitarian sentiments of Stone and the Christian movement, asserting that "to ascertain the sentiments of one sect, will be to ascertain the sentiments of both."

To bolster his accusation, Landis quoted Campbell's positive reaction to the news of the 1832 union of the Stone and Campbell churches in Lexington, Kentucky. In reality, however, Landis had completely misunderstood Campbell's words. When Campbell said he was happy that the Christians "now go for the Apostolic Institutions," he was actually taking a jab at the Stoneites, who, he was hinting, must have *dropped* their peculiar views of God and other nonevangelical beliefs by uniting with *his* followers![26]

After denouncing Campbell's alleged Unitarianism, Landis spent fourteen pages repudiating Campbell's translation. He first charged Campbell with deliberately misidentifying the Congregationalist scholar Philip Doddridge as a member of the Church of Scotland—a Presbyterian—to sell more books.[27] He accused Campbell of being arrogant, quoting Campbell's statement in the preface that he had no sectarian agenda. Landis scoffed at Campbell's claims that he was one of the rare individuals "whose genius, independence of mind, honesty and candor" could produce a solid translation, and that his translation was "more intelligible than any version in our language."[28]

He then tried to establish that Campbell had lied about his translation being the work of George Campbell, James Macknight, and Philip Doddridge. This was Alexander Campbell's work alone, Landis insisted. Campbell's dishonesty in claiming the three distinguished Scottish scholars as the authors was a maneuver to gain credibility for his own perversion. This, Landis exclaimed, was "a crime in no way differing from actual forgery." He quoted Campbell's assurances that any changes he made would "not depart in any instance from the meaning" of the three scholars, then proceeded to

26. Landis, "Campbellism," 308; Alexander Campbell, "The Christian Messenger," *Millennial Harbinger,* March 1832, 139.

27. Landis, "Campbellism," 313.

28. Landis, "Campbellism," 313, 315–16.

show that in fact Campbell had changed dozens of passages contrary to the Scottish scholars' work, mutilating or omitting "hundreds of passages which they regarded as inspired."[29]

Landis then proceeded to denounce Campbell for sloppiness and lack of careful editing. He cited examples of notes in Campbell's appendix explaining why he had omitted certain passages, yet the passages were still in the text. The charge of Unitarianism came up again as Landis asserted that Campbell's omissions reflected, and even went further than, those in the Unitarian "Improved Version" of 1808.[30] Furthermore, he asserted that Unitarians preferred Griesbach's Greek text, casting doubt on Griesbach's theological commitments. He then listed passages that supported the doctrine of the Trinity that Campbell had omitted but that the three Scottish scholars had kept.[31]

Landis closed his treatise urging anyone who had been enticed to buy Campbell's "dreadfully corrupt version" to stop using it, take a legitimate translation of the Word of God, and seriously examine the material in his article. If they did this with prayer and reliance on God's Spirit, they could be saved from the "fatal delusion" of Campbellism.[32]

This was not the first time Campbell had sparred with Landis. In 1835 Landis had published articles in the *Christian Gazette* of Philadelphia labeling Campbell's understanding of baptism "fraught with absurdity." Campbell had responded in kind, sweeping away Landis's remarks as "stale criticisms in favor of his own Calvinism."[33] Later that year Campbell gloated that the *Christian Gazette* had gone out of business, along with a number of other papers that had been "inveterate opposers of the Reformation."[34]

Campbell read Landis's two 1839 articles in July, declaring that nothing so false, dishonest, and malevolent had ever been printed against him. He then wrote Absalom Peters, the editor of the *American Biblical Repository*, in which Landis's articles appeared, requesting space to defend himself but re-

29. Landis, "Campbellism," 314–19.

30. Thomas Belsham et al., *The New Testament, in an Improved Version, upon the Basis of Archbishop Newcome's New Translation: with a Corrected Text, and Notes Critical and Explanatory* (London: Richard Taylor & Co., 1808). William Wells of Boston distributed an American edition in 1809.

31. Landis, "Campbellism," 319–25.

32. Landis, "Campbellism," 327.

33. Alexander Campbell, "The Rev. R. W. Landis, of Delaware, on Acts xxii. 16," *Millennial Harbinger*, February 1835, 67–71.

34. Alexander Campbell, "Poor Encouragement for Publishers," *Millennial Harbinger*, May 1835, 134.

ceived no response.[35] Campbell did not wait to hear from Peters. In October he published a special "extra" edition of the *Millennial Harbinger* in which he began a scathing review of Landis's review of Campbellism that continued for forty-eight pages into the next regular issue in November.

As in his encounter with Landis four years earlier, Campbell's response matched his opponent's denunciation. "We fear not the tribunals, nor the canons, nor the decisions of enlightened high-minded, honest criticism, however severe; but the petulant cavils of saucy sectarians, the acrimonious quibblings of cynical piquancy, the mawkish disdain of affected sanctity, and the supercilious denunciations of wounded pride—of *ex cathedra*, swollen, pampered orthodoxy, I can not endure; especially when it constitutes itself court, and jury, and witness, and hastens to pronounce sentence without privilege of a reply, or of an appeal."[36]

Campbell then proceeded to defend his views of faith and the connection of immersion to regeneration. Landis's descriptions of his beliefs were so off base, he exclaimed, that it would be "impossible that any man of common education and common sense, who has ever read one volume of my writings, could honestly impute to me such a tissue of nonsense and absurdity as he gravely accumulates in the whole extent of the review."[37] In an odd move, Campbell mentioned that he had it on good authority that Landis himself had been immersed for the remission of his sins, making him as much a Campbellite as anyone![38] Landis later confirmed that he had been immersed as a youth in his parents' Baptist church but later renounced immersion as the only legitimate baptism and become a Presbyterian.[39]

Campbell characterized Landis's critique of his translation as more hostile than anything said thus far. Its maliciousness, he exclaimed, was surpassed only by its absolute powerlessness to label him a Unitarian and his translation a deception. Only a "malignant slanderer" would accuse him of such. Campbell maintained that the members of his reform used the com-

---

35. Alexander Campbell, "American Biblical Repository," *Millennial Harbinger*, July 1839, 335.

36. Alexander Campbell, "A Review of a Review of Something Called 'Campbellism,'" special issue, *Millennial Harbinger*, October 1839, 481.

37. Alexander Campbell, "A Review of a Review of Something Called 'Campbellism,'" 495.

38. Alexander Campbell, "A Review of a Review of Something Called 'Campbellism,'" 503.

39. R. W. Landis, "A Brief Reply to the 'Remarks' of Alexander Campbell in Defence of the Doctrines of 'Campbellism': Am. Bib. Repository for April, 1840, Vol III, p. 469, seq.," *American Biblical Repository*, July 1840, 208.

mon—King James—version "as authoritative in all matters of controversy," contrary to Landis's accusation that they used his translation exclusively.[40]

As for his mistaken identification of Congregationalist Philip Doddridge as Presbyterian, Campbell explained that since Presbyterian scholars often quoted Doddridge approvingly, he had assumed he was one. Furthermore, in the United States the Presbyterian and New England Congregationalist denominations had been united until the previous year.[41] It was an innocent mistake, corrected as soon as he learned about it, not a devious move to sell books, as charged by Landis. The fact that some passages were flagged to be omitted in the appendix but were included in the text anyway was an inadvertent error of the kind that occurs in every Bible because of the massive amount of material. He defended his use of Griesbach as reflecting more texts and older Greek texts not available to the King James translators.

Then Campbell again defended himself against the charge of Unitarianism. Even Landis had admitted, Campbell pointed out, that not one of the doctrines of Christianity was weakened by the omission of spurious passages. The most thorough expurgation of spurious passages could not weaken the evidence for the "underived godhead of my Lord and Redeemer," he affirmed.

He then launched into a defense of his views of God. Although he repudiated both scholastic Trinitarian and Unitarian vocabulary as "uncouth, barbarous, unmeaning jargon," he would never interpret anything said about the Redeemer to imply subordination. Furthermore, in no uncertain terms he emphasized the following: "To deny the doctrine of three names—of three relations—of three participants in one godhead is to deny the possibility of saving sinners, and of putting down sin forever."[42]

Campbell closed with what appeared to be a threat of further action if Landis and Peters did not retract their attacks on him. They had maliciously attempted to destroy his character by publicly accusing him of criminal deception. They had violated, Campbell insisted, the law of Moses, the law of Christ, and the laws of the states of New York and Pennsylvania. He would

40. Alexander Campbell, "A Review of a Review of Something Called 'Campbellism,'" 504.

41. The Plan of Union of 1801 provided for interchangeable ministers and allowed congregations to choose their polity as an aid to frontier evangelism. In the division of the Presbyterian Church in 1837, Old School presbyteries withdrew from the union.

42. Alexander Campbell, "A Review of a Review," *Millennial Harbinger*, November 1839, 525.

now give them the opportunity to repent, "or perchance you may repent when it is too late."[43]

The following February, having received no response from Landis or Peters, Campbell issued a formal appeal to the Presbytery of Philadelphia, under whose jurisdiction Landis served. It was not Landis's challenge to his beliefs that prompted the appeal, Campbell stated, though Landis had grossly misrepresented them. It was the attacks on his honesty, fairness, and moral character, as well as the "wicked and outrageous attempts at fastening upon me the infamy of Unitarianism."

Though Campbell enclosed a copy of his review of Landis's articles with the appeal, he proceeded to summarize and refute Landis's slanders. Finally, Campbell gave a rationale why the presbytery should act even though he was not a member of the Presbyterian church. He was a man, an American citizen, and a defender of Christianity against infidels and Catholics, he declared. "I have as good a right to your protection, in this case, from the violence and malice of one of your body, as an American citizen would have in England from any outrage committed by one of her Majesty's subjects against him."[44]

Campbell said he would not appeal to any other court until the presbytery had had enough time to deal with the matter, hinting that he would initiate a civil suit for libel in the state of Pennsylvania if the presbytery failed to act. He had faith, he said, that they would not pollute their consciences nor jeopardize their character by rejecting his appeal. They would have to answer for their actions to "the American people, and to the Judge of the living and the dead."[45]

Later in the same issue of the *Millennial Harbinger*, Campbell reported that he had just received a letter from Absalom Peters offering him space in the *American Biblical Repository* to answer Landis. Campbell said he would do so immediately. He sent much of what had appeared in his lengthy articles in the *Millennial Harbinger* to Peters, who published most of the material, though he said he had intended to print only a few pages. However, Peters introduced Campbell's remarks with a lengthy statement and a copy of his letter to Campbell. Throughout Campbell's rebuttal Peters added notes that supported Landis's original charges.[46]

43. Alexander Campbell, "A Review of a Review," 528.

44. Alexander Campbell, "The Calumnies of R. W. Landis," *Millennial Harbinger*, February 1840, 51.

45. Alexander Campbell, "Calumnies," 51-52.

46. Alexander Campbell, "Remarks on an Article Denominated 'Campbellism' by Rev. R. W. Landis," *American Biblical Repository*, 2nd ser., 3 (April 1840): 469-502.

When Campbell saw what Peters had printed, as well as another article by Landis in July, he was furious. He accused Peters of cutting off the head and extremities of his article and of mangling the body—just as had been done to the martyrs of old. The treatment he had received from those who were supposedly learned and fair Presbyterian ministers and scholars would be apparent to honest readers, he exclaimed, and he released the journal from any further obligation. It was to the presbytery alone that he now left Landis.[47] Campbell's appeal to the Presbytery of Philadelphia apparently fell on deaf ears, however. No record of the appeal appeared in the minutes of the presbytery, and Campbell seems simply to have dropped the matter, though other opponents would repeat Landis's accusations for some time.[48]

While the Landis incident was perhaps the most intense personal attack on Campbell's translation, it was by no means the only one. Episcopal editor George Smith joined the voices insisting that Campbell could not be trusted because of his Unitarianism.[49] Congregationalist Dennis Platt condemned Campbell as an "erratic genius" who falsely claimed that George Campbell, Macknight, and Doddridge were the authors of what was actually his translation. None of the Scottish scholars had used "immerse" in their work as Campbell had, Platt pointed out, so Alexander Campbell had lied when he attached their names to his version.[50]

Baptist Opposition to Campbell's Version

The most sustained criticism, however, came from Baptist churches. As mentioned, many Baptists supported Campbell's translation. Campbell was doing his work of reform primarily within Baptist circles when the first edition of his translation came out, and its immersionist character drew many to use it. One purpose of Dennis Platt's attack was to shock "respectable and orthodox Baptist ministers" who were distributing and promoting it into

47. Alexander Campbell, "Dr. Peters and the Biblical Repository," *Millennial Harbinger*, May 1840, 221–26.

48. See, for example, Alexander Campbell, "Excursion into Ohio," *Millennial Harbinger*, October 1842, 457.

49. George Smith, *Episcopal Recorder*, 1834, cited in Thomas, *Alexander Campbell*, 75–79.

50. Dennis Platt, *The Foundations Examined; or, Plain Scriptural Reasons for Refusing to Become a Baptist*, 2nd ed. (Skaneateles, NY: M. A. Kinney, 1840), 47–48.

realizing that they were promoting "all the superstition, and delusion, and fanaticism of Campbellism."[51]

The fact that certain Baptists were among the strongest opponents of Campbell's translation can be partly explained by differences among Baptists at the time. The Baptist churches among whom Campbell worked were part of a union of Regular Baptists, who were strict Calvinists, and Separate Baptists, who had emerged in the first Great Awakening and tended to be more open to Arminian theology. The Separates opposed creeds and confessions of faith because of the tyrannical authority they exercised over the minds of believers. Their churches were "constituted on the Bible" and not any human creed.[52] Their eventual cautious adoption of the Calvinistic Philadelphia Confession of Faith of 1742 allowed them to unite with the Regular Baptists in 1787, though most remained deeply suspicious of such statements.[53]

Many of Campbell's reform ideas, especially his attacks on Calvinist beliefs like the special operation of the Holy Spirit in conversion, predestination, and a separate clergy class, increased the friction between Campbell and orthodox Calvinists. The division that began to occur between Baptists sympathetic to Campbell's reform and those who opposed him was largely along the old lines of Separate and Regular Baptists.[54]

The earliest instance on record of a Baptist church condemning and prohibiting the use of Campbell's translation was the Lulbegrud congregation of the North District Association of Kentucky in 1827—the year after the first edition appeared.[55] By 1830 the Appomattox (Virginia) Association had also condemned Campbell and his translation, advising the churches of the association not to tolerate Campbell's new version or allow anyone sympathizing with his views into their pulpits.[56] Despite the opposition, Campbell's "Sacred Oracles" continued to sell and, though never dominant even among

51. Platt, *The Foundations Examined*, 46.

52. Garnett Ryland, *The Baptists of Virginia, 1699–1926* (Richmond, VA: Virginia Baptist Board of Missions and Education, 1955), 121; Robert A. Baker, *A Baptist Source Book with Particular Reference to Southern Baptists* (Nashville: Broadman, 1966), 16–24.

53. Errett Gates, *The Early Relation and Separation of Baptists and Disciples* (Chicago: Christian Century Co., 1904), 76–78.

54. Gates, *Early Relation*, 78–79.

55. Gates, *Early Relation*, 69–70.

56. Abner W. Clopton, "Extract from the Minutes of the Appomattox Baptist Association, Held at Wolf Creek Meeting House, on 15th, 16th and 17th May, 1830," *Columbian Star and Christian Index* 2 (June 5, 1830): 363. See James L. Gorman's treatment of Baptist condemnations of Campbell's translation in "From Burning to Blessings: Baptist Reception of Alexander Campbell's New Translation," *Stone-Campbell Journal* 16 (Fall 2013): 181–88.

members of his own movement, continued to be used by preachers and scholars through the next two centuries.

Campbell's Translation of the Book of Acts

Significant changes began to occur in American Bible translation in 1836 — changes that would impel Campbell toward his last effort in this arena. That year a number of prominent Baptists left the American Bible Society when it refused to publish Baptist missionary Adoniram Judson's Burmese translation that used the Burmese word for "immerse" for the Greek *baptizo*. Campbell printed a long letter written to him by "D.A." that was strongly complimentary of the defecting Baptists who had formed a new organization for Bible translation. Campbell must be gratified, D.A. suggested, to see that the Baptists, who had once condemned his translation, were now moving to produce their own immersionist version in English.[57] What neither D.A. nor Campbell admitted, however, was that many Baptists still doggedly objected to Campbell's baptismal theology.

The Baptists who withdrew from the American Bible Society in 1836 immediately formed the American and Foreign Bible Society (AFBS) in New York. Campbell published the speech of the new body's president, Spencer H. Cone, given at the group's first anniversary meeting in 1837.[58] Five years later Campbell revealed that he was a "life member" of both the American Bible Society and the American and Foreign Bible Society. Since there was no Bible society in his movement, he urged members to support the new society that was populated by "our more intelligent, pious, and benevolent Baptist brethren."[59]

Campbell's comment about his movement's lack of a Bible society prompted a small group under the leadership of David S. Burnet to form the American Christian Bible Society (ACBS) in Cincinnati in 1845.[60] Campbell, however, opposed it, partly because he was afraid the new organiza-

---

57. Alexander Campbell, "American Bible Society," *Millennial Harbinger*, April 1836, 185–86; D.A., "Diffusion of Truth," *Millennial Harbinger*, July 1836, 314–21.

58. Still, he criticized Cone's statement affirming plenary verbal inspiration, which Campbell labeled "ultraism," a claim that Scripture did not make for itself and that would hinder the efforts of those who defended biblical inspiration.

59. Alexander Campbell, "Bible Society," *Millennial Harbinger*, July 1842, 315–16.

60. Alexander Campbell, "Five Arguments for Church Organization," *Millennial Harbinger*, November 1842, 523.

tion would divert funds from his recently established Bethany College and needlessly duplicate the work of the AFBS. Friction between Campbell and Burnet was palpable during the late 1840s. The ACBS continued to limp along until 1856, when it became part of the American Christian Missionary Society that began in 1849 and of which Campbell was president.[61]

In 1850 a showdown occurred between members of the AFBS who insisted that the body should produce a new immersionist version in English and those who insisted their work should be limited to translating the Scriptures into other languages for use on the mission field. When notices began to arrive in Bethany concerning the fight within the AFBS, Campbell was distraught. By refusing to produce a new English immersionist Bible, the body had effectively destroyed any reason to exist, he exclaimed. They should go back to the American Bible Society and ask forgiveness for wasting so much time and money and for fomenting bad feelings "for the sake of a sham battle."[62]

Soon, however, leaders who rejected the AFBS's policy prohibiting a new English translation withdrew and formed the American Bible Union (ABU)—a body explicitly committed to publishing such a book. Campbell immediately threw his support to it.[63] Two of the primary leaders of the AFBS, Spencer H. Cone and W. H. Wyckoff, knew Campbell for his earlier translation work as well as his consistent support of the AFBS. They now served as president and corresponding secretary of the new ABU.

In August 1850, Wyckoff wrote Campbell to ask him on behalf of the organization's board to address the Union's first annual meeting in New York that October on "the necessity and importance of a new, or corrected version, of the English Scriptures." Campbell did attend and speak, thus beginning a relationship with the ABU that would include service as a vice president, being a frequent speaker at annual meetings, recruitment of others from his movement as members and officers, and production of a new translation from Greek of the book of Acts.

Campbell was again elated that Baptists, who had opposed his earlier translation so vigorously, now accepted him as an evangelical Christian and

61. Noel L. Keith, *The Story of D. S. Burnet: Undeserved Obscurity* (St. Louis: Bethany, 1954), 72–76, 117, 152–53.

62. Alexander Campbell, "A Most Portentous Discussion and Decision," *Millennial Harbinger*, July 1850, 396.

63. Gutjahr, *An American Bible*, 106–9; Alexander Campbell, "American Bible Union," *Millennial Harbinger*, September 1850, 514–17.

biblical scholar capable of doing significant translation work![64] James L. Gorman has suggested that this shift was partly due to the separation of the Campbell reformers from the Baptists, lessening the antagonism between the groups. With diminished tensions, Campbell was able to participate actively in the American Bible Union led primarily by Baptists.[65] Yet as had been true in the 1820s and 1830s, some Baptists were willing to enlist Campbell's help in the ABU's efforts while others continued to oppose him. The difference seems to have been as much regional as chronological. Northern Baptists were by far the majority in the ABU. The Baptists who were most antagonistic to Campbell were the Regular Baptists of the South, who lost significant numbers to his reform.[66]

Yet, even in the north many Baptists resisted any contribution from a man they considered a heretic. Two years into the operation of the ABU, the pastor of the Amity Street Baptist Church in New York, William R. Williams, wrote a scathing response to a letter from William Wyckoff asking for support. Williams started with a defense of the King James Version— despite its minor flaws, it had "rare and indisputable merits." The argument for using "immerse" rather than "baptize" for *baptizo* was an illegitimate one, Williams insisted, since "baptize" as fully signified "the submerging of a convert in water, and his emerging" as any word could. He expressed other objections to abandoning the KJV typical of those who opposed all new English translations.[67]

Then Williams launched into a direct attack on the Bible Union's "alliance" with the adherents of Alexander Campbell. This was a group, he exclaimed, with which "in its doctrines, ministry, and membership, our own churches have long held no fellowship." While the Campbellites had many peculiarities, the chief objection was to their doctrine of what amounted

---

64. Campbell's speeches and list of offices he held appear in William H. Wyckoff and Charles A. Buckbee, eds., *Documentary History of the American Bible Union: Consisting of the Reprint of its Constitution, Annual Reports, Quarterly Papers, Select Addresses, Tracts, etc., etc., in the Form of the Bible Union Quarterly* (New York: American Bible Union, 1857), available at https://catalog.hathitrust.org/Record/012308410.

65. Gorman, "From Burning to Blessings," 190–91.

66. Southern Baptists provided almost no support for the ABU. The fact that ABU members included Episcopalians, Presbyterians, and German Reformed further alienated strict Baptists. See Michael Kuykendall, "The Quest for a Baptist Bible: The Rise and Demise of the American Bible Union, 1850–1883," *Baptist History & Heritage* 51 (Summer 2016): 41.

67. William R. Williams, "Correspondence Between the American Bible Union and Rev. William R. Williams, D.D. In Behalf of the Amity Street Baptist Church," *Bible Union Quarterly*, August 1852, 357–61. See Gutjahr, *An American Bible*, 91.

to baptismal regeneration. This teaching wronged the Holy Spirit and perverted the whole gospel, Williams asserted. He repeated the charge that Campbell and his followers were Unitarians and Arians since they rejected the label Trinitarian and were united with the Christian Connexion. Such heresies had taken hold whenever a group, like Campbell's, denounced creeds. Furthermore, Campbellite teaching denied the operation of the Holy Spirit in conversion other than to create "historical" faith through the words of Scripture.

Williams noted that while other Bible societies had permitted Arians and Unitarians to be members, they had never employed them as translators or revisers. Yet Campbellites showed up in every corner of the Bible Union's leadership. Because of the prominent place they occupied, Williams insisted, although the Union did not reveal the names of its translators, there had to be members of the body doing that work too. With such people actively engaged in the Bible Union's work, for Amity Baptist Church to maintain its allegiance to Christ and to truth, it could not give it its sympathy, confidence, nor aid to the ABU.[68]

The American Bible Union responded in a lengthy article by a committee of three headed by President Spencer Cone. Regarding the charge of using Campbell and others from his reform as translators, the writers insisted that they hired no one for that work except those who were "firm believers in all the cardinal doctrines of Christianity, as held by Baptists and other evangelical denominations." Even if Campbellites were heretics, no translation tainted with Arianism, Unitarianism, or other doctrinal errors could ever be approved by the Bible Union, they insisted. Translations were not the product of any individual but were vetted in a meticulous process that involved many layers of critique and approval.[69]

The reply included excerpts of previously published explicit denials by Alexander Campbell and James Shannon of holding the heretical beliefs they were accused of. Campbell repeated what he had said many times, that while he rejected the speculative dogma of the Trinity formulated by Greek Orthodox and Roman Catholic theologians and was committed to calling Bible things by Bible names, he believed in the "equal Godhead or Divinity of the Father, and of the Son, and of the Holy Spirit. 'God the Father,' 'God the Word' incarnate, and God the Holy Spirit." He rejected Unitarian, Arian,

---

68. Williams, "Correspondence," 361–64.

69. "Reply of the American Bible Union to the Amity Street Baptist Church," *Bible Union Quarterly*, August 1852, 365–86.

and Sabellian ideas as heartless and hopeless philosophy. Furthermore, he denied the accusation that he rejected the active work of the Holy Spirit in conversion. "It is the Spirit that quickens, renews, re-creates; and neither breath nor word, neither blood nor water." He repudiated the idea that he had ever advocated "Papal or Episcopal" teachings of water regeneration, and pointed out that neither Jesus nor Paul ever said that being begotten of the Spirit was predicated on first being begotten of water. "Paul makes baptism only the washing of the new birth, and not the renewing of the Spirit."[70]

Even Baptist minister Samuel W. Lynd, with whom Campbell had sparred in 1837 over baptismal regeneration, came to Campbell's defense in response to criticisms of the ABU for using Campbell in the Bible translation work. Campbell and others from his movement had been active in the AFBS, he said, and it was only right that they be involved now in the ABU. While he did not know whether or not Campbell and Shannon had been contracted as revisers, if they had, he was fully confident they would act "honestly and independently in the discharge of their duty."[71]

Campbell began working on his translation of the book of Acts after the Bible Union's convention of 1852 when basic rules and procedures were put in place.[72] Campbell never mentioned his translation work in the *Millennial Harbinger*, apparently because of the ABU's policy not to make public the names of specific translators, since every individual's work would go through an extensive editing process before publication.[73]

But the work did not progress as expected. In January 1854, Campbell acknowledged his tardiness in completing the translation of Acts to ABU president William Wyckoff and told him to "expect my revision of the Acts in some three weeks from this date. I am having it transcribed. Insuperable difficulties growing out of my many relations to Society domestic and foreign have been the occasion of my slow progress."[74] It would be more than a year before Campbell actually finished the work and submitted his manuscript

70. Alexander Campbell, "Replies of Campbell and Shannon to the Charge of Heterodoxy," *Bible Union Quarterly*, August 1852, 402–3.

71. S. W. Lynd, "Bible Union's Plan of Revision Vindicated," *Bible Union Quarterly*, February 1853, 464.

72. "Bible Union Convention," *Millennial Harbinger*, May 1852, 286–93.

73. Cecil Thomas surveys extensively the scholarly resources Campbell used in producing his revision as well as main characteristics of his work. Thomas, *Alexander Campbell*, 92–110.

74. Alexander Campbell to Wyckoff, January 25, 1854, Campbell Collection, Bethany College Archives, Bethany, West Virginia.

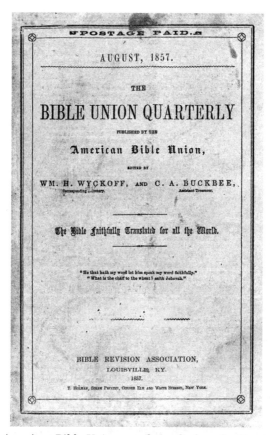

⌖POSTAGE PAID.⌖

AUGUST, 1857.

THE

BIBLE UNION QUARTERLY

PUBLISHED BY THE

American Bible Union,

EDITED BY

WM. H. WYCKOFF, AND C. A. BUCKBEE,
Corresponding Secretary.   Assistant Treasurer.

𝔗𝔥𝔢 𝔅𝔦𝔟𝔩𝔢 𝔣𝔞𝔦𝔱𝔥𝔣𝔲𝔩𝔩𝔶 𝔗𝔯𝔞𝔫𝔰𝔩𝔞𝔱𝔢𝔡 𝔣𝔬𝔯 𝔞𝔩𝔩 𝔱𝔥𝔢 𝔚𝔬𝔯𝔩𝔡.

" He that hath my word let him speak my word faithfully."
" What is the chaff to the wheat? saith Jehovah."

BIBLE REVISION ASSOCIATION,
LOUISVILLE, KY.
1857.
T. Holman, Steam Printer, Corner Elm and White Streets, New York.

The American Bible Union was formed when the Baptist-led American and Foreign Bible Society refused to produce a revised English version with the word "immerse" instead of "baptize." The Bible Union asked Alexander Campbell to do the translation of the book of Acts for its new version, the first parts of which appeared in 1862. Courtesy of the Center for Restoration Studies, Abilene Christian University, Abilene, Texas.

to the Bible Union. Robert Richardson remarked that the strenuous effort he put into the translation of Acts, added to all his other duties, seriously affected both Campbell's mental and physical health.[75]

By the end of the 1850s, Campbell was worn out from the wear and tear of the translation work. His weariness was intensified by the unexpected

75. Richardson, *Memoirs of Alexander Campbell*, 2:619–22.

Campbell's handwritten "Preamble" to his translation of Acts, defending the new version against those who insisted on the King James Version. "To make a new version at all desirable, it must be more truthful, or more perspicuous, or more definite, and consequently more intelligible than that now in use." Used with permission from the Disciples of Christ Historical Society, Bethany, West Virginia.

urgency to rebuild Bethany College after a devastating fire in 1857 and growing alarm at what appeared to be the approaching dissolution of the nation.

In 1858, Campbell attended the meeting of the American Bible Union committee that was editing his translation of Acts. In a letter to his wife Selina, he reported that he had declined the invitation to be part of the deliberations. Some had urged him to participate and "lobby" for his ideas, but he insisted on recusing himself. He explained to her, however, that he had been consulted "on all the premises of importance during the meeting so far, and I find my positions are sustained and affirmed by the leading men in the board, and their shyness and party spirit yields and softens and seems to be forgotten in all matters which we discuss. My being present at this time is very gratifying to many friends here and I presume to say that it will be nothing to our disadvantage as a people that I am here."[76] Nevertheless, when Campbell's Acts did appear, the ABU's Committee on Revision had ruled against many of his translation choices.

The next year, Duncan R. Campbell, president of Georgetown College in Kentucky, alleged that the committee's changes to Campbell's work were due to Campbell's incompetence as a scholar. Campbell shot back that his detractor was actually the incompetent one. The Bible Union had published his work the same way it did every book it produced. Each book would still have to undergo a final evaluation before a final edition of the New Testament was compiled, he explained. He called his attacker, among other things, "a crafty charlatan, a mere clerical pretender, of limited learning," as well as a person of coarse and vulgar bearing with a crude and superficial knowledge of Greek.[77] Despite his fatigue, Campbell could still defend himself passionately against attacks on his integrity and competence.

In spite of continued opposition to Campbellism and widespread suspicion toward Campbell's doctrinal positions, even former detractors were now willing to accept him as a scholar and an "evangelical Christian." He had come a long way.

76. Alexander Campbell to Selina Campbell, written from New York, September 29, 1858, Campbell Collection, Bethany College Archives, Bethany, West Virginia.

77. Alexander Campbell, "Response to Dr. D. R. Campbell," *Millennial Harbinger*, August 1859, 457–60.

CHAPTER 8

The Defender
of Protestant Christianity

After his first debate with John Walker in 1820, Alexander Campbell embraced such public contests as powerful tools to spread his reformation. During his career he conducted five formal public discussions, several written debates, and countless less-formal clashes with religious opponents in his periodicals.[1]

Two public debates significantly shaped Campbell's career at midstage. The first pitted Christianity against skepticism, as Campbell took on the genial Welsh anti-Christian social reformer Robert Owen in 1829. The second, in 1837, matched Campbell as the champion of Protestantism with the Roman Catholic bishop of Cincinnati, John Baptist Purcell. While many hailed Campbell as the defender of Protestant Christianity against skepticism and Catholicism, Campbell clearly understood these contests as tools to promote his restoration of the ancient gospel and order of things.

The Debate with Robert Owen

America seemed to be, at least at some levels, thoroughly "Christian." Local and state laws excluded atheists from running for political office or serving on juries, and unbelievers seldom admitted it for fear of ostracism and loss of reputation. Yet a small but significant rebellion against traditional religion had been growing at least since the American Revolution. Thomas Jefferson

---

1. Campbell's formal public debates included the two discussed in this chapter as well as those with Presbyterians John Walker (1820), William L. Maccalla (1823), and Nathan L. Rice (1849). Among his written debates were those with Universalist Dolphus Skinner (1835) and with "skeptics" Irad Kelley and Samuel Underhill (1836).

and others who were not themselves skeptics advocated toleration for all, including non-Christians and atheists.[2]

In the mid-1820s advocates of "skepticism" (often labeled Deism) began openly attacking Christianity and challenging orthodox beliefs. Among the most widely known skeptics of the day was Welsh social reformer Robert Owen. Owen's career had begun with a set of experimental reforms at the New Lanark cotton mill in South Lanarkshire, Scotland, today a UNESCO World Heritage Site.[3] Owen envisioned New Lanark, begun by his father-in-law, David Dale, as a model for how to treat workers and their families with kindness and generosity and for how to train them to treat everyone that way. He believed that the spread of this "gospel" would solve the world's ills.[4] Resistance to his humanitarian program led Owen to conclude that religion was the source of all exploitation, greed, and wars in the world.

To Owen, Christianity was no better or worse than other religions. In his 1857 autobiography, completed the year before he died, he recalled his early quest to find "the true religion."

> I studied and studied, and carefully compared one with another, for I was very religiously inclined, and desired most anxiously to be in the right way. . . . It was with the greatest reluctance, and after long contests in my mind, that I was compelled to abandon my first and deep-rooted impressions in favour of Christianity. But being obliged to give up my faith in this sect, I was at the same time compelled to reject all others, for I had discovered that all had been based on the same absurd imagination, "that each one formed his own qualities, determined his own thoughts, will, and action, and was responsible for them to God and to his fellow-men." My own reflections compelled me to come to very different conclusions. . . . My language, religion, and habits were forced upon me by Society; and that I was entirely the child of Nature and Society. . . . Thus was I forced, through seeing the error of their foundation, to abandon all belief in every religion which had been taught to man. But my religious feelings were immediately replaced by the spirit of universal charity—not for a sect or a party, or for

2. Leigh Eric Schmidt, *Village Atheists: How America's Unbelievers Made Their Way in a Godly Nation* (Princeton: Princeton University Press, 2016), 7.

3. See New Lanark World Heritage Site at http://www.newlanark.org/world-heritage-site/#virtualtour.

4. I am greatly indebted in this section to Richard Cherok for his insights into the background, content, and effects of the Campbell-Owen debate in his book *Debating for God* (Abilene, TX: Abilene Christian University Press, 2008).

a country or a colour, but for the human race, and with a real and ardent desire to do them good.[5]

Owen's goal was to eliminate the world's evils through the elimination of religion. He sincerely believed he could create a system of education (or reeducation) that would train people to care for one another rather than use each other for self-advancement. His model community in New Lanark, Scotland, elevated the lives of mill workers through higher wages, access to healthy food, education for their children, and protection from unregulated labor practices he believed proved the truth of his ideas. Religion— Christianity, in his personal experience—was the main force blocking the spread of such beneficial outcomes and the creation of a just society. Owen and his ideas received considerable publicity. His personal kindness and generosity set him apart from other, more abrasive skeptics, and for many he provided an attractive alternative to traditional Christian values. He was, therefore, dangerous.

One of Campbell's first responses to skepticism appeared as a response to a letter published in the September 1826 *Christian Baptist.* Although the letter's author had written "Private" across the top, Campbell published it anyway, along with six lengthy replies over the next four months. He excused this breach of confidence with the explanation that he believed many could benefit from his responses. He identified the writer only as "D," thereby maintaining his privacy.

The letter seemed to express a sincere plea for Campbell to dispel the author's doubts about Christianity, particularly the idea that a good God would construct a system in which the majority of humanity would end up in eternal torment. Campbell's responses, however, were often biting. In a convoluted and rambling first reply, he argued that if God had constructed a system in which there were no possibility of moral evil, there would have been no possibility of God being governor—a role essential to human happiness. He also argued that without the possibility of choosing to rebel against God and being punished for it, there would be no meaning to being rewarded for being righteous. "If God had not given birth to a system in which it was possible for some to be miserable hereafter," he asserted, "it would

---

5. *The Life of Robert Owen, Written by Himself* (London: Effingham Wilson, 1857), quoted in Frank Podmore, *Robert Owen: A Biography* (London: Hutchinson & Co., 1906), 19–20.

have been impossible to have given birth to a system in which any could have been eternally and perfectly happy."[6]

In the other five articles, Campbell repeated this point and accused "D" of falling into the inconsistency of other skeptics—assuming biblical premises about God's nature, sin, and punishment even as they attacked the Bible. In Campbell's final article, he advised "D" to take up the Bible (preferably his recently published translation) and give it a close reading "about a dozen of times, and then tell me what you think of it."[7]

The less-than-convincing articles against the anonymous "D" were Campbell's first extended response to skepticism. He would soon, however, give his attention to the "king of skeptics." In 1825 Robert Owen had purchased the land and buildings of a failed utopian millennial group named Rappites (after founder George Rapp) or Harmonists at New Harmony, Indiana. Owen planned to use the site as a springboard to spread his ideas in the New World (he also attempted to obtain land in Mexico for a massive community). He believed America was especially ripe for his ideas because of the possibility of "mental independence" from old ways of thinking.[8] In October he began the *New Harmony Gazette* to promote his new community and his antireligion ideas.

In April 1827 Campbell began a series of five articles attacking Owen's program.[9] In the second, he challenged the "enlightened deists of New Harmony" to respond to his defense of the existence of God, the immortality of the human spirit, and humanity's state of happiness or torment after death.[10] These articles continued through October 1827. That month Campbell's thirty-six-year-old wife Margaret died, and he dropped the topic for several months.[11] In May 1828, however, he renewed the assault by reprinting

6. Alexander Campbell, "Replication—No. I," *Christian Baptist* 4 (September 7, 1826): 43.

7. Alexander Campbell, "To Mr. D, A Sceptic. Replication—No. VI," *Christian Baptist* 4 (January 1, 1827): 140.

8. Robert Owen, "Oration Containing a Declaration of Mental Independence" (Public Hall, New Harmony, Indiana, July, 4, 1826), text available at http://www.indiana.edu/~kdhist/H105-documents-web/week11/Owen1826.html.

9. At the time, Campbell did not object to communitarian ideas, then a major part of Owen's vision. Alexander Campbell, "Mr. Robert Owen and the Social System. No. I," *Christian Baptist* 4 (April 1827): 209–12. Not until his sharp encounters with Mormon communitarianism in the 1830s did Campbell reject such ideas.

10. Alexander Campbell, "The Social System and Deism. No. II," *Christian Baptist* 4 (June 1827): 259.

11. "Obituary Notice," *Christian Baptist* 5 (November 1827): 96.

a challenge to Christian clergy Owen had made after a series of lectures in New Orleans.

Owen's New Harmony experiment never quite got off the ground, and by 1827 he began attending to other projects. After a three-month trip back to Britain between August and November, he returned to the United States and embarked on a speaking tour starting in New York. In January 1828 he was back in New Orleans, where he presented several lectures focusing especially on the plight of African Americans as further evidence of religion's negative effect on society. Most who heard him in New Orleans were hostile to Owen's positions, but Owen pushed back. He announced that he was ready to debate the evils of religion with any Christian clergyman who would accept his invitation.[12]

Before hearing of Owen's challenge, Campbell had received an invitation to debate an Ohio skeptic named Samuel Underhill. In April 1828 Campbell printed a letter from Canton, Ohio, describing Underhill's attacks on Christianity and success in converting many to Owen's ideas. The writer urged Campbell to take on Underhill, but he refused. Underhill was too obscure to merit his attention, he said. It was only the "king of the skeptics," Robert Owen, that he would take on.[13]

The *New Harmony Gazette* printed this challenge from Campbell, assuring readers that Owen would respond soon.[14] In the meantime, Campbell read Owen's New Orleans offer to debate any Christian minister and immediately printed his acceptance in the May *Christian Baptist*. Owen responded by suggesting a meeting of skeptics and Christians to discuss his ideas. Campbell said no. He was accepting the New Orleans challenge for a one-on-one debate, he informed Owen, not making a new proposal. When Owen finally saw all the correspondence, he agreed to defend his ideas against Campbell and quickly made a trip to Bethany so the two could arrange details. This first meeting began a lasting friendship despite deep differences in belief.[15]

The two agreed to meet in Cincinnati the following April.[16] Owen

12. Ian Donnachie, *Robert Owen: Owen of New Lanark and New Harmony* (East Lothian, Scotland: Tuckwell, 2000), 252.

13. Alexander Campbell, "Canton, Ohio, February 22, 1828," *Christian Baptist* 5 (April 1828): 207–8.

14. "From the Christian Baptist," *New Harmony Gazette*, April 30, 1828, 215.

15. See, for example, Robert Richardson, *Memoirs of Alexander Campbell*, 2 vols. (Philadelphia: J. B. Lippincott & Co., 1868–1870), 1:543.

16. Owen returned to Britain on a planned trip but was caught up in an opportunity

would defend the five propositions issued to Christian clergy during his visit to New Orleans: (1) That all religions were founded on human ignorance; (2) that they are directly opposed to the universal laws of human nature; (3) that they have been, and are, the real sources of all vice, disunion, and misery; (4) that they are a barrier to the formation of a society of virtue, intelligence, sincerity, and benevolence; and (5) that they can no longer be maintained except through the ignorance of the masses and the tyranny of the few over them.

Anticipating large crowds, Cincinnati officials attempted to secure the largest meeting place possible for the debate. Their first choice was the Presbyterian meetinghouse—the largest venue in town. But when the minister refused, likely because of antagonism toward Campbell, they got permission from the Methodist church. Their building had a seating capacity of about a thousand, though up to twelve hundred crowded in most days. Publicity for the debate generated so much excitement that spectators from at least seven states besides Ohio came to watch.

When the contest began on April 13, it quickly became obvious that the two antagonists had very different concepts of what it was supposed to be. Despite the agreement that Owen would take the affirmative on the five propositions in his New Orleans challenge, he instead launched into an explanation of his twelve laws of human nature, a set of propositions apparently developed for the government of the Mexican province of Texas, where he hoped to establish more of his cooperative villages.[17]

Owen's laws started with the assertion that individuals have no control over their personality or the circumstances into which they are born. Every individual had, he claimed, the capacity at birth to learn ideas and habits—both good and bad—and simply acted on the strongest impressions received, with no personal choice involved. When people were born with an inferior disposition into bad circumstances, they developed the worst possible character. When they were born with a mixture of good and bad makeup and circumstances, they developed a medium character. The highest development occurred when both personality and circumstances were superior. Owen's vision was to provide everyone with circumstances that produced positive

---

to obtain land in Mexico for his experimental communities. He spent almost four months pursuing the possibility with Mexican officials, with no concrete results. Donnachie, *Robert Owen*, 253–57.

17. Donnachie, *Robert Owen*, 255.

DEBATE

ON THE

EVIDENCES OF CHRISTIANITY;

CONTAINING

AN EXAMINATION

OF THE

"SOCIAL SYSTEM,"

AND OF

ALL THE SYSTEMS OF SCEPTICISM OF ANCIENT AND
MODERN TIMES.

HELD IN THE CITY OF CINCINNATI, OHIO, FROM THE 13th
TO THE 21st OF APRIL, 1829; BETWEEN

ROBERT OWEN,

OF NEW LANARK, SCOTLAND, AND

ALEXANDER CAMPBELL,

OF BETHANY, VIRGINIA.

Reported by CHARLES H. SIMS, *Stenographer.*

WITH

AN APPENDIX,

WRITTEN BY THE PARTIES.

VOL. I.

What then is unbelief?—'Tis an exploit,
A strenuous enterprize. To gain it man
Must burst through every bar of common sense,
Of common shame—magnanimously wrong!

——Who most examine, most believe;
Parts, like half sentences, confound.
Read his whole volume, Sceptic, *then* reply!

O Lord of Hosts! blessed is the man that trusteth in thee!

YOUNG.

DAVID.

BETHANY, VA.
PRINTED AND PUBLISHED BY ALEXANDER CAMPBELL.
1829.

Robert Owen relinquished to Campbell all rights to publish their
debate, giving Campbell the opportunity to begin making his case
in verse against "skepticism" on the title page. Used with permission
from the Disciples of Christ Historical Society, Bethany, West Virginia.

impressions and caused them to develop their highest possible character.
This was the only sure way to elevate the human race to its highest levels.[18]

18. Robert Owen and Alexander Campbell, *Debate on the Evidences of Christianity*,
2 vols. (Bethany, VA: Alexander Campbell, 1829), 1:109–10. Hereafter, page references from
this work will be given in parentheses in the text.

Campbell repeatedly reminded Owen of the original terms of the debate, to no avail. Finally, on Friday morning the seventeenth, the fifth day of the eight-day event, Owen stated that he had said all that he had to say. He then gave Campbell permission to speak uninterrupted for as long as it took to make all his arguments. When the debate reconvened after lunch, the moderators had approved the new procedure. Campbell then proceeded to speak for twelve hours, divided into two-hour sessions starting that afternoon and ending Monday morning (no sessions were held on Sunday). In essence, Campbell gave a sweeping defense of Christianity, discussing historical and prophetic evidences and its positive effects on the world, concluding with a strong critique of Owen's social system (2:12–141).

Despite their radically different views, the two agreed on three things, at least partially. First, Campbell admitted that much that was taught and practiced in religion did tend toward evil. The reason for this, however, was that all the religions of the world (besides Judaism—and it had its own corruptions) were "mere systems of abstract opinions and speculations." Greek, Roman, and Eastern philosophy had crept into all religions, filling them with "air-built and visionary schemes about matter and mind, creation and providence" (2:108).

Because so many through the centuries had been converted to Christianity from these false systems, Campbell asserted, Christianity itself became polluted and turned into a system of speculation, no different from speculation on the ideas of Plato or Socrates. "From these unhallowed commixtures sprang the creed systems of ancient and modern times, so that finally almost every vestige of the ancient simplicity and the true genius of Christianity disappeared; and various schemes of sectarian and philosophic Christianity succeeded and supplanted it." The point of his reformation, he insisted, was to strip Christianity of those perversions.

When Campbell launched into such critiques, it surely made his Protestant supporters uncomfortable. "We are assured that the progress of scepticism is neither owing to the weakness nor the paucity of the evidences of Christianity; but to a profession of it unauthorized by, and incompatible with, the Christian scriptures" (1:14).

Campbell declared that if Scripture had not predicted these very departures from truth just as clearly as it had the birth of Christ, he would have been prepared to join Owen in standing against all religions. However, he had been "taught to distinguish a thing from the abuse of it; and never to condemn any thing until . . . fully acquainted with it" (2:88–89). The divisions and hostility between Christians had been one of the most convincing evidences to Owen of Christianity's falsehood. "When Mr. Owen assails us, my friends, through the medium of our sectarian divisions and discords, 'tis then he wounds us most sensibly." It was here that Christians were most vulnerable, Campbell admitted. The adversarial spirit and "foolish and absurd dogmas of the fashionable systems of religion" gave skeptics their strongest argument. Yet even here they were attacking the abuse of Christianity rather than the real thing (2:165)!

Second, both envisioned a bright millennial future toward which America and the world were headed. As seen earlier, though Campbell's optimistic postmillennialism was not always dominant, his overarching sense of God's unique plans for America reflected a deep conviction that humanity had the God-given ability and responsibility to eradicate poverty, crime, exploitation, and misery.

Owen clearly held the same conviction. According to biographer J. F. C. Harrison, "At the same time he denounced all existing religions he began to use the language of millennialism."[19] Millennial ideas abounded in nineteenth-century American and British evangelical Christian groups. But it was from groups like the Shakers, who based their millennial vision on communitarianism, that Owen drew inspiration for his communitarian ideas. They showed the viability of disciplined, self-sufficient communities without traditional family structures. In the 1820s and 1830s, Owenism developed into a secular millennial sect, with its own meetings, hymns, and rituals. Many leaders in Owen's movement came to understand it as "practical millennial Christianity."[20]

And finally, before, during, and after the debate, both men made it clear that they regarded the other as a person of integrity and good will. Owen was almost effusive in his praise of Campbell in his closing response to Campbell's long oration.

> My friends, Mr. Campbell appears to me to have done his duty manfully, and with a zeal that would have been creditable to any of the primitive fathers of the church. His learning, his industry, and some very extraordinary talents for supporting the cause which he advocates, have been conspicuous; and for one trained in the fiery notion produced by the free-will doctrines, he has restrained his temper beyond my most sanguine expectations. That, however, which I admire in him above all, is his downright honesty and fairness in what he believes to be the cause of truth. . . . Now, [his] is a straightforward proceeding in the investigation of truth, which I have long

19. J. F. C. Harrison, *Robert Owen and the Owenites in Britain and America: The Quest for the New Moral World* (London: Routledge and Kegan Paul, 1969), 92–93.

20. Harrison, *Robert Owen and the Owenites*, 125.

sought for, but which until now, I have sought for in vain. The friends of truth, therefore, on whichever side of the question it may be found, are now more indebted to Mr. Campbell than any other Christian minister of the present day.[21]

Owen did go on to say that he was still absolutely convinced that Christianity was false and that it was anything but beneficial to humanity. Perhaps it was that Campbell's "version" of the religion seemed more agreeable to him.

Such politeness was apparently a consistent characteristic of Owen. A remarkable description of Owen's demeanor in the debate appeared in Frances Trollope's *Domestic Manners of the Americans*. Trollope immigrated to America from England in 1827 to join the Nashoba Community near Memphis, Tennessee. When that Owen-inspired effort to educate and emancipate slaves failed, she moved to Cincinnati with her family. While there, she attended sessions of the Campbell-Owen debate, publishing her account in 1832 after returning to England. Trollope reported that despite his insistence that Christianity was utterly false, a fraud devised to control the masses, Owen's presentations did not provoke outrage from the audience. "The gentle tone of his voice; his mild, sometimes playful, but never ironical manner; the absence of every vehement or harsh expression; the affectionate interest expressed for 'the whole human family;' the air of candour with which he expressed his wish to be convinced he was wrong, if he indeed were so—his kind smile—the mild expression of his eyes—in short, his whole manner, disarmed zeal, and produced a degree of tolerance that those who did not hear him would hardly believe possible."[22] Owen's utterly gentlemanly demeanor and the lack of overt antagonism toward his ideas by the spectators seem to have made Campbell nervous that observers might get the impression Owen had convinced the people of his claims.

After Campbell's twelve-hour speech, Owen, who had said earlier that a couple of hours would be plenty to respond, now seemed to want more. He spoke the rest of the evening Monday and all morning Tuesday. That afternoon the two went back and forth about how long Owen would have to speak, when finally Campbell ended the proceedings with a surprise move. Rather than risk anyone mistaking the audience's "good and Christian deportment" for assent to Owen's ideas, Campbell asked all who

---

21. Owen and Campbell, *Debate on the Evidences of Christianity*, 2:142.

22. Mrs. [Frances] Trollope, *Domestic Manners of the Americans* (London: Whittaker, Treacher & Co., 1832), 127.

believed in the truth of Christianity and wanted it to spread throughout the world to stand. The stenographer noted that there was "an almost universal rising up." When Campbell then asked all who rejected Christianity and opposed its spread to stand, three people did so. Owen briefly thanked the moderators, congratulated Campbell on his "little maneuver," and concluded by saying that truth required no such support. The debate was over.[23]

Because Owen's New Harmony community had failed and his hopes to acquire land in Mexico did not materialize, he prepared to return to England immediately. But before he did, he made a quick trip to Bethany to proof and edit his parts of the debate transcript, having sold all rights to the book to Campbell. Owen's warmth and complete lack of discourtesy and arrogance continued to impress Campbell deeply. For the rest of his life he spoke of Owen consistently in affectionate terms. Their only other actual meeting was in New York in 1847 as Campbell was about to depart for a tour of Scotland and Ireland. Owen, back in America to promote his ideas, made a point to come and visit. Campbell described the meeting in a letter to his daughter, describing Owen as "my old friend." During the visit Owen never mentioned the debate, asking how Campbell's work was going and especially how his father, Thomas, was. Campbell spoke of Owen's "unyielding good nature" and repeated what he had said many times before—that he was "the most fair, candid, and gentlemanly disputant I have yet met with; and a saint in morality compared with some of my opponents."[24]

Campbell learned of Owen's death in 1858, while glancing at the table of contents of a Bethany College student publication. There he saw an announcement of a biography of Owen that spoke, among other things, of his innovation in childhood education. Campbell, perhaps a bit nostalgic in the midst of the looming crisis of the Civil War and his own decline, had no criticism of Owen at all. "In our protracted discussion of the evidences and claims of the Christian Gospel, and the Christian Scriptures, he never lost his equanimity and courtesy, and well sustained the character and candor of a gentleman and a philosopher."[25]

The discussion with Owen and the publicity surrounding it arguably

23. Owen and Campbell, *Debate on the Evidences of Christianity*, 2:200–201.

24. Alexander Campbell, "Letters from Europe—No. I," *Millennial Harbinger*, July 1847, 420.

25. Alexander Campbell, "The Neotrophian Magazine," *Millennial Harbinger*, March 1859, 173.

propelled Campbell into the national spotlight as never before. The debate book went through several printings in 1829—it was printed in Bethany and Cincinnati, and then in London a decade later. No fewer than sixteen subsequent editions appeared between 1852 (when Campbell edited the book for a new printing) and 1957, from publishers representing all streams of the North American Stone-Campbell Movement. Campbell gained the reputation among many Christian leaders, even among those who rejected his reforms, as a successful defender of Christianity against skepticism—as successful as anyone at the time.[26]

The Debate with Bishop John Baptist Purcell

Though not the only debate in American Christian history between a Protestant and a Roman Catholic leader, this event was unusual enough to create a major stir.[27] John Baptist Purcell, first bishop (and later archbishop) of the burgeoning Catholic community in Cincinnati and the Ohio Valley, was one of several important US Catholic leaders who held ideas that later in the nineteenth century the Vatican would condemn as "Americanism."[28]

Americanist understandings arose early in US Catholic history. The first Roman Catholic bishop in America, John Carroll (1735–1815), insisted that Roman Catholicism had nothing to fear from American democratic ideas but could actually thrive best in that environment. He actively supported the American Revolution, published in 1784 *An Address to the Roman Catholics of the United States of North America* endorsing religious freedom and open dialogue, and insisted on being elected bishop by the nation's priests rather than simply being appointed bishop by the pope. He also set in place a "trustee system" whereby a lay council in each local Catholic parish owned

---

26. For example, see the comment attributed to Presbyterian leader Robert Breckinridge, who refused to oppose Campbell in the 1843 debate discussed in chapter 14 because he esteemed him too highly for his defense of Christianity against infidelity and Protestantism against Catholicism. See J. J. Haley, *Debates That Made History* (St. Louis: Christian Board of Publication, 1920), 178.

27. Haley, *Debates That Made History*, 128. Purcell himself later conducted a written debate with Congregationalist minister Thomas Vickers in 1867–1868 in the pages of the *Catholic Telegraph* and the *Cincinnati Gazette*.

28. Thomas Timothy McAvoy, *The Americanist Heresy in Roman Catholicism, 1895–1900* (Notre Dame: University of Notre Dame Press, 1963); Patrick W. Carey, *Catholics in America: A History* (Westport, CT: Praeger, 2004), 55–66.

and administered the church property.[29] Another early advocate of these ideas was John England (1786–1842), first Catholic bishop of the Carolinas and Georgia. England wrote a constitution to govern his diocese, convened annual conventions of clergy and laity to make decisions, and was largely responsible for calling the first American Council of Bishops in 1829.[30]

John Baptist Purcell was of the same mind. An Irish immigrant to America in 1818, he did his priestly training in France, where ideas of "Enlightenment Catholicism" emerging from the French Revolution shaped his thought. When he returned to America in 1827, he had embraced the idea that Catholicism was perfectly harmonious with the American system of religious freedom. Catholicism was, in fact, more in keeping with American ideals than the chaos of Protestantism.[31] He sought to present "Catholicism as a reasonable and public faith, one open to the critical scrutiny that their Protestant interlocutors had been claiming it could not withstand."[32]

American Protestant insistence that all Catholics owed political allegiance to the pope, that Jesuits were plotting to take over the country, and that priests and nuns were universally guilty of gross immorality was a real obstacle for Purcell. The debate with Campbell actually provided a perfect opportunity for him to make his case before both a local and—through newspaper reports and publication of the debate—a national audience. Yet Purcell's defense of Catholicism was as much for his own Catholic flock as for anti-Catholic Protestants. They needed to be fortified in their faith and equipped to defend it from the constant and sometimes violent attacks of Protestants. Lyman Beecher's virulently anti-Catholic *Cincinnati Journal*, for example, published a steady stream of accusations that Catholicism was inherently un-American and immoral.

Campbell's personal attitude toward Catholicism had been shaped by his early experiences in Northern Ireland. As noted, Campbell lived through

---

29. Joseph Agonito, *The Building of an American Catholic Church: The Episcopacy of John Carroll* (New York: Garland, 1988), 100–123.

30. Andrew Joseph Eck, "The Americanism of Bishop John England as an Organizer of Catholicity in the Diocese of Charleston, South Carolina" (MA thesis, St. Mary's Seminary & University, 1928); Sister Jose Murphy, "Americanism of John England: First Bishop of Charleston, S.C. 1820–1842" (MA thesis, Boston College, 1942).

31. Margaret C. DePalma, *Dialogue on the Frontier: Catholic and Protestant Relations, 1793–1883* (Kent, OH: Kent State University Press, 2004), 79–80. DePalma charts Purcell's career in three extensive chapters. One of his chief campaigns was for public schools to allow Catholic children to use Catholic translations of the Bible.

32. Herbert Dean Miller, "Enacting Theology, Americanism, and Friendship: The 1837 Debate on Roman Catholicism between Alexander Campbell and Bishop John Purcell" (PhD diss., University of Dayton, 2015), 49, 53.

a period of violent conflicts between Catholics and Protestants, and was formed by the anti-Catholic sentiment of his Presbyterian father and uncles. His frequent comparisons between the backward and repressive nations dominated by Roman Catholicism and those dominated by Protestant ideals reflected commonplace sentiments in Britain and British America.[33]

Campbell reflected these fears in an address to the Western Literary Institute and College of Teachers meeting in Cincinnati in October 1836. Speaking of immigrants then flooding into America, he insisted that they would need solid white Protestant education to make them at least compatible with American genius. "Every wind is carrying to our shores, hundreds and thousands of human beings from distant and oppressed countries, alike ignorant of things human and divine, calling for our sympathies and our means of promoting their cultivation, both in things intellectual and moral; and shall we suffer them to appeal to our humanity and our religion in vain? Our own interests, indeed, our political safety, our personal security from wrong and outrage, demand our best efforts to neutralize that mass of ignorance and corruption which otherwise must accumulate on our borders, or grow up in the bosom of our society."[34] Most of those ignorant and corrupt immigrants were Catholics.

As Catholic historian Jay Dolan noted, new Catholic leaders in America in the 1820s and 1830s favored strict control of the American church by Rome.[35] Campbell was becoming increasingly alarmed at the growing number of American Catholics, and in the 1836 *Millennial Harbinger* challenged any informed Catholic leader to debate him on the un-American, tyrannical, and immoral nature of Catholicism. D. S. Burnet of Cincinnati reprinted the challenge in his own magazine and personally delivered a copy to Purcell with the challenge marked.[36]

Purcell and Campbell actually met for the first time at the 1836 meeting of the Western Literary Institute and College of Teachers mentioned above.

---

33. Robert Emmett Curran, *Papist Devils: Catholics in British America, 1574–1783* (Washington, DC: Catholic University of America Press, 2014).

34. Alexander Campbell, "Closing Address," in *Transactions of the Sixth Annual Meeting of the Western Literary Institute and College of Teachers*, ed. D. L. Talbott (Cincinnati: Published by the Executive Committee, 1837), 255.

35. Jay P. Dolan, *In Search of an American Catholicism: A History of Religion and Culture in Tension* (New York: Oxford University Press, 2002), 47–51.

36. Alexander Campbell, "Editorial Remarks on W.A.'s Communication," *Millennial Harbinger*, March 1836, 117; John B. Purcell, "Letter 1—No Title," *Catholic Telegraph*, December 22, 1836, quoted in Miller, "Enacting Theology," 64–65.

Purcell was a member of the organization and delivered a speech titled "On the Philosophy of the Human Mind." In it Purcell attacked skepticism, a point his audience would have agreed with; but he also criticized Scottish commonsense philosophy. Purcell insisted that such philosophical empiricism led to the same conclusion as skepticism. This argument would be important for his debate with Campbell the next year.

Campbell responded to Purcell's speech by pointing out that overt religious discussions were not within that body's purview and invited Purcell to engage in a discussion with him on these matters in another venue, but Purcell politely declined. Campbell then announced that he would give a speech on Catholicism Monday evening, October 10. Purcell attended, but when Campbell invited him to respond, Purcell announced he would speak the next night. After Purcell's address the following evening, Campbell again invited the bishop to participate in a formal debate, and he again declined, citing diminished health and heavy pastoral responsibilities.

Campbell planned to speak once more on Catholicism and then depart for home. Before he could leave Cincinnati, however, he agreed to a petition written by a group of "Concerned Cincinnatians" to conduct a public debate. Before his departure, he issued a challenge to debate any Catholic of equal or higher rank than Purcell, in any state. He promised to be back in January and either publicly debate whoever stepped forward or give a series of lectures on six propositions concerning Catholicism (reduced from an earlier list of nine) he had drawn up after his final message in the city.[37]

Though at first hesitant to engage Campbell in debate after the encounter at the College of Teachers, Purcell came to see a public discussion with Campbell as an opportunity to clarify misunderstandings of and defend American Catholicism. On December 22, Purcell announced that he would debate Campbell after all. When Campbell returned to Cincinnati on January 11, the two met to negotiate terms. They tinkered again with Campbell's list of propositions, reducing it to seven—all couched in anti-Catholic language. Campbell asserted, among other things, that the Catholic Church was not the true church but an apostasy from it, the fulfillment of prophecy of the falling away; that the claim of apostolic succession of Catholic bishops was spurious; that the Catholic sacramental system was illegitimate; and that the Catholic Church's claim that it had produced the Bible was false. The final proposition, which took up more time in the debate than any other, was that

---

37. "Roman Catholic Discussion," *Millennial Harbinger*, December 1836, 551–54.

Roman Catholicism was inherently and unchangeably opposed to American freedom and republican government.[38]

The debate ran from Friday, January 13, 1837, through Saturday, January 21, at the Campbell group's meeting house on Sycamore Street. Campbell began by asserting that the New Testament authorized none of Catholicism's chief teachings and practices. Purcell responded by asking, Where is the true church from which the Roman Catholic Church supposedly departed? Interestingly, Campbell came back with a classic statement of the "trail of blood" argument, characteristic of Landmark Baptists. Any groups historically persecuted by the Catholic Church were actually the true church, including the Novatians, Donatists, Cathari, Waldensians, and Protestant Reformers.[39] Many Protestants in attendance would have been very uncomfortable with such a claim.

Campbell challenged the assertion that Christ appointed Peter as the supreme leader of the church in Matthew 16. Using standard Protestant arguments, he insisted that the foundation upon which Christ built his church was not Peter but the truth of his divinity. Any leadership role Peter exercised was not divinely designated but merely reflected Peter's historical function in preaching the first "gospel sermon" on Pentecost. Campbell went on to contend from historical records, quoting from Edward Gibbon's history of the Roman Empire, that Boniface III in 606 was the first pope as we know the office today.[40]

Campbell then attacked the Catholic claim of having produced and infallibly safeguarded the Bible and its teachings through the centuries. He asserted that the Bible authenticates itself and does not need authentication or interpretation by the church. Campbell next attacked the doctrine of purgatory, claiming that at its heart it denied the all-sufficiency of the work of Christ in salvation—the heresy of all heresies.

Then the disputants engaged the question of whether the church or the Bible was the ultimate source of religious authority. Purcell pointed out that

38. *A Debate on the Roman Catholic Religion between Alexander Campbell and Rt. Rev. John B. Purcell* (New York and Cincinnati: Benziger Brothers, 1837), vii–viii. Note: many editions of the debate were published in the nineteenth and twentieth centuries, often with different pagination and extra content. Page numbers here are from the edition available at https://archive.org/stream/debateonromancatoocampiala#page/n3/search /Western+hemisphere.

39. See William M. Shea, *The Lion and the Lamb: Evangelicals and Catholics in America* (New York: Oxford University Press, 2004), 111–13; *A Debate on the Roman Catholic Religion*, 65–68.

40. *A Debate on the Roman Catholic Religion*, 68–75.

the Protestant use of commonsense rationalism when seeking truth in Scripture produced disagreement and division that ultimately had the same effect as Deism (skepticism)—indifference toward religious truth claims. Campbell attacked the Catholic concept that infallibility was invested in the church. Infallibility was a matter of method instead of abstract "objective infallibility" vested in a document or an institution. Protestants claimed an infallible Bible, and Catholics claimed an infallible church; but neither the Bible nor the church as detached object can *be* infallible, Campbell claimed. What was relevant was that we have a "perfect" rule—the Bible. If we apply the perfect rule perfectly, he insisted, "it will make us perfect."[41]

An odd part of the debate involved Campbell's quoting from the *Moral Theology* of Alphonsus Liguori, a prominent eighteenth-century Catholic teacher, to prove his accusation that priests regularly violated their vow of celibacy with church approval. The translation of Liguori Campbell used was by Samuel Smith of New York, an anti-Catholic editor who claimed to be a former priest.[42] Campbell quoted a passage that spoke of bishops' use of fines collected from "non-resident Clergymen, or upon those clergymen who keep concubines." This was actually the last of a long list of immoralities Campbell alleged were approved by Catholic teaching.[43]

Purcell immediately challenged the Liguori quotation. The source of Campbell's quote was Smith, Slocum, and Company of New York, known for its extreme anti-Catholic slurs. He asserted that he had three full copies of Liguori's work in the original Latin, and that the phrase Campbell quoted was nowhere to be found in them. This controversy sparked a bizarre exchange that lasted well after the debate.

On Friday afternoon, January 20, Purcell produced a local Swedenborgian classics scholar, Alexander Kinmont, who had examined the original Latin version of Liguori's work. Much to Purcell's delight, this scholarly "disinterested party" pronounced that the only mention of priests involved in concubinage was the requirement that if they continued after two reprimands and severe penalties, they were to be removed from the priesthood.

Campbell's only reply was that while he had quoted many damning passages from Liguori that still stood, Purcell had challenged only this one. Fur-

41. *A Debate on the Roman Catholic Religion*, 168.

42. Shea, *Lion and the Lamb*, 121.

43. *A Debate on the Roman Catholic Religion*, 218–19. Oddly, the first version of the quotation by Campbell used the phrase "clergy who keep nieces." Purcell in his response used "concubines." Hereafter, page references from this work will be given in parentheses in the text.

thermore, Campbell asserted, other passages in official Catholic documents teach the same thing, whether or not the Liguori passage was legitimate. Nevertheless, Campbell's inability to corroborate this accusation opened the possibility that he could be mistaken on others. Campbell refused to back off, however, and promised he would contact Samuel Smith to find out the exact location of the concubine passage (318–21).

Campbell did indeed receive a note from Smith after the debate with the exact location of the damning quote and another translation, verified and signed by six New York Protestant clergy. Campbell promptly borrowed one of Bishop Purcell's Latin translations, took it to Kinmont, who had earlier attested to the spurious nature of the words, who then certified that the passage said exactly what Campbell (and Smith) had alleged. This exchange was included in later editions of the published debate.

In the first edition, however, a fifteen-page "appendix"—omitted from later editions—praised Purcell for his defense of the Catholic religion. This included a long letter written by Purcell and published in the *Catholic Telegraph*, the official newspaper of the Archdiocese of Cincinnati. Purcell accused Smith, Campbell, and the New York clergy of either trying to deceive or being deceived. He denied Campbell's accusation that the passage made concubinage "a trifling offence and allowable on payment of a fine." Then Purcell added another wrinkle to the argument. The passage was not from Liguori's *Moral Theology* at all, he announced, but was written later and appended to Liguori's work by a printer trying to make the size of the volumes of the series uniform. Purcell then proceeded to debunk Campbell's and Smith's accusation that the Council of Trent allowed priests and bishops to have concubines if they paid a fine, producing Kinmont's signed statement from May 22, 1837:

> Most unquestionably it is not so to be regarded; and any person may satisfy himself on that point, who will turn to pages 319–20 (in the first edition of the book), where, on being called on, I gave an abstract of the decree of the Council here referred to by Liguori. . . . There is certainly nothing in the passage here quoted, or in any one in Liguori (which I could find), to countenance the allegation, that Priests may keep Concubines by paying a fine, unless it be considered that to punish an offence is to permit or encourage it. (appendix, xxviii)

This bizarre distraction, while adding little of substance to the content of the debate, highlighted the deep anti-Catholic assumptions of rampant immorality among Catholic leaders and Purcell's categorical denial that the church ever sanctioned or condoned sexual immorality by priests or bishops.

In the final and longest section of the debate, Campbell tried to establish that Roman Catholicism was by its very nature a threat to American freedoms and democratic government. He quoted at length from official Catholic documents that claimed power over all temporal governments and that the pope was "by divine right Lord of thrones and all earthly things" (322–34). He pointed to the Inquisition as representative of the Catholic Church's justification of torture and coercion of anyone who dared challenge the power of the pope and the church. He dared Purcell to deny that his very bishop's oath included a clause that he would "increase and advance the authority of the Pope," and that this oath undeniably superseded Bishop Purcell's oath of allegiance to the United States and its government (323).

Purcell countered with the argument that Catholics where he was from (Ireland) were themselves the subjects of vicious persecution by Protestants. That, he asserted, was one reason he came to America! He consistently denied that the pope had any worldly power outside of the Papal States, implying that the political situation of the Middle Ages reflected in Campbell's quotes no longer existed. His loyalty to the government of the United States, Purcell stated categorically, was in no way compromised by his religious oaths. In fact, he pointed to the Catholics of Maryland as the first to proclaim "freedom of conscience in the Western hemisphere!!" (317).

William Shea points out that while neither Purcell nor Campbell fully grasped it, Purcell's remarks were an admission that Christendom had disappeared—that the world that produced the documents Campbell quoted no longer existed. Purcell admitted that though some nineteenth-century papal decrees condemned modern thought and sought to reassert medieval European Christendom, it could never happen; that system was gone. Purcell argued that none of the so-called anti-American decrees were the infallible doctrine of the church because they were not declared so in the first thousand years of the church's existence (338).

Campbell still insisted that declarations made by, for example, Boniface VIII in *Unam Sanctam* in 1302 and the decrees of the Council of Trent in the mid-sixteenth century claimed to be infallible, universal, and unchangeable truth. These claims Campbell labeled an inherent defect of the Catholic system that made it dangerous to America. Neither Campbell nor many in the Catholic Church could admit the implications of Purcell's defense—that regardless of the wording, such statements were neither universal nor infallible (334–46).

Though Campbell and Purcell differed sharply on many theological points during the weeklong debate, the relative lack of vicious anti-Catholic diatribe is striking. To be sure, Campbell tried to portray the Catholic system as antagonistic to American political and cultural ideals. But he was also clear that he believed Catholics as people and as Americans were not scheming spies for the Vatican. He refused to use the most lurid anti-Catholic attacks like the sensational "Maria Monk" literature that alleged gross sexual immorality and abuse by priests and nuns.[44] Campbell also believed that Catholicism could be "rehabilitated" in the American context, not a commonly held notion in the increasingly anti-Catholic paranoia already present in organized political efforts in New York, Boston, and Philadelphia.[45]

Part of the reason for Campbell's relatively moderate tone was surely the clear and repeated avowals by Purcell of loyalty to America and commitment to the advance of civilization and prosperity in Ohio. Part of his argument was that Catholicism properly understood would actually advance American ideals. Campbell admitted that the Catholics who supported the American Revolution did have a "love of liberty," though he disputed that as absolute proof of the loyalty of all Catholic Americans.[46] Mark Weedman observed that while the Purcell debate made Campbell "famous as an anti-Catholic debater," his anti-Catholic writing actually dropped off significantly after the debate.[47]

Shortly before Purcell's death in 1883, Indiana Stone-Campbell minister-turned-politician Ira Joy Chase interviewed the bishop. Chase may have conducted the interview while traveling on behalf of the Indiana chapter of the Grand Army of the Republic, which he served as chaplain. His account of the interview was published in the December 1889 issue of the *Christian-Evangelist*. Chase quoted extensively from Purcell's evaluation of Campbell, who, according to Chase, he regarded as a friend and fellow Christian.

> From the very first day of our acquaintance to the day of his death, I always entertained the kindliest feelings toward that gentleman. Oh! he was a most

---

44. In John Tracy Ellis, *American Catholicism*, 2nd ed., revised (Chicago: University of Chicago Press, 1969), 151; Philip Jenkins, *The New Anti-Catholicism: The Last Acceptable Prejudice* (New York: Oxford University Press, 2003) 23. See also Mark S. Massa, *Anti-Catholicism in America: The Last Acceptable Prejudice* (New York: Crossroad, 2003).

45. *A Debate on the Roman Catholic Religion*, 170.

46. "For my part, I incline to the opinion that the hatred of England was at least as strong an impulse to their efforts as the love of liberty." *A Debate on the Roman Catholic Religion*, 352.

47. Mark Weedman, "History as Authority in Alexander Campbell's Debate with Bishop Purcell," *Fides et Historia* 28 (Summer 1996): 18n5.

lovable character, indeed, and treated me in every way and on all occasions like a brother.

Was he not my brother in the Lord? Was he not like me a follower of the meek and lowly Jesus? Did he not believe in the resurrection of the dead and of the life beyond the grave where we shall all meet to part no more?

It is true, we differed in some matters—for instance, on church government, prayers for the departed, confessions of sin to the priest, the celibacy of the clergy—what of that? These were all minor matters. In the essentials of Christianity we entirely agreed.[48]

Though after reading the published debate some might quibble with Purcell's assessment that there was not even "a particle of ill-feeling or bitterness" between them, a genuine friendliness did seem to develop between the two. Purcell's evaluation of Campbell's work, perhaps somewhat overstated in the memory of the eighty-something-year-old, was that historians would place him alongside Luther, Calvin, and Wesley. If Campbell had been born in earlier times (apparently before the Protestant Reformation), Purcell continued, he would have been canonized and placed in the list of saints for the significant good he had accomplished![49]

Campbell's fourth major public debate increased his national fame as a skilled defender of Protestant Christianity. Yet, as in the Owen debate, careful listeners and readers could also discern that he continued to criticize the corruptions of Protestantism as strongly as skepticism and Roman Catholicism. Over the next decade he would give considerable energy and time to the creation of two institutions that would further advance his reformation in significant ways.

---

48. I(ra) C(hase), "Archbishop Purcell on Alexander Campbell and His Work: An Interview with the Catholic Prelate," *Christian-Evangelist* 35 (December 1, 1889): 680.

49. Chase, "Archbishop Purcell on Alexander Campbell," 681.

CHAPTER 9

The Creation of Two Crucial Institutions

Campbell's notoriety grew from local to regional to national during the 1820s and 1830s. His frenetic travel and speaking schedule as well as his prodigious writing provided ever-widening exposure for him and his ideas. His service in the Virginia Constitutional Convention of 1829–1830 introduced him to some of the nation's most prominent figures, including former presidents James Madison and James Monroe and chief justice of the United States Supreme Court John Marshall. According to one source, Madison, though often disagreeing with Campbell and his democratic ideas, said that, surprisingly, Campbell had been the most impressive and skillful debater of the convention.[1] His debates with Robert Owen (1829) and John Baptist Purcell (1837), while alarming to some because of his harsh criticisms of Protestantism, nonetheless expanded his fame.

The sheer amount of Campbell's activity coupled with the scope of subjects he tackled in his public lectures and articles tended to mask the details of his reform agenda to noninsiders. To those who knew his fundamental commitment to the restoration of the ancient gospel and order of things, however, it was clear that everything he said and did was geared toward its advancement. This is especially true of one of his greatest passions—education.

Much has been written about Campbell's philosophy and theories of education, including his advocacy of public schools for all white citizens, the education of women, and making Scripture a part of the educational curriculum. Clearly Campbell was a major voice for educational reform in America. Yet most treatments of his educational ideas miss the point of his passion. Only by educating people to be intelligent, virtuous, and patriotic,

1. William M. Moorhouse, "Alexander Campbell and the Virginia Constitutional Convention of 1829–30," *Virginia Cavalcade*, Spring 1975, 190.

only by teaching them to think rightly and freeing them from human philosophies, speculations, and sectarian dogmatism, would they be equipped to grasp the ancient gospel and order. Properly educated, they would be able to hear, understand, and obey the clear biblical teachings that alone could bring the needed reform of church and society. With this understanding, people could order their lives according to God's direction and move the nation and the world toward the millennium.

Not surprisingly, then, Campbell was always involved with schools. He had taught in the schools run by his father and his uncle in Ireland and operated his own Buffaloe Academy from 1818 through 1822. While in Glasgow before coming to America, Campbell heard debates over the benefits and dangers of state-sponsored public education. Aristocrats argued against it because they feared an educated public would rebel against established authority.[2] Campbell surely agreed with them at one level—public education would indeed enable people to resist religious authorities who controlled access to biblical teaching.

Campbell's sharp criticism of popular American understandings of education in his "Bonus Homo" articles surfaced again in his own Buffaloe Seminary. His goal for the school—to produce preachers for his reformation—never materialized because the students were mostly interested in worldly careers. He closed the school at the end of December 1822 after only four years.

The duties of running the school had interfered with the constant calls to preach in Baptist churches. He was still working out the details of his reform then, and his success in publishing and selling the Walker debate led him to believe that starting his own publishing operation would have more impact than the school. Yet as the restoration of the ancient gospel and order took concrete shape and compelled him to take this insight to the world, the importance of education began to weigh on his mind again.

At the Virginia Constitutional Convention he submitted a resolution—which didn't pass—for the state to "patronize and encourage" a system of common schools for all youth to receive "such an education as may promote the common good."[3] He was committed to public schools to educate all white children—boys and girls—in the Scriptures, sciences, literature, and moral principles. This would equip them to be useful and productive citizens.

But his aim was not simply to produce cultured moral citizens. It was

2. See, for example, R. D. Anderson, "Education and the State in Nineteenth-Century Scotland," *Economic History Review* 36 (November 1983): 518–34.

3. Moorhouse, "Alexander Campbell," 191.

to produce people educated to think and reason properly for themselves, able to see through the deceptions of sectarian teachers and see the truth of the ancient gospel and order. That alone could bring church and society up to the New Testament standard that had been obscured for so long. This educated and converted America would serve as the staging ground to take this true knowledge—this true science—to the entire world.

For Campbell, education of the intellect alone could not equip learners to discern true knowledge; a legitimate education would combine the intellectual and the moral. He argued to the College of Teachers in Cincinnati in 1836 that true education involved the "full development and proper training of all the human powers," both intellectual and moral. Furthermore, the moral powers were the most important part of the equation.[4]

Campbell complained bitterly that moral education had been neglected in the American system. The deplorable divisions among Christians had pushed Americans to assign religion and morality to the private sphere. To avoid making things worse in already religiously alienated communities, they had removed all religious and moral education from the schools. Parents and religious leaders were responsible for those matters, not the schools and colleges. Campbell proposed an alternative. What if Protestants could move beyond partisan divisions and create a common religion? That would remove any fear of schools purveying sectarian indoctrination through teaching religion and morality.[5] For Campbell, the ancient gospel and order of things was that common religion.

Campbell's agenda was not evident to most of his hearers when he insisted that the teaching of "true religion"—to which "true morality" was inseparably joined—should be taught in all the nation's schools.

> Let the simple facts, without the theories of religious belief—let the belief of God, of Christ, of immortality, of eternal life and eternal death, without any partisan theory—let temperance, righteousness, benevolence, and judgment to come, without metaphysics, be inculcated on one, on all, by every parent, guardian, teacher, and in every school and college and university in our land—and we may have—nay, we shall have—quite another and a better state of things. The evidences, the absolute certainty and divine

---

4. Alexander Campbell, "Address on the Importance of Uniting the Moral with the Intellectual Culture of the Mind," in *Popular Lectures and Addresses by Rev. A. Campbell* (St. Louis: Christian Publishing Co., 1861), 456, 462.

5. Campbell, "Address on the Importance," 473–74.

authority, of the Christian religion, of the Old and New Testaments, ought to be taught and inculcated, as an essential part of a good and liberal and polite education, in every high-school in Christendom.[6]

In Campbell's mind, this true religion, from its core to all the beliefs and practices flowing from it, was his concept of the ancient gospel and order of things in its fullness and beauty, clearly taught by the Bible now freed from sectarian and partisan distortions.

For Campbell, public schools that would provide proper moral and intellectual training for everyone were the best tools for parents to fulfill their obligations to their children. In the prospectus for the *Millennial Harbinger*, he listed issues to which the new paper would give priority. Second in the list was "The inadequacy of all the present systems of education, literary (intellectual) and moral, to develop the powers of the human mind, and to prepare man for rational and social happiness."[7] Proper education was key to restoring the ancient gospel and order of things, which would bring the unity of all Christians and the conversion of the world, thus ushering in the millennium.

Public education that included teaching the Bible daily was the only hope for the United States to reach its potential as the emanating point for the "true science." He thought and talked about public schools constantly and developed specific proposals for establishing them in Virginia and other states, all emphasizing the central role of teaching the Bible.[8] Here again most people did not fully understand Campbell's point. He did not mean simply reading the Bible in the public school classroom without commentary, as Unitarian educational reformer Horace Mann had proposed.[9] He believed it was necessary for teachers to explain the Scriptures.

But Campbell distinguished between explaining the plain facts of a text of Scripture and theologizing about it. Theology was inherently filled with human sectarian ideas. What he proposed, he insisted, was simply explaining the facts of Scripture. "The Bible being a book of facts, and not of theories, it may in these be studied, believed, obeyed, and enjoyed, without one speculative oracle, on the part of teacher or pupil."[10] In Campbell's mind, this

6. Campbell, "Address on the Importance," 474.

7. Alexander Campbell, "Prospectus," *Millennial Harbinger*, January 1830, 1.

8. See especially Alexander Campbell, "On Common Schools. An Address Delivered at Clarksburg, VA., 1841," in *Popular Lectures and Addresses by Rev. A. Campbell*, 247–71.

9. James Riley Estep Jr., "The Bible in the Classroom: Campbell's View of Public Education," *Restoration Quarterly* 40, no. 4 (1998): 266–69.

10. Alexander Campbell, "Address on Education. Cincinnati, 1856," in *Popular Lectures and Addresses by Rev. A. Campbell*, 235.

approach would remedy the problems of partisan teaching of Scripture and allow the Bible to shape students as it was meant to.

In May 1836 Campbell published a circular letter dated March 10 from two church leaders in Jacksonville, Illinois, that made a strong case for the establishment of a college for the "Brethren of the Reformation." The writers definitely reflected Campbell's sentiments when they insisted that the success of the reformation required a proper education for everyone. "The religion which we advocate, and desire to practice, recommends itself by its purity to the consciences of all men, not upon the ground of enthusiasm and mysticism, but upon the principles of reason and philosophy. Therefore, for the future propagation and reception of this religion, we should endeavor to prepare the way by the establishment of colleges, high schools, and primary schools."[11]

All the parties and sects around them had such institutions to advance their partisan interests, they continued. Wasn't it time for those who "have renounced all modern denominative names, and sectarian peculiarities, and have taken the sacred oracles as the only sure and sufficient guide in all the concerns of faith and morals" to have a college of their own? They explicitly rejected establishing a theological school to produce clergy. Instead, it would teach "true science," general knowledge that would equip students to be productive and morally shaped citizens, but more importantly would give them the tools to properly "investigate the sacred writings, and to understand the genius of the Christian religion."[12]

The writers then called for a meeting of representatives from as many churches as possible "that hold the apostolic unity of one body, one spirit, one Lord, one faith, one immersion, one hope, and one God and Father of all; and observe the institutions of Christ as delivered to us by his Apostles"—the churches of the Campbell reformation. They proposed Louisville, Kentucky, as the location and September 28 as the date.

Campbell responded that he thought September was too soon to examine all the issues at stake. He seemed concerned that a project he had been contemplating for years might be preempted by such a meeting, especially since the writers suggested Louisville as the location for such a school. Campbell then listed key ideas about education he believed they all agreed on and discussed some of his educational principles.

First, in good Lockean terms he stated that since children were born with nothing but capacities, they had to be educated. Education was neces-

---

11. Guerdon Gates and J. T. Jones, "Literary Institutions—No. 1," *Millennial Harbinger*, May 1836, 198.

12. Gates and Jones, "Literary Institutions—No. 1," 199–200.

sary for intellectual greatness and moral goodness. Parents were primarily responsible for their children's education, and schools and colleges were the best way for parents to achieve that. Furthermore, Christians had the duty to ensure that the education provided in the schools was good and true rather than false and bad. Schools of theology substituted errors and corruptions of all sorts for biblical teaching, and most existing colleges and high schools had simply taken the Bible out of the curriculum. It was imperative that those devoted to the Bible alone and to the principles of simple apostolic Christianity provide access to "the best models of fine taste, true eloquence, and sound practical knowledge, or science properly so called," which necessarily included what he understood as the nonsectarian teaching of Scripture.[13] Campbell's strong caution against a quick meeting apparently squelched the proposed Louisville gathering.

In October 1839 Campbell finally revealed his idea for a new educational institution that would eventually become Bethany College. He explained that while he had been thinking about such an endeavor for some time, he had delayed moving ahead to avoid diverting support from Bacon College, established in Georgetown, Kentucky, in 1836. That school was now successfully launched. But even more importantly, Campbell claimed he was proposing a school of an entirely different character.[14]

He then described what he labeled "the union of four institutions in one." Besides a college proper, he included a group home for children seven to fourteen years old, a primary school for children of the same age preparing for college, and a "church" that he compared to a military school where students would put the things they learned into practice. He insisted that the course of instruction would be different from that of any other educational institution in the country, not so much in the courses taught—though "the immoral and profane poets and writers would be excluded"—but in the way the subjects would be taught.

> We want no scholastic or traditionary theology. We desire, however, a much more intimate, critical, and thorough knowledge of the Bible, the whole Bible as the Book of God—the Book of Life and of human destiny, than is usually, or indeed can be, obtained in what are called Theological Schools. As we make the Bible, the whole Bible, and nothing but the Bible our creed,

13. Alexander Campbell, "Remarks," *Millennial Harbinger*, May 1836, 201–2.

14. Alexander Campbell, "A New Institution," *Millennial Harbinger*, October 1839, 450–51.

our standard of religion and of all moral science, we have no hesitation in saying that this institution, from the nursery class upward to the church classes, shall make that volume a constant study. All science, all literature, all nature, all art, all attainments shall be made tributary to the Bible and man's ultimate temporal and eternal destiny.[15]

During 1840 Campbell published a series of brief articles concerning aspects of his proposed "new institution," and in April gave the text of the school's charter that had just been granted by the Virginia legislature.[16] In the same issue he reported the first donation to the school of one thousand dollars from the estate of Philip B. Pendleton, followed in the May issue by an all-out appeal to "the wealthy and philanthropic portion of the community" who were "conscious of their responsibilities."[17] In November Campbell alluded to the difficult economic times brought on by the Panic of 1837 and the tumultuous 1840 presidential election that would put William Henry Harrison in the White House. Though he published notes from the college's board meetings, he felt it best to wait until there was less political turmoil to begin raising the funds needed to actually begin operations.[18]

The following June Campbell reported that the board had approved the first Monday in November as the college's opening date. In somewhat different terms than what he outlined in his 1839 proposal, he described four departments for the school: preparatory and elementary schools for boys seven to fourteen years old, an Academy of Arts and Sciences for older boys, the college proper, and a normal school for training teachers. He also announced the amount of donations received. Actual cash in hand was $1,405, though pledges for another $9,649 scheduled over the next several years had also come in. Clearly disappointed, Campbell criticized the lack of generosity by wealthy donors. "Simpleton that I was, I expected some hundred or two sons of consolation, real philanthropists, to step forward and subscribe each his 1000 dollars." Instead, the ones most capable of funding the college had failed to come through. He would now turn to the middle class.[19]

15. Campbell, "A New Institution," 448.

16. "A Bill Incorporating the Bethany College," *Millennial Harbinger*, April 1840, 176–79.

17. Alexander Campbell, "New Institution—No. IV," *Millennial Harbinger*, May 1840, 220.

18. Alexander Campbell, "Bethany College," *Millennial Harbinger*, November 1840, 508.

19. Alexander Campbell, "Bethany College," *Millennial Harbinger*, June 1841, 269, 273.

In August he reported that the college buildings were under construction and that about one hundred students could be accommodated that first school year. The next month he published directions on how to get to Bethany.[20] In January 1842 he gave an account of the successful opening, despite delays in completing the main classroom building and in the arrival of some students. He continued to express irritation at the low level of financial support the school had received thus far, especially in comparison to Baptist schools like Georgetown College in Kentucky.[21] Still, despite delays and disappointment at funding, the school was a reality.

When Bethany College began operation in November 1841 on land carved out of his rural farm, the curriculum reflected Campbell's idea of what was needed to form a person into a rational thinking moral being. This was not a traditional education that focused on classical literature and languages. Rather, it was founded on the daily teaching of Scripture as Campbell conceived of it—6:30 a.m. Bible lectures and worship for the entire student body, regardless of vocational goals. Course offerings included ancient languages, ancient history, English grammar and logic, as well as "sacred history" and evidences of Christianity. But unlike the vast majority of schools of the day, half of Bethany's curriculum was focused on scientific studies—chemistry, geology, physics, astronomy, zoology, botany, physiology, and mathematics.[22]

On the basis of Campbell's description of his motivation and goals for the school, it could appear that he was establishing a school that was just as sectarian as the ones he decried—a "nonsectarian sectarian" school, so to speak. Such a self-delusion that he was free from any partisan leanings would produce a curriculum tainted by the very kind of indoctrination Campbell so opposed. Yet Campbell's optimism about the capacity of the properly educated person to come to right conclusions without coercion or indoctrination, his deep commitment to free and open thinking (assuming the person had been trained to think properly), underlay all his educational efforts at Bethany and his advocacy for creating a public education system.

It was naïve of Campbell to believe that people who were "properly educated" would agree with his conclusions—what he was absolutely convinced were clear and evident truths. Yet he truly wanted to train people to

20. Alexander Campbell, "Bethany College," *Millennial Harbinger*, August 1841, 378; September 1841, 432.

21. Alexander Campbell, "Commencement of Bethany College," *Millennial Harbinger*, January 1842, 34–36; "Congratulations of Bethany College," *Millennial Harbinger*, January 1842, 36–38.

22. Campbell, "Bethany College," *Millennial Harbinger*, August 1841, 377–78.

The land on which Bethany College was built in 1840 was carved out of Alexander Campbell's extensive farmland. The surrounding property remained rural and used for farming. Used with permission from the Disciples of Christ Historical Society, Bethany, West Virginia.

think carefully, expansively, rightly. As a result, Bethany became one of the premier educational institutions of its day. Campbell sought out the best teachers in every area of study—especially the sciences. Again, a cynical view of Campbell's aim could dismiss him as claiming to provide the best possible liberal education while actually indoctrinating people so that they agreed with him. In reality, Bethany provided a magnificent education, as evidenced in the statesmen, scientists, and religious leaders it produced.[23]

Nevertheless, producing such notable leaders was a by-product of Campbell's educational vision, not the goal itself. In an article distinguishing Bethany from the recently established Northwestern Christian University as an antislavery alternative, Campbell elaborated on his reason for establishing

23. D. Duane Cummins, *Bethany College: A Liberal Arts Odyssey* (St. Louis: Chalice, 2013), 76–77, 328–29; William Kirk Woolery, *Bethany Years: The Story of Old Bethany from Her Founding Years through a Century of Trial and Triumph* (Huntington, WV: Standard, 1941), 104.

his school. It was "the cause of education—intellectual, moral, religious ed-ucation—the cause of Reformation, in its connexion with literature, science and art—the conviction that educated minds must govern the world and the church—that God had made men of learning, talent and character, his great instruments of human redemption, from the days of Moses and Aaron to the days of Paul and Apollos—that originated the idea of Bethany College."[24]

No college in the world had done what Bethany College was doing, he insisted—teaching the Bible to the world "in a rational manner, in harmony with itself," and making it "the basis of all literary, scientific, moral and religious education." The Bible was as much the foundation for the college as it was for the church "in all the liberal science and learning that can give exaltation and moral grandeur to a human being." The proof was the number of evangelists who had gone out from Bethany to preach the ancient gospel and order across the United States. These were not professional clergy but Christians trained in all areas of knowledge, with the Bible as the underpinning for all learning and life.[25]

Now another crucial piece of Campbell's program for bringing in the millennium was in place. In his preface to the 1842 *Millennial Harbinger*, Campbell reflected on his twenty years of editorial and preaching work. These things had contributed to meeting "the demands of society in this great moral regeneration now advancing with every pulse of life in every part of the civilized world." But education was the special burden of the age, and that subject would receive his chief attention in the coming year's volume.

But then Campbell remarked that the next important matter to receive his attention would be church organization. He explained that while we use the terms "cooperation," "organization," and "order" in our talk about the church, we don't really know what the words mean. This topic would get its full share of his attention in the coming year.[26] In reality, church organization would assume a major place in Campbell's agenda for the entire decade, culminating in 1849 with the creation of the first national annual gathering and missionary organization for his growing movement.

During the separation of the Campbell reformers and the Baptist churches, some of the Baptist associations dominated by supporters of Campbell had simply dissolved themselves as unscriptural bodies. In some cases, however, such as the former Mahoning Association, the churches that

24. Alexander Campbell, "The North-Western Christian University," *Millennial Harbinger*, June 1850, 333.
25. Campbell, "The North-Western Christian University," 334-35.
26. Alexander Campbell, "Preface," *Millennial Harbinger*, January 1842, 3-4.

had been members continued to hold annual meetings for mutual edification and cooperative evangelism. By the end of the 1830s, state and regional meetings of churches had also become common.

While Campbell was certainly in favor of cooperation between churches, these efforts operated independently of one another and, in his estimation, were uneven in leadership and effectiveness. He had a growing sense of the need for something more coordinated to advance the reform, including a national gathering to facilitate cooperation among all the churches. In 1842 he published eight articles in a series begun the previous November titled "The Nature of the Christian Organization." The series went through July 1843 and totaled twenty-five articles.

From the beginning of the series he was clear: the only way the churches that made up Christ's kingdom could maintain unity and expand was by consultation and systematic cooperation. The churches of the reformation as a whole were woefully lacking those crucial mechanisms necessary for protection against false preachers and false teachings. "Every sort of doctrine has been proclaimed by almost all sorts of preachers under the broad banners and with the supposed sanction of the . . . reformation." Campbell believed this had damaged the cause and had to be changed.[27]

He developed his ideas on organization fairly extensively in the long series, but in a half-page statement in November 1842 he summarized his position succinctly and forcefully.

1. We can do comparatively nothing in distributing the Bible abroad without co-operation. 2. We can do comparatively but little in the great missionary field of the world either at home or abroad without co-operation. 3. We can do little or nothing to improve and elevate the Christian ministry without co-operation. 4. We can do but little to check, restrain, and remove the flood of imposture and fraud committed upon the benevolence of the brethren by irresponsible, plausible, and deceptious persons, without co-operation. 5. We cannot concentrate the action of the tens of thousands of Israel, in any great Christian effort, but by co-operation. 5. We can have no thorough co-operation without a more ample, extensive, and thorough church organization.[28]

27. Alexander Campbell, "The Nature of the Christian Organization. No. II," *Millennial Harbinger*, February 1842, 60, 64.

28. Alexander Campbell, "Five Arguments for Church Organization," *Millennial Harbinger*, November 1842, 523. The repeated number "5" in the list is in the source.

Campbell continued to talk about church organization in theoretical terms until the beginning of 1849. In January he published letters concerning a register of church statistics for the movement published by Alexander Hall the previous year that many complained was inaccurate. He said this was one more piece of evidence of the need for a more "scriptural, rational, and efficient organization." No individual should take on such authoritative projects on his own initiative, he insisted.[29]

Campbell proposed forming a committee to examine the subject of organization that would report back in the next issue of the *Millennial Harbinger*. Two months later, however, he had nothing to report since the committee had been able to meet only once. Instead he continued his own thoughts in several more articles. At the end of the fourth installment in May, he proposed a general meeting of the churches of the reformation for Cincinnati, Lexington, Louisville, or Pittsburgh.[30]

About that time a call for a general meeting in Cincinnati in October appeared in Walter Scott's paper, the *Christian Age and Unionist*. Campbell reprinted the call in the *Millennial Harbinger* in July but said October would not work because a cholera outbreak in Cincinnati would likely not have subsided by then.[31] He agreed that Cincinnati was the best place, but that the following May would be the best date to ensure the absence of cholera. In the meantime, he said, there should be a free and open exchange of ideas about what the most effective organization might be.[32]

Despite Campbell's admonition to wait, organizers went ahead and scheduled the meeting in Cincinnati for October 23–27. Campbell had insisted that any national meeting should be a gathering of "messengers" sent by the churches—like in the Baptist association meetings—not an assembly of editors or publishers, or even of individuals who came on their own. He wanted a truly representative convention. Campbell's fear that people would stay away from an October meeting was at least partially realized— only about 150 people attended, and most were there simply as interested individuals. Yet the meeting proceeded and succeeded in accomplishing

29. Alexander Campbell, "The Christian Register," *Millennial Harbinger*, January 1849, 51–54; see "A Case of Discipline in the Church at Bethany," *Millennial Harbinger*, July 1849, 385.

30. Alexander Campbell, "Church Organization—No. IV," *Millennial Harbinger*, May 1849, 273.

31. Alexander Campbell, "Convention. A Suggestion," *Millennial Harbinger*, July 1849, 418–19.

32. Alexander Campbell, "Convention," *Millennial Harbinger*, August 1849, 475–76.

what Campbell had been talking about for a decade—the establishment of a cooperative organization for the churches.

Even though the organizers had proceeded without his endorsement, Campbell printed a glowing report of the meeting written by his coworker and son-in-law W. K. Pendleton in the December *Millennial Harbinger*. Campbell explained that although he had not attended due to "an unusually severe indisposition," his hopes for the convention had been more than realized. Those who gathered had established the first truly national organization for his movement—the American Christian Missionary Society—predictably electing Campbell president in absentia. This, along with the American Christian Bible Society organized four years earlier, gave Campbell great satisfaction, he said. "These Societies we cannot but hail as greatly contributing to the cause we have been so long pleading before God and the people."[33]

In one sense, the missionary and Bible efforts were not new. There had always been support for financing evangelists and distributing the Scriptures to spread the gospel. Now, however, for the first time, Campbell's reform had a formal national structure that provided a means for the movement to execute those vital tasks together. This was essential, Campbell believed, for the widespread and sustained success of the movement. Because of what the general convention had accomplished, Campbell exclaimed, "our horizon and with it our expectations, are greatly enlarged."[34]

In reality, the organization raised alarms among some who viewed it as unscriptural and potentially coercive. This would become a central issue in the movement's division following the Civil War. Those who challenged the legitimacy of the missionary society accused Campbell of abandoning his opposition to such structures expressed in the *Christian Baptist*. He denied, however, that he had ever opposed the churches cooperating in good works and evangelism. The gathering that had formed the American Christian Missionary Society was entirely consistent with Christian law.[35]

And so, by the end of the third decade of the creation and propagation

---

33. Alexander Campbell, *Millennial Harbinger*, December 1849, 694–95. Campbell had originally opposed the American Christian Bible Society but accepted it when its leaders agreed to work through the American and Foreign Bible Society under the umbrella of the American Christian Missionary Society—which Campbell headed. Campbell, *Millennial Harbinger*, December 1849, 649.

34. Campbell, *Millennial Harbinger*, December 1849, 695.

35. Alexander Campbell, "The Christian Religion," *Christian Baptist* 1 (August 1823): 20; Alexander Campbell and Jacob Creath, "Conventions—No. V," *Millennial Harbinger*, November 1850, 637–41.

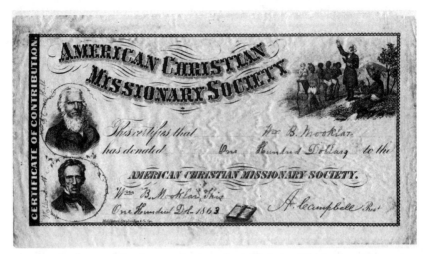

Receipt for contributions to the American Christian Missionary Society with Campbell's likeness and signature. Used with permission from the Disciples of Christ Historical Society, Bethany, West Virginia.

of the restoration of the ancient gospel and order, Campbell had navigated his movement toward the creation of an important educational institution— Bethany College—and the first truly national organization for the churches— the American Christian Missionary Society. Though both would become entangled in the disintegration of America that centered on slavery and resulted in civil war, these institutions marked a maturing of Alexander Campbell's movement that would have great significance for the rest of his career.

Defense and Conflict

A hundred minor spirits supposed that they must do as Brother Campbell did. Thus they waged a war on nearly the whole creation.

—Arthur Crihfield, *The Orthodox Preacher*, 1844

CAMPBELLISM
Its History and Heresies

By BOB L. ROSS

ALEXANDER CAMPBELL
The "Master-Spirit" of Campbellism

PRICE $1.00

"Campbellism" continued to be a focus of attack well into the twentieth century, especially from among conservative independent Baptists such as Bob Ross. Courtesy of the Center for Restoration Studies, Abilene Christian University, Abilene, Texas.

CHAPTER 10

The Rise of Anti-Campbellism

As soon as Campbell had formed and begun to spread his concept of the ancient gospel and order of things, opposition arose. Much of the hostility was in reaction to his accusations that other religious leaders had perverted New Testament Christianity. Strong counterattacks labeled Campbell the real corrupter of religion. As he formulated the core doctrines of his reformation, Campbell's first major clashes were with the groups he was closest to—the Presbyterians, who had shaped his earliest religious convictions, and the Baptists, with whom he had affiliated. Sometime in the mid-1820s, starting from within Baptist circles, his detractors began to label his teachings "Campbellism" and his followers "Campbellites," terms that continued in use even in the twenty-first century.[1]

The earliest printed use of the term "Campbellite" appeared in a booklet published in September 1824 by Baptist minister Lawrence Greatrake. Following the publication of Campbell's debate with William Maccalla, Greatrake warned fellow Baptists against what he regarded as Campbell's false gospel: Campbell denied the Holy Spirit's work in conversion and ridiculed the heartfelt Christian experience that was so much a part of Baptist spirituality.

> It ought not to be a matter of question for one moment, with any regular Baptist, or any real and spiritual Christian, as to who and what that man is, who, as a minister of the gospel, even neglects to preach the doctrine of the new birth by the Holy Ghost sent down from heaven. No, nor will it be

---

1. See, for example, Larry Wessels and Bob L. Ross, "Campbellism Review: Is the 'Church of Christ' the Real Church?," video available at https://www.youtube.com/watch?v=8-e7QZxXNk4.

a matter of question with any intelligent, spiritual Christian, of whatever denomination they may be! they will one and all pronounce him to be an unregenerated man, and an impostor. . . . The Devil, brethren, is never so dangerous, as when he assumes the form of an angel of light, and comes into the churches with great profession of zeal for ordinances, and some part of the truth: but not the whole truth.

Greatrake compared Campbell and his followers to the Jews whose veiled hearts prevented them from recognizing Jesus as the promised Messiah. In the same way, if "Campbellites . . . were to swear that there was no Holy Ghost now, to operate specially, and immediately upon the human soul, it must only be considered as an evidence, that they were equally as blind and wretched in their spiritual condition as the Jews!"[2] Campbell responded immediately in a series of articles in the *Christian Baptist* and in a pamphlet the following February titled *Lawrence Greatrake's Calumnies Repelled*. But he did not specifically react to Greatrake's use of "Campbellite."[3]

Campbell's first printed notice of the term "Campbellism" appeared in the June 1828 *Christian Baptist* when he reported receiving a letter from Kentucky asking him to define it. Campbell's reply was succinct and forceful. "It is a nickname of reproach invented and adopted by those whose views, feelings, and desires are all sectarian; who cannot conceive of Christianity in any other light than an *ism*." Anyone who would use such a term when the recipient repudiated it, Campbell continued, was simply a "railer or reviler, and placed among the haters of God and those who have no lot in the kingdom of heaven."

Those sectarians were using the term to slander him and all those "who prefer the scriptures to any human creed, and the kingdom of Jesus the Messiah to any sect." They would answer to God for their wickedness. Campbell closed with an admonition to his followers: "We wish all the friends of the ancient gospel and the ancient order of things, to remember that our motto is, and we hope ever will be, to *call no man Master or Father*, in the things pertaining to the kingdom of our Lord."[4]

Later that year Campbell published a satirical letter from a correspondent who identified himself as Old Farmer. Whenever people began to read

2. [Lawrence Greatrake], *Letters to Alexander Campbell. By a Regular Baptist* (Pittsburgh: Eichbaum & Johnston, 1824), 19, 23.

3. His first response to Greatrake was "An Address to the Public," *Christian Baptist* 2 (September 1824): 37–46.

4. Alexander Campbell, "Campbellism," *Christian Baptist* 5 (June 1828): 262–63.

Campbell's work, the writer noted, "a hydrophobial fear" arose among his enemies that readers would catch "Campbellism." These physicians were trying to stop Campbell by identifying him as a contagious pest that infected all he contacted with his hateful and destructive "ism." The Old Farmer assumed, however, that such persecution would not stop Campbell but would rather provoke curiosity and sympathy among the people, causing the disease to become an epidemic.

The way to inoculate against Campbellism, the Old Farmer continued, was to take a dose of New Testamentism three times a day. That would get rid of all human doctrines and crude systematic theology, bringing healing and peace. Implying that this was exactly what the so-called Campbellites had been doing in the first place, the writer reminded readers that Jesus himself was charged with "devilism, Herodism, Cesarism, and blasphemism." Just like the labels hurled at Christ, "Campbellism" was a false designation. The remedy for all "isms," he concluded, was "New Testamentism."[5]

Campbell had used the term "New Testamentism" in the first volume of the *Christian Baptist* five years earlier when he insisted that this alone was the system he advocated. "We have no system of our own, nor of others to substitute in lieu of the reigning systems. We only aim at substituting the New Testament in lieu of every creed in existence. . . . We neither advocate Calvinism, Arminianism, Arianism, Socinianism, Trinitarianism, Unitarianism, Deism, or Sectarianism, but Newtestamentism. We wish, cordially wish, to take the New Testament out of the abuses of the clergy, and put it into the hands of the people."[6] The use of the term and the satirical style of the "Old Farmer's" letter indicate that Campbell himself may have been the author.

Over the next decades Campbell's opponents published a torrent of anti-Campbellism books and pamphlets. Titles ranged from *Campbellism Unmasked* (1834), *Campbellism Examined* (1855), and *Campbellism Exposed* (1870), to *Campbellism Refuted and Truth Vindicated* (1833), *Campbellism Not of the Bible* (1852), and *Campbellism Not of God* (1889).[7] Campbell regarded the term as an insult to himself and to all who supported the reformation—a

---

5. Old Farmer, "New Testamentism, a Cure for and Preventative against Campbellism, and All Other Isms," *Christian Baptist* 6 (September 1828): 45–46.

6. Alexander Campbell, "Address to the Readers of the Christian Baptist. No. 1," *Christian Baptist* 1 (December 1823): 120.

7. Over sixty-five publications with "Campbellism" or "Campbellite" in their titles appear in the Online Computer Library Center's database, with publication dates ranging from the 1830s to the 1990s.

tactic by the enemies of truth to stigmatize and obstruct the progress of the ancient gospel and order.

In the eyes of his opponents, the fatal flaw at the center of Campbell's theology was his doctrine of baptism. Presbyterians and others who baptized infants by sprinkling or pouring rejected Campbell's insistence on adult immersion. Yet it was his understanding of baptism's essential connection to salvation that proved to be the deepest difference, especially with other immersionists.

Lawrence Greatrake lamented that Campbell was seducing Baptists to believe he was one of them because of his insistence on immersion. In reality, he was deceiving them with his deadly teaching that equated baptism with conversion, regeneration, and the washing away of sins. He accused Campbell of proselytizing Baptists, whom he and his followers then deluded into believing "that baptism is salvation." Greatrake feared that many would discover the delusion only when they got to hell.[8]

Presbyterian Thomas T. Skillman, editor of the *Banner of Truth*, published in Lexington, Kentucky, ridiculed Campbell's claim to have discovered the long-obscured meaning of baptism. This was equivalent to saying that God's revelation was inadequate to shed light on this subject "without the amazing skill and co-operation of this modern luminary in the western wilds of Virginia!" Campbell's insistence that baptism was necessary for the remission of sins was in direct contradiction to the apostle Peter's teaching that "whosoever believeth in [Christ] shall receive remission of sins" (Acts 10:43) and that "*in every nation*, he that feareth God and worketh righteousness, *is accepted with him*" (Acts 10:35). Despite these clear teachings, Skillman asserted, Campbell taught that Peter did not preach that the Jews on Pentecost were forgiven of their sins by faith, "but by an *act of faith*, by a believing immersion into the Lord Jesus." Skillman exclaimed sarcastically, "Here is the whole front and facing of this wonderful affair—the wonderful secret—the golden gem just raked up from the rubbish of human traditions of hundreds of years standing."[9] Opponents attacked Campbell in sermons and print wherever he went.

Yet not all adversaries were outsiders to his reformation. Some of his most ferocious conflicts were with insiders—some who stayed and some who would leave to form rival religious movements. One of the leading figures in the early formation of Campbell's reform was former Baptist Sidney Rigdon. Campbell came to suspect him of seeking preeminence in the

---

8. Greatrake, *Letters to Alexander Campbell*, 8.

9. Thomas T. Skillman, "Campbellism—No. III," *Banner of Truth* 1 (January 1833): 17.

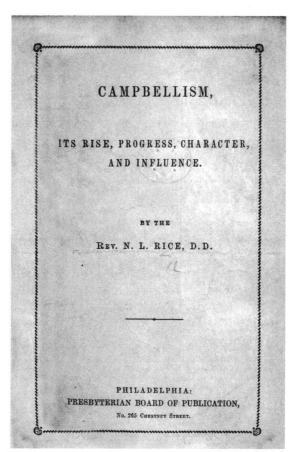

CAMPBELLISM,

ITS RISE, PROGRESS, CHARACTER,
AND INFLUENCE.

BY THE

REV. N. L. RICE, D.D.

PHILADELPHIA:
PRESBYTERIAN BOARD OF PUBLICATION,
No. 265 CHESTNUT STREET.

Presbyterian leader Nathan L. Rice (1807–1877) was one of
scores who wrote books, pamphlets, and articles against Campbell and his teachings. In 1843, Rice was Campbell's last opponent in a public debate, an especially hostile encounter.

movement and disagreed with him about the need to establish communal
societies. Campbell marginalized Rigdon, who moved out of the movement
and into a prominent leadership position for a time in Joseph Smith's Latter
Day Saints. John Thomas, a British medical doctor who was an enthusiastic
convert to the ancient gospel and order, took Campbell's baptismal theology beyond where Campbell himself was willing to go. Campbell eventually
denounced Thomas, who left to form the Christadelphians.

Two of Campbell's closest allies in the reform, Walter Scott and Barton W. Stone, would also become embroiled in sharp disagreements and

fierce conflict with him, to the point of significant disruption of the movement. In these often-intense internal clashes, a few suggested that maybe Campbell secretly liked the name "Campbellism," since he was so intent on maintaining control of "his reformation."

These conflicts and many others marked Alexander Campbell's long career. The clashes we now examine, each of which Campbell viewed as a defense of the truth of his reform, had a significant impact on Campbell's movement and provide important insights into Campbell's ideas and character.

CHAPTER 11

John Thomas and
the Lunenburg Letter

No single incident in Alexander Campbell's career revealed his deepest commitments and his most perplexing ambiguities more sharply than a set of events beginning in September 1837. Campbell's statements provoked over three years of heated discussion about baptism, salvation, and the boundaries of the church, all with profound implications for the identity of his reform.

A letter to Campbell from a "conscientious sister" in Lunenburg, Virginia, provoked the controversy. The writer challenged a comment Campbell made in the August 1837 *Millennial Harbinger* to James Wallis, leader of a British movement sympathetic to Campbell's and editor of the *British Millennial Harbinger*. Campbell had written to assure Wallis of his support, including for Wallis's reprinting of many of Campbell's writings. He promised to write monthly letters to advise the British churches and provide news of the reformation in America.[1]

Wallis had asked Campbell whether or not he believed Christians should participate in organizations like missionary, antislavery, and temperance societies. Campbell explained that the churches of the reformation in America generally did not form or participate in such bodies because they often included non-Christians. They were human institutions doing work the church should be doing. However, Campbell continued, he had no objections to individual Christians cooperating with other Christians in such worthy causes, *"whether or not they belong to our churches."* "I find," Campbell stated, "in all Protestant parties Christians as exemplary as ourselves according to their

---

1. The *British Millennial Harbinger* succeeded the *Millennial Harbinger and Voluntary Church Advocate* published by Scotch Baptist William Jones in 1835–1836. Jones, a staunch Calvinist, initially sympathized with the Campbell reform but broke with Campbell over theological differences and ceased publication.

and our relative knowledge and opportunities," and he assured Wallis that he could "with as good conscience and as perfect freedom as I once did," pray with Protestant leaders despite theological differences.[2]

The correspondent from Lunenburg took offense at these statements and shot back several pointed questions.[3] After expressing shock that Campbell recognized "the Protestant parties as Christian," she demanded, "Will you be so good as to let me know how anyone becomes a Christian? . . . Does the name of Christ or Christian belong to any but those who believe the gospel, repent, and are buried by baptism into the death of Christ?"[4]

As usual, Campbell was in the midst of several controversies when this letter arrived. He had begun a written debate with Universalist Dolphus Skinner in April; he was sparring with Catholic bishop John Baptist Purcell over details of the publication of their debate in Cincinnati the previous January; and he had recently received a public rebuke from an unidentified leader in his movement—likely Dr. John Thomas—criticizing him for representing apostate Protestantism in that debate. To round out the conflicts, he was engaged in disputes with Baptist minister Samuel W. Lynd over the role of the Holy Spirit in conversion and with two Baptist papers that accused his new translation of being non-Trinitarian.

The conflict underlying the Lunenburg letter had been heating up for several years between Campbell and John Thomas, a medical doctor who emigrated from England in 1832 and quickly become part of the Campbell movement. At first Campbell endorsed Thomas as a gifted and worthy evangelist, advising him to give full time to the movement. After preaching in Philadelphia for about a year, Thomas moved to Richmond and in May 1834 began the *Apostolic Advocate*.

Thomas stayed in Campbell's good graces until he published a series of articles explaining his views of the soul, resurrection, and baptism. Thomas had become convinced that the human soul was nothing more than the animated body itself—it had no separate existence. Only those who had heard the gospel would be resurrected, with everyone else remaining in "soul sleep" after death. Furthermore, in his zeal for teaching baptism for

2. Alexander Campbell, "Letters to England No. I," *Millennial Harbinger*, June 1837, 272, 274.

3. The writer was Luisa Anderson, wife of Virginia church leader Albert Anderson. Both were supporters of John Thomas. See David Lertis Matson, "Who Wrote the Lunenburg Letter? The Untold Story of the 'Conscientious Sister' of Lunenburg," *Stone-Campbell Journal* 11 (Spring 2008): 3–28.

4. Alexander Campbell, "Any Christians among Protestant Parties," *Millennial Harbinger*, September 1837, 411.

John Thomas (1805–1871) was a British medical doctor who came to America in 1832 and became part of Campbell's reformation. He eventually broke with Campbell over a number of doctrinal issues, especially views of the church and the end of time. He was rebaptized in 1847 and eventually founded the Christadelphians. Used with permission from the Disciples of Christ Historical Society, Bethany, West Virginia.

the remission of sins, he began reimmersing Baptists who wanted to become members of a reform church.

Campbell condemned Thomas's position on rebaptism, his "materialist" view of the soul, and his view of the resurrection. The controversy continued into the 1840s, with a final break in 1844 when Thomas withdrew his Richmond congregation from the Campbell movement, forming the Brethren in Christ, later known as the Christadelphians.[5]

In July 1837, the month before his letter to James Wallis, Campbell published a letter from an evangelist in eastern Virginia, Albert Anderson, who

5. Terry Cowan, "Thomas, John," in *The Encyclopedia of the Stone-Campbell Movement*, ed. Douglas A. Foster et al. (Grand Rapids: Eerdmans, 2004), 741–42; Matson, "Who Wrote the Lunenburg Letter?," 6–12.

rebuked both Campbell and Thomas for their conduct in the dispute. Both were at fault, Anderson contended; both had engaged too much in personalities. They should act like Christians and treat one another with tenderness and love. But, as Anderson closed his admonition, he aimed a special rebuke at Campbell. As the older and more experienced, he asserted, Campbell was more culpable than Thomas for his bad behavior.

In his reply, Campbell insisted that he was not aware of anything he had written for which he should apologize. He had not violated truth or propriety but had merely moved to stop Thomas's divisive actions and writings in the *Apostolic Advocate*.[6] These events formed the backdrop for the letter from Lunenburg and Campbell's strong response.

Campbell began his response to the Lunenburg letter with the proposition that if there were no Christians among the Protestant churches, there were certainly none among the Catholics, Jews, Turks, and pagans. That would mean that there had been no Christians in the world for centuries "except ourselves, or such of us as keep, or strive to keep, all the commandments of Jesus." But that was not possible if one believed Jesus's promise that even the gates of hell would never prevail against his church.

As for identifying who is a Christian, Campbell gave a simple definition that to many seemed contradictory to the position he had taken since the formulation of the ancient gospel and order. "But who is a Christian? I answer, every one that believes in his heart that Jesus of Nazareth is the Messiah, the Son of God; repents of his sins and obeys him in all things according to his measure of knowledge of his will."[7]

He then made a sharp distinction between deliberate disobedience or willful ignorance and being honestly mistaken. Many who were mistaken about baptism were deeply devoted to Christ and were obedient as far as they understood Christ's commands. "I cannot, therefore, make any one duty the standard of Christian state or character, not even immersion into the name of the Father, Son and Holy Spirit, and in my heart regard all who have been sprinkled in infancy without their own knowledge and consent, as aliens from Christ and the well-grounded hope of heaven."[8]

For Campbell, something even more fundamental than the crucial act of baptism was the ultimate proof that one was a Christian: "It is the image of Christ the Christian looks for and loves, and this does not consist of be-

---

6. Albert Anderson, "Special Correspondence," *Millennial Harbinger*, July 1837, 330–33.

7. Campbell, "Any Christians among Protestant Parties," 411.

8. Campbell, "Any Christians among Protestant Parties," 412.

ing exact in a few items, but in general devotion to the whole truth as far as known. . . . He that infers that none are Christians but the immersed, as greatly errs as he who affirms that none are alive but those of clear and full vision." If he had to choose between someone who had been sprinkled as an infant, who was "more intelligent in the Christian Scriptures, more spiritually minded and more devoted to the Lord," and one who agreed with his understanding of immersion, "I could not hesitate a moment in giving the preference of my heart to him who loveth most."[9]

The article provoked a number of negative responses. Campbell published an article titled "Opinionism" in the October *Millennial Harbinger* that censured those who, like Thomas and his followers, insisted on forcing their aberrant opinions on others. But he could not ignore the growing criticism of his statements in response to the conscientious sister. He admitted that in the early church the term "Christian" was given only to immersed believers. But, he continued, "we do not think it was given to them because they were immersed, but because they had put on Christ." He raised Paul's contention in Romans 2:29 that the true Jew was one inwardly, and that true circumcision was of the heart by the Spirit, not the letter. He asked, "may we not have the *inward* and *outward* Christians?" He always taught that both the inward and outward were important. Yet he was convinced, just as Paul said regarding circumcision, that it was possible for someone who honestly mistook the outward baptism to have the inward.[10]

Campbell had made it clear well before the Lunenburg letter articles that he regarded as "wholly unauthorized by the New Testament" the reimmersion for the remission of sins of those who were already "citizens of the kingdom of Jesus Christ."[11] His antirebaptism stance was undoubtedly formed in response to the growing support for the practice among followers of John Thomas. In November he insisted that he had always believed these things and had expressed them whenever called on, referring readers to his first "Extra on Remission" in 1830 as an example.[12]

It was, however, in the Lunenburg letter articles that some of his most eloquent and forceful language regarding salvation emerged. In December he exclaimed:

9. Campbell, "Any Christians among Protestant Parties," 412–14.

10. Alexander Campbell, "Christians among the Sects," *Millennial Harbinger*, November 1837, 506–7.

11. See, for example, Alexander Campbell, "Re-Immersion. Letter from a Correspondent in Eastern Virginia," *Millennial Harbinger*, August 1835, 419.

12. Campbell, "Christians among the Sects," 506.

The case is this: when I see a person who would die for Christ; whose brotherly kindness, sympathy, and active benevolence know no bounds but his circumstances; whose seat in the Christian assembly is never empty; whose inward piety and devotion are attested by punctual obedience to every known duty; whose family is educated in the fear of the Lord; whose constant companion is the Bible: I say, when I see such a one ranked amongst heathen men and publicans because he never happened to inquire, but always took it for granted that he had been scripturally baptized; and that, too, by one greatly destitute of all these public and private virtues, whose chief or exclusive recommendation is that he has been immersed, and that he holds a scriptural theory of the gospel: I feel no disposition to flatter such a one; but rather to disabuse him of his error. And while I would not lead the most excellent professor in any sect to disparage the least of all the commandments of Jesus, I would say to my immersed brother as Paul said to his Jewish brother who gloried in a system which he did not adorn: "Sir, will not his uncircumcision, or unbaptism, be counted to him as baptism? and will he not condemn you, who, though having the literal and true baptism, yet does transgress or neglect the statutes of your King?"[13]

Campbell knew very well what was behind the "conscientious sister's" letter—she was a supporter of John Thomas. Thomas denied the name Christian to any who had not been immersed explicitly *for the remission of sins*. Even immersed believers whose baptism had not been understood by administrator and recipient to be for the remission of sins remained outside of Christ. Campbell was disgusted by reports that supporters of Thomas in churches of his reform in eastern Virginia were hurling gross and unwarranted insults at Christians in other bodies. He condemned Thomas's labeling John Calvin "the Arch Perverter of the faith of Christ," the Methodist clergy "Draconic Lambs," and all Protestant bodies "Synagogues of Satan."[14] Campbell's denunciation of those who, though perhaps right about immersion, were nowhere near as godly and holy as the ones they were denouncing was in response to such abusive language.

Campbell admitted that knowing the motivation behind the Lunenburg letter had made his response stronger and more narrowly focused than it

---

13. Alexander Campbell, "Any Christians among the Sects?" *Millennial Harbinger*, December 1837, 565.

14. Campbell, "Any Christians among the Sects?," 566; Alexander Campbell, "Extra, No. I.—New Series," *Millennial Harbinger*, December 1837, 580, 588.

might have been otherwise, "perhaps more bold than on any former occasion."[15] It would become clear over the next three years, however, that though he did hold the beliefs expressed in his answers to the Lunenburg letter and never retracted them, they were not the main emphasis of his teaching. In many ways the exchange reflected a struggle over the very identity of his reform, and he sensed it.

While Campbell defended the inclusive statements in the Lunenburg letter articles as having always been his conviction, he was also clear that his views did not include those who were willfully ignorant or disobedient. Perhaps surprised by the level of criticism he had received, he began to repeat his strong convictions concerning baptism as immersion for the remission of sins. The shift began at the end of the third article. If he had not been responding to those who were abusing the sects and making "Christianity to turn more upon immersion than upon *universal holiness*," he would have answered the letter differently, he asserted.

He then explained how he was using the term "Christian." The scriptural meaning was one who "*habitually believes all that Christ says, and habitually does all that he bids him.*"[16] Readers would have assumed correctly that this included immersion for the remission of sins following repentance and confession of faith. He had used "Christian" in his initial reply to the letter, he said, not in its strictest biblical meaning but in the way most people used it, that is, as applied to people who live Christlike lives regardless of their doctrinal positions. In that sense, he insisted, "I think there are many, in most Protestant parties, whose errors and mistakes I hope the Lord will forgive; and although they should not enter into all the blessings of the kingdom on earth, I do fondly expect they may participate in the resurrection of the just." He then reminded readers that "we are all learning and progressing toward perfection."[17]

In December 1837 Campbell felt he needed to publish an extra issue of the *Millennial Harbinger* to give a history of his controversy with John Thomas, to identify Thomas as a false teacher, and to justify again his statements in the earlier articles. He compared Thomas to Sidney Rigdon, who had defected from Campbell's reform to become a leader in the Mormon movement. He reminded readers that he had declared nonfellowship with

---

15. Campbell, "Any Christians among the Sects?," 564–67; Campbell, "Christians among the Sects," 506.

16. Campbell, "Any Christians among the Sects?," 566–67.

17. Campbell, "Any Christians among the Sects?," 567.

Thomas the previous November "for having become a factionist and having departed, in part at least, from the faith of the New Testament."[18] He labeled Thomas's practice of requiring a confession of faith and reimmersion of Baptists who wished to join the movement as "unprecedented" and denounced his extreme verbal abuse of those in churches that did not practice believers' immersion for remission of sins.[19]

He then attacked two of Thomas's teachings as departures from central Christian beliefs: that there would be no general resurrection of the dead and no universal judgment of the world. These conclusions were based on Thomas's view that the human soul was simply the animated body itself—a view Campbell labeled "materialism."[20] Campbell issued a clear ultimatum in the last paragraph of the extra issue. Thomas's only hope for regaining his lost reputation and effectiveness as a leader was to abandon his dogmatism, retrace his steps, and write no more on the disputed matters.[21]

For the next two years Campbell wrote practically nothing about the dispute. Instead, he allowed the conversation to continue between one of his supporters identified only as "Christianos"—most likely Campbell's brother-in-law Archibald McKeever—and Thomas sympathizers Thomas M. Henley and Matthias Winans. Christianos attacked the Thomasite position with vigor, defending and expanding Campbell's earlier statements. He insisted, for example, that "The [one] whose will and affections are bowed to the divine will (however imperfectly he may understand that will), is an acceptable worshipper of God."[22] Henley and Winans responded by insisting that baptism for remission of sins was the clear and unmistakable teaching of Scripture. The inescapable conclusion, therefore, was that those not immersed for remission of sins were not Christians and were not saved.[23] Campbell allowed the discussion to play out without comment but promised that he would write an evaluation of both sides' statements whenever the series finished.

Christianos published ten articles titled "Christians among the Sects"

---

18. Campbell, "Extra, No. I—New Series," 578.

19. Campbell, "Extra, No. I—New Series," 580, 588.

20. Campbell, "Extra, No. I—New Series," 582.

21. Campbell, "Extra, No. I—New Series," 588.

22. Christianos, "Christians among the Sects," *Millennial Harbinger*, January 1839, 44.

23. See, for example, Thomas M. Henley, "Christians among the Sects—No. I," *Millennial Harbinger*, March 1839, 124–25. Henley and Winans wrote multiple articles arguing their point.

and three related pieces titled "Our Name," "Baptism," and "Positive Or-dinances," the last in July 1840. But even before then Campbell felt he had published all he cared to about "Christians among the sects." In April he made good on his promise to evaluate the ideas of Christianos and the two correspondents who opposed him. While all three had said good things, Campbell began, they, like Job's friends, were wrong more in the application of their premises than in the premises themselves. He criticized Winans for being a "severe and rectangular logician," and Henley as an "uncompromis-ing arbiter," complimenting Christianos's beliefs as "much more consola-tory" than those of the other two. Though we may not be able to identify for certain all sincere followers of Jesus who through no fault of their own had mistaken the form of baptism, God knew; and we could assume that there were many such persons.[24]

Yet, surprisingly, the thrust of Campbell's critique was against Chris-tianos. Every Christian who had a Bible, Campbell asserted—and that would be practically everyone—had little justification for ignorance con-cerning baptism, "whether the lack may be in sense or honesty." While Campbell agreed with Christianos that the state of one's heart was "ev-erything," he went on to ask how one's heart could be in a proper state without the ordinances of the gospel? Merely having a proper disposition to receive the gospel ordinances was not the same thing as "the Christian state."

Similar to his earlier definitions of "Christian," Campbell distinguished between national, sectarian, and scriptural uses of the name. Clearly there were Christians in state churches and denominations—in fact, many of them were more devout than the immersed persons who denied them the name Christian. But in the scriptural sense, he continued, only those who believed in Jesus; repented; were immersed in the name of the Father, Son, and Holy Spirit; and followed Christ in all things could legitimately have the name Christian applied to them.[25] His emphasis seemed intended to avoid offend-ing those who took John Thomas's position and to halt further defections from his movement to Thomas's.

Campbell insisted there was a vast difference between simply being mistaken about gospel ordinances like baptism and neglecting or disdain-ing them. Any clear thinking believer, he contended, could have the hope

---

24. Alexander Campbell, "Review of Christians among the Sects—No. I," *Millennial Harbinger*, April 1840, 162–63.

25. Campbell, "Review of Christians among the Sects—No. I," 164.

that God would forgive those who were honestly mistaken. But he closed his evaluation of Christianos with a statement that diminished the force of his assertions of 1837. "In this day of increasing light, I confess that, in my opinion, the cases of involuntary ignorance are becoming fewer and more few; and that the hope of remission for many who do not, who will not examine and obey from the heart the Saviour's precepts, becomes more and more feeble."[26]

The continuous assaults on his reform from both outsiders and insiders were taking a toll on Campbell's tolerance. After years of hammering out and disseminating the doctrine of immersion for the remission of sins, Campbell felt that most of those who had not been immersed but claimed to be followers of Christ were without excuse.

Embedded in the controversy with Thomas and his followers was a dispute over what name Campbell's reform should use. This question was a crucial part of the struggle for the movement's identity. The discussion began in response to a request in the May 1839 *Millennial Harbinger* from T. W. Rucker of Elbert County, Georgia, who begged Campbell to say something about what the churches should call themselves.[27] Campbell began his response in August, listing and evaluating the names that had been used, including Christian Baptists, Reformers, and Campbellites. He concluded that only two labels were scriptural—Disciples and Christians. He promised to give his judgment on them in the next article.[28]

In September he proposed that of the two scriptural terms, Disciples of Christ was better for four reasons. First, "Disciples" was more ancient, since the disciples were not called Christians until many years after Pentecost. Second, it was a more accurate description than "Christian," which could be understood as more of a national designation—such as "Christian nation"—rather than simply a follower or student of Christ. Third, it was more scriptural since "Christian" only appeared twice in Acts and then only in the mouths of non-Christians in Antioch and Herod Agrippa. "Disciples," on the other hand, occurred more than thirty times and was the most common self-designation for followers of Christ. Finally, Campbell feared that if the churches of his reformation used the name "Christian," people would mistake them for Unitarians and Arians who did not baptize for remission

26. Campbell, "Review of Christians among the Sects—No. I," 164.

27. T. W. Rucker, "News from the Churches," *Millennial Harbinger*, May 1839, 236.

28. Alexander Campbell, "Our Name: Disciples, Christians, Reformers, Campbellites," *Millennial Harbinger*, August 1839, 337–39.

of sins or take the Lord's Supper every Sunday. Since no other group used "Disciples of Christ," it was, he insisted, the best choice.[29]

A number of leaders disagreed with him on this, including his own father and Barton W. Stone. Stone and Alexander Campbell had discussed this several years earlier when the churches of their respective movements began to unite in many places. Stone felt personally attacked by Campbell's fourth reason for preferring "Disciples." Though Stone denied being a "Unitarian," he was clearly not Trinitarian in any traditional sense. When he baptized, he admitted, he did not use the words "I baptize for remission," though he believed in the doctrine of baptism for the remission of sins as much as Campbell did. He did not use those words because he believed that many had already received remission before their immersion. You believe the same thing, Stone charged, since you believe there are Christians among the sects. An unpardoned person could not be called a Christian; therefore, those who are Christians in the sects have already received remission of sins and should not be immersed for that purpose.

Stone was afraid that Campbell, though he consistently denied it, was creating a new church known as Disciples of Christ. He pressed Campbell for clarification: "I do hope . . . that you do not design to establish another sectarian party—that you do not design to cooperate with Trinitarians against Unitarians—that you do not design unchristianizing those who cordially embrace the Apostles' Creed; especially those who take the Bible alone for their rule of faith and practice—that you do not make the opinion of a pious believer, differing from your opinion, a bar to fellowship. Do, my brother, inform me."[30]

In his reply Campbell expressed surprise at the objections to his opinion on the name. Because some people gave too much authority to his opinions, he complained, others became jealous and seemed compelled to challenge him—though he was quick to clarify that he did not mean his father or Stone. He apologized to Stone if he had offended him but criticized him for being overly sensitive. He then continued to develop his reasons for preferring "Disciples," concluding with a response to Stone's admission that he did not say "for the remission of sins" when he baptized. "I do not believe but in one baptism, and that for the remission of sins. . . . If one of these sectarian Christians . . . should happen to come to me desiring baptism, I would immerse him for the remission of his sectarian sins,

29. Alexander Campbell, "Our Name," *Millennial Harbinger*, September 1839, 401–3.
30. Barton W. Stone, "Communication," *Millennial Harbinger*, January 1840, 21–22.

and especially for his sinful ignorance of the Lord's ordinances and long neglect of duty."[31]

The tone of this reply was very different from the tone of his articles two years earlier. Now he was striking out at anything or anyone that threatened to weaken the teaching of baptism for remission of sins and its essential role in salvation and the unity of the church.

What do the events of 1837–1840 reveal about Campbell's theology of salvation and the church, a theology that profoundly shaped his reformation then and now? Many have seen Campbell as clearly inconsistent, appearing at times very positive toward the "pious unimmersed" but quite the opposite at other times. Taken at face value, what he says does seem contradictory. Was he aware of inconsistencies? Did he reverse his position but was unwilling to admit it? Was he afraid of compromising the unique theological insights of his movement and therefore backed off of his more open and inclusive statements? Or did he hold together what seemed to be contradictory beliefs in a creative tension—a paradox—that would provide fodder for those who came later to claim he supported them regardless of their views?

It is wrong to dismiss Campbell as grossly inconsistent or changing his positions under pressure. All his statements responded to the specific threat he saw as most dangerous at the time. He does develop his baptismal theology over time, as can be seen in his changing positions in the debates with Presbyterians John Walker and William Maccalla. Indisputably he would come to the solid conviction that biblical baptism was immersion of believers for the remission of sins, even asserting at times that that *was* conversion.

In an article titled "Union" in the November 1840 *Millennial Harbinger*, Campbell showed the intimate connection he saw between immersion for remission of sins and the goal of visible Christian unity: "I argue that it is the duty of all the true and loyal friends of Jesus to preach and teach one Lord, one faith, and one immersion into Christ for the remission of sins. *For twelve hundred years after Christ immersion for the remission of sins was the practice of the whole Christian world—Hebrews, Greeks, and Romans.* Remember I have said it, and can prove it from the most authentic records on earth."[32]

By the time Campbell published *Christian Baptism: With Its Antecedents and Consequents* in 1851, only glimmers of his inclusive statements from the

---

31. Alexander Campbell, "And Our Name," *Millennial Harbinger*, January 1840, 29.

32. Alexander Campbell, "Union," *Millennial Harbinger*, November 1840, 486.

Alexander Campbell at age forty-one. Used with permission from the Disciples of Christ Historical Society, Bethany, West Virginia.

Lunenburg letter articles remained, chiefly in the answers to three questions in the catechism at the end of the book. In answer to question 126—"Have not many Christians had their infants sprinkled or baptized in infancy?"—he admitted that many *Christians* did in fact engage in the practice of infant baptism. In the next answer he stated that many who baptize their infants and practice other "traditions of men" were good people. And in response to question 128 concerning the effectiveness of infant sprinkling, he contrasted performing an act thinking it was right with doing it while doubting its correctness or knowing it to be wrong. "The former is a simple mistake; the latter a willful transgression." Yet he would go on to say in item 129 that all who could know the truth if they would just access it but did not, were guilty of willful transgression. No one except those immersed in the name of the Father, Son, and Holy Spirit could claim to have been truly baptized, he asserted in item 131.[33]

No one was stronger than Campbell on the necessity of immersion for the remission of sins. Yet his understanding of the theological significance of baptism expressed in the Lunenburg letter articles reveals other commitments that, regardless of his strict view of baptism, allowed him to avoid the seemingly inevitable legalistic and divisive conclusions promoted by John Thomas and his followers. He held together what seemed to be contradictory understandings in a tension still felt among his heirs today.

33. Alexander Campbell, *Christian Baptism: With Its Antecedents and Consequents* (Bethany, VA: Alexander Campbell, 1851), 433–34.

CHAPTER 12

Campbell versus the Mormons

Another intense conflict between Campbell and a coworker contributed to the creation of a restoration movement that would rival Campbell's as the fastest-growing and largest indigenous American religious body. In comparison to his long-running battles with Baptists and Presbyterians, Campbell's battle with early Mormon leaders was relatively brief. Yet in this clash between two new religious movements, the profound effect of the American experience on each of them can be seen with striking clarity.[1]

No religious leader elicited more scathing denunciations and attacks from Alexander Campbell than Joseph Smith, founding prophet of the Church of Jesus Christ of Latter-day Saints. Campbell was the first to publish an examination of the Book of Mormon, labeling it the fabrication of a deluded or deliberately deceitful person. One thing motivating Campbell's intense criticism was the fact that Sidney Rigdon, a leader of the Campbell movement in Ohio, had embraced Smith's ideas in 1830 after reading the newly published Book of Mormon. Rigdon would go on to become one of Joseph Smith's closest advisers and fellow leaders.[2]

In fact, many of Mormonism's key early leaders had been part of Alexander Campbell's reform, including Rigdon and Oliver Cowdery (two of the witnesses who certified they had seen the golden plates from which Smith

1. For a careful study comparing Alexander Campbell and Joseph Smith from the standpoint of a Mormon scholar, see RoseAnn Benson, *Alexander Campbell and Joseph Smith: 19th Century Restorationists* (Provo, UT: Brigham Young University Press, 2015).

2. Anti-Mormon writers would accuse Rigdon of stealing the manuscript of a novel by Solomon Spaulding that told of ancient civilizations in America and along with Smith and Oliver Cowdery crafting it into the Book of Mormon. See appendix B, "The Spaulding-Rigdon Theory," in Fawn M. Brodie, *No Man Knows My History*, 2nd ed., revised and enlarged (New York: Vintage Books, 1995), 442–56.

Sidney Rigdon (1793–1876) was a preacher among the churches of the Campbell reformation in Ohio before becoming a major leader of Joseph Smith's
new "restoration" movement. After Smith's murder, Rigdon lost to Brigham
Young in a power struggle and organized a rival group of Latter Day Saints
in Pennsylvania. Photo courtesy of Community of Christ Archives.

translated the Book of Mormon), as well as Parley and Orson Pratt. They
previously had been preachers among the "Reformed Baptists" or Disciples
in Ohio and were influential in bringing several thousand members of those
churches into Mormonism.

Campbell was the first to publish an attack on the authenticity of the Book
of Mormon and the movement that claimed it as scripture. Appearing first as an
article in the February 1831 *Millennial Harbinger* and republished the following
year in Boston by Joshua V. Himes, "Delusions" was a no-holds-barred, insulting assault on the Book of Mormon and Joseph Smith. Campbell identified

what he regarded as blatant contradictions of biblical history and unfounded claims of a new priesthood. His tone, though, was personal and sarcastic.

Campbell began with examples of imposters who had claimed to speak for God through the ages. Smith, he asserted, was only the most recent of such frauds. He then proceeded to give the names of the books of the Book of Mormon and tell the story recounted in each—interspersed with biting comments. At the end of the sketch of the contents of the Book of Mormon, he concluded:

> Such is an analysis of the book of Mormon, the bible of the Mormonites. For noticing of which I would have asked forgiveness from all my readers, had not several hundred persons of different denominations believed in it. On this account alone has it become necessary to notice it, and for the same reason we must examine its pretensions to divine authority.
>
> Smith, its real author, as ignorant and impudent a knave as ever wrote a book, betrays the cloven foot in basing his whole book upon a false fact, or a pretended fact, which makes God a liar.[3]

The false claim to which Campbell referred was that Lehi, a descendant of the patriarch Joseph, had been made a priest, in clear contradiction to the restriction in the book of Numbers of the priesthood to the tribe of Levi for all time.

Campbell then listed ten internal evidences he believed demonstrated the utter falsity of the Book of Mormon. The illegitimacy of the new Mormon priesthood and the promise of a different promised land (America) to the renegade migrant Jews topped his list of absurdities. These were clear contradictions, he contended, of the commands and promises of God.

He then attacked the book's description of a royal dynasty not from the divinely designated tribe of Judah, the construction of a new temple with no recognition of the temple in Jerusalem, quotations from New Testament books centuries before they were written, and discussions of every religious controversy then being discussed in America—all of which indicated the book's contemporary origin. Campbell then pointed to factual errors (Jesus was born in Jerusalem), anachronisms (the navigational instrument used to get to America was not invented until centuries later), and the identification of Americans as Christians centuries before Jesus was born.[4]

Next Campbell listed what he called "Smithisms" that showed the book's

3. Alexander Campbell, "Delusions," *Millennial Harbinger*, February 1831, 91.
4. Campbell, "Delusions," 92–93.

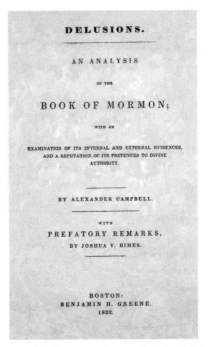

Campbell was the first to write a refutation of the claims of divine inspiration for the Book of Mormon in his tract "Delusions" in 1831. Joshua Himes, who would later become the chief promoter of the millennial teachings of William Miller, reprinted Campbell's work the following year.

scurrilous nature. Awkward and repetitive use of phrases from the King James Version of the Bible made it, Campbell charged, "the meanest book in the English language. . . . It has not one good sentence in it, save the profanation of those sentences quoted from the Oracles of the Living God. . . . It is as certainly Smith's fabrication as Satan is the father of lies."[5]

Campbell then dismissed as unreliable the witnesses who attested to having seen the plates from which Smith translated. Some of them, he charged, had an economic interest in the sales of the book. He closed with a warning to the followers of Joseph Smith that if they had any reason left in them they should abandon this delusion and return to the true God.[6] Despite Campbell's utter incredulity about Smith's claims of revelation from God,

5. Campbell, "Delusions," 95.
6. Campbell, "Delusions," 96.

the loss of several thousand members in Ohio to the Latter Day Saints in the early 1830s made the Mormons a significant threat to Campbell.[7]

The losses to the Mormons prompted Campbell to make a twenty-two-day preaching trip from Bethany to the center of the defections in Ohio in May or June 1831. Earlier in February, in the same issue of the *Millennial Harbinger* in which "Delusions" appeared, he had denounced Rigdon as having "fallen into the snare of the Devil in joining the Mormonites."[8] In July he claimed that many adherents of Mormonism "had begun to recover their reason, and desert the ranks of the new Apostle."[9]

But Rigdon's conversion to Mormonism was especially disturbing to Campbell. Because of Rigdon's influential role in Campbell's reform, he was compelled to explain what had happened. Rigdon, Campbell claimed, had suffered from mental illness for some time and had been getting progressively worse. This was manifested in fits of melancholy and enthusiasm, nervous spasms and swoonings—events that Rigdon interpreted as the work of the Holy Spirit. If you set out to experience signs, omens, and visits from angels, Campbell asserted, you will find them, just as those who set out to find witches see one in every "unseemly old woman." The need now, he said, was to teach the foundations of the faith found in Scripture and to learn from the experiences of the past year.[10]

Smith and the Mormons received little sustained attention from Campbell over the next decade, though disparaging statements appeared from time to time. In a footnote to the April 1834 installment of Samuel L. Mc-Corkle's series "Signs of the Times," Campbell exclaimed: "'tis a disgrace to the Christian character, to the name, to any man who has ever read a Bible, to believe that absurd book called 'the book of Mormon.' It must have been written by an ATHEIST, who did not believe that God would ever call him to judgment for lying in his name. The author must have studied barrenness of sentiment and expression, a poverty of style, without an equal in the English language, for the purpose of deception."[11]

Though Smith was no stranger to caustic religious rhetoric, he apparently did not respond immediately to Campbell's "Delusions" article in 1831 nor to its republication the next year as a stand-alone pamphlet by Boston Christian

---

7. Mark Lyman Staker, *Hearken, O Ye People: The Historical Setting for Joseph Smith's Ohio Revelations* (Salt Lake City: Greg Kofford Books, 2009), 284–88, 377–78.

8. Alexander Campbell, "Sidney Rigdon," *Millennial Harbinger*, February 1831, 100.

9. Alexander Campbell, "Mormonism," *Millennial Harbinger*, July 1831, 331.

10. Campbell, "Sidney Rigdon," 100–101.

11. Samuel L. McCorkle, "Signs of the Times," *Millennial Harbinger*, April 1834, 148.

leader Joshua V. Himes.[12] He did read, at least occasionally, some of Campbell's writings, however. Perhaps partly in response to the derogatory footnote just quoted, in September 1834 Smith wrote a letter to Oliver Cowdery. In the letter, which was published in the *Evening and the Morning Star*, edited by Cowdery, Smith mentioned reading the *Millennial Harbinger*. He was always grieved, he stated, to see corrupt-hearted men like Campbell "step forward and pretend to teach the ways of God." Yet Smith thanked God that he had been the instrument of showing the world Campbell's true spirit. Though he had never met Campbell, he remarked, "the GREAT MAN, not infrequently condescends to notice an individual of obscure birth as myself." Requesting that Cowdery print his letter as a response to Campbell's attacks, Smith concluded:

> I take this course to inform the gentleman, that while he is breathing out scurrility he is effectually showing the motives and principles by which he is governed, and often causes men to investigate and embrace the book of Mormon, who might otherwise never have perused it. I am satisfied, therefore he should continue his scurrility; indeed, I am more than gratified, because his cry of Joe Smith! Joe Smith! false prophet! false prophet! must manifest to all men the spirit he is of, and serves to open the eyes of the people.
>
> I wish to inform him further, that as he has, for a length of time, smitten me upon one cheek, and I have offered no resistance, I have turned the other also, to obey the commandment of our Savior; and am content to sit awhile longer in silence and see the great work of God roll on, amid the opposition of this world in the face of every scandal and falsehood which may be invented and put in circulation.[13]

Six months later Cowdery published an article in the *Messenger and Advocate* titled "Delusion," in which he responded point by point to Campbell's "Delusions," which continued to be circulated. Cowdery closed with an offer to supply more examples of Campbell's scandalous writing to any readers who wanted to see them, "and then close with this gentleman forever."[14]

Mormonism shared many core beliefs and practices with Campbell's re-

12. *Delusions: An Analysis of the Book of Mormon; with an Examination of its Internal and External Evidences, and a Refutation of its Pretenses to Divine Authority. By Alexander Campbell. With Prefatory Remarks, by Joshua V. Himes* (Boston: Benjamin H. Greene, 1832).

13. Joseph Smith Jr., *The Evening and the Morning Star* 2 (September 1834): 192, http://www.centerplace.org/history/ems/v2n24.htm.

14. Oliver Cowdery, "Delusion," *Messenger and Advocate* 6 (March 1835): 90–93.

form: white America as God's chosen land, the central importance of restoring ancient Christianity, the practice of immersion. This made Mormonism an attractive option to many in Campbell movement churches, especially where influential leaders like Rigdon, Parley Pratt, and Orson Hyde embraced and advocated Mormonism.[15] Yet there were also vast differences. Smith believed he was the divinely inspired prophet chosen to restore lost truths through the Book of Mormon. Furthermore, his movement claimed to have restored (1) the authority to perform ordinances in the Aaronic and Melchizedek priesthoods; (2) the structure of the church—including the office of apostle; (3) the teaching that God would soon gather the Latter Day Saints to an American Zion for Christ's reordering of all things; and, most importantly, (4) the restoration of continuing revelation from God. Campbell's complete rejection of all these claims made it clear that, despite the similarities, Mormonism was as far from his "restoration of the ancient gospel and order of things" as anything could be.

When Mormon political strength began to make national news, Campbell resumed his attacks. From September through December 1842, then in four additional installments in 1843, Campbell reprinted a sixty-four-page pamphlet by Methodist leader LaRoy Sunderland published in 1842 in New York titled *Mormonism Exposed*. Among other things, the booklet claimed to provide evidence that Smith and Mormonism were guilty of treason against the United States.[16] Campbell completed the reprint in the August issue and gave his assessment. "I have now paid my share of attention to the meanest, vilest, and most infamous humbug ever promulgated in any age, language or country under these broad and high heavens. . . . It would be more difficult to exaggerate its enormous wickedness than any other species of delusion, fraud, or fiction ever palmed upon the world. . . . Meanwhile, we must refer all future inquirers to the documents already spread upon our pages, from which, if they cannot learn its monstrous impiety, they could not be taught by any human tongue."[17]

Joseph Smith declared himself a candidate for the US presidency in 1844. This, along with other events, increased antagonism toward Smith

15. Staker, *Hearken, O Ye People*, 320–21.

16. See especially "Mormonism," *Millennial Harbinger*, January 1843, 24–28; April 1843, 152–57. Original booklet available online at https://babel.hathitrust.org/cgi/pt?id=hvd .hwyprp;view=1up;seq=5. Sunderland had printed an earlier attack on Mormonism in 1838 titled "Mormonism Exposed and Refuted," of which the 1842 booklet was a revision and expansion.

17. Alexander Campbell, "Remarks on the Mormon Expose," *Millennial Harbinger*, August 1843, 351.

from both inside and outside Mormon ranks and led to the murder of Smith and his brother Hyrum at the hands of a Carthage, Illinois, mob in June 1844.[18]

Campbell's notice of the murders reflected his utter contempt of Smith and his movement. "Joseph Smith and his brother Hiram have been providentially cut off in the midst of their diabolical career. . . . The money-digger, the juggler, and the founder of the Golden Bible delusion, has been hurried away in the midst of his madness to his final account. An outlaw himself, God cut him off by outlaws. He requited him according to his works. It was neither more nor less than the assassination of one whose career was in open rebellion against God and man."[19] Campbell thereafter gave almost no notice to Mormonism in the pages of his journal. Curiously, he printed, without comment, a notice from a group that had unsuccessfully supported Sidney Rigdon as successor to Joseph Smith. He titled the short piece "Mormon Church Extinct," based on the document's contention that the "Church of Jesus Christ of Latter Day Saints does no longer exist" except in connection with Rigdon.[20] The notice referred to the internal power struggle after Joseph Smith's murder that led to Rigdon's marginalization by Brigham Young and his supporters, and the formation of a faction that for a time supported Rigdon's claim to successorship. Contrary to Campbell's statement, Mormonism was not extinct. It would continue to grow until it equaled the number of members of Stone-Campbell churches in the United States.[21]

18. See especially chapter 29 of Richard Lyman Bushman, *Joseph Smith: Rough Stone Rolling* (New York: Knopf, 2005), 526–50.

19. Alexander Campbell, "Death of J. Smith, the Mormon Impostor," *Millennial Harbinger*, September 1844, 410.

20. "Mormonism Extinct," *Millennial Harbinger*, December 1844, 618–19.

21. See "Religious Landscape Study," Pew Research Center, http://www.pewfo rum.org/religious-landscape-study/. The "Restorationist Family" under the "Evangelical Protestant" category and the Mormon category each claimed 1.6 percent of the American population.

CHAPTER 13

Campbell versus
the Presbyterians—Again

Alexander Campbell's last public debate contrasted sharply with the decorum of the Owen and Purcell discussions. Neither of those opponents had provoked Campbell to the levels of abrasive language of which he was capable by questioning his motives or intelligence. The debate with Nathan L. Rice, however, was shot through with personal attacks and insinuations of dishonesty by both contestants.

In the 1830s Campbell's movement had proven to be a formidable competitor to Presbyterianism in Kentucky. In a report of a preaching trip to Kentucky and Ohio in August 1842, Campbell related that the churches in Frankfort and Lexington were building large meetinghouses and that the number of baptisms had been substantial—with over a thousand in the Lexington area during the two months before he arrived, and 350 in the Green River area southwest of Lexington. Even in Danville, a Presbyterian stronghold and location of Presbyterian Centre College, Campbell reported 40 or 50 recent baptisms.[1]

In the second article of the report Campbell made a disparaging remark about Presbyterian minister Nathan Rice in his account of passing through Bardstown, Kentucky. Two years earlier, the minister of the Christian Church in the city had informed Campbell of Rice's aggressive challenges to the reformation. Campbell had intended to respond to Rice's attacks at the time, he said, but it slipped his mind. Later in the article he repeated a rumor that Rice had backed down from a debate on baptism with reformer Aylette Rains in Paris, Kentucky, insinuating that Rice was afraid he would

---

1. Alexander Campbell, "Notes on a Late Tour—No. I," *Millennial Harbinger*, October 1842, 449–51.

be unable to win.[2] Campbell had no idea that he would soon be engaged with Rice in the most acrimonious debate of his career.

The debate originated when Campbell was visiting Richmond, Kentucky. John H. Brown, the Presbyterian minister there, approached him to propose a public discussion on the doctrinal differences between Campbell's reformation and Presbyterianism. Campbell at first insisted that the Kentucky leaders of his movement were fully capable of defending their teachings. But when Brown countered that only Campbell's word would carry the full weight of the reform, Campbell agreed to pursue the matter. He told Brown to draw up a formal proposal and send it to him; he would respond after he returned home from his trip.[3]

Brown immediately wrote a proposal and sent it to Campbell on September 19. Based on the conversation the two had already had, Brown suggested that they form a committee of two or three from each side that would meet in November to make specific plans for the debate. He asked Campbell to send him names from his side and to propose a meeting date. Brown added that their correspondence was to remain private until both agreed to make it public.

Campbell responded that he had expected to hear earlier from Brown, and that he didn't think a committee should be given the responsibility to make decisions about the content of the debate. He then set out five propositions, apparently assuming that Brown would be his opponent.[4] Three focused on baptism—whether infant baptism and sprinkling were legitimate, and whether baptism was for the remission of sins. The other two dealt with whether Presbyterian structure and the doctrines of the Westminster Confession were found in the New Testament. This began eleven months of bickering over who said what in the initial conversation, who would serve on the committee for the Presbyterians, whether there would be one debater or a group on each side, and whether the Presbyterian debaters would be officially appointed by the synod. The exact points to be debated also became a major problem, with repeated rewriting and nuancing by Campbell and Brown.

Campbell later claimed that Brown had assured him—though Brown denied it—that if there were to be one Presbyterian debater it would be John C. Young, president of Centre College, for whom Campbell had great respect.

---

2. Alexander Campbell, "Notes on a Late Tour—No. II," *Millennial Harbinger*, November 1842, 502, 507.

3. Campbell, "Notes on a Late Tour—No. II," 505–6.

4. *A Debate Between Rev. A. Campbell and Rev. N. L. Rice* (Lexington, KY: A. T. Skillman & Son, 1844), 11–12.

When Young's failing health prevented this and a second person acceptable to Campbell, J. R. Breckinridge, refused to debate Campbell because Campbell had championed Christianity and Protestantism in the earlier debates,[5] Brown named Nathan Rice as the Presbyterian representative. In response Campbell threatened to withdraw from the contest altogether. He accused Brown and the synod of dishonesty, intending to put Rice forward as his opponent from the beginning. Campbell's reply sparked the rumor among Presbyterians that Campbell was backing out of the debate, which he strongly denied in an article printed in May.[6]

Both committees finally agreed to meet in Lexington, Kentucky, in early August to finalize details. The antagonism between them had grown so great, however, that even after they all arrived the groups refused to meet for six days. Instead, they sent messages back and forth, apparently carried by runners, until August 7, when they finally came together. Brown proposed that their entire correspondence be published immediately, apparently thinking it would show Campbell in a bad light. Campbell refused. Not until the publication of the debate volume would the long and rancorous process be revealed to the public.[7]

In February 1843, in the midst of the correspondence with Brown, Nathan Rice responded to Campbell's uncomplimentary statements in his *Millennial Harbinger* report the previous November. Campbell published Rice's letter and answered it with further disparaging remarks. While he had always encouraged open, courteous discussion of disputed points of belief, Campbell declared, it was "the rude and wanton attacks of the bigoted sectary, sworn to his errors and his party" that he condemned. This was Rice's offense, not his differences with the reformers.[8] Between the increasingly unfriendly correspondence between Campbell and Rev. John Brown and his hostile editorial exchanges with Rice, an extremely different tone had been set for the final formal debate of Campbell's career.

In September 1843 the *Millennial Harbinger* announced final details. The debate would take place at the Reformed Church in Lexington, Kentucky,

5. This claim appeared in a funeral sermon for Campbell preached by Joseph King and published in the May 1866 *Millennial Harbinger* and was widely reported afterward. John Brown, however, said in his December 2, 1842, letter to Campbell that Breckinridge was not in Kentucky at the time of the discussion and thus unable to participate. *A Debate Between Rev. A. Campbell and Rev. N. L. Rice*, 17.

6. Alexander Campbell, "Contemplated Discussion," *Millennial Harbinger*, May 1843, 199–200.

7. *A Debate Between Rev. A. Campbell and Rev. N. L. Rice*, 13–46.

8. "Letter from Rev. N. L. Rice," *Millennial Harbinger*, February 1843, 86–88.

REVᵈ. N. L. RICE,
of the Presbyterian Church.
PARIS, KY.

REVᵈ. A. CAMPBELL,
BETHANY, VA.

Frontispiece of the Campbell-Rice Debate. Courtesy of the Center for Restoration Studies, Abilene Christian University, Abilene, Texas.

beginning November 15. There would be six propositions. The first four were to focus on baptism—whether immersion of believers was the only valid form, whether infant baptism was scriptural, whether baptism was for the remission of sins, and whether only ordained bishops or presbyters could administer it. The other two propositions examined the role of the Holy Spirit in conversion and sanctification, and the legitimacy of creeds.[9]

The debate began on Wednesday, November 15, and continued every day but Sunday, from 10 a.m. to 2 p.m., through Saturday, December 2. Campbell initially assumed there would be six hours of speeches per day for ten or eleven days, but when Rice said he could do only four hours a day, Campbell agreed to extra days. The questions surrounding baptism took up the majority of the debate. In the final published volume, they occupied 562 pages of the 912-page, small-print tome. The hateful spirit that had characterized the fourteen months of planning carried over fully into the debate.

In his first speech Campbell remarked that many might think the topics

9. A. Campbell and N. L. Rice, "Contemplated Debate, Lexington, Kentucky," *Millennial Harbinger*, September 1843, 425.

at issue were minor matters—like whether you were to have a small basin or a large one for baptism. He insisted, however, that what was at stake was essential to the fate of America, Europe, and the world. The Catholic Church was adding hundreds of millions of subjects through the practice of infant baptism. The Protestant Reformation had challenged that power and tyranny in the sixteenth century but had been seduced by the favor of governments to continue the false practice. He intended to show from the most authoritative sources that baptism was immersion of believers, launching into an extensive exposition of the Greek word *baptizo*. He also reminded hearers that it had been the Presbyterians who wanted to debate, not him—a fact that seemed to annoy him and intensify his exasperation with the entire affair.

Rice replied that his views had the support of countless wise Christian leaders past and present. If Campbell's assertion that believers' immersion was the only valid baptism were true, then the great Protestant Reformers Campbell had just praised had "failed to discover one of the most important features of the christian system; and they and their followers were alike un-baptized, and were aliens from the church of Christ. Nay, if this doctrine be true, there is not now a true church on earth, save the few who have 'been so happy as to make this remarkable discovery'!"[10]

Rice asserted that he had no responsibility for calling for the debate, quoting from the correspondence between John Brown and Campbell to show that it had been a "Campbellite" reformer, a Mr. Duncan, who was the initiator. Furthermore, he challenged Campbell's claim that Scripture was absolutely clear about the doctrine of believers' immersion, quoting from authorities who took the opposite position. "When he asserts, that it . . . is so clearly taught, that nothing but folly or perverseness can prevent the discovery of it; we are bound to believe, either that he is wholly mistaken, or that the multitudes of apparently wise and good men of whom I have spoken, were in truth most perversely rebellious or most profoundly stupid!"[11]

Ironically, Rice's words were reminiscent of Thomas Campbell's early misgivings about taking the position that immersion of believers was the only valid baptism. He had warned that while immersion might be the "regular and appointed way," they should not put anyone baptized as an infant "out of the church merely for the purpose of coming in again."[12] Alexander himself had made a similar point in his Lunenburg letter articles in 1837.

---

10. *A Debate Between Rev. A. Campbell and Rev. N. L. Rice*, 63.

11. *A Debate Between Rev. A. Campbell and Rev. N. L. Rice*, 66.

12. Quoted in Robert Richardson, *Memoirs of Alexander Campbell*, 2 vols. (Philadelphia: J. B. Lippincott & Co., 1868–1870), 1:393.

"I cannot, therefore, make any one duty the standard of Christian state or character, not even immersion into the name of the Father, of the Son, and of the Holy Spirit, and in my heart regard all that have been sprinkled in infancy without their own knowledge and consent, as aliens from Christ and the well-grounded hope of heaven."[13] Rice then quoted from the same lexicons Campbell had used earlier to find uses of the Greek root translated "baptism" that did not exclusively mean immersion.

In many ways the arguments Campbell made concerning baptism in the Rice debate represent his most developed understandings and teachings. Thirteen years earlier, in July 1830, Campbell had published an "extra" issue of the *Millennial Harbinger* on "remission of sins." In the last of ten propositions in that issue he asserted, "Immersion and regeneration are two Bible names for the same act." This had provided fuel for those who accused Campbell of teaching baptismal regeneration—a position rejected by both Presbyterians and Baptists.[14] The debate with Rice provided a forum to present his mature views, including an explanation of his understanding of baptismal regeneration.[15]

Rice complained that Campbell had been less than clear in his opening speech concerning immersion being necessary for salvation. In essence, he charged Campbell with downplaying his true beliefs that amounted to baptismal regeneration. Rice then quoted from Campbell's writings, including an article from the *Christian Baptist* and a passage from *Christianity Restored* in which Campbell had described baptism as "the gospel in water," labeling the act of baptism the line of demarcation between condemnation and salvation.[16]

Campbell, however, denied that he made baptism invariably necessary for salvation. There might be cases, he admitted, in which a penitent believer could still be saved even though baptism was not possible. "I do not make baptism absolutely essential to salvation in any case" (519). Rice retorted that Campbell's admission that some could be saved without immersion was

---

13. Alexander Campbell, "Any Christians among Protestant Parties," *Millennial Harbinger*, September 1837, 412.

14. Alexander Campbell, "Remission of Sins," special issue, *Millennial Harbinger*, June 5, 1830, 27.

15. He would publish his final and most extensive treatment of baptism in 1851 in a carefully structured volume titled *Christian Baptism: With Its Antecedents and Consequents* (Bethany, VA: Alexander Campbell, 1851).

16. *A Debate Between Rev. A. Campbell and Rev. N. L. Rice*, 443–44. Hereafter, page references from this work will be given in parentheses in the text.

contradictory to what he had said in print many times—that no adult could be saved without repentance and immersion.

When time ran out at 2 p.m., the disputants agreed that the arguments on this proposition were too important to delay. They resumed the debate from 6 to 9 p.m. that Friday, November 24. Even then, both had to be stopped by the moderators because of time. In his closing remarks, Campbell insisted that his position was the "catholic" view of baptism. Everyone agreed that immersion was valid baptism, not everyone accepted sprinkling or pouring. Everyone agreed that penitent believers were proper subjects for baptism, but many rejected the idea that infants were.

Finally, Campbell insisted that while each idea about the purpose of baptism had some adherents, "the whole world," he asserted, "Greek, Roman and all," were united in the belief that baptism was "a pledge of remission of sins, and of our in-grafting into Christ." Any other view was sectarian because not everyone agreed on it. "Why not, then, sacrifice that which is so sectarian, and unite in one Lord, one faith, and one immersion?" (560). Ironically, Rice would use this same logic in the fourth proposition on the proper administrator of baptism. All would agree, he said, that ordained bishops or presbyters were proper administrators of baptism, but not all would agree that laypersons were (575).

Bill Humble suggested that the real difference between Campbell and Rice was that Campbell gave broad comprehensive overviews and principles while Rice simply looked for exceptions to Campbell's sweeping statements. This interpretation is not without merit, but Humble's point seems to be to explain why Campbell had such difficulty with Rice's arguments and became so petulant during the debate. In the often excruciatingly hostile language of the published debate, both Campbell and Rice spent huge amounts of time questioning the honesty and integrity of the other.

Rice quoted extensively from Campbell's writings to show that he had contradicted himself. Campbell conceded that it had been several years since he had read his earlier writings, and that whenever he wrote about a subject he did not feel compelled to check on what he had said before. "I am at no such pains to prevent contradictions, real or apparent." But, he continued, he had certain fundamental principles about the Christian religion so fixed in his mind that he could never contradict them. Whether he had always expressed himself in the clearest and most precise way was another matter, he admitted. Nevertheless, he was adamant that the positions he was expressing in the debate were the sure and catholic ones (643).

On Monday morning, November 27, the topic shifted from baptism to the operation of the Holy Spirit in conversion. Campbell affirmed that the Holy Spirit worked only through Scripture in conversion. Rice agreed that the Spirit usually worked in conjunction with "the Truth" but could work in other ways too. Rice, in his reply to Campbell's first speech, accused him of giving an eloquent discourse on a variety of topics that had nothing to do with the actual proposition. Furthermore, he charged that Campbell had made exclusive, sectarian claims of having the only truth about conversion that sounded more like "the pride of Rome, than the Spirit of the gospel" (625).

In Campbell's response, he angrily reproached Rice for his refusal to respond to his arguments, which he had numbered and clearly stated in his first speech. Rice's accusation that he had failed to state the issue they were then debating or the specific differences with Rice was absurd. "Did I not read the proposition? Did I not distinctly affirm 'That the Spirit of God operates in conversion and sanctification only through the truth'? This I solemnly affirm as my belief. This he denies" (640). The reason Rice avoided answering his arguments, Campbell asserted, was that he could not—there were no effective answers to his points. He accused Rice of using *ad captandum* arguments—unsound, sham rhetoric designed to prey on the gullibility of the audience using emotion rather than reason. Furthermore, Campbell charged, "Neither as affirmant or respondent will he keep to the Bible."

Campbell then lashed out at the whole affair. He had come at considerable sacrifice, he said, expecting a fair exchange of ideas. Instead, he found a massive effort on the part of Rice and the Presbyterians to manipulate public opinion into thinking they had won a "glorious victory" over Campbell. While he knew that the desire to triumph over one's opponent was common in such situations, and he had expected it here, what he was experiencing exceeded "every thing I have ever known or witnessed." He accused his opponents of planting a "laughing committee" in the balcony to encourage Rice and manipulate the audience's sentiments. I, in contrast, did not come here to win, he snapped, but to uphold the truth (641–42).

Rice retorted, "Mr. Campbell cannot moderate me," and called on the debate moderators to judge whether or not he had followed the agreed-to rules. He charged Campbell with violating the rules of common courtesy in accusing him of dishonesty. Rice began a list of examples of Campbell's slanders, including the use of terms like "licentiousness of the tongue" and "base aspersions." Campbell interrupted, saying he was not describing Rice when he used those terms but the sources from which Rice was quoting. One of the moderators agreed that he too had understood the descriptions to be about the authors quoted, not Rice personally. Rice, however, disputed the judgment, saying that he had only quoted two writers and that the charge was clearly aimed at him. "When a man so accustomed to debate as Mr. Campbell, and so remarkable for his coolness and self-possession, displays so much temper, as the audience witnessed in his last speech, there is sad evidence that something is wrong. Men do not ordinarily lose their temper, when successful in argument. I verily believe, that the sole cause of his trouble is, that I adhere too closely to the point. Every argument I have advanced bears directly on the subject in debate" (645).

He then cited examples of Campbell having wandered from the assigned topic, followed by a point-by-point response to Campbell's seven points on the Holy Spirit. Rice said that he had already given these arguments, though without using Campbell's numbering. And furthermore, the Presbyterians were not manufacturing public sentiment, he exclaimed. Instead, the arguments he had given were strong enough to persuade the public of the truth of his positions and the weakness of Campbell's.

When Rice ended his speech a few minutes early, Campbell challenged the moderators to enforce the rule that the respondent had to answer the points of the affirmant. Two moderators spoke. The first said that respondents were allowed to give their arguments in whatever form they chose. The only matter on which the moderators could rule was whether or not the material presented was extraneous or irrelevant to the proposition. Campbell pressed, "Is it not usual for the respondent to reply in some way or other to the matter presented by the affirmant?" The first moderator said yes, but a second rose to address the debaters and the audience. Several times in the debate the opponents had "very nearly trodden upon" the boundaries of good order. He strongly advised the two to avoid all statements about the other's character. The first moderator added that they should stick strictly to the propositions, introducing only authorities and argument into the discussion, not the defects of the other debater (651).

Despite the admonitions, they continued to take personal jabs at each other with accusations of deliberate misrepresentation of the other's positions. They seemed unable to stop. The next day they fought over whether or not Campbell's remarks had been made in anger. When Campbell denied it, Rice asserted that they would have been more excusable if they had been made in anger rather than deliberately. Then, in an odd diversion, the discussion of the Holy Spirit was partially sidetracked for several days over whether or not a Presbyterian leader twenty years earlier had admitted that Campbell had won the debate with Baptist William Maccalla.

The personal attacks continued even on the final day of the debate. On

Saturday, December 2, the two addressed whether creeds were inherently heretical and divisive. After Rice's first presentation Campbell declared that he had never heard "such a tissue of misrepresentation and abuse, from anyone professing piety." Rice responded that Campbell, despite his "pretty speeches," had merely made exhortations, avoiding arguments relevant to the topic. Mercifully, sometime after 2 p.m., the moderators called the debate to a close.

In his brief account of the debate in the January 1844 *Millennial Harbinger*, Campbell disparaged the Presbyterians' exuberant claim of victory. "It was decidedly the most partisan discussion in which I have ever been engaged," he concluded. Even though the Presbyterian press declared "that sprinkling gloriously triumphed over dipping," he insisted that it would be premature for anyone to claim a victory before the book with the full debate had been published. Since the Presbyterian boasting was based on "raw and unsupported assertion," he did not need to provide a substantial refutation. Just read the book, he said, and you will see who came out on top.[17]

Unlike his other debates, Campbell gave few clues concerning how the manuscript was finalized for publication. Based on the inclusion of several sections critical of Campbell that the moderators had agreed should be omitted, as well as Campbell's comment that he found numerous typographical errors in the first edition, Campbell apparently had little to do with it. Both debaters, however, signed a certificate authenticating it as "a full exhibition of the facts, documents, and arguments used by us on the several questions debated." Campbell had insisted early on that all proceeds from sales of the book be given to the two American Bible societies.[18]

The first copies of the debate appeared in March or April 1844, published in five cities by five publishers. Campbell said he had sold all rights to the book to John H. Brown—the minister who had initially proposed the debate—for $2,100.[19] Campbell wanted nothing to do with the publication and sales of the volume. Sales among Presbyterians were evidently not robust, leading Brown to sell the rights to a church leader in the Campbell

17. Alexander Campbell, "The Late Debate," *Millennial Harbinger*, January 1844, 6, 9.
18. *A Debate Between Rev. A. Campbell and Rev. N. L. Rice*, [10]; Alexander Campbell, "The Lexington Debate," *Millennial Harbinger*, 1844, 180. The two societies were the American Bible Society and the American and Foreign Bible Society, the Baptist group with which Campbell worked that split from the American Bible Society in 1836 when the ABS insisted on continuing to transliterate βαπτιζο in its English Bible as "baptize" rather than translate it "immerse."
19. Campbell, "The Lexington Debate," 180.

Bust of Alexander Campbell made in 1843, the year of his debate with N. L. Rice. It was sculpted by W. H. Edge in the James Carr Pottery workshop, New York, and displayed at the Philadelphia Centennial Exhibition, which opened on May 10, 1876, to represent American ceramic pottery. Used with permission from Bethany College, T. W. Phillips Memorial Library, Archives and Special Collections, Bethany, West Virginia.

movement, C. D. Roberts, who published the first of numerous reprints in 1857 from Jacksonville, Illinois.

Campbell and Rice continued to disparage and attack each other long after the debate was over. Competing articles continued through 1844, with

Campbell closing the December *Millennial Harbinger* with descriptions of Rice's malicious insinuations, suppression of the truth, absolute fabrications, and perversions of fact.[20] Campbell's final printed mention of Rice appeared in 1857. Describing Robert Owen as his only honorable opponent in debate, Campbell said Owen was the "literal antithesis of Dr. N. L. Rice," who deserved the "highest niche in the temple of Jesuitical casuistry" with his ability to make bad reasoning appear good.[21]

Why did Campbell remain so enraged and defensive over the Rice debate for the rest of his life? Obviously, there was significant antagonism between Kentucky Presbyterian leadership and Campbell. Campbell was fifty-five years old when he engaged Rice in debate. Three years earlier he had taken on the responsibility of getting Bethany College up and running with adequate staff and funding—a duty that occupied much of his time for the rest of his life. His writing and editing as well as his extensive preaching tours continued unabated. He had not sought the debate with Rice but felt he had been badgered into it. Clearly Rice and the Kentucky Presbyterian leaders were looking for an opportunity to slow the growth of the Campbell reform, regardless of their oft-stated, pure motives of simply seeking truth.

But that would go both ways—Campbell had been lured into a petulance and pettiness that were at best unflattering and, at worst, showed a side of him that highlighted his elitism and arrogance. Perhaps he was embarrassed at what the debate had devolved into—a constant harping at each other and accusations of avoiding the question and dishonesty. The postdebate boasting by each side, claiming victory and a great defeat of the enemy, highlighted Campbell's strong aversion to admitting that he was as guilty of setting the tone as Rice was.

Apart from Campbell's near obsession with it, the Rice debate marked an incident in his career that revealed potential weaknesses in his program of reform. His 1847 trip to Scotland and imprisonment in a controversy over slavery, along with other events in the 1850s, would heighten Campbell's growing fear that something ominous was taking shape. These events would lead him to reassess his vision of the advance and triumph of the ancient gospel and order of things in his blessed nation.

---

20. Alexander Campbell, "Mr. Rice Again," *Millennial Harbinger*, 1844, 613.
21. Alexander Campbell, "An End of the Controversy," *Millennial Harbinger*, 1857, 170.

CHAPTER 14

Bitter Clashes with Baptists

Campbell's reformation shared many key beliefs with the Baptists—so many that it seemed natural for him to do his reform work within Baptist churches for almost two decades. The dogged commitment to Scripture; the emphasis on the local church and rejection of hierarchical structures; the practice of believers' immersion—these shared stances created a like-mindedness between Campbell and his Baptist allies that in the eyes of many boded well for constructing a common cause that would sweep the country.[1]

Yet many Baptist leaders quickly realized that Alexander Campbell held beliefs that were at odds with central Baptist principles. "Anathemas" issued against Campbell and any who followed his teachings by the Beaver (1829), Tate's Creek (1830), and Dover (1830) Baptist associations spelled out irreconcilable differences—both real and exaggerated. All focused on Baptist perceptions of Campbell's view of salvation, including the role of the Holy Spirit, human responsibility, and baptism.

The Beaver anathema accused the Mahoning Association (where Campbell then held membership) of "disbelieving and denying many of the doctrines of the Holy Scriptures," including teaching "that there is no promise of salvation without baptism, that baptism should be administered to all who say they believe that Jesus Christ is the Son of God, without examination on

---

1. When he was informed on his deathbed of a "union" discussion between Baptists and Disciples in Virginia, Campbell wept with joy and stated that if all baptized believers could be united, it "would work wonders in regard to the spread of the truth and the conversion of the world." Robert Richardson, "Union of Christians," *Millennial Harbinger*, March 1866, 97. See John Moss, *Campbell and the Baptists* (Huntsville, AL: John Moss, 1994), and Douglas A. Foster, "Efforts at Repairing the Breach: Twentieth Century Dialogues of the Churches of the Stone-Campbell Movement with Baptists and Presbyterians," *Discipliana* 63 (Winter 2003): 101–2.

any other point; that there is no direct operation of the Holy Spirit on the mind prior to baptism; and that baptism procures the remission of sins and the gift of the Holy Spirit." Furthermore, the reformers taught "that no creed is necessary for the church, but the Scriptures as they stand." The Dover Association's anathema added the charges that Campbell taught there was no special call to the ministry, no mystery in the Scriptures, no legitimacy in religious experience, and no authority in the Mosaic law.[2]

The anathemas pressed church members, congregations, and associations to side with either the Campbell reformers or the anti-Campbell Baptist leaders, leading to painful and often rancorous separations. Thomas Campbell was convinced that the separation should never have happened, urging Campbell churches to aid and encourage their Baptist brothers and sisters and rejoice when their churches increased. It was, he insisted, "a few proud partizans [sic] in the Redstone Association" that had precipitated the division.[3] The fact that the Campbell reformers and Baptists were so close in worldview and theology, however, made the differences stand out more starkly and deepened the rivalry.

While members of Baptist and Campbell movement churches met several times during the nineteenth century to explore the possibility of union,[4] Baptist-"Campbellite" conflict remained very much alive. The anathemas of the late 1820s and 1830s had codified the theological objections to Campbell's teachings, and articles against Campbell and his ideas frequently appeared in Baptist papers. It was in the 1850s, however, when two flamboyant Baptist leaders, Jeremiah Bell Jeter (1802–1880) and James Robinson Graves (1820–1893), mounted an intensified and bitter anti-Campbell campaign.

2. See the list of heresies at the website of the Primitive Baptist Library of Carthage, Illinois, http://pblib.org/Redstone.html.

3. "I am much gratified with the account of your labors, and of their success, especially among our baptist brethren, between whom and us there never should have been any difference: nor indeed would there, had it not been for a few proud partizans in the Redstone Association, of which once we were all members. . . . We have always considered and treated them as our Brethren, and, as far as I am concerned, always hope to do so. I would humbly advise you to treat them with all Christian respect as brethren; and of course, do anything within your power to build up and edify their societies. The first Christian duty to fellow creatures is to love the brethren for Christ's sake, as he has loved us. And by this shall all know that we are his disciples; if we manifest this love to one another. (John 13: 34, 35)." Thomas Campbell to Samuel Riddle Jones, January 17, 1844, Thomas Campbell papers, Disciples of Christ Historical Society, Bethany, West Virginia.

4. Foster, "Efforts at Repairing the Breach," 101–2.

Influential Tennessee Baptist leader James Robinson Graves (1820–1893) became one of Campbell's most relentless and bitter foes. Many Baptists opposed Graves because of his leadership in the controversial Landmark movement. Courtesy Southern Baptist Historical Library and Archives, Nashville, Tennessee.

Campbell and the Clash with James Robinson Graves

James Robinson Graves was a highly influential southern Baptist leader and editor, and the acknowledged founder of the Landmark Baptist movement. Born in Vermont in 1820, Graves moved to Nashville, Tennessee, in 1845 after his ordination as a Baptist minister three years earlier in Kentucky. He served briefly as pastor of Second Baptist Church in Nashville and became editor of the *Tennessee Baptist* in 1846, a role he continued to fill until 1889.[5]

Graves's religious censures were by no means confined to Alexander Campbell. He gave considerable attention to fighting the Methodists, another major religious body in Nashville,[6] as well as Roman Catholics and Presbyterians.[7] Furthermore, he had just as much reproach for other Baptists who he believed were unfaithful to the marks of the true church, and was the most militant proponent of Landmarkism among Southern Baptists.[8] Yet his experience in Kentucky, where Baptist churches lost significant numbers to the Campbell movement, and his awareness of the disruption Campbellism had caused to Baptist life in Nashville before he got there and after he became minister of Second Baptist Church, gave his attacks on Campbell and Campbellism a particularly vitriolic tone.

Graves set the stage in 1851 for the battle with Campbell that would begin in earnest two years later. In the December 20 issue of the *Tennessee Baptist*, Graves printed a short letter in the "Ladies' Department" from a correspondent who signed her letter Florence. She asked Graves to explain why he refused to commune with Campbellites so that she could "silence their cavils" in her neighborhood. Graves responded that he could have no fellowship with Campbellites because though they had been immersed, they had not been scripturally baptized, since the Holy Spirit had not regenerated them before immersion nor did a proper officer in a scriptural church perform it.[9]

Eight weeks later Graves printed a letter from a member of a Christian Church in McMinnville, Tennessee, challenging Graves's depiction of "Campbellite" conversion and demanding a correction. Graves responded that he had merely repeated what the teachers in those churches said. If that

---

5. James A. Patterson, *James Robinson Graves: Setting the Boundaries of Baptist Identity* (Nashville: B&H, 2012), 7–29.

6. Graves wrote extensive attacks on Methodist theology and polity, particularly in his *The Great Iron Wheel; or, Republicanism Backwards and Christianity Reversed* (Nashville: Graves & Marks, 1855) and two sequels.

7. Patterson, *James Robinson Graves*, 59–71.

8. James Leo Garrett Jr., *Baptist Theology: A Four-Century Study* (Macon, GA: Mercer University Press, 2009), 212–25. Landmarkism is the belief that strict Baptists constituted the true church and had existed in unbroken continuity since the apostolic age. These churches had remained faithful to the "old landmarks" and were therefore persecuted by Catholic leaders and other apostate churches through the centuries. Campbell himself used a similar idea in his debate with Bishop Purcell for his movement.

9. James Robinson Graves, "Bro. Graves," *Tennessee Baptist*, December 20, 1851, 4.

was a misrepresentation, they misrepresented themselves. He then issued a counterchallenge—why had a Christian Church minister in Memphis recently rebaptized several Baptists who came to his church?[10]

The discussion continued the following September when Graves reprinted a challenge from the *Christian Magazine* published by Jesse B. Ferguson, preacher of the Nashville Christian Church. The writer offered to pay Graves one hundred dollars if he could prove that Campbell taught no one could be pardoned from sin without being immersed. Graves proceeded to give thirty-five quotes from Campbell and other writers in his movement that he believed demonstrated definitively their teaching of baptismal regeneration.[11] The dispute spilled over into 1853 when in January Graves revealed that the author of the original challenge had been Phillip Fall, pastor of Nashville's First Baptist Church from 1825 to 1830, who had, in Graves's mind, hijacked the congregation into Campbellism.[12] The sparring continued into February, with Graves unsuccessfully challenging Fall to a public debate.

Articles attacking Campbellism had become by now a standard part of the *Tennessee Baptist*. Graves began a series against Jesse Ferguson, who, though advocating Universalist ideas, remained minister of the Nashville Christian Church until 1856. In October 1853, Campbell published a letter from a correspondent identified only as "S" that quoted a particularly nasty article by Graves from the July 16 *Tennessee Baptist*. "We do not consider that there are any more points of identity or even similarity between Baptists and Campbellites than between Baptists and Mormons," Graves had exclaimed, then predicted that Campbell's "kingdom of water, without the Holy Spirit," would soon cease to exist.[13] "S" was insistent that Campbell make an immediate reply to Graves, but Campbell remained silent.

In the November issue of the *Millennial Harbinger*, however, Campbell finally did reply. He first reprinted an article by Phillip Fall with a blow-by-

---

10. Jesse Barnes, "Mr. Graves," *Tennessee Baptist*, February 14, 1852, 3. Many churches of the Campbell movement used the generic terms "Christian Church" and "Church of Christ," especially after the union in the 1830s with many of the Barton W. Stone Christian Churches. Campbell personally preferred the designation "Disciples of Christ."

11. J. R. Graves, "The Offer of $100 Accepted," *Tennessee Baptist*, September 11, 1852, 2. Digitized copies of the *Tennessee Baptist* can be found at the website of the Southern Baptist Historical Library and Archives at http://www.sbhla.org/tb_archive/.

12. Herman Norton, *Tennessee Christians: A History of the Christian Church (Disciples of Christ) in Tennessee* (Nashville: Reed & Co., 1971), 19–24.

13. "The Tennessee Baptist," *Millennial Harbinger*, October 1853, 569–71; "Truly Said," *Tennessee Baptist*, July 16, 1853, 2.

blow account of the failed proposals for a debate between Fall and Graves. Fall had sent it first to Graves's offices in Nashville, but it had been returned marked "refused." Campbell then began a four-and-a-half page rant dismissing Graves as an arrogant, self-important youth who was neither a gentleman, a scholar, nor a Christian. "I have not time nor inclination to expose the flimsy sophistry in which he veils himself." Then Campbell gave a brief statement of his view of conversion to show his orthodoxy, concluding with: "grace, blood, faith, repentance, baptism, constitute the five golden links in the chain of Divine grace," all perfected in the act of baptism. He closed with an offer to give Graves equal space in the *Millennial Harbinger* if he would print Campbell's remarks in the *Tennessee Baptist*.[14] This article began a journalistic battle with Graves that elicited some of the most personal, caustic, and extreme language in Campbell's writing career.

Graves published several articles in early 1854 attacking Campbell and his teachings, including a series by James M. Hart titled "Campbellism in Trouble." In April Campbell took another swipe at Graves, attacking him for accusing Campbell of views as preposterous as those of the Qur'an. In fact, Campbell asserted, there was more truth in the Qur'an than in Graves's misrepresentation of Campbell's beliefs. Graves had accused him of teaching so many things he had never taught that the Baptist editor could not be believed even if he tried to tell the truth.

Campbell spent considerable time establishing his Christian orthodoxy, quoting respected Baptist theologians like Robert Hall, Andrew Fuller, Archibald McClean, and Alexander Carson as holding the same views he did. "I am, to say the least, in the true sense and import of the true orthodoxy of the True Baptists," as orthodox as any of those leaders. Even though Baptist friends had told him not to take Graves seriously, Campbell still offered to print anything Graves said in response if he would print Campbell's defense in the *Tennessee Baptist*.[15]

The next month Campbell lashed out at Graves and the *Tennessee Baptist* in even more extreme terms. In response to the series by James M. Hart and Graves's failure to print Campbell's defense from the previous month, he exclaimed, "He is either the most stupid, or the most reckless of truth, of any sectarian editor known to me in the United States." Campbell pressed

14. Alexander Campbell, "The Tennessee Baptist & Its Chivalrous Editor," *Millennial Harbinger*, November 1853, 636–47.

15. Alexander Campbell, "American Bible Union," *Millennial Harbinger*, April 1854, 229–30.

even harder for Graves to print his responses to the accusations against him, asserting that if Graves did not do so, it would be an admission that he was unable to support his positions. He also restated his charge that most honest Baptists knew Graves was misrepresenting his positions and that they therefore had no respect for Graves.[16] The article was immediately followed by a brief "Advertisement"—a formal challenge to Graves to print Campbell's articles exposing Graves's errors just as Campbell had printed Graves's accusations of him for his readers.[17]

Campbell's assertion that the number of Baptists in Tennessee who sympathized with him was growing was at least partly true and surely one reason behind Graves's increased assaults on Campbell. Graves was becoming a leading spokesperson for Baptists and a major thought-shaper in defining Baptist identity. Losses to Campbell among Baptists as well as increased attacks from the Methodists in Tennessee pushed Graves to define the boundaries of the Baptist church as identical to the boundaries of the whole church. He held to Baptist successionism—that there was an unbroken chain of true (Baptist) churches since the days of the apostles, and that Baptist churches could not recognize baptisms performed outside the Baptist church as legitimate. Only Baptist churches were churches—all others were merely religious societies.

A group of Baptist leaders meeting at the Cotton Grove, Tennessee, Baptist Church on June 24, 1851, compiled and approved Graves's views into a set of resolutions. His colleague James Madison Pendleton published these principles in 1854 in a booklet titled *An Old Landmark Reset*, which gave Landmarkism its name.[18] Graves's militant advocacy for the Landmark position would actually alienate him from a significant number of Baptists who refused to take his radical position, a fact Campbell would later use against Graves.

Two months passed before the dispute with Graves appeared again. In the August *Millennial Harbinger*, in an article titled "Tracts for Tennessee Baptists. No. I," Campbell complained bitterly that while Graves had finally published his April article in which he defended his beliefs, Graves had written seven times the number of words in response and demanded that Campbell fulfill his promise to print it in the *Millennial Harbinger*. Campbell reminded Graves that he had promised to provide *equal* space, not print everything Graves might write. Still, he proceeded to give his readers Graves's

16. Alexander Campbell, "The Tennessee Baptist," *Millennial Harbinger*, May 1854, 280–81.

17. Patterson, *James Robinson Graves*, 72–73. Also see 75n49.

18. Joe Early Jr., "The Cotton Grove Resolutions," *Tennessee Baptist History*, Fall 2005, 41–52; Garrett, *Baptist Theology*, 212–48, chap. 6, "Baptist Landmarkism."

"massive columns of words and calumnies, interspersed . . . with a few corrections and expositions."[19]

Graves began by explaining that when he had first noticed Campbell's April article, it was so full of personal attacks against him and devoid of any substantive argument that he had simply filed it away. When he saw mention of it later in another journal and reread it, he was outraged at the "tirade of abuse and denunciation, and reckless assertions" that Campbell had made despite claiming never to have met him or known anything about him. Graves dismissed Campbell's assertion that Baptists did not support him; it was a tactic to distract from the *Tennessee Baptist*'s exposure of the "utter rottenness and deceptiveness of your system . . . ; the *great apostasy* of the nineteenth century."[20] Graves continued by explaining why he had been forced to oppose the work of the American Bible Union to produce a modern English immersionist translation. The Baptists who were leaders in the Union had declared Campbellism orthodox when in reality it was heretical in its teaching of baptism for the remission of sins.

Campbell then spent almost ten pages showing that his beliefs were the same as the beliefs and practices of ancient Christianity, which he insisted most of the contemporary Christian world agreed with. He closed by attacking Graves for distorting, caricaturing, and mystifying his teachings. Any Baptist who had read his *Christian System* or *Christian Baptism* carefully, he asserted, would not be convinced by Graves's "evangelical Vandalism."[21]

The September issue of the *Millennial Harbinger* included the second of Campbell's "tracts," a nineteen-page back-and-forth of acerbic accusations and labeling. Graves continued to use the *Tennessee Baptist* to try to stop Campbell's reformation, quoting Baptist theologian Alexander Carson against Campbell's views on baptism. Campbell made fun of Graves's inflated view of his impact on Baptist thought through the *Tennessee Baptist* and again defended his orthodoxy regarding baptism and regeneration.[22]

The third tract in October was more of the same. Graves attempted to refute Campbell's claim that respected Baptist leaders endorsed his theological positions as orthodox evangelicalism. "I cannot believe one 'jot' or 'tittle' of it," exclaimed Graves, saying that he could only attribute Campbell's claim to

19. Alexander Campbell, "Tracts for Tennessee Baptists. No. I," *Millennial Harbinger*, August 1854, 437.

20. Campbell, "Tracts for Tennessee Baptists. No. I," 438–39.

21. Campbell, "Tracts for Tennessee Baptists. No. I," 451.

22. Alexander Campbell, "Tracts for Tennessee Baptists. No. II," *Millennial Harbinger*, September 1854, 493–511.

"a treacherous or failing memory," though most Baptists would consider it an intentional fabrication. Campbell shot back that if Graves did not retract this accusation of lying, he would publish nothing else from Graves in the *Harbinger*. Furthermore, when the series of reviews of each other's articles was completed, he would have nothing more to do with Graves, unless it was in a public debate with a panel of judges.[23]

The next month Campbell began a new series titled "Letters to Tennessee Baptists." The first article consisted of a private letter written in 1853 to Graves by a Baptist sympathizer of Campbell's views, H. O. Smith. In it Smith chastised Graves for misrepresenting Campbell. Graves had refused to print it in the *Tennessee Baptist*, but apparently Smith had sent Campbell a copy of the original letter along with Graves's response.

Smith insisted that Graves had characterized Campbell inaccurately as being opposed to fundamental Baptist teachings. True, Campbell believed that all could hear and believe the gospel and that baptism was "the door through which we enter Christ's kingdom," but that was precisely what orthodox Baptists believed. Actually, this and similar teachings held by Baptists were precisely what Graves was trying to purge from Baptist belief in his Landmark campaign. In his reply, Graves responded to Smith, dismissing Campbellism as "an exploded dogma" that had run its course. Campbell printed both letters, commenting only that Graves's low and despicable sophistry deserved no reply. But he also revealed that he had come into possession of a couple of other exchanges between Smith and Graves that he would publish in the next issue.[24]

Later in the same issue Campbell accused Graves of retreating from the battlefield, acknowledging his defeat by refusing to print any of Campbell's recent articles against him. He promised his readers, however, that he would provide more statements from Tennessee Baptists attacking Graves's theology and conduct. These were anti-Landmark Baptists with whom Campbell was in fellowship.[25]

Interestingly, at the end of that issue, in a brief statement in small print, Campbell cryptically announced that he had some documents that, though he would not be wrong in publishing them, he had resolved to withhold for

23. Alexander Campbell, "Tracts for Tennessee Baptists. No. III," *Millennial Harbinger*, October 1854, 569.

24. Alexander Campbell, "Letters to Tennessee Baptists. No. I," *Millennial Harbinger*, November 1854, 616–23.

25. Alexander Campbell, "Mr. Graves' Retreat," *Millennial Harbinger*, November 1854, 649–51.

Title page of Graves's *Campbell and Campbellism Exposed: A Series of Replies*, 1854. Courtesy of James P. Boyce Centennial Library, The Southern Baptist Theological Seminary, Louisville, Kentucky.

the time being. He insinuated that some of his supporters had urged him to back off his harsh attacks, so he could not be accused of being like "vainglorious aspirants for notoriety." He also noted that urgent calls for him to visit Nashville and other places in Tennessee had led him to contemplate a visit there in November and December. The main reason for going to Nashville was to help stabilize the Nashville Christian Church that had suffered a major division after its minister, Jesse B. Ferguson, had embraced Universalism and spiritualism.[26] Yet Campbell's clash with Graves—who also lived in

26. Alexander Campbell, "A Contemplated Visit to Nashville" and "Deferred Docu-

Nashville—had pushed him to print some of the harshest, most rancorous, and overblown language of his writing career.

The warnings against becoming like the "vainglorious aspirants for notoriety" ultimately had little effect on Campbell. In the next month's issue he pulled out all the stops with another insulting description of Graves's "silence" as a de facto admission of defeat. He also published a second letter from H. O. Smith and Graves's response, a letter from Jacob Creath commending Campbell's stand against the *Tennessee Baptist* and endorsing his view of regeneration, a mocking report of the Duck River Baptist Association's endorsement of Graves and condemnation of Campbell, and a brief article on the term "regeneration." Clearly Campbell was taking this very personally, and despite his claims to wash his hands of the controversy, he could not do so.

In the February 1855 issue of the *Millennial Harbinger*, Campbell briefly noted that though he had received nothing from Graves for several weeks, he heard that Graves had censured H. O. Smith, apparently for giving Campbell his correspondence with Graves. Campbell printed a letter from Baptist minister J. H. High, who asserted that though the majority of Baptists in Tennessee might still hold "the old Baptist metaphysical theory of spiritual influences, regeneration, and the like," the most representative congregations in west Tennessee believed what Smith (and Campbell) did.[27]

As part of a report of his visit to Nashville, Campbell reported that several Baptists at Russellville, Kentucky, who were regular readers of the *Millennial Harbinger*, had apologized to him for Graves's conduct. Campbell stated that he could not regard Graves as a Christian, in contrast with these Baptist friends who were both truthful and honorable.[28]

In April, Campbell announced that in the next issue he would expose Graves's most recent assault on him, and after that would drop any further notice of him. He described Graves as "one of the best definitions of total depravity, in a living and formal development of the term" he had seen in his forty years of ministry. Even J. B. Jeter, toward whom Campbell had begun to turn his ire, would be ashamed to associate with Graves, Campbell said.

Even so, at the end of the promised "final" article that challenged

---

ments," *Millennial Harbinger*, November 1854, 660. See chapter 17 for a discussion of the clash with Jesse B. Ferguson.

27. Alexander Campbell, "Letter from a Tennessee Baptist," *Millennial Harbinger*, February 1855, 108–9.

28. Alexander Campbell, "Our Visit to Nashville," *Millennial Harbinger*, March 1855, 155.

Graves's representation of Alexander Carson's view of Campbell, he could not resist one more challenge. If Graves would allow both sides to be fully published in his paper, follow the rules of honorable discussion, and secure the endorsement of "three respectable Baptist brethren," Campbell would exchange articles with him "line for line and page for page" on any doctrinal issue in the Christian religion.[29]

A few notices of Graves continued to appear in the *Millennial Harbinger*. In September, Campbell's coeditor, W. K. Pendleton (not related to Graves's Landmarkist associate J. M. Pendleton), refuted a rumor that Campbell had died in New Orleans and reprinted a letter from the *Tennessee Baptist* defending Campbell, written by Dr. Samuel W. Lynd, then serving as moderator of the General Association of Baptists of Kentucky. In November and December Campbell noted some articles attacking him in other Baptist papers, but he dismissed them as people trying to ingratiate themselves to Graves, "a peace offering to the redoubtable Mr. Graves and his brother Pendleton!!"[30]

In 1860 Graves included an assault on Campbell's reform in a discussion of the teachings and practice of baptism. Campbell had never dreamed of the notion that baptism procured the remission of sins and regeneration of heart when he was immersed in 1812, Graves asserted. Since Campbell was now claiming that Baptist churches were false, "Mr. Campbell himself, being his own judge, was never scripturally baptized, nor were any of his first ministers or followers, and consequently since a pure stream cannot flow from an impure fountain, the Campbellites of this age are all unbaptized and without authority to baptize. . . . Therefore the whole denomination, being unbaptized, are no church of Christ in any sense."[31]

Campbell and the Clash with Jeremiah Bell Jeter

But by this time another prominent Baptist leader had mounted an attack on Campbell. Jeremiah Bell Jeter's *Campbellism Examined* appeared first in 1855, with a second printing in 1858, and in 1860 a ninety-four-page supplement titled *Campbellism Re-examined* was printed with the original text.

29. Alexander Campbell, "Misrepresentation of Mr. Carson by the Tennessee Baptist," *Millennial Harbinger*, May 1855, 269–74.

30. Alexander Campbell, "Letters to a Reformer, *Alias* Campbellite," *Millennial Harbinger*, November 1855, 614.

31. J. R. Graves, *The Trilemma; or, Death by Three Horns* (Nashville: Southwestern Publishing House, 1860), 195–96.

Jeter had served as minister of several Virginia Baptist churches, including First Baptist Church in Richmond, and after the Civil War would serve as coeditor of the *Religious Herald*, the Virginia Baptist paper.

In 1852 Jeter had published a sixty-page memoir of the life of respected Baptist leader Andrew Broaddus in a book of Broaddus's sermons and letters.[32] Jeter's memoir devoted considerable space to Broaddus's interactions with Alexander Campbell and the reformers, and Broaddus's eventual rejection of Campbell's views of "baptismal regeneration." According to Broaddus, Campbell's false doctrines included the sufficiency of intellectual assent to the facts of the gospel without supernatural action by the Holy Spirit, conversion and regeneration occurring in the act of baptism, and reception of the Holy Spirit only after baptism.[33]

Jeter's brief treatment of Campbell in the Broaddus memoir prompted a group of twelve Baptist leaders to petition him to write a more extensive treatment of the "the rise, progress, character, and influence of the sect of Christians called Disciples, or Campbellites."[34] *Campbellism Examined* was Jeter's response. Jeter first challenged Campbell's use of the terms "reformation" and "ancient gospel" for his movement, then defended his own use of "Campbellism" as the most accurate term for the false doctrine he intended to expose. He then examined the beginnings, development, teachings, and tendencies of Campbellism, with a summary conclusion.

Jeter stated that he first met Campbell in 1825 and since that time had carefully followed his writings and influence. He quoted Campbell's writings and sermons extensively to back up his evaluations.[35] While admitting that Campbell was an able editor and that his reform was not intended to form another sect, Jeter insisted that his attitude and peculiar doctrines clearly tended toward just that. Jeter examined Campbell's attacks on clergy and creeds and his insistence on the illegitimacy of extracongregational structures. All these things, Jeter insisted, hindered the spread of the gospel and the aid of those in need, and produced unrest among Baptist leaders. He then examined Campbell's derisive, sarcastic style that ridiculed religious experience and sacred ceremonies such as the ordination of ministers and missionaries.

---

32. *The Sermons and Other Writings of the Rev. Andrew Broaddus with a Memoir of His Life by J. B. Jeter, D.D.*, ed. A. Broaddus (New York: Lewis Colby, 1852).

33. *Sermons and Other Writings of the Rev. Andrew Broaddus*, 23–31.

34. Jeremiah B. Jeter, *Campbellism Examined* (New York: Sheldon, Lamport, & Blakeman, 1855), v.

35. See *Campbellism Examined*, where he cites the *Christian Baptist* and *The Christian System* extensively.

Jeremiah Bell Jeter (1802–1880) opposed J. R. Graves's Landmarkism, but joined him in his attacks on Campbell. Courtesy Southern
Baptist Historical Library and Archives, Nashville, Tennessee.

Jeter next explained why it was necessary to force the disruptive Campbellite reformers out for the sake of the ministry of the Baptist churches. The
combination of false teachings regarding the work of the Holy Spirit and the
nature of baptism and of the church, along with the conflict Campbell's doctrines stirred up, could only hinder the spread of the gospel and the Baptist
church. He gave a history of the separation of the Campbell reformers from
the Baptists using the Dover Baptist Association as a case study—a separation Jeter himself had helped facilitate.

In a section titled "Campbellism in Its Principles," Jeter began by commending Campbell for his commitment to the most important principles of
Christianity held in common with all Christians. Campbell's debate with Robert Owen, Jeter insisted, showed Campbell's consistent faith in the authenticity
and inspiration of Scripture and the "vital principles of Christianity." His debate
with Catholic bishop John Baptist Purcell further confirmed Campbell's adher-

ence to the "many truths held in common with all Protestants." And frankly, Jeter admitted, Campbell had been a champion of some key Baptist principles, especially believers' immersion and the importance of church membership.[36]

It was, however, Campbell's "scripturally unfounded" teachings that poisoned his reform movement and made him and his followers a dangerous and disruptive force. Jeter then identified the fatal errors of the Campbellites, starting with their teaching that the Holy Spirit had no direct role in conversion other than through the words of Scripture. Jeter continued with the charge that Campbell equated regeneration, conversion, and baptism, and then in succession listed other Campbellite falsehoods, including the contention that prayer is not a duty of the unbaptized and that communion should be celebrated weekly.

In the section "Campbellism in Its Discipline" Jeter examined what he believed was the faulty basis for Christian unity promoted by Campbell—a platform that would encourage such destructive heresies as Arianism, Unitarianism, and Universalism. Furthermore, Jeter accused Campbell of ridiculing those who held sound Trinitarian views and of hindering the spread of the gospel through opposition to associations, colleges, and an educated ministry. He concluded with a call for Campbell to apologize to the Christian world and to repudiate his "heterodox sentiments."

As soon as he got a copy of Jeter's book, Campbell began writing an extensive refutation. In the February 1855 *Millennial Harbinger*, Campbell quoted parts of Jeter's introduction and charged that Jeter was not qualified "by nature, by grace, or by education" to do what he claimed to be doing. Campbell recalled meeting Jeter in 1825 at a meeting of the Dover Baptist Association, where he had noticed in the young man a desire to attain "clerical distinction."[37]

Jeter was no follower of Landmarkism—he published articles critical of Graves's view of the church. Still, his critique of Campbell's teaching on conversion and baptism mirrored that of J. R. Graves.[38] Campbell's responses naturally argued the same things he had with Graves. Unlike in the responses to Graves, however, Campbell stated early on that he regarded Jeter to be a brother. He called him a friend and a "very estimable man," though unequal to the task of refuting Campbell.[39]

---

36. Jeter, *Campbellism Examined*, 114–15.

37. Alexander Campbell, "Campbellism Examined," *Millennial Harbinger*, February 1855, 61–75.

38. Patterson, *James Robinson Graves*, 78.

39. Campbell, "Campbellism Examined," 61–75.

Campbell challenged Jeter's view of the Holy Spirit's role in conversion, disputed the accusation that he taught baptismal regeneration, and attacked Jeter's views on religious experience and regeneration. Despite his earlier high estimation of Jeter, Campbell's articles increasingly accused Jeter of dishonesty toward and ignorance of his beliefs. Yet in October, in the final article of the series, Campbell confessed that he had not done a good job of dealing with Jeter's points. His many other responsibilities had distracted him, he grumbled, describing what he had written as disconnected and repetitious. Though Jeter's book was filled with perversions, misconceptions, and misrepresentations and had little merit of its own, so many Baptist clergy had endorsed it, he believed it deserved a book-length examination. So he proposed to suspend the series in the *Harbinger* for two or three months and write just such a book.[40]

Five months later, in the March 1856 issue of the *Millennial Harbinger*, Campbell repeated that he was preparing a formal response to Jeter and even published an introduction to the proposed book.[41] But the book never appeared. In June Campbell published a brief note complaining about his jam-packed schedule that included teaching six days a week, writing and editing articles for his paper, reading and responding to voluminous correspondence, as well as reading widely in the religious press. Jeter had published his follow-up book of ninety-four pages titled *Campbellism Re-examined* a few weeks earlier. Campbell admitted that he had not had time to read more than a couple of pages of it, since he had "more grave and important critical labors" to take care of. He asked his readers to have patience with him on the Jeter response.[42]

Finally, however, Campbell gave up. He announced in February 1857 that he had asked a young graduate of Bethany College, Moses E. Lard, to write a review of *Campbellism Examined*, to be published later that year in Philadelphia. Lard began his review with a disclaimer: clearly he could not do as good a job as Campbell would have had he not been overwhelmed by more important duties. There had been no urgency in writing the book, Lard explained, since Jeter's work had been out for two years and had caused no disruption whatsoever to the progress of the Disciples. In a brief introduction to Lard's volume, Campbell asserted that the reason Jeter had written

40. Alexander Campbell, "'Campbellism Examined'—No. IX," *Millennial Harbinger*, October 1855, 553-54.

41. Alexander Campbell, "Dr. Jeter's Campbellism," *Millennial Harbinger*, March 1856, 163-69.

42. Alexander Campbell, "A Response to One Hundred Questions," *Millennial Harbinger*, June 1856, 359.

Moses E. Lard (1818–1880) was an 1849 graduate of Bethany
College. Campbell asked him to write a refutation of J. B.
Jeter's 1855 *Campbellism Examined*. Lard's 1857 *Review of
J. B. Jeter's Book* took on the bitter sarcastic tone of Campbell's previous responses in the *Millennial Harbinger*. Used
with permission from the Disciples of Christ Historical Society, Bethany, West Virginia.

Campbellism Examined in the first place was his alarm at the large number of
Baptists who had dropped the requirement to relate a conversion experience
before baptism, baptizing people on a simple confession of faith in Jesus.[43]

Lard took his cue from Campbell for the tone of his work. He described
Jeter's book as "dull and haggled" in style, "its thoughts narrow, its arguments
absolutely nil, its reflections trite and shallow, its air vain and pretending, its
spirit dissembled and mean." Nevertheless, he continued, this examination

43. Moses E. Lard, *A Review of Rev. J. B. Jeter's Book Entitled "Campbellism Examined"*
(Philadelphia: J. B. Lippincott & Co., 1857), iv, v, x, 9.

was needed to give an accurate picture to the world of Campbell's beliefs instead of the garbled form in Jeter's book.[44] In the second and third chapters, Lard listed and refuted the arguments in *Campbellism Examined* regarding Campbell's view of the work of the Holy Spirit in conversion. Next he examined Jeter's attacks on Campbell's teaching on baptism, followed again by an exposition of what Campbell actually believed and a refutation of objections to these beliefs by Jeter. He ended the book by refuting charges of Arminianism and a growing Campbellite desire to be seen as orthodox, closing with the claim that Jeter's book was "bad without one compensating trait."

In 1860, J. R. Graves's Southwestern Publishing House issued the final piece in the Jeter-Campbell controversy. Missouri Baptist Alvin Peter Williams responded to Lard's *Review* in a book titled *Campbellism Exposed*. Williams continued the personal slurs in a tedious rehashing of the arguments seen throughout the interchange.[45]

The decade of the 1850s took a tremendous toll on Campbell. From 1853 to 1855 he experienced the most concerted assault on his beliefs by Baptists since the separation of the 1830s. In 1855 a crisis in the Nashville church over Jesse B. Ferguson's spiritualist and Universalist ideas and a major disturbance over slavery among the students at Bethany College increased the anxiety of the sixty-seven-year-old "bishop." Though he tried to ignore it, such events were eroding Campbell's hopeful expectation of the triumph of the ancient gospel and order of things.

44. Lard, *A Review of Rev. J. B. Jeter's Book*, 12–13.
45. Alvin Peter Williams, *Campbellism Exposed, in an Examination of Lard's Review of Jeter* (Nashville: Southwestern Publishing House, 1860).

CHAPTER 15

The Clash with Walter Scott

One of the most disturbing clashes of Campbell's career was with his close fellow laborer in the reformation, Walter Scott. After study at the University of Edinburgh, Scott arrived in New York to live with his uncle in 1818. After teaching for a few months, he moved to Pittsburgh and became part of a school and church led by George Forrester, a follower of Scottish Independents James and Robert Haldane. When Forrester drowned in 1820, Scott became leader of both the school and the church. The next year, however, he traveled back to New York to seek out Henry Errett, leader of a Scotch Baptist church who had published a pamphlet on baptism for the remission of sins. Though Errett's tract convinced him, Scott found the church to be narrow and stagnant and left New York sadly disappointed.[1]

Soon afterward, he accepted an offer from the father of Robert Richardson, one of his former students at Forrester's school, to return to Pittsburgh and become tutor to Robert and a few other boys. Richardson had studied under Thomas Campbell when he operated an academy in Pittsburgh in 1816, and the Campbells were frequent guests in the Richardson home. It was there in late 1821 that Scott and Alexander Campbell first met.[2] The two immediately formed a strong connection based on their shared commitment to religious reform.

Though Scott's biographer, William Baxter, portrayed this first meeting in positive terms, he hinted at an attitude that would become the centerpiece of the clash between Campbell and Scott. The two were surprised, Baxter explained, "to find that they occupied common ground, when each had here-

---

1. William Baxter, *Life of Elder Walter Scott* (Cincinnati: Bosworth, Chase & Hall, 1874), 53–54.
2. Baxter, *Life of Elder Walter Scott*, 64–68.

tofore regarded himself as almost alone in his views of the Christian religion and of the remedy for the divisions and party strifes by which the religious world was agitated."[3] In the years ahead, despite their intimate partnership in the formation and expansion of the Campbell reformation, each would seek to be known as the chief catalyst for the movement's success.

The heating up of the Campbell-Scott conflict was connected with Campbell's clash with John Thomas. In the May 1838 issue of the *Apostolic Advocate*, Thomas published two letters from Francis W. Emmons designed to show that Campbell's answer to the Lunenburg letter on "Christians in the sects" was inconsistent with his earlier statements advocating baptism for the remission of sins. In the letter, Emmons quoted Campbell as saying that the true meaning and design of baptism had first been proclaimed in America in 1823, presumably referring to Campbell's debate with William Maccalla. In a footnote, Emmons remarked that Walter Scott had claimed in his book *The Gospel Restored* that the true gospel had been restored in 1827, alluding to Scott's work as evangelist for the Mahoning Baptist Association.[4]

Emmons's insinuation that Scott and Campbell had contradicted each other provoked Scott to print a response. At first Scott appeared simply to refute any charge of contradiction, but his subsequent comments sparked open conflict with Campbell. To say that baptism for remission of sins was "in 1823 first promulgated in America," Scott explained, was not the same as saying that the gospel was restored then. "The restoration of the whole gospel in 1827, can never be confounded with the definition of a single one of its terms in 1823, or in any year preceding it." Scott acknowledged that even his arrangement of the terms of salvation in the proper order was still not the restoration of the gospel. The gospel was restored, he contended, when penitent believers were immersed "publicly and avowedly" into the church for the remission of sins and reception of the Holy Spirit.[5]

Campbell correctly understood that Scott was referring to the beginning of his practice of baptism explicitly for the remission of sins. This was the key element of Scott's "plan"—faith, repentance, baptism, remission of sins, the Holy Spirit, and eternal life. In both the preface and the note to the reader at the end of his 1836 book *The Gospel Restored*, Scott claimed that he had done precisely that in 1827. While Campbell had proposed the "ancient order" in

---

3. Baxter, *Life of Elder Walter Scott*, 64–65.

4. F. W. Emmons, "Brother F. W. Emmons on the Crisis," *Apostolic Advocate* 5 (May 1838): 22.

5. Walter Scott, "Brother Francis W. Emmons," *Evangelist* 6 (August 1, 1838): 180–81.

1823 in the debate with Maccalla, Scott had restored the "True Gospel" in 1827. Scott titled his book *The Gospel Restored* "because it contains the substance of those things, which were brought before the public in 1827, and which, at that time and since, have been recognized as a republication of the true Gospel of Jesus Christ."[6] Though defending Campbell against Emmons's criticism of his actions in the rebaptism controversy with John Thomas, he suggested that, regarding the date of the restoration, Campbell might have committed "an error of memory or of the feelings in which the heart is not even remotely engaged."[7]

Campbell reprinted most of Scott's article in October with a terse response. He started by saying that he would not give an opinion on Emmons's or Scott's account of his motivation for his statements on baptism, though it quickly became clear what he thought. Emmons's assertion was just one more attack on his statements in the Lunenburg letter articles. He agreed with Scott that Emmons's accusation that he and Scott had contradicted each other concerning the date of the "restoration of the ancient gospel" was false. He had never said it was restored in either 1823 or 1827. But then he turned his attention to Scott. To make the claim to have restored the gospel, he contended, was a serious matter. It would imply that the gospel had been lost, and even that the church had ceased to exist. In a clear swipe at Scott, he said that he was thankful he had never titled anything he wrote "Christianity Restored" or "Gospel Restored." (Twice in the article he explained that the words "Christianity Restored" on the spine of his 1835 book later known as *The Christian System* had been placed there by the publisher without his knowledge!)[8]

Campbell went on to say that although he had spoken often about restoring the ancient order of things to the church, talking about restoring the gospel was something else altogether. True, at one point he had referred to Scott's arranging and teaching parts of the gospel in the specific order he used on the Western Reserve in 1827 as the "Ancient Gospel," but he had never meant that to be understood as crediting Scott with restoring the gospel to existence. He and a host of others had been working at "restoring to the elect of God . . . the original order of things." But whether that had yet been accomplished he could not say.[9]

Campbell then took another shot at both John Thomas's followers and

6. Walter Scott, *The Gospel Restored* (Cincinnati: O. H. Donogh, 1836) v, 573.

7. Scott, *The Gospel Restored*, 181.

8. Alexander Campbell, "Events of 1823 and 1827," *Millennial Harbinger*, October 1838, 465–66, 471.

9. Campbell, "Events of 1823 and 1827," 467.

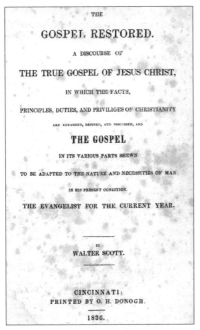

Walter Scott suspended publication of his monthly journal the *Evangelist* for 1836 to write and publish his masterpiece *The Gospel Restored.* Campbell would reprimand Scott for claiming to have restored the ancient gospel. Courtesy of the Center for Restoration Studies, Abilene Christian University, Abilene, Texas.

Despite the printer's inscribing the words "Christianity Restored" on the spine of the first edition of Campbell's *Christian System*, in the dispute with Walter Scott Campbell rejected the idea that Christianity had ceased to exist and that anyone in his movement had restored it. Photo courtesy of Mac Ice, Abilene, Texas.

Scott. If anyone wanted to fix a date and a place of the restoration of the gospel, it would be whenever and wherever "a penitent sinner made the apostolic confession of faith in order to [receive] immersion, and was immersed on that confession alone—not for any particular purpose, as the personal remission of sins; but for all the blessings of the Christian covenant."[10] That is exactly what he did when Matthias Luce immersed him in 1812.

He stated that he had first begun to understand the connection between baptism and remission of sins during his debate with William Walker in 1820.

10. Campbell, "Events of 1823 and 1827," 467. The apostolic confession was "Jesus is the Christ, the Son of God."

As he prepared for the October 1823 debate with William Maccalla, he and his father had discussed the teaching but told no one about their ideas until a few months before the debate, when Walter Scott visited them. In other words, Campbell implied that he was actually the one who had introduced Scott to baptism for the remission of sins. In his August article, Scott had dismissed the idea that Campbell had restored the ancient gospel during the Maccalla debate, since Campbell had stated the doctrine then merely to put down his opponent. Campbell bristled at that description and countered that he had taught baptism for remission as the truth, not to score points against Maccalla. His intent was to urge Baptist ministers to immerse penitent believers immediately for the remission of their sins.[11]

Campbell proceeded to give his version of what happened in 1827. He visited Scott, who was then running a school in Steubenville, Ohio, and urged him to join him at the annual meeting of the Mahoning Baptist Association, which was dominated by Campbell supporters. As things turned out, the association offered to support Scott as a traveling evangelist, which he accepted. That appointment gave Scott the platform to begin teaching and actually practicing baptism for remission of sins—the doctrine he had learned from Campbell four years earlier. Campbell also stated that Scott had begun to use a different baptismal formula than the one used by Baptists, baptizing in the name of the Father, Son, and Holy Spirit for the remission of sins and the gift of the Holy Spirit.[12]

Campbell then analyzed Scott's new baptismal confession, which included explicit use of "for the remission of sins" at the time of the immersion. This had been a matter of expediency that he was willing to go along with, Campbell explained, "not as a matter of authority, but to signify to the spectators the value of the institution." Yet Campbell implied that Scott's insistence on using the phrase every time he immersed someone had actually laid the basis for the crisis with John Thomas. Because some people mistakenly attached divine authority to Scott's new formula, those who had been baptized "on a simple profession of faith," like himself, were being forced to be reimmersed under the new formula "upon pain of their forfeiture of Christian standing and character." This practice Campbell regarded as a distortion of "the true meaning of baptism given in my debate."

Campbell then added two more arguments for why nothing that happened in 1823 or 1827 merited the designation of a restoration of the original

11. Campbell, "Events of 1823 and 1827," 468–69.
12. Campbell, "Events of 1823 and 1827," 469.

WALTER SCOTT   DR. ROBERT RICHARDSON

Two of Campbell's closest friends, Walter Scott and Robert Richardson, were also recipients of his deeply felt need to protect his reformation from anyone who might challenge it. Photo courtesy of Mac Ice, Abilene, Texas.

gospel. First, any penitent believer immersed in water in the name of the Father, Son, and Holy Spirit received remission of sins—as well as all the other blessings associated with baptism—whether the term "remission" was mentioned at the time of the baptism or not. Even if the person performing the baptism did not believe it was for the remission of sins, the penitent believer's faith in Christ was the key to baptism's effectiveness, not a formula or the intentions of the baptizer.[13] Campbell explained his ungracious language in the article as a response to the long-running and now acute propensity of some—clearly meaning Scott—to devalue the work of others and to give too much significance to certain past events.

Campbell closed with an admonition to stop trying to claim "comparative honors" but to be like his father, Thomas, who said, "If the Lord will graciously forgive all that I have done wrong in pleading his cause, I shall be perfectly content with the humblest place in his everlasting kingdom, and to unite with all my brethren in lauding that mysterious and overwhelming grace which condescended to save our sinful persons and accept such unworthy services at

13. Campbell, "Events of 1823 and 1827," 470–71.

our hands."[14] Campbell's sharp rebuke of Scott's statements did not suddenly appear from nowhere—resentment had been seething for some time and was made worse by the controversy with John Thomas. Scott had claimed through the years that he had restored the ancient gospel in his evangelistic work beginning in 1827, and some had granted the claim, much to Campbell's displeasure.

Scott replied at great length to Campbell's rebuke in the December issue of his journal the *Evangelist*. Rather than launch immediately into a rejoinder, however, he printed a short letter dated July 6, 1838, from John T. Johnson of Georgetown, Kentucky, longtime leader in the Campbell reform. Johnson gave a brief report of his recent evangelistic work, then asked Scott to give an account of how he had arrived at the arrangement of the "ancient gospel." Under the guise of answering Johnson, Scott responded to Campbell. He had intended to write Johnson about this privately, Scott began, since answering would involve focusing on his accomplishments when he ought to have been preaching the gospel and not becoming a historian. However, since his "true yoke-fellow brother Campbell" had chosen to speak about these events, he was happy now to put it all in print.[15]

Scott then printed seven letters that contained his answer to Johnson. He recounted his intimate association with both Thomas and Alexander Campbell from the earliest days of the reform and exclaimed that after all they had done, spoken, written, and suffered together "in the cause," surely no one would seek to drive a wedge between them. But, he continued, "bro. Alexander at least has decided upon a better way."[16]

He then examined each part of Campbell's article to point out distortions, omissions, contradictions, and factual errors and to give evidence for his having restored the ancient gospel in 1827. His first witness was none other than Thomas Campbell himself. He printed parts of an article he had published five years earlier in which he quoted Thomas Campbell as saying that "the *direct* exhibition and *practical* application of [the ancient gospel] as a whole, did not occur until 1827," when Scott first preached that believing penitents could respond immediately to the gospel by being immersed for the remission of sins.

In the fifth letter Scott quoted three additional witnesses who attested to his having restored the ancient gospel in 1827—evangelists Adamson Bentley

14. Campbell, "Events of 1823 and 1827," 471.
15. Walter Scott, "Letters on the Events of 1823 and 1827," *Evangelist*, December 1838, 266–67.
16. Scott, "Letters on the Events," 269.

and Aylette Raines, and Alexander Campbell himself! He quoted Campbell from the October 1831 *Millennial Harbinger*, that Scott had in the "Fall of 1827, arranged the several items of Faith, Repentance, Baptism, Remission of Sins, the Holy Spirit and Eternal Life, restored them in this order to the church under the title of *Ancient Gospel*, and successfully preached it for the conversion of the world."[17] But now, Scott pointed out, Campbell was claiming he never said the ancient gospel was restored in 1827 *or* 1823.

He labeled childish Campbell's statement that if anyone had restored the gospel to the English-speaking people, it had been John Wickliffe by translating the Scriptures. Furthermore, he sharply disputed Campbell's assertion that several parties, including evangelist Jeremiah Vardeman, the Christian movement preacher John Secrest, and even the Episcopal Church, could all rightfully claim they had known the true gospel apart from anything Scott ever said. None of these had called on hearers to arise and be immersed for the remission of sins before he had in 1827, Scott exclaimed. And besides, Wickliffe had not restored Scripture to the people anyway—his translation was not made available for centuries. As for Vardeman and Secrest, they had abandoned the movement and were not credible.

Scott then attacked Campbell's claim that every person he had baptized since 1823 had been baptized for the remission of sins. Several of those people had not understood it that way, Scott retorted, since they had been reimmersed for the remission of sins after 1827 when that teaching began to be clearly understood. Campbell's baptism on a simple apostolic confession of faith in Christ did not come up to what Scott had required penitents to do in 1827. He dismissed the claim that Secrest had baptized for remission of sins before Scott had by reporting that Secrest had actually come to Scott's home in Lisbon, Ohio, to learn the doctrine from him.[18]

In the seventh letter Scott accused Campbell of delaying publishing a notice by his father, Thomas, in 1827 detailing Scott's amazing success on the Western Reserve in baptizing for remission of sins. The younger Campbell was then preparing a series on the "ancient gospel" for the *Christian Baptist* and, instead of publishing his father's glowing report, waited until after he had published two of his own articles. Scott again gave his account of how he restored the ancient gospel in 1827. His unheard-of success, he stated, finally forced "my beloved Alexander Campbell" to describe him as "the ac-

17. Alexander Campbell, "Brother Walter Scott," *Millennial Harbinger*, October 1831, 480.

18. Scott, "Letters on the Events," 276.

tive agent of the most important revolutions and conversions in the present day, as far as has come to my ears."[19]

Thomas Campbell had written an extensive account of Scott's work that fully endorsed his preaching—which Alexander never published. Scott accused Alexander of failing to tell the real story of what happened in 1827. Campbell had described his success as the result of a "very great excitement" and Scott's "new formulary" as offering nothing new—Protestants already understood the purpose of baptism as for remission of sins and reception of the Holy Spirit.[20]

Scott charged that Campbell was trying to elevate his role by claiming credit for Scott's attending the Mahoning Association meeting that appointed him evangelist. Furthermore, Campbell claimed he had begun his series on Christian immersion titled "The Ancient Gospel" to protect the true meaning of baptism from excesses and innovations. Scott angrily challenged Campbell's claim, asserting that he had actually given the title to Campbell in his parlor in 1827, a fact Campbell had apparently forgotten. And it was actually Campbell who was guilty of "innovation" by his introduction of the unfortunate phrase "the gospel in water" for baptism, resulting in a mocking poem that now greeted "the Evangelist of the true gospel" (Scott) everywhere he went.[21]

Scott defended himself against other slights he perceived in Campbell's article, resisting any claim that Campbell had precedence in the doctrine of baptism for remission of sins. Scott did concede that Campbell had introduced what he had taught and practiced on the Western Reserve in the debate with Maccalla, but "it would be criminal to confound his deeds with mine, or mine with his."

To prove that both he and Campbell had been familiar with the doctrine of baptism for the remission of sins by at least 1821, he reprinted the tract

19. Scott, "Letters on the Events," 280; Scott was quoting Campbell's introduction to an article titled "The Beaver Anathema," *Christian Baptist* 7 (July 1830): 269.

20. In fact, many Protestants did connect baptism with the forgiveness of sins, though they did not practice immersion of believers. These included Anglicans, Methodists, and Lutherans, for example, though each with their own theological nuancing.

21. Alexander Campbell, "Ancient Gospel—No. II, Immersion," *Christian Baptist* 5 (February 1828): 158–61. The satirical poem "The Gospel in the Water" Scott mentioned appeared in a booklet titled *Alexander the Great; or, The Learned Camel*, published in 1830, http://digital2.library.pitt.edu/islandora/object/pitt%3A31735054851641/viewer#page/4/mode/2up. The author is identified as Methodist minister William Phillips in James B. Finley, *Sketches of Western Methodism: Biographical, Historical, and Miscellaneous Illustrative of Pioneer Life* (Cincinnati: Methodist Book Concern, 1854), 482–86.

by Henry Errett they each had received that year. He closed the lengthy article saying that while he deplored calling anyone's veracity into question needlessly or inappropriately, Thomas Campbell never said that the ancient gospel had been restored in 1823, contrary to Alexander's claim.[22]

Open hostility between Scott and Campbell diminished the next year, though it clearly continued to seethe. In the only major print confrontation, Scott published a biting critique of Campbell's articles on "our name" that advocated "Disciples of Christ" to designate the movement. In his refutation of Campbell's reasons, Scott insinuated that Campbell was using the term as a sectarian denominator.[23]

Later in the same issue Scott ridiculed Campbell's argument that "Christian" was not based on the Savior's actual name but on his title "anointed one." If they were going to use his actual name as a label, Campbell had reasoned, it would have to be "Jesuit." Since that was already taken, the only real alternative was "Disciples of Christ." Scott retorted that "Christ" *had* actually become part of the Savior's name, and that the real alternatives were "Christians" or "Campbellites." That was really what Campbell was pushing for, Scott asserted, under the title Disciples of Christ. Scott charged that Campbell, based on his faulty reasoning, would even prefer "Jesuit" to "Christian"—the name for which untold numbers had suffered persecution through the ages.[24]

By this time, many church leaders believed the feud had gotten completely out of hand. In December 1839, a group of elders in Cincinnati arranged a reconciliation meeting between Scott and Campbell. Little is known of the specifics of the meeting, except that brief letters from the two protagonists dated December 2, 1839, appeared (oddly enough) in the November issue of Scott's paper the *Evangelist*.[25] He introduced the letters at the end of his third article on "the name." He gave a brief report of the meeting and promised that nothing like what he had published against Campbell in the October articles would ever again appear in the pages of the *Evangelist*.

In his letter Scott stated that he sincerely regretted what he had published about Campbell in the long December 1838 article. The material had put them both in a bad light and hindered the cause they had cooperated in

22. Scott, "Letters on the Events," 288.

23. Walter Scott, "Our Name, No. 1," *Evangelist* 7 (October 1839): 219.

24. Walter Scott, "From the Millennial Harbinger. Our Name," *Evangelist* 7 (October 1839): 230–33.

25. "Letters from Brother Campbell and Brother Scott," *Evangelist* 7 (November 1839): 259.

for so long. He closed with a pledge that it would not happen again. In his letter, Campbell stated that he still could not call anything he or Scott did in 1823 or 1827 a "restoration of the gospel of Christ." Nevertheless, he conceded that Scott had carried out more fully and successfully than anyone before him the principles Campbell first published in the *Christian Baptist* and in his debate with Maccalla, and had therefore "eminently advanced the cause of reformation."[26]

Immediately following Scott's account of the reconciliation meeting and the text of the letters, he published a letter from Barton Stone that was extremely critical of Campbell's advocacy of the name Disciples of Christ. Stone exclaimed that though Campbell could choose whatever name he wanted for himself, "we deny his right to choose a name for us, and call it 'Our Name;' because we have not chosen him as our dictator nor leader." Stone then examined Campbell's reasons for advocating "Disciples," refuting each one as Scott had done the previous October. Stone was especially offended by Campbell's rejection of the label "Christian" because Unitarians in the Northeast used it—people with whom Stone was in full fellowship.[27]

For several months Campbell said nothing in the *Millennial Harbinger* about the reconciliation meeting and letters. Instead he published two brief articles that Scott would take to be attacks on him. At the end of the November 1839 issue of the *Evangelist*, in which the news of the reconciliation had appeared, Scott published a brief call for increased subscriptions to his journal. While he had never been in favor of a large number of periodicals in the movement, he confessed, he had become convinced that "a plurality of periodicals is absolutely indispensible."[28] This seemingly innocuous statement would anger Campbell and prompt a harsh response, effectively nullifying the supposed reconciliation.

Campbell began his counterattack with two articles in the February *Millennial Harbinger*. In "Embryo Heresy" Campbell told the story of the large, prosperous church at ancient Palmyra. A group of members had appealed to the younger bishop against the older one rather than addressing the older directly with their grievances. The younger became the representative of the disaffected and eventually made an open break that divided and ruined the Palmyra church and all the churches in the region.

In "Heretical Periodicals," Campbell asserted that in the past there had

---

26. "Letters from Brother Campbell and Brother Scott," 259.

27. Barton W. Stone, "Letters," *Evangelist* 7 (November 1839): 259–62.

28. Walter Scott, "Improvement of the Evangelist," *Evangelist* 7 (November 1839): 264.

been, with one exception, perfect harmony between those working in the reformation—even among the "numerous periodicals that have from time to time risen up to assist us." In a clear reference to Scott's remarks, Campbell said that some had justified a "plurality of periodicals" because of the need for an opposition voice. If anyone had a grievance against him, Campbell declared, the person should send it to him and he would publish it. If anyone published a grievance against him in a rival publication, however, he would regard the person as disorderly, "a *heresy-maker* in fact, if not in intention." As long as he held a pen, "the brethren will never need a second periodical to oppose me: they shall have mine. Therefore, I will neither hear nor notice them in any other."[29] The implication was that he would ignore any further articles in Scott's paper that were critical of him.

The following April, Scott responded. The fact that Campbell had placed his remarks under the caption "Heretical Periodicals" was, at best, unkind, at worst, bearing false witness against him and breaking their recently made pledges of peace. Just as frustrating was Campbell's statement that until recently there had generally been perfect harmony among those working for the reformation, including among the many periodicals that had arisen "to assist us in this grandest and noblest of enterprizes."[30] The *Evangelist* had not been started to assist Campbell, Scott snapped; its purpose was to help the Lord and the truth, and to publish the doctrine of the apostles, not as Campbell saw it but as he understood it.

He then explained that the reconciliation letter he wrote in December expressing regret for publishing what he did about Campbell was never intended to deny the truth of his restoration of the ancient gospel in 1827. He was sorry that he had published what he did, but it had been necessary to correct inaccuracies published by Campbell. As for Campbell's letter repeating the denial that anyone had restored anything in either 1823 or 1827, he had published it as a concession to Campbell and would make no further comment about it.

Then Scott brought up an anonymous article published in the December 1839 *Millennial Harbinger* that many had seen as intentionally designed to malign him.[31] The author, identified only as D.A., was later identified as a man living near Bethany and doing business with Campbell. The article was

29. Alexander Campbell, "Heretical Periodicals," *Millennial Harbinger*, February 1840, 69–70.

30. Campbell, "Heretical Periodicals," 69.

31. Walter Scott, "Unity of Spirit. Explanations and Corrections," *Evangelist* 8 (April 1840): 79–81.

one of the many Campbell published that discussed the best name for the movement. The offending section described a person who,

> desiring to have the preeminence, and preferring the praise of men to the praise of God, seeks every opportunity to plume himself with the well-earned reputation of his brother. . . . Presuming upon the nearness of the relation, he seeks every occasion to jeer, insult, and abuse him, supposing that, as a matter of course, it must all be taken on good part. And while under the hood of brotherly affection he hides the two faces of jealousy and pride, he thinks that under a disguise so amiable he is free to follow his inclinations. Does such a one as this deserve to be called Christian in the modern sense of that word? And I am surprised that such a one should wish to have this title adopted.[32]

Since the conflict between Scott and Campbell had been fully aired in the pages of their respective papers, the conclusion seemed inescapable to many that D.A. was describing Scott. When Scott protested, Campbell replied that the article had been put in the paper while he was away and had been written before the reconciliation meeting, so he had nothing more to say about it. He refused to reveal the name of the author, despite Scott's pressure.[33]

Four months after the fact, Campbell finally acknowledged the "reconciliation" meeting. He introduced the event with the statement that even people with good intentions could attach more importance to their accomplishments than was warranted, then censure anyone who did not give them the credit they wanted. Nevertheless, he deeply desired to restore the harmony that had existed between him and Scott in the past. He then reprinted Scott's description of the meeting along with the two brief letters.[34]

At that very moment, Scott's critique of Campbell's "false testimony" about him in the heretical periodicals article was going into print. Each accused the other of violating the peace—though with condescending caveats that they might be wrong in their evaluations of the other's words and motives. Throughout 1840, Campbell and Scott continued to fight. Campbell accused Scott of false accusations against him, of publishing material about him that was unchristian, of breaking the peace he had pledged himself to

32. D.A., "Our Name," *Millennial Harbinger*, December 1839, 556–57.

33. Alexander Campbell, "The Evangelist," *Millennial Harbinger*, June 1840, 286.

34. Alexander Campbell, "Extracts from the Evangelist," *Millennial Harbinger*, April 1849, 187–88.

maintain, and of flagrantly violating Christian courtesy and decorum.[35] Scott countered that Campbell desired the preeminence, always depicting him and every other leader in the reform as having come to Campbell's assistance. Furthermore, he accused Campbell of totally misunderstanding the nature of his "peace" letter. All he said, Scott insisted, was that he would no longer point out Campbell's desire for preeminence; he never pledged not to defend himself against Campbell's slurs. Describing the article by D.A., Scott said "a more flagrant injustice and wickedness has not been done any individual in this reformation since it commenced."[36]

Campbell's response in September summarily dismissed Scott's accusation that the anonymous article was about him. The article never mentioned Scott, and Scott never asked whether he was the one being described—he just assumed it. He should have asked, and if Campbell and the author had said no, that would have been the end of it. But even if they had said yes, the question would then be, was it deserved?

Campbell then stated that this was the end of his involvement in the dispute. It had been carried out in an unscriptural and unchristian way in the tribunal of the papers—a tribunal he did not recognize. Therefore, he would present to the Bethany Church of Christ, of which he was a member, all the documents and let them examine the case. Scott was invited to be present to sustain his accusations and bring proof.[37]

Scott immediately rejected the notion that the church at Bethany had any jurisdiction over him and listed again his chief grievances against Campbell. Yet the tenor of the article seemed conciliatory in comparison to those over the past three years. He ended it saying that it was his duty to lay aside all anger, to be meek and unresisting, humble and holy, as well as to love all his fellow Christians and always seek their good. However much Campbell may have wounded him, he said, "I forgive it all, and I can forget it all, thanks be to God; and, I trust, that he, like the Evangelist, longs and pants after the perfection of his nature, after a divine and heavenly character."[38]

Campbell's final notice of the controversy was a brief mention the following month that many friends had advised him to stop publishing on "the name" and to stop responding to material about him in the *Evangelist*. As for

---

35. Campbell, "The Evangelist," *Millennial Harbinger*, June 1840, 286.

36. Walter Scott, "The Harbinger," *Evangelist* 8 (July 1840): 157–61.

37. Alexander Campbell, "The Evangelist," *Millennial Harbinger*, September 1840, 415–19.

38. Walter Scott, "The Harbinger," *Evangelist* 8 (September 1840): 201–3.

One of the many likenesses of Campbell based on the painting by
New York portrait painter James Bogle, circa 1850. Used with permission from Bethany College, T. W. Phillips Memorial Library, Archives
and Special Collections, Bethany, West Virginia.

responding to Scott, Campbell said, that was already decided—he would say
no more.[39] In November, Scott responded by saying that since everything he
had written in the dispute had been in response to the *Millennial Harbinger*,
he would follow suit "The question of our personal differences may, therefore, be considered as dismissed from our pages."[40]

39. Alexander Campbell, "Our Course," *Millennial Harbinger*, October 1840, 474.
40. Walter Scott, "Our Course," *Evangelist* 8 (November 1840): 241.

Personal contact between Campbell and Scott was minimal over the next years. Campbell published the prospectus for Scott's paper in the June 1842 *Millennial Harbinger,* as Scott tried unsuccessfully to increase his subscription base.[41] Scott was present at a general cooperation meeting in September 1842 at Bethany representing the church at Smithfield, Ohio, at which Alexander Campbell was also present.[42] In the preface to the 1843 volume of the *Millennial Harbinger,* Campbell gave a brief overview of the beginning and advance of the reformation in which he seemed at times conciliatory toward Scott. Yet he assigned responsibility for the schism with the Baptist associations to the "great excitement" fueled by Scott's "fervid spirit and glowing eloquence" and again described both Scott and Barton Stone as having joined the work he was already doing.[43]

Over the next few years Campbell occasionally took notice of Scott in his writings. He criticized Scott for his millennial views that reflected those of William Miller in the early 1840s. In 1844 he disputed Scott's statement that Mormonism had gotten its doctrine of immersion for remission of sins from him by way of Sidney Rigdon. He printed the prospectus of Scott's new paper, the *Protestant Unionist,* in October 1844 and January 1848.[44] When Campbell published stories of the early history of the movement in 1848 and 1849, he recounted the story of having convinced Scott to attend the 1827 Mahoning Baptist Association meeting where Scott was appointed traveling evangelist. When Scott took the field, Campbell explained, they had both already agreed to preach immediate immersion for remission of sins to inquirers. But now with Scott actually in the field, it was like a "new revelation" to him. Scott's amazing success likely included, Campbell continued, "too great warmth of a lawful enthusiasm and the eccentricities of a fervent zeal" but much less than in other revivals.[45]

41. Scott continued publishing the *Evangelist* (renamed *Carthage Evangelist* in 1843 since he was living in Carthage, Ohio) through March 1844. It may be that his reputation had suffered in the dispute with Campbell and led to decreased subscriptions. He ceased publication and moved to Allegheny City, Pennsylvania, in April 1844.

42. "General Meeting," *Millennial Harbinger,* December 1842, 570.

43. Alexander Campbell, "Preface," *Millennial Harbinger,* January 1843, 4–7.

44. One historian surmised that Scott's shift to include all of evangelical Protestantism was partly due to his disappointment at having been marginalized by some in the movement. David Edwin Harrell Jr., "Protestant Unionist, The," in *The Encyclopedia of the Stone-Campbell Movement,* ed. Douglas A. Foster et al. (Grand Rapids: Eerdmans, 2004), s.v.

45. Alexander Campbell, "Anecdotes, Incidents, and Facts, Connected with the History of the Current Reformation, Never Before Published—No. VI," *Millennial Harbinger,* January 1849, 46–48.

News of the bitter fight between Campbell and Scott even spilled over into publications of other religious groups. In 1848, J. L. Waller, editor of the Frankfort, Kentucky, *Western Baptist Review,* was engaged in a written discussion with John T. Johnson, an evangelist in the Campbell reform. In one of his letters to Johnson, Waller claimed that "If Mr. Campbell had not come, your party had never been." Scott saw it and responded in a blistering article against Waller published in his new paper, the *Protestant Unionist.* He accused Waller of "consummate ignorance" of the history of the movement. First, it was not the coming of any man but the practical application of a great truth that brought the movement into existence. And furthermore, Campbell was not the one who had been the first to introduce the practice or to move it forward. Scott himself had restored "the original advocacy of the gospel." He had acted the part of Peter, Campbell of Paul. Leaving his work out of the history of the reform would be like deliberately leaving Peter out of the book of Acts.

Waller had a heyday with Scott's article, seizing on the friction between Scott and Campbell. Expanding the Peter and Paul analogy, Waller ridiculed Scott, saying that he had been fully aware of Scott's "pretensions to the authorship of the reformation. We have read full many a weary line of his insipid twaddle on this very subject, until we have become thoroughly disgusted with his inflated egotism and self-conceit." Campbell was the one who was the "sun" of the reformation, Waller stated; "Scott a mere subordinate planet." Waller gleefully fueled the dispute, and his complimentary statements about Campbell's intellect and abilities were designed to back up his charge that the movement was a product of Campbell's peculiar ideas rather than orthodox Christian belief—justifying the label Campbellism.[46]

Indications of better relations between the two began to appear in 1849. Campbell had been in Scott's home in Pittsburgh not long before Scott's wife died in April of that year, and he published a kind and sympathetic obituary of her in May. Both men were active in the American Christian Missionary Society from its beginning in October (though Campbell was not present at the founding meeting) and were often together at annual meetings. In August 1851, the two by chance found themselves traveling together in Ohio and, according to Campbell's report, spent several pleasant days together. By 1853 Campbell was calling Scott "one of the best living preachers that I know," and the next year he strongly endorsed Scott's work at the Covington, Kentucky, Female Institute, describing his "genius, learning and piety

---

46. J. L. Waller, "Walter Scott, of the 'Protestant Unionist,'" *Western Baptist Review* 3 (March 1848): 272–75.

... eloquence in the pulpit, and ... admirable talent for communicating instruction" as admired by all who knew him.

The events of the 1850s that divided the nation and moved it toward civil war clearly had a massive impact on the attitudes of both men. As the decade advanced, they seemed less inclined to insist on their preeminence in the reformation and more inclined toward reconciliation. Increasingly when others wrote about or referred to the history of the reform, they regarded both as "founders" of the movement.[47]

Campbell's personal despair over the outbreak of the Civil War was compounded by the news in 1861 that Scott had died on April 23, eleven days after the attack on federal forces at Fort Sumter, South Carolina. He was devastated. The sharp, sometimes condescending tone toward Scott so common in their long and bitter conflict was gone.

> No death in my horizon, out of my own family, came more unexpectedly or more ungratefully to my ears than this of our much beloved and highly appreciated Walter Scott; and none awoke more tender sympathies and regrets. Next to my father, he was my most cordial and indefatigable fellow laborer in the origin and progress of the present reformation. . . . He had his moods and tenses, as men of genius generally have. . . . He was, in his palmiest days, a powerful and successful advocate of the Lord Messiah on the heart and life of everyone who had recognized his person and mission. . . . I knew him well. I knew him long, I loved him much. We might not, indeed, agree on every opinion nor in every point of expediency. But we never loved each other less. . . . By the eye of faith and the eye of hope, methinks I see him in Abraham's bosom.[48]

Campbell's first biographer, Robert Richardson, alluded to the conflict with Scott several times in his *Memoirs of Alexander Campbell*. Richardson, however, minimized the fight's significance, mentioning it specifically only once when he explained that Scott had given in to "a tendency, for a time,

47. For example, an obituary published after the death of both Campbell and Scott stated, "In the days when Alexander Campbell and Walter Scott, the Paul and Apollos of the 19th century, preached the 'ancient gospel and order of things' in the grand valley of the Mahoning, her home was their home. . . . In her religious history the names of Campbell and Scott were inseparably connected." F. M. Green, "Obituary of Mrs. E. Sackett," *Millennial Harbinger*, September 1869, 539.

48. Alexander Campbell, "Elder Walter Scott's Demise," *Millennial Harbinger*, May 1861, 296–97.

to exalt beyond measure the importance of the practical restoration of the design of baptism and to claim that this was in reality the restoration of the gospel." Campbell, with his "more enlarged views," Richardson continued, could not accept such a claim for Scott's work or any other specific event in the reform. Campbell had corrected the errors and eccentricities, apparently of Scott, through his series "Letters of Epaphras" so that the success of the reformation was not compromised.[49]

Richardson gave no other overt indication of the clash. He praised Scott as the one who had made the doctrine of immersion for the remission of sins a chief point of the reform. Interestingly, the second volume of Richardson's *Memoirs of Alexander Campbell*, published in 1870, carried a plate in the front with Scott's likeness and the caption in Scott's handwriting, "The Lord bless your labours." This same plate appeared in the front of Scott's biography in 1874.

Scott's biographer William Baxter was even less clear about the conflict. Like Richardson, he emphasized the close collaboration of Campbell and Scott and even seemed to imply Campbell's preeminent position in originating the reform. Yet he pointed out that while Campbell's early thrust was to attack "partyism," it was Scott who had realized and remedied the flawed presentation of the gospel prevalent among professed Christians.[50] He compared Campbell's intellectual preaching style with Scott's more emotional tone and mentioned briefly their difference over the name for the movement, but with no hint of the larger acrimonious controversy. Baxter's last description of the relationship was couched in the story of a trip Scott made to Bethany in 1855.

> In the last week of 1855, he paid a visit to Bethany, and his spirit was greatly refreshed. He says he was received with the greatest cordiality and hospitality, and that it would have been impossible for any one to have showed him greater kindness than was manifested by Mr. Campbell and family. He remained there several days, and delivered several addresses to the students at the college. Mr. Campbell and himself had been engaged in an earnest effort to restore primitive Christianity since their early manhood, but now Mr. Scott was about three-score, and his fellow-laborer verging upon three-score and ten; together they had borne the heat and burden of the day; they both felt that the evening was at hand and their work nearly done; but when

49. Richardson, *Memoirs of Alexander Campbell*, 2:442–43.
50. Baxter, *Life of Elder Walter Scott*, 15–16.

they looked at the mighty results which had grown out of their united and untiring labors, they could not but be grateful to him who had made their lives and labors such a blessing to their race.[51]

The effect of the two biographies was to obscure the significant clash that occurred between these key leaders.

Whatever we make of this incident in Campbell's career, it reflects several recurring patterns. First was Campbell's desire to protect his reputation as the one who started and was responsible for the reform movement. Second, the clash brought Campbell's egotism to the forefront in a strong way. Many insiders feared the fight would disrupt the progress of the reformation. Unlike John Thomas or Jesse B. Ferguson, however, Scott did not defect. Neither did he distance himself from Campbell, as would Barton W. Stone. As the two intimate colleagues lost their youthful enthusiasm and ego in the 1850s, the clash faded, and later members of the movement generally knew nothing about it. Yet with different actors and different issues, their spiritual heirs would reenact such conflicts many times during the next two centuries.

51. Baxter, *Life of Elder Walter Scott*, 421–22.

CHAPTER 16

Alexander Campbell
and Barton W. Stone

The person usually seen as Campbell's most important ally in the reformation—along with his father, Thomas, and Walter Scott—is Barton W. Stone. The global tradition that has grown from his nineteenth-century efforts has even become known in scholarly work as the Stone-Campbell Movement. In reality, however, Alexander Campbell's relationship with Barton Stone was always uneasy at best, and at worst represented a persistent battle for the heart and mind of the movement.

Stone and a group of fellow Presbyterian ministers began a religious reform in Kentucky at the beginning of the nineteenth century, several years before Alexander Campbell's arrival in America in 1809. Yet Stone's opposition to "human" creeds and confessions, his dogged commitment to simple Christianity ruled by Scripture alone, and his passion for the visible unity of the church produced a strong affinity with Campbell and his reform.

Stone entered David Caldwell's academy in Guilford County, North Carolina, in 1790 to study law. The following year the preaching of Presbyterian revivalist James McGready convicted him of his sinful state. In keeping with Calvinist theology, the sensitive Stone agonized for months over whether or not he was among the elect—those chosen by God for salvation. His excruciating uncertainty actually made him sick. Several weeks later, however, a sermon by another New Light Presbyterian minister, William Hodge, on the theme "God is love," gave Stone hope. Still uncertain of his salvation, he went into the nearby woods alone to pray and study Scripture. That night he accepted God's love and salvation. He changed his studies to become a minister and continued his education until 1793. After teaching in a Methodist academy in Washington, Georgia, he returned to North Carolina in 1796, where the Orange Presbytery licensed him to preach. The following year he

The reform of Barton W. Stone (1772–1844) preceded that of the Campbells. Like theirs, his reformation focused on Christian unity and Scripture alone as authority in religion. Campbell generally distanced himself from Stone because he did not want his reformation to be confused with the Stoneites. Used with permission from the Disciples of Christ Historical Society, Bethany, West Virginia.

moved west to become the minister of two rural Presbyterian churches near Paris, Kentucky—Cane Ridge and Concord.[1]

Despite his growing doubts about several key Presbyterian doctrines, including the Trinity, predestination, and the use of formal confessions of faith, he was ordained to the ministry by the Presbytery of Transylvania in

1. *The Biography of Eld. Barton Warren Stone, Written by Himself, with Additions and Reflections by Elder John Rogers* (Cincinnati: J. A. and U. P. James, 1847), 6–30.

October 1798. He was increasingly frustrated, however, with what he saw as oppressive Calvinist theology about God, human nature, and salvation. This "old light" attitude, he believed, was partly responsible for the lack of vital faith in his own congregations and in society generally.

In 1801 he began to hear amazing stories about large numbers of conversions happening under the preaching of James McGready in northern middle Tennessee. He determined to travel the roughly two hundred miles to see what was happening. There he witnessed powerful preaching designed to prepare church members to celebrate the Lord's Supper, a practice with long precedent among Presbyterians.[2] The preaching was triggering emotional religious "exercises" that converted and transformed hearers into devoted Christians. Though this was a strange and new experience for Stone, he became convinced that it was a work of God to revitalize the church, and he returned to his congregations determined to bring revival to them as well.[3]

As in the Great Awakening decades before, this revival provoked charges of heresy from strict Calvinists. Revivalists seemed to imply that anyone could respond to the gospel—not just the "elect." Stone began planning for a sacramental meeting like the one he had seen a few weeks earlier for the first week of August at Cane Ridge. By all accounts, several thousand gathered and experienced the same emotional fervor seen in McGready's meetings and other sacramental meetings that summer. Hundreds were converted, and Stone challenged the divisions between Presbyterians, Methodists, and Baptists, advocating a unity of all Christians as part of the great work of God then happening.[4]

The Cane Ridge meeting provoked a response by Kentucky Presbyterian leadership, most of whom were "Old Lights" opposed to the revivals. Over the next two years, Stone and his revivalist colleagues found themselves increasingly at odds with orthodox Presbyterianism. At the September 1803 meeting of the Synod of Kentucky, Stone and four other ministers withdrew and formed their own Springfield Presbytery. Within a year, however, they had killed the new body with what is now considered the first founding document of the Stone-Campbell Movement: "The Last Will and Testament of Springfield Presbytery."[5]

2. See, for example, Leigh Eric Schmidt, *Holy Fairs: Scottish Communions and American Revivals in the Early Modern Period* (Princeton: Princeton University Press, 1989).

3. *The Biography of Eld. Barton Warren Stone*, 34–42.

4. D. Newell Williams, *Barton Stone: A Spiritual Biography* (St. Louis: Chalice, 2000), 55–63.

5. *The Biography of Eld. Barton Warren Stone*, 44–55. Springfield was near Cincinnati and is now named Springdale.

The document willed that all the members and churches of the former Springfield Presbytery "sink into union with the body of Christ at large." It proclaimed that they would no longer acknowledge divisions between Christians, would oppose all church structures and rules not clearly taught in the New Testament, and would insist on the right of each local congregation to choose and examine its minister. The document then called for Christians to unite as a necessary prerequisite for the conversion of the world and the coming of the millennium. By design it had no detailed doctrinal statements; it merely affirmed an absolute commitment to Scripture alone and to the unity of Christ's church, free from all unscriptural coercive powers.[6]

Adopting the name Christian, Stone's reform appealed to people who wanted relief from the anxiety produced by Calvinist teaching about salvation. The movement grew and spread, though not without setbacks. Two of the original five ministers returned to Presbyterianism out of frustration with the new movement's lack of doctrinal and structural precision. Two others became leaders in another radical movement—the Shakers. Only Stone was left, and he became the recognized leader of the "western Christians." Stone's movement immediately connected with other "Christian" groups in the East led by James O'Kelly and in New England led by Elias Smith and Abner Jones.[7]

Stone's misgivings about several traditional theological beliefs had begun early and can be seen in his rejection at his ordination of the confession's statement on the doctrine of the Trinity. He believed that Scripture was plain and accessible and that doctrines not explicitly taught in the New Testament or that in his view contradicted biblical teaching could not be true. False leaders desiring to control Christians had invented them. Soon after dissolving the Springfield Presbytery, Stone began expressing doctrinal positions that Alexander Campbell would regard as dangerous and a barrier to any union of the two reform movements.

Stone expressed the first of these beliefs in his 1805 booklet, *Atonement: The Substance of Two Letters Written to a Friend*. In his autobiography Stone recounted being "embarrassed" at the orthodox doctrine of substitutionary atonement. He regarded the idea that Christ died to reconcile sinful humans

6. Full text of the "Last Will and Testament of Springfield Presbytery" is available at https://webfiles.acu.edu/departments/Library/HR/restmov_nov11/www.mun.ca/rels /restmov/texts/jmathes/webws/WEBWS02.HTM.

7. Williams, *Barton Stone*, 121–37; William Garrett West, *Barton Warren Stone: Early American Advocate of Christian Unity* (Nashville: Disciples of Christ Historical Society, 1954), 176–88.

to an offended God as absurd. God sent Christ out of pure love for humanity, not out of wounded pride or anger. If Christ's death substituted for the spiritual death of sinful humans, either all humans would be saved or Christ did not die for everyone. Scripture opposed the Universalist teaching that all would be saved, he insisted, and Scripture clearly taught that Christ died for all (2 Cor 5:14–15). Therefore he rejected substitutionary atonement. Stone believed that Christ's work on the cross changed humans, not God. The news of God's love shown in the life, death, and resurrection of Christ would capture and draw hearers to accept the free gift of salvation. His view was in essence the classical moral theory of the atonement.[8]

The second major "problem" in Stone's theology, related to the first, was his view of God. Stone came to reject vigorously and consistently the orthodox doctrine of the Trinity; he believed it was unscriptural, absurd, and divisive. He insisted that there was one eternal God; that Jesus was the eternal God's only begotten Son who possessed the fullness of the Godhead when he came in flesh; and that the Holy Spirit was simply the spirit of the eternal God—not a separate person.[9] These unorthodox views remained a major barrier to Campbell's full embrace of Stone and his movement, despite the numerous shared commitments and the union of many of the congregations of the two movements beginning in the 1830s.

In his autobiography, written shortly before he died in 1844, Stone recalled his first meeting with Campbell near Stone's home in Georgetown, Kentucky, in 1824. Stone, who was almost seventeen years older than Campbell, had led a Christian reform movement in that region for over twenty years. Yet he recalled being impressed with the younger Campbell and, despite significant doctrinal differences, would come to describe him as his most capable fellow reformer.

> When he came into Kentucky, I heard him often in public and in private. I was pleased with his manner and matter. I saw no distinctive feature between the doctrine he preached and that which we had preached for many years, except on baptism for remission of sins. Even this I had once received and taught, as before stated, but had strangely let it go from my

---

8. *The Biography of Eld. Barton Warren Stone*, 56–60; Williams, *Barton Stone*, 107–20; West, *Barton Warren Stone*, 160–62.

9. *The Biography of Eld. Barton Warren Stone*, 276–78; Williams, *Barton Stone*, 144–48, 151–54; Kelly D. Carter, *The Trinity in the Stone-Campbell Movement: Restoring the Heart of Christian Faith* (Abilene, TX: Abilene Christian University Press, 2015), 90–111.

mind, till brother Campbell revived it afresh. I thought then that he was not sufficiently explicit on the influences of the Spirit, which led many honest Christians to think he denied them. . . . In a few things I dissented from him, but was agreed to disagree.[10]

Campbell's initial impression of Stone was not as positive. Campbell was in Kentucky on a three-month preaching tour begun after the September 1824 meeting of the Mahoning Baptist Association. He had received invitations from church leaders in the state who had read his debate with William Maccalla and were reading his *Christian Baptist*. Stone's Christian movement had been expanding for twenty years and was strong in several parts of Kentucky. But Stone's beliefs on the Trinity, the deity of Christ, and the atonement were widely regarded as heretical, putting Campbell on his guard.

Campbell clearly came to view Stone and his reform as deficient, if not heretical, on key Christian beliefs and practices. Campbell's Baptist supporters and opponents alike warned him that association with Stone would hurt his reform. In 1827, for example, the editor of the *Baptist Recorder*, Spencer Clack, no friend of Campbell's "ancient gospel and order," rebuked Campbell for failing to refute Stone's denial that Jesus Christ was God. "Beware, my brother, lest you be ensnared, lest you be caught in the net of Mr. Stone."[11]

That many in Kentucky had begun to see similarities between Campbell's movement and Stone's made Campbell uneasy, to say the least. In October 1827 Stone quoted from the minutes of the Franklin (Kentucky) Baptist Association that assumed he and Alexander Campbell had joined in attacking a circular published by the association the previous year. The document justified creeds written by "voluntary associations of Christians" as opposed to those enforced by civil authority, a stance that Stone and Campbell would both have opposed. Stone, however, denied that he had ever seen, read, or attacked the circular. The fact that the Baptist association seemed naturally to associate the two leaders and their movements must have intensified Campbell's anxiety.[12]

Based on the details of Campbell and Stone's relationship from the time they met until Stone's death in 1844, Robert Richardson's description of their

---

10. *The Biography of Eld. Barton Warren Stone*, 75–76.

11. Spencer Clack, "Letters Addressed to A. Campbell. Letter V," *Baptist Recorder*, quoted in *Christian Messenger* 2 (December 1827): 29.

12. Barton W. Stone, "From the Minutes of the 13th Anniversary of the Franklin Association of Baptists in August 1827," *Christian Messenger* 1 (October 1827): 269–71.

first meeting is a strong glossing over of reality. The *Memoirs* describes Stone as a man known as much for "his eminent Christian virtues as for his efforts to effect in Kentucky a religious reformation almost identical in its leading principles and aims with that in which Mr. Campbell was himself engaged." Richardson describes the "warm personal attachment" that continued for the rest of their lives, and that contributed to the union between their two movements.[13]

Actually, Campbell and Stone seem to have had almost no direct contact for three years after their initial meeting. In November 1826 Stone had begun publishing the *Christian Messenger*, giving him for the first time an outlet to propagate his ideas widely. In July 1827 Stone published an open letter to Campbell criticizing an article in the *Christian Baptist* in which Campbell had given his views of the nature of Christ. The article was written in response to a Kentucky correspondent identified as "Timothy," who asked Campbell to put in print what he had said about the Trinity in a "fireside chat" sometime earlier. Campbell reminded Timothy that he had said the topic was "so awfully sacred" that to talk about it risked putting one's Christian reputation in danger. Nevertheless, he was not afraid to discuss it as long as readers understood what he said as speculation and not as his teaching.[14]

Campbell then gave an exposition of John 1:1: "In the beginning was the Word, and the Word was with God, and the Word was God." "The Word," he explained, was the term the Holy Spirit chose to describe the relationship between the Savior and God before time and creation. In the style of John Locke, he stated that a word is an exact image of a thought or idea. An idea and a word have the same age yet are distinct from each other. Therefore, the Savior is coeternal with God and not a creation. The Calvinist terminology of "eternal Son," Campbell insisted, does not give the Savior the full glory deserved—"son" implies inequality. The terms we use most often for the Savior actually describe a relationship with God that began only when he was born of Mary and began the work of salvation as the Christ, Campbell asserted. "There was no Jesus, no Messiah, no Christ, no Son of God, no Only Begotten, before the reign of Augustus Caesar."[15]

Campbell ended the article by explaining why he had agreed to write on this topic after all his denunciations of religious speculation. "I have acceded to your request with more ease than I could have done, had it not been for

---

13. Robert Richardson, *Memoirs of Alexander Campbell*, 2 vols. (Philadelphia: J. B. Lippincott & Co., 1868–1870), 2:118.

14. Alexander Campbell, "The Trinitarian System," *Christian Baptist* 4 (May 1827): 230–34.

15. Campbell, "The Trinitarian System," 231–32.

a few prating bodies who are always striving to undo my influence by the cry of Unitarianism, or Socinianism, or some other obnoxious *ism*." Stone's movement had the reputation of being Unitarian. The increasing association of his movement with Stone's, along with criticism that his New Testament published earlier that year had Unitarian tendencies, pushed Campbell to make it clear that he believed that God and Christ were "coeternal," though in rather nontraditional terms.

Stone reported being surprised and sorrowful when he saw Campbell's article. He began his response by expressing how much he respected Campbell's learning, his battle against religious division and human creeds, and his crusade against theological speculation. He had "generally approved" of Campbell's course, shared many of Campbell's religious views, and was even grateful for the reprieve Campbell's efforts had provided; "to you is turned the attention of creed-makers and party spirits, and on you is hurled their ghostly thunder. We enjoy a temporary peace and respite from war where you are known."[16]

But then Stone accused Campbell of violating his own principle against religious speculation. "You have speculated and theorized on the most important point in theology, and in a manner more mysterious and metaphysical than your predecessors." While Stone acknowledged that Campbell had long ago rejected the Calvinist teaching of Jesus as the "eternal Son of God," as had he and his followers, Stone confessed that he could see no real difference between that and Campbell's view. The Calvinists used "eternal Son of God," Campbell used "Word," but both believed the Word was "the one, self-existent, and eternal God himself." In effect, Stone was accusing Campbell of being a full-blown Trinitarian despite his renunciation of the name.

Stone then asked Campbell seven questions designed to show the scriptural absurdity of Campbell's idea that the relationship of Son and Father did not exist before the birth of Christ. How could Jesus say in John 6:38, for example, that he came from heaven to do the will of the one who sent him, if he was, according to Campbell's logic, himself the eternal God? Was Jesus praying to himself in John 17:5 when he asked the Father to glorify him with the glory he had shared with the eternal One before creation? And what sense would Ephesians 3:9 and Colossians 1:16 make when they say that God created everything by or through Jesus Christ if Christ was God?[17]

Campbell ignored Stone's letter for three months, then reprinted it and replied condescendingly. The reason I can call you brother, Campbell went

16. Barton W. Stone, "To the Christian Baptist," *Christian Messenger* 1 (July 1827): 204.
17. Stone, "To the Christian Baptist," 207–8.

on to say, is that you once told me that you could "conscientiously and devoutly pray to the Lord Jesus Christ as though there was no other God in the universe than he." That is exactly what the Calvinists do, Campbell exclaimed, throwing Stone's critique of him back at his questioner—you differ from the Calvinists in theory, but in practice you are the same. Campbell went on to say patronizingly that he did not think it was strange that Stone, "in running post haste out of Babylon, should have, in some angles of your course, run past Jerusalem." In fact, Campbell said, he was astonished that Stone had "made so few aberrations."[18]

Again turning Stone's criticism of him back on his accuser, Campbell said that he regretted that Stone had written about this topic. If he disagreed with Campbell's discussion on John 1:1, he should simply have said so and dropped the matter. He reminded Stone that at the beginning of his article he had admitted that it was speculation and he would never insist that anyone accept his views. All he was doing was exploring what ideas might be behind the Holy Spirit's term "word" for the relationship "between him that 'was made flesh' and him who sent him."[19]

Campbell then explained that Christians should interpret biblical "terms" just as they would any term—according to normal use and reason. "Things," on the other hand, were simply to be accepted because God had revealed them. There was nothing "unreasonable" about the Trinitarian hypothesis, Campbell declared. He had no more desire to defend speculative Trinitarian views than he had to defend those of Unitarians or Socinians. Yet it was a fact that the Bible taught the existence of one God, and it taught something about three beings. Since humans know nothing about how spirits exist, we cannot rule out that one could exist in three beings. No one can rationally prove or disprove Trinitarianism or Unitarianism; the only sure solution to this difficult subject was simply to use terms found in Scripture without elaboration.[20]

Campbell then leveled an accusation at Stone that would have hurt him deeply—you are abandoning your commitment to Christian unity. The group called Christian or Church of Christ—Stone's movement—was assuming the "sectarian badge" of Arianism or Unitarianism along with peculiar views of the atonement. Campbell warned Stone that if this were not stopped quickly, the name Christian would become as sectarian as Lutheran, Methodist, or

---

18. Alexander Campbell, "To the Christian Messenger," *Christian Baptist* 5 (October 1827): 64.

19. Campbell, "To the Christian Messenger," 64–65.

20. Campbell, "To the Christian Messenger," 66.

Presbyterian. He closed, "Wishing you favor, mercy, and peace, from God our Father, and the Lord Jesus Christ, and that you may never set up a new sect, I am yours in the Lord."[21]

Stone replied in November. He quickly moved to correct what he assumed was an honest mistake in Campbell's understanding of his view of Christ. While he was sorry to jeopardize Campbell's regard for him as a Christian brother, for the sake of honesty he had to clarify that he did not pray to Jesus "as though there were no other God in the universe than he," nor did he worship him "supremely." He worshiped the Son of God, he stated, according to the Scriptures. He had always thought that Campbell recognized as fellow Christians "all who believe that Jesus Christ was the Son of God, and who were willingly obedient to his commands." Had he misunderstood Campbell, or had Campbell changed his mind? Stone asked.[22]

Stone insisted that he had always tried to receive every doctrine revealed by God, regardless of how mysterious it might seem. He knew that Campbell was equally committed to this. Stone said that he rejected the doctrine of the Trinity not because it was unreasonable, as Campbell had insinuated, but because it was not revealed in the Bible. Campbell's contention that the idea of one spiritual entity somehow existing as three was not unreasonable, Stone declared, "appears to my mind too weak to produce conviction." Then he turned Campbell's statement back on him: "Why not abide in the use of Bible terms alone?"

Stone thanked Campbell for his warning against letting "Christian" become a sectarian label. However, he responded, he had no control over his opponents and could not stop them from attaching any names they chose to his movement. The fact that their enemies called them Arians and Unitarians did not make them such. Stone gave a vigorous "Amen" to Campbell's concluding prayer for him, adding that he prayed the same blessings for his friend and brother, undoubtedly including that Campbell never set up a new sect.[23] Over the next two months, Stone published two lengthy replies to Spencer Clack detailing his belief that Christ was not the one God but the Son of God, and therefore worthy of worship as Messiah and Redeemer.[24] These explanations were as much for Campbell as they were for Clack.

---

21. Campbell, "To the Christian Messenger," 66–67. This was the reply that Campbell's Baptist critic Spencer Clack thought totally inadequate in refuting Stone's errors.

22. Barton W. Stone, "Reply," *Christian Messenger* 2 (November 1827): 10–11.

23. Stone, "Reply," 13.

24. Barton W. Stone, "Reply: To Elder Spencer Clack, Editor of the Baptist Recorder,"

For Campbell this ended the first round of conflict with Stone. He had other serious matters to attend to. In October, his beloved wife, Margaret, died at age thirty-six after contracting tuberculosis. He was well into the crucial series on restoring "the ancient order of things." Also, in January 1828 he would begin his series on "the ancient gospel" in response to concerns about Walter Scott's spectacular success in teaching and practicing immersion for the remission of sins on the Western Reserve. And his ongoing battle with Baptist leaders, including with Spencer Clack, moved the Campbell movement ever closer to final separation from the Baptists.

The most intensely confrontational exchange between the two reformers would take place in 1830 and 1831. Many from the Campbell and Stone movements in Kentucky seemed on the brink of uniting in communities around the state, a prospect that made Campbell very nervous as he struggled to solidify the nature and identity of his reform. He was finishing the seventh and final volume of the *Christian Baptist* and beginning his new *Millennial Harbinger*, publishing both from January through July 1830. The condemnation of Campbell and his reform issued by the Beaver Baptist Association in 1829 was being adopted and expanded by other associations and Baptist churches.

Stone triggered this second major dispute with Campbell in a September 1829 response to a question from a Baptist reader asking why Stone's group and the "New Testament Baptists" did not unite. Stone repeated what he had said often before, that there was no scriptural reason why all Christians of every name should not unite. Then he got to the point. As far as he knew, there was no essential difference between his movement and Campbell's. "We have nothing in us to prevent a union," Stone declared, "and if they have nothing in them in opposition to it, we are in spirit one."[25]

Campbell did not respond to Stone's comments about the "union in spirit" for eight months. But in May 1830 he published without comment a letter from a correspondent identified only as "F." that described the Stone church in the town to which he had recently moved. "The Christian church, I am told, numbers about 100 members—is Unitarian in sentiment, and from the other information received concerning them, I should judge very ignorant and enthusiastic. Were it not for the *abuse* of this holy name I would be called by no other; but, as it is, I shall for the present, I think, hold on

---

Christian Messenger 2 (December 1827): 29–36; Barton W. Stone, "Letter II—To Elder S. Clack," *Christian Messenger* 2 (January 1828): 52–57.

25. Barton W. Stone, *Christian Messenger* 3 (September 1829): 261–62.

to my letters of commendation, certificates, etc. which call me a *Baptist.*"[26] F.'s comments undoubtedly reflected Campbell's feelings about the Stone movement and his concern about public perception of his movement's relationship with it.

The following August Stone published yet another article calling for Christian unity. Though he did not specifically mention Campbell, he challenged Campbell's attitude toward the Christians by insisting that for thirty years he and his movement had taught the authority of Scripture and the unity of Christians exactly as the Baptist reformers did. He did admit, however, that he was afraid the reforming Baptists would make their views of immersion for the remission of sins a test of Christian fellowship and thereby become a sect—the very thing Campbell had warned Stone about with his use of the name Christian. Despite fears some had about a union of his Christians and the Campbell reformers—including the Christians' denial of the Trinity—Stone repeated that he was ready to unite with everyone who took the Bible as the only source of faith and rejected all sectarian names. "We will unite in fellowship with all holy, obedient believers in Jesus, without regard to their opinions."[27]

Campbell quickly shot back at Stone's comments concerning immersion. First Campbell published another note from "F." designed to put the Christians in a bad light, describing how they had shunned him when they found out he was a Baptist. Then Campbell strongly challenged Stone's statement that his views of immersion were an opinion. His teaching and practice of baptism were not human opinion, Campbell declared, but obedience to the clear commands of Jesus. He advised Stone that if he would read his "Extra, No. 1" on the remission of sins, he would get the point.[28]

To admit unimmersed persons into the church, Campbell maintained, would make it like Noah's ark—"full of vermin and ravenous beasts, their noise and clamor (to say nothing of their filth and uncleanness)." That was not the true church of Christ. Campbell then questioned Stone's commitment to immersion for remission of sins. To teach it as a theory but drop it in practice was to treat Christ's authority with contempt. Campbell then repeated that he loved the name Christian, but since it was associated with

26. F., "To the Editor of the Millennial Harbinger," *Millennial Harbinger*, May 1830, 199–200.

27. Barton W. Stone, *Christian Messenger* 4 (August 1830): 201–2.

28. Alexander Campbell, "The Remission of Sins," special issue, *Millennial Harbinger*, July 5, 1830, 1–88. Campbell published special extra issues of the paper when he felt a subject needed more extensive development than was possible in the regular monthly issue. This extra appeared in the first volume of his new *Millennial Harbinger*.

people who did not believe or practice what the ancient Christians did, he preferred the older name "disciple" and recommended they all be known simply as "the disciples of Christ."[29]

Editorial exchanges continued through September and October. Campbell approved of Stone's commitment to weekly Lord's Supper but pressed Stone on his inconsistency on immersion. During a preaching trip to Kentucky in November, Campbell had what he described as "an interesting conversation" with Stone and a small group of leaders in their respective movements about the reformation. Campbell gave no other details of the meeting, but Stone later reported that Campbell had expressed fear that if the two groups united it would damage the progress of his reformation.[30]

Eight months of silence followed, when finally in August 1831 Stone published an article titled simply "Union." People were asking why his people and the Reformed Baptists (a common designation for the followers of the Campbell reform) had not united, and he repeated what he had said before—"in spirit we are united, and no reason existed on our side to prevent the union in form." He explained that the Reformed Baptists had come to accept many of the doctrines the Christians had been teaching for thirty years: Christians should abandon authoritative creeds and confessions because they promoted sectarianism, and the gospel message alone without any special operation of the Spirit was powerful enough to produce saving faith in anyone who heard it. He also explained that many in his movement had long taught that baptism with faith and repentance was for the remission of sins, though the Campbell movement had made immersion even more central than the Christians had. Furthermore, both groups believed "Christian" was a proper designation, though the Campbell people preferred a different name.[31]

Stone went on to explain that while the groups differed in some matters of opinion, the Christians, unlike the reformers, did not make those opinions matters of fellowship. He then named the two chief differences he could see: the Christians had fellowship with unimmersed persons and admitted them to communion while the reformers did not, and the two groups went by different names. Stone then clarified why the Christians could not break fellowship with the unimmersed. Such an action, he insisted, would imply

---

29. Alexander Campbell, "The Name Christian," *Millennial Harbinger*, August 1830, 371–73.

30. Alexander Campbell, "Notes on a Tour, &c.—No. III," *Millennial Harbinger*, January 1831, 27.

31. Barton W. Stone, "Union," *Christian Messenger* 5 (August 1831): 180.

that millions who had assumed they obeyed Christ in baptism and who had lived faithful Christian lives were then suffering eternal punishment in hell—because they inadvertently failed to obey the command to be immersed.

Stone then expressed his belief that the churches of Campbell's reform had taken the name Disciples specifically to distinguish themselves from the Christians. He was not opposed to the name Disciple—it was scriptural. But the reason they had chosen it was to separate themselves from other followers of Christ, in essence to create their own sect, and that was wrong. Stone then made the case that "Christian" was actually the divinely given name for the followers of Christ. He examined every occurrence in the New Testament of the Greek word *chrematizo*, translated "called" or "named" in Acts 11:26 ("And the disciples were called Christians first in Antioch"). In every instance God did the calling or naming.

Stone closed with an attack on the Campbell movement's practice of closed communion—admitting only the immersed to the Lord's Supper. Campbell actually seemed to struggle at times with the closed communion stance, even sounding similar to Stone at times—that no human had the right to invite or debar "any pious, holy believer from the Lord's table."[32] And in the famous Lunenburg letter articles of 1837 and 1838, Campbell would insist that pious believers who innocently neglected the command to be immersed for the remission of sins should not be counted as outside the covenant of grace.[33]

In Campbell's extensive reply the next month, he took on every issue Stone cited as blocking their "union in form." Campbell first attacked Stone's terms. What could Stone possibly mean by "union in form"? Was it a formal confederation of ministers, a general convention of messengers, a general assembly of all the members from both groups, or a couple of individuals (apparently Campbell and Stone) who would bring this about? Would they draw up articles of agreement to create and regulate such a union? Since Stone had not specified, Campbell declared, his brother had no right to complain that there was not yet a formal union.[34]

32. Alexander Campbell, in *Christian Messenger and Family Magazine*, 1845, 40–41; *British Millennial Harbinger*, 1860, 451–52, cited in David Thompson, *Let Sects and Parties Fall: A Short History of the Association of Churches of Christ in Great Britain and Ireland* (Birmingham, UK: Berean, 1980). He later condemned the exclusion of persons from the table because of doctrinal or political differences. Alexander Campbell, "Christian Communion.—No. 1," *Millennial Harbinger*, December 1862, 529.

33. See the discussion in chapter 12.

34. Alexander Campbell, "Reply on Union, Communion, and the Name Christian," *Millennial Harbinger*, September 1831, 389.

Campbell then criticized Stone's claim that the reformers had accepted the doctrines the Christians had been proclaiming for years before the Campbells showed up. Stone was greatly mistaken, Campbell retorted, if he thought that the reformers were pleading what Stone's movement had begun pleading in Kentucky thirty years earlier. Campbell admitted that the Christians had begun attacking creeds as terms of communion "and some other abuses," but what did that have to do with his reformation? "The greatest heretics in Christendom have inveighed against creeds, councils and human dogmas," but that was not what his movement was about. It was the "ancient gospel and ancient order of things" that made his movement different from every other reform since the great apostasy.[35]

In a sarcastic paragraph, Campbell altered his oft-repeated statement that a union with the Stone churches would hurt the spread of his reform among other groups. He reported that Stone had told him, apparently at the meeting the previous November, that he had just as much to lose by uniting with the Campbell movement. Many of the "orthodox," Stone had claimed, held him and his movement in higher esteem than they did the Campbell reformers. How noble of Stone to condescend to associate with the Disciples, he snapped. While it would be an honor to unite with the Christians, Campbell continued, "If our union with them, though so advantageous to us, would merge 'the ancient gospel and ancient order of things' in the long-vexed question of simple anti-trinitarianism, anti-creedalism, or anti-sectarianism, I should be ashamed of myself in the presence of him whose '*well done, good and faithful servant*,' is worth the universe to me. We all could have had honorable alliances with honorable sectaries, many years since, had this been our object."[36]

Campbell then remarked that Stone must not have been in his right mind when he wrote the "Union" article, admitting that he himself was not in his when he read it. One of the so-called opinions Stone cited as a barrier to union was not an opinion at all but a practice—accepting unimmersed persons into fellowship and communion. He accused Stone of nullifying the command to be scripturally baptized by taking people into the kingdom of Jesus who had not been legitimately born. He then ridiculed Stone's illustration of the innocently mistaken pedobaptist. He sympathized with such persons too, he insisted. But that was not the question. "Are we authorized to make the sincerity and honesty of a person's mind a rule of our conduct? . . .

---

35. Campbell, "Reply on Union," 390.
36. Campbell, "Reply on Union," 391.

We can never justify ourselves before God or man in presuming in our 'judgment of charity' to set aside his commandment, and for accepting for it a human substitute."[37]

Campbell expressed surprise at Stone's statement that he could not give up the name Christian to unite with the Disciples. No one ever asked him to do that, he asserted. He then spent several pages refuting Stone's claim that the name Christian had been given by God, insisting that "disciples" was actually older and more humble. Campbell closed by explaining that he had written as bluntly as he had because Stone, by the tone he had taken in his "Union" article, had asked for it. Nevertheless, he asserted that he respected Stone and those of his movement and that he could unite "in spirit and form" with many of them he knew.[38]

Stone's reply two months later was equally frank. Clearly alluding to Campbell, he started with a saying he had heard from an old Baptist preacher, that "the enemies of Christian union, were the world, the flesh, and the Devil; and I will add, said he, the fourth, more mischievous than all, the preachers." He lamented that so many preachers were out to make a great name for themselves and predicted that until such an attitude were eliminated, there was little hope of Christian unity.[39]

He then clarified what he meant by "union in form." All he had in mind was that where groups of Christians and reformers existed in local neighborhoods, they should come together formally into one congregation, especially where their numbers were low and they could do little alone. Campbell should have known, Stone chided, that he had long since rejected the authority of confederations of churches and other "unscriptural" associations.

As for Campbell's detecting "a squinting at some sort of precedence" in Stone's statement, did he think it would be degrading to them to admit that Stone's churches had taught the same doctrines before they did? Campbell's assertion that his "ancient gospel and ancient order of things" was different from every other reform since the great apostasy was pretentious. The only difference Stone saw between what his movement had taught for three decades and what Campbell's movement believed was that the Disciples attached more importance to baptism than the Christians and minimized the work of the Holy Spirit.[40]

37. Campbell, "Reply on Union," 393.
38. Campbell, "Reply on Union," 393–95.
39. Barton W. Stone, "Remarks on A. Campbell's Reply on Union, Communion, and the Name Christian," *Christian Messenger* 5 (November 1831): 248–49.
40. Stone, "Remarks on A. Campbell's Reply," 250–52.

Then Stone repeated that he believed and practiced immersion for the remission of sins as much as Campbell did; he simply could not condemn to hell the people of God who "had been long in the wilderness." He believed that admitting the unimmersed to fellowship while teaching the truth in love would be the best way to bring them to the biblical understanding. He again defended his view that "Christian" was the divinely selected name and derided Campbell's distinction between "Christian" and "Disciple." Both were scriptural and meant the same thing, he insisted.[41]

This was the final straw for Campbell. When he acknowledged Stone's remarks the next month, he said that if he were to reply in the same spirit in which Stone had written, "many would regret that we had noticed his writings at all on the subject." He deeply resented Stone's insinuation that he was out to make a great name for himself. Such statements lowered his esteem for Stone, he exclaimed. He expected such discourteous treatment from his opponents, but he thought he would receive better from those who claimed fellowship with him. "I solicited a free, candid, and *affectionate* correspondence on any points of difference. But in asking for *bread* I did not expect a *stone*."[42]

Campbell then in essence washed his hands of the whole matter. He had treated the sectarian peculiarities of the Christians delicately for years, he said. He was happy that many of the Christians in the West were becoming more informed in the Scriptures and as sound on the nature of Christ as any congregations he knew. As an individual, he was already united with and could cooperate with those Christians. Furthermore, he would be overjoyed if all immersed disciples took the name Christian and walked "in all the commands of the Lord and Saviour." He closed, however, with this emphatic declaration aimed at Stone and his churches: "*If my uniting with any one sect would shut me out from all others which hold the Christian institutions ever so imperfectly, I would choose rather to stand aloof from that sect than from all others.*"[43]

Yet even as Campbell penned his harsh response to Stone, the union effort in Kentucky was moving swiftly forward. In January 1832 Stone jubilantly announced the union of the Christians and reformers in Georgetown and Lexington. Furthermore, John T. Johnson, a leader in Campbell's movement in Kentucky, would be assuming the role of coeditor of the *Christian*

---

41. Stone, "Remarks on A. Campbell's Reply," 252–57.

42. Alexander Campbell, "The Christian Messenger," *Millennial Harbinger*, December 1831, 557.

43. Campbell, "The Christian Messenger," 558.

John T. Johnson was a leader of the Campbell movement in Kentucky. He became very close to Barton W. Stone, and in 1832 he became coeditor of Stone's journal the *Christian Messenger,* symbolizing the union between many of the churches of the Campbell and Stone movements. Used with permission from the Disciples of Christ Historical Society, Bethany, West Virginia.

Messenger with Stone. John Smith from the Campbell movement and John Rogers from the Christians had been appointed, supported by money raised from both groups, to travel to all the churches urging them to unite as well.[44]

Two months later, Campbell reprinted parts of the articles from the *Christian Messenger* announcing Johnson's editorial work with Stone, the union of the Kentucky congregations, and the sending out of Smith and Rogers to promote the union elsewhere. He wished Smith and Rogers success in their work because he knew they would not merely baptize people and then persuade them to protest against creeds and extol the sufficiency of the Bible. They would instead, he was confident, teach the ancient gospel and order of things and advocate no union except a union in and with truth. He was happy that everyone from both groups had renounced their religious speculations and now promoted only the "apostolic institutions."[45] Though

44. Barton W. Stone and John T. Johnson, "Union of Christians," *Christian Messenger* 6 (January 1832): 6–8. See the extensive treatment of the events leading up to and following the 1832 union in Williams, *Barton Stone,* 183–202.

45. Alexander Campbell, "The Christian Messenger," *Millennial Harbinger,* March 1832, 137–39.

it was muted, Campbell was giving his approval to the union because the Christians had accepted his ancient gospel and order.

Robert Richardson described the union of the churches in 1831 and 1832 as a natural outgrowth of the "warm mutual sympathy" and "high personal regard" between Stone and Campbell. Though acknowledging differences, Richardson ignored or minimized the sharp disputes between the two leaders, including Campbell's determination to distinguish his movement from Stone's. "He thought sufficient time had not perhaps been allowed for a thorough comprehension of the principles of the Reformation, and dreaded lest these should in any wise be overruled or lost sight of in so sudden and unceremonious an arrangement. His misgivings, however, proved to be entirely groundless."[46]

Richardson's softening of Campbell's uneasiness toward Stone reflected Richardson more than it did Campbell. While many Kentucky Christians did accept Campbell's "ancient gospel and order," a different spirit often existed in the churches with roots in the Stone movement—including more exuberant worship, belief in an active role of the Holy Spirit in believers' lives, and a more open attitude toward admission to the Lord's Supper. Campbell held that any meaningful unity must be based on agreement on a set of core beliefs, not a loose federation with no clear standard. For Campbell the standard was his "ancient gospel and order of things." Those who did not accept or understand it must be brought to accept it for true unity to exist.[47]

In April Campbell printed a letter from "H.C.C." giving news of a "blow up" in the united Lexington congregation over who could administer the Lord's Supper. The Christians insisted it would have to be a properly ordained elder (essentially a minister—called a "teaching elder" in Presbyterian structure), a proposition the reformers rejected. Somewhat triumphantly, Campbell commented on the account the following month. The Stonite Christians in Lexington were so steeped in their human traditions that they could not accept the New Testament alone as the bond of union, he exclaimed. "Until the christians have more love to Jesus Christ, and more veneration for his Apostles, than for fine oratory . . . ; until they prefer communion with the Father and his Son Jesus Christ, in keeping his institutions, to the formalities of the kingdom of the clergy, it will be in vain to profess reformation, or a love for the union of christians upon New Testament premises."[48]

46. Richardson, *Memoirs of Alexander Campbell,* 2:370, 387.

47. See the discussion of the commonalities and differences between the Stone and Campbell movements in Richard L. Harrison Jr., *From Camp Meeting to Church: A History of the Christian Church (Disciples of Christ) in Kentucky* (n.p.: Christian Board of Publication, 1992), 64–70.

48. Alexander Campbell, "The Union," *Millennial Harbinger,* May 1832, 194.

Campbell lashed out at the Christians for holding to practices like mourning benches, camp meetings, ordinations, orations, and religious shows rather than to the ancient order. Union-like sincerity was an evil when all it did was unite sects. When sects (implying the Christians in Lexington) contend for their views against others, it is better that the Lord scatters them like the builders of the tower of Babel. He closed his evaluation of the Lexington situation by calling for the real Christians in all the sects to leave those bodies and unite. The only way that could happen, he believed, was "to propound the ancient gospel and order of things in the words and sentences found in the apostolic writings—to abandon all usages and traditions not found in the Record, and to make no human terms of communion."[49]

Though he could not stop the union, and he eventually grudgingly accepted it, Campbell always spoke of it in terms of the members of Stone's reform having renounced their speculations and accepted the principles of his reformation—the ancient gospel and order. He repeated his belief that no one who had read what had been published on the ancient gospel and order for the last ten years could possibly confuse that for what the Christians had taught decades earlier. Despite protests from leaders in both his movement and Stone's, this would remain Campbell's stance.[50]

Stone insisted that the "ancient gospel and order" was precisely what his movement had taught for thirty years. He did not understand those terms to mean Campbell's set of principles, but rather the simple story of God's love manifested in the death of Jesus as Savior that produces love and faith in penitent hearers. There was no detailed set of beliefs or church structures; just Christians who tried to live like Christ and who came together in local congregations to work and worship. Campbell, however, saw much more, and consistently chafed at embracing churches from the Stone movement that did not overtly adopt his program.

Over the next decade, Stone and Campbell interacted in their journals on two issues: the best name for the movement and the nature of the atonement. The second became a fifteen-month written debate in 1840–1841.[51] Campbell told readers at the end of a February 1840 article on Unitarianism that he had proposed to Stone that they conduct a written discussion on mat-

---

49. Campbell, "The Union," 195.

50. Barton W. Stone and John T. Johnson, "Advice," *Christian Messenger* 6 (April 1832): 110–11; L. F., "A Complaint," *Millennial Harbinger*, May 1832, 237–38; Alexander Campbell, "Remarks on the Complaint," *Millennial Harbinger*, June 1832, 279.

51. A PDF file with the text of the articles on the atonement is at http://archive.tr churchofchrist.com/resources/Restoration%20Studies/Stone_Campbell_Atonement.PDF.

ters connected with the atonement. Stone responded in March that besides being too old and slow of mind, he was afraid such a discussion would lead to conflict and division. Nevertheless, he said, several friends had relieved his fears, and he would therefore take up Campbell's "invitation."[52]

As seen earlier, Stone viewed Christ's death as the ultimate proof of God's infinite love, not as a means to satisfy God's anger at human sin. The atonement did not change God; it changed sinners who heard and believed the good news. Campbell believed that this understanding undermined the very need for Christ's death—God could simply have forgiven sin without Christ's death if it effected no change in God at all.[53] In the end, nothing new emerged from the 1840–1841 debate. Despite Stone's continued doubts that the debate could accomplish any good, he conceded in his third article that if the exchange did nothing else, it would show how Christians could differ and yet love one another and remain in union.[54]

In May 1841 Stone published—at the request of Campbell—an article by a writer who basically labeled Stone's teaching a "low, Socinian, God-dishonoring doctrine." In his commentary following the article, Stone wondered why Campbell would ask him to publish such a thing, implying that it must simply be to insult his movement. It was time to close the debate, he concluded, since a fair exchange didn't seem possible after all. He proposed that they each write a synopsis of their beliefs and then devote their energies to reforming the church and saving the world.[55]

In November Campbell published a note from Stone saying that he had thought more about it and decided it would add nothing to the discussion for him to write a synopsis of his views. He would write no more on the subject in the *Christian Messenger*—Campbell could do what he thought best in his paper. He would spend the rest of his days "preparing himself and others for eternity."

After Stone's note Campbell added a brief note of his own that included

52. Alexander Campbell, "Definitions and Answers to Questions—No. I," *Millennial Harbinger*, February 1840, 81–83; Barton W. Stone, "Atonement," *Millennial Harbinger*, June 1840, 243. Stone had ceased publication of the *Christian Messenger* in 1836 but resumed it in September 1840 and began to print both his and Campbell's articles, as Campbell was already doing in the *Millennial Harbinger*.

53. For a detailed discussion of the beliefs of each, see John Mark Hicks, "What Did Christ Accomplish on the Cross? Atonement in Campbell, Stone, and Scott," *Lexington Theological Quarterly* 30 (January 1995): 145–70.

54. Barton W. Stone, "Letter III. Review of Brother Campbell's III Letter. (continued)," *Christian Messenger* 11 (February 1841): 181.

55. Barton W. Stone, "Notice," *Christian Messenger* 11 (May 1841): 310–12.

the news that Stone had suffered a stroke and was likely already dead. Under the circumstances, he would also end his discussion of the atonement, at least for the time being. He expressed his disappointment that Stone had failed to repudiate Unitarianism in his articles or to give an explanation of how his beliefs were in keeping with those of Campbell's "current reformation." Nevertheless, he was willing to make allowances for Stone's deeply ingrained ways of speaking and thinking.[56]

Perhaps assuming Stone's death, at the end of his comments Campbell made a remarkable concession. "As we are not saved by the strength and comprehension of our views, but through obeying from the heart the apostolic mould of doctrine, more stress ought to be laid on moral excellence than upon abstract orthodoxy; especially when all the great facts and documents of Christianity are cordially believed and cherished."[57]

Stone, however, was not dead. Though partially paralyzed, he would live for three more years. Campbell basically ignored Stone after the 1841 notice. However, an incident during Campbell's debate with Presbyterian leader Nathan Rice in September 1843 revealed Campbell's continued disdain for the Stone movement. Rice had attacked Campbell for being in fellowship with people who held heretical doctrines, including Unitarians. He quoted Stone from the *Christian Baptist* as denying that Christ was the only true God or that he existed from eternity, then added material from the recent articles in the *Millennial Harbinger* where Stone denied that Christ bore the punishment for human sin on the cross. He charged Campbell with compromising key doctrines of Christianity by being united with Stone and his followers.[58]

In response Campbell explained his version of the history of the Springfield Presbytery that Stone and his colleagues had formed after withdrawing from the Synod of Kentucky. Part of it, he said, had become Arian while the other had joined the Shakers. Campbell asserted that the framers of Rice's cherished Westminster Confession would have executed Barton Stone for his views. He, on the other hand, preferred to save lives by the gospel and had tried to save people like Stone, so much so that some of his friends began to think he sympathized with their speculations. While he did not approve of all that Stone believed, he was sure that his staying in fellowship with Stone and his followers "has been, and is pursuing a most salutary and redeem-

56. Alexander Campbell, "Note," *Millennial Harbinger*, November 1841, 538.
57. Campbell, "Note," 538–39.
58. *A Debate Between Rev. A. Campbell and Rev. N. L. Rice* (Lexington, KY: A. T. Skillman & Son, 1844), 852–55.

ing policy." It was not until the reformers appeared that the unscriptural speculations of the Newlights (Stone's group) were eradicated. Rice and the Presbyterians should thank Campbell and his reform for correcting what the Presbyterians had been unable to.[59]

The disparaging remarks regarding Stone provoked strong protests from church leaders in Kentucky with roots in both the Stone and Campbell movements. One letter, signed by four evangelists and nine elders, criticized Campbell for failing to defend Stone from Rice's unjust remarks and for making statements that made things worse. You did not save Brother Stone and his associates any more than they saved you and yours, they declared. True, each side held opinions different from the other's, but none were damning or subversive of the Christian faith, as Rice had said of Stone and his followers. They ended with a call to maintain the peace that had resulted from the union of the groups. A second letter from longtime Campbell associate John T. Johnson echoed the charges already made and chided Campbell for apparently intentionally omitting Stone's paper from his list of approved periodicals.[60]

Campbell printed the two letters, but his only response was that his omission of the *Christian Messenger* from his list of "our periodicals" was purely accidental, and he had put it back in a later list. Both letters from Kentucky had asked Campbell to reprint an exchange that had appeared in the *Christian Messenger* about the reproachful description of Stone in the Rice debate. Campbell said he would be happy to do so if someone would send him a copy. He had seen it earlier, he admitted, but he couldn't seem to find a copy now.[61]

On the following page of the *Millennial Harbinger*, Campbell copied a brief notice from the *Christian Messenger* that the editors intended to publish a volume with the discussion between him and Stone on the atonement with an extended appendix by Stone. Campbell replied that he had no objection, provided he would also be allowed to add an extended appendix. Readers would remember, he said, that he had been forced to end the discussion before it was over because he thought Stone was near death after his stroke.

---

59. *A Debate Between Rev. A. Campbell and Rev. N. L. Rice*, 864–65.

60. John Rogers and others, "Elder Barton W. Stone," *Millennial Harbinger*, September 1844, 414–16.

61. Alexander Campbell, *Millennial Harbinger*, September 1844, 416. He finally published the material a year later, after being reminded of it by someone from Kentucky. See "Charge of Unitarianism," *Millennial Harbinger*, November 1845, 495–99.

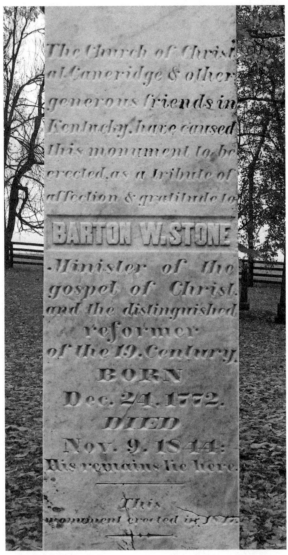

The Church of Christ at Caneridge & other generous friends in Kentucky have caused this monument to be erected, as a tribute of affection & gratitude to

BARTON W. STONE

Minister of the gospel of Christ, and the distinguished reformer of the 19. Century.

BORN
Dec. 24. 1772.
DIED
Nov. 9. 1844.
His remains lie here.

This monument erected in

Barton W. Stone was buried three times—first immediately after his death in November 1844 near his daughter's house in Jacksonville, Illinois; then at the Antioch Christian Church cemetery near Jacksonville in January 1846; and finally at the Cane Ridge Church cemetery in Kentucky in March 1847. Alexander Campbell supposedly objected to the inscription on this monument, crediting Stone with being "the" distinguished reformer of the nineteenth century. Photo courtesy of James Trader, Curator, The Cane Ridge Meeting House, Cane Ridge, Kentucky.

He would approve of such a volume only if he were given equal space to respond to Stone's extra comments.[62]

The proposed volume was never published. A few weeks later, on November 9, 1844, Stone died at the home of his daughter in Hannibal, Missouri. The next month Campbell printed a letter from evangelist Jacob Creath giving an account of Stone's last days, followed by a brief paragraph of his own. Stone may have gone too far on some controversial points, he said, but he had been an instrument of God to bring many to the Bible as their only rule of faith and life. He hoped to give more of Stone's history in a future article.[63]

But no such article ever appeared. Campbell was engaged in more pressing matters. Sectional divisions of the Baptist and Methodist denominations over slavery pushed him to publish a seven-part series entitled "Our Position to American Slavery" in 1845. He gave increased attention to a more extensive organization for the movement, a discussion that would lead to the creation of the American Christian Missionary Society in 1849. When reminded in late fall that he had failed to print the notice of a proposed biography of Stone, Campbell responded that with so many other things to be published, he had simply forgotten about it.[64]

After Stone's death, he virtually disappeared from Campbell's notice. When Stone's body was moved to Cane Ridge from the cemetery of the Antioch Christian Church near Jacksonville, Illinois, church members in Kentucky raised funds to erect a monument. The inscription read in part, "Barton W. Stone, Minister of the gospel of Christ and the distinguished reformer of the 19 Century." Though possibly apocryphal, the story is certainly believable that when Campbell read the epitaph, he retorted that it should read "a" reformer instead of "the." The irony of the wide acceptance in the twentieth century of the scholarly designation "Stone-Campbell Movement" for the global Christian tradition that emerged partly from his reform would surely be a distressing surprise to Campbell.

62. Alexander Campbell, "Discussion," *Millennial Harbinger*, September 1844, 417.
63. Alexander Campbell, *Millennial Harbinger*, December 1844, 622.
64. "Charge of Unitarianism," 495–96.

CHAPTER 17

The Ferguson-Fanning-Richardson Affair

There were other conflicts in Campbell's long career—many of them. Arthur Crihfield's observation that Brother Campbell was at war with the whole world sometimes seemed indisputable. True, he was tireless in pursuing every method available to advance his reform: writing and publishing articles and books; debating key tenets of his plea; translating Scripture; operating a school; traveling thousands of miles annually to speak in churches and other public venues on subjects as diverse as phrenology, public education, and prison reform; advising the churches of his movement; and serving as president of the American Christian Missionary Society.

Yet, as already seen, spread throughout this immense activity were constant and unrelenting conflicts with opponents and colleagues alike. Virtually no issue of the *Christian Baptist* or the *Millennial Harbinger*, among the most comprehensive and reliable records of his life and work, was free from controversy. And though he understood the fights as necessary to defend and advance his reform (as well as to protect himself against charges of dishonesty and deception and to preserve his chief role in the reform), as Crihfield observed, the endless clashes set a tone for many others in his movement.

Among other battles was a rancorous discussion with Nashville Presbyterian minister Obadiah Jennings in December 1830. After hearing Campbell preach a couple of times, Jennings publicly challenged Campbell's denial of the role of "religious experience" in conversion and his teaching that baptism was the new birth and regeneration. On Christmas Day the two met in Jennings's church for a debate on these and other doctrines characteristic of Campbell's reformation.

Two years later Jennings's nephew S. C. Jennings, editor of the Pittsburgh *Christian Herald*, published an account of the debate written by his uncle, who had died the previous January. The book began with a memoir of Jennings's life, followed by a brief note "to the reader" by the editor. But it was Obadiah Jennings's introductory paragraph that set the tone.

> That the system of Mr. Alexander Campbell, of Bethany, Brook County, Virginia, is calculated and designed to exclude all true spirituality from the religion of the Bible, must be apparent to every impartial and intelligent inquirer for truth, who seriously examines it; that it is in fact a system of infidelity somewhat disguised, it is conceived, he himself has lately given, both in his writings and public harangues, the most decisive proof. This more plenary evidence of the true nature and design of his religious sentiments, was not, however, necessary to fasten upon the minds of a great majority of the pious community, the conviction, which has long been felt, that he is one of the most dangerous "false teachers" that has appeared in our country.[1]

Right after Jennings died, Campbell had published a brief but respectful obituary in the February *Millennial Harbinger*.[2] When he read his opponent's account of the debate, however, he was infuriated. In response, Campbell issued an "extra" issue of the *Millennial Harbinger* in August entirely dedicated to denouncing what he considered Jennings's completely false description of the debate. His opening sentences equaled Jennings's in contempt.

> I have risen from the perusal of this work with a worse opinion of human nature, and of what Doctor Owen called the "indwelling sin of Christians," than I have been conscious of, on the reading of any book of controversy which has ever fallen into my hands. I can say, in all sincerity, before God and man, if such be the fruits, the proper fruits, of the metaphysical regeneration of the holy spirit of Doctors of Divinity and of the schools, from such may the good Spirit deliver me! If the spirit of slander, detraction, and false accusation, be the spirit of truth, then is this book written under the direction, and infused with large measures of the spirit of truth.[3]

If the way to defend Presbyterianism was to abuse and attack the reputation of anyone who questioned its teachings, Jennings was entitled to

1. Obadiah Jennings, *Debate on Campbellism; Held at Nashville, Tennessee. In Which the Principles of Alexander Campbell are Confuted, and His Conduct Examined* (Pittsburgh: D. & M. Maclean, 1832), 29.
2. Alexander Campbell, "Obituary Notice," *Millennial Harbinger*, February 1832, 95.
3. Alexander Campbell, "Character of 'The Debate on Campbellism, by Obadiah Jennings, D.D.,'" *Millennial Harbinger*, August 1832, 422.

Presbyterians' gratitude and admiration, Campbell exclaimed. He continued with a series of articles designed to refute Jennings's criticism of Campbell's New Testament titled "New Version Defended; and O. Jennings, D.D. Exposed." By December, Campbell was ready to move on. He had received a "very well-written critique" of the Jennings book, he said, but it was not worth further notice.[4]

Another battle was a written debate with Universalist Dolphus Skinner between 1837 and 1839. The exchange was filled with bickering and mutual accusations of dishonesty and misrepresentation. Even after the debate, there were fights about its publication. Campbell had offered Skinner the rights, but when it came out in 1840, Campbell said the book was "unfaithfully published" because of Skinner's additions of an appendix and comments on some of Campbell's letters not in the original articles.[5]

But by far the most perplexing and painful dispute as Campbell neared the end of his career was with another of his closest colleagues in the reformation—coeditor of the *Millennial Harbinger*, cofounder of Bethany College, longtime professor of science, and eventually his biographer, Robert Richardson.

The controversy did not start with Richardson at all. It began in a dispute with Jesse B. Ferguson, the charismatic minister of the church in Nashville, Tennessee. Ferguson had gained a reputation as an excellent preacher and minister as a young man in Ohio and Kentucky. After he preached in two "protracted meetings" at the Nashville church in 1842 and 1844, the members strongly urged him to become their regular minister. Though he resisted, after continued urging he finally agreed to work with the church half-time in 1846. In March 1847 he moved his family to Nashville to become the full-time minister at the age of twenty-eight.[6]

In October Ferguson issued a prospectus for a new paper to be titled the *Christian Magazine*, though it was actually the continuation of the *Christian Review* begun by Tolbert Fanning in 1844. Though he remained a coeditor, Fanning had decided to turn the journal over to the gifted young minister of

4. Alexander Campbell, "Apology," *Millennial Harbinger*, December 1832, 618. See the account in Robert Richardson, *Memoirs of Alexander Campbell*, 2 vols. (Philadelphia: J. B. Lippincott & Co., 1868–1870), 2:338–43.

5. Alexander Campbell, "Debate on Universalism," *Millennial Harbinger*, September 1840, 432. Alexander Campbell and Dolphus Skinner, *Discussion of the Doctrines of Endless Misery and Universal Salvation* (Utica, NY: C. C. P. Grosh, Printer, 1840).

6. Jesse B. Ferguson, *History of the Relation of the Pastor to the Christian Church of Nashville* (Nashville: McKennie and Brown, 1855), 3–4.

Jesse B. Ferguson (1819–1870) was the charismatic minister of the Nashville Christian Church whose public embrace of Universalism, Unitarianism, and spiritualism in the 1850s divided the church. Campbell's sharp response to Ferguson eventually fomented alienation with his colleagues Robert Richardson and Tolbert Fanning. Used with permission from the Disciples of Christ Historical Society, Bethany, West Virginia.

his congregation because of his heavy responsibilities as president of Franklin College. When Campbell published Ferguson's notice of the new paper in December, he spoke of Ferguson's good sense and courtesy. "We doubt not that he will be found a vigorous, edifying, and spirited writer," Campbell exclaimed, and that the proposed magazine would be "a useful and successful auxiliary in the great cause of Reformation."[7]

Ferguson's success and fame continued to grow, and by 1852 the church's building was too small for the crowds he attracted every Sunday. The congregation built a new structure to accommodate up to twelve hundred people

7. Alexander Campbell, "Prospectus of the Christian Magazine," *Millennial Harbinger*, December 1847, 718.

at the enormous cost of thirty thousand dollars.[8] Ferguson was then the youngest and most popular minister in the city.[9] In the very year of this success, however, Ferguson published an article in the *Christian Magazine* that would embroil him in a fierce struggle with Campbell and lead to the perplexing hostility between Campbell and Richardson.

The controversial article appeared in the April 1852 *Christian Magazine* with Ferguson's interpretation of 1 Peter 3:18–20: "For Christ also hath once suffered for sins, the just for the unjust, that he might bring us to God, being put to death in the flesh, but quickened by the Spirit: By which also he went and preached unto the spirits in prison; Which sometime were disobedient, when once the longsuffering of God waited in the days of Noah, while the ark was a-preparing, wherein few, that is, eight souls were saved by water" (KJV). Ferguson's understanding of the passage was that Christ in spirit form had descended into the realm of the dead after his death and resurrection and preached the gospel to all who had never had the opportunity to hear it during life. While Ferguson admitted that his ideas were different from anything held in the churches of the reform or by most Protestants, the many requests to publish his interpretation, which he said he had held for eight years, finally persuaded him to do so. While he believed this was the plain meaning of the text, he also revealed another motivation: "we pity the spiritual darkness of any man or sect of men whose earthly and selfish views limit the benefits of the mission of Christ to the comparatively few who hear of him and learn his ways while they remain in the flesh."[10] To many this sounded like Universalism.

In June Campbell responded with a vengeance. He reprinted Ferguson's article under the title "A New Discovery," then proceeded in a fourteen-page reply to attack and discredit Ferguson and his exposition. Such an interpretation would give solace to those who had rejected Christ in life and destroy any motivation for Christian mission on earth. Surely every spirit in Hades would respond immediately to the first sermon that gave them a chance to get out, he scoffed. Actually, Ferguson did not say that Christ would preach to all who died without obeying the gospel but only to those who never had the opportunity to hear it in life.

Several times Campbell alluded to Ferguson's lack of maturity and rea-

8. Jesse B. Ferguson, "Opening of Our New House of Worship," *Christian Magazine* 5 (August 1852): 237–39.

9. H. Leo Boles, *Biographical Sketches of Gospel Preachers* (Nashville: Gospel Advocate Co., 1932), 189.

10. Jesse B. Ferguson, "The Spirits in Prison," *Christian Magazine* 5 (April 1852): 115.

son, labeling his arguments far-fetched. In contrast, Campbell's interpretation, which he claimed was based on a literal translation of the Greek, was that the Holy Spirit through Noah preached to the disobedient people who were living while the ark was being built. That Jesus preached to disembodied spirits in Hades was pure fiction invented by Ferguson's poetic but baseless imagination, Campbell proclaimed. Then he summed up: "This speculation saps the whole foundation—the strongest argument for obeying the gospel. We have never read, from any quarter in our ranks, an essay of a more vulnerable or a more censurable character."[11]

Over the next three years Campbell continued his condemnation of Ferguson and was joined by a chorus of others. Samuel Church of Pittsburgh, for example, said Ferguson had "a maggot in his brain" that had destroyed his usefulness and led him to teach a "damnable heresy."[12] Ferguson defended his right to hold a private opinion and lashed out at heresy hunters, quoting Campbell's own earlier defense against his critics that he answered only to the church at Bethany where he was a member.[13] The majority of Ferguson's Nashville congregation continued to support him, despite the attacks and his move toward Universalist beliefs that all would be saved.[14]

Ferguson had stopped publication of the *Christian Magazine* at the end of 1853, but the Nashville newspapers continued to print news of his ideas because of his wide popularity in the city. By 1854 the charges against him had expanded to include being a Universalist, a Unitarian, and a spiritualist. Ferguson announced in the *Nashville Union and American* that on July 16 he would preach a sermon at his church answering these accusations and explaining his beliefs. That day he openly avowed that he believed all three. The sermon was then published as a booklet and widely distributed.[15]

The members of the Nashville church who opposed Ferguson had asked Campbell to come to the city and aid them in stopping Ferguson's destruction of their congregation. He arrived on Friday, November 24, and after resting and visiting friends on Saturday, he began eight days of almost nonstop speaking against Ferguson and his beliefs, first in McKendree Methodist

11. Alexander Campbell, "A New Discovery," *Millennial Harbinger*, June 1852, 316–29.

12. Alexander Campbell, "The Spirits in Prison," *Millennial Harbinger*, July 1852, 414.

13. Jesse B. Ferguson, special issue, *Christian Magazine*, December 1852, 26. See also Jesse B. Ferguson, "The Attack of the *Millennial Harbinger* upon the *Christian Magazine* and Its Editor," *Christian Magazine* 5 (August 1852): 241–46; (September 1852): 274–79.

14. Ferguson, *History of the Relation*, 4–5.

15. J. B. Ferguson, *Relation of Pastor and People: Statement of Belief on Unitarianism, Universalism, and Spiritualism* (Nashville: Union and American Steam Press, 1854).

Church, then in the Cherry Street building where Ferguson was the preacher. As for Ferguson, he reported that the spirit of William Ellery Channing had warned him to stay away from Campbell, so the two never met.[16]

Campbell's visit encouraged Ferguson's opponents, but his supporters at the Cherry Street church kept him as minister until July 1856. That month he resigned in the wake of a lawsuit brought by the opposing members for possession of the building. With Ferguson gone, the lawsuit became unnecessary, and the dissenters returned to the building in December. They called a former minister, Phillip S. Fall, to return to the congregation, but the magnificent Cherry Street building burned to the ground on April 8, 1857, sparked by a fire in a nearby carpenter's shop.[17]

Like the clash with John Thomas two decades earlier, the conflict with Ferguson ended with his clear separation from the movement. Under the leadership of Tolbert Fanning and others, the Nashville church slowly began to recover from this major disruption. But Ferguson's departure did not end the matter.

Tolbert Fanning, influential evangelist, editor, and educator, triggered the next part of the clash. Alexander Campbell had been a major influence on Fanning's theology and ministry, igniting in him a passion for restoring the ancient gospel and order. In 1835 and 1836 Fanning had accompanied Campbell on preaching tours and was a frequent correspondent in the *Millennial Harbinger*. Campbell had endorsed Fanning's Franklin College and his paper the *Gospel Advocate*, and the two seemed to be on good terms.[18]

But the Ferguson affair had been a major ordeal for Fanning. He had been a leader of the group that rejected Ferguson's teachings, and he suffered greatly over the division of the Nashville church. He was on heightened alert for any sources of what he considered dangerous false teachings.

In September 1856 Robert Richardson had begun a series in the *Millennial Harbinger* titled "The Misinterpretation of Scripture." In the first article he laid down his basic premises for understanding the Bible properly. First, he said, Christians must allow the Bible to interpret itself, going to Scripture itself to compare "spiritual things with spiritual." This was not merely an intellectual exercise, Richardson explained. It was essential to approach

16. W. K. Pendleton, "A. Campbell in Nashville," *Millennial Harbinger*, January 1855, 42–45; Alexander Campbell, "Our Visit to Nashville," *Millennial Harbinger*, February 1855, 96–107.

17. "The Christian Church Burnt," *Nashville Union and American*, April 9, 1857, 3.

18. Alexander Campbell, "Our Colleges," *Millennial Harbinger*, September 1845, 420; "Prospectus for the Gospel Advocate," *Millennial Harbinger*, June 1855, 358.

Tolbert Fanning (1810–1874) led in the opposition to Jesse B. Ferguson. His *Gospel Advocate* would become the most influential paper among the Southern churches after the Civil War. Courtesy of Mac Ice.

the text with "an humble, teachable, and prayerful spirit, conscious of dependence upon the Divine Author." "Spiritual truths admit only of being spiritually discerned. The Scriptures themselves do not reveal them to him who relies upon his understanding alone, and who, judging only according to things sensible and external, historical, grammatical and logical—the mere machinery of revelation, would make the acquisition of religious truth, if not a mere mechanical affair, at least a natural and simple result of ordinary external causes entirely under his own control. The moral sensibilities and spiritual affections of the soul, must be aroused before the things of the Spirit can be truly perceived or comprehended."[19]

19. Robert Richardson, "Misinterpretations of Scripture—No. I," *Millennial Harbinger*, September 1856, 503.

While Richardson insisted he would never devalue the letter of God's written revelation, he condemned any philosophy that made human understanding the sole legitimate interpreter of Scripture. In reality, only one's human spirit could perceive spiritual truths. Reason alone could never discover or grasp even one such truth. "All attempts, then, to reduce spiritual truths to the forms of the understanding, must be futile, and derogatory to that Divine word which addresses itself to our higher spiritual nature."[20]

Richardson was talking about what he saw as an alarming tendency in the movement to approach Scripture from a purely Lockean perspective. True, Locke taught that Scripture was a revelation from God that human senses alone could never discover. Yet he also insisted that we learn the divine truths of the Bible just as we learn any other information—by right use of the human intellect. While Scripture was supernatural in origin, one could understand it by proper use of human reason without added supernatural or spiritual force. Richardson saw the Lockean approach to Scripture as powerless to discern spiritual truths.

To Fanning, then in the last stages of the Ferguson affair, Richardson's statements were extremely alarming. Fanning believed that they could be used to justify Ferguson's destructive interpretations, and he was not going to let things get as far with Richardson as they had with his former minister. Fanning had begun the *Gospel Advocate* in 1855, partly to counter Ferguson's *Christian Magazine*. In October 1856 Fanning began a series of four articles titled "Metaphysical Discussions" attacking what he saw as Richardson's dangerous ideas. In essence, Fanning accused Richardson of following speculative human philosophy in his approach to Scripture rather than a simple rational approach to the clear teachings of Scripture.[21]

Richardson responded with his own series in the *Millennial Harbinger* titled "Faith versus Philosophy." He started by seemingly agreeing with Fanning. It was wrong, he said, to make Scripture conform to a human philosophical theory of religion. The present reformation began with the premise that Christians should abandon those theories and unite on the Bible alone. This movement advocated the ancient gospel and ancient order

20. Richardson, "Misinterpretations of Scripture—No. I," 505. Richardson had already written about his fears that the movement had lost a sense of the work of God's Spirit in the lives of Christians in seven articles in 1842 and 1843 titled "The Spirit of God."

21. Tolbert Fanning, "Metaphysical Discussions—No. I," *Gospel Advocate* 2 (October 1856): 314; "Metaphysical Discussions—No. 2," *Gospel Advocate* 2 (November 1856): 327–28; "Metaphysical Discussions—No. 3," *Gospel Advocate* 2 (December 1856): 357–59; "Metaphysical Discussions—No. 4," *Gospel Advocate* 3 (January 1857): 3–4.

of things—*"the only religious body that professes and maintains them in their primitive purity and simplicity."*[22]

Yet something was wrong. While the movement's principles were perfect, the way they had been applied was flawed. The fact is, Richardson declared, the faith had been contaminated with human philosophy—not on purpose or even knowingly, but it nevertheless had been. He identified Tolbert Fanning as a prime example of how human philosophy had crept in and perverted the gospel. Fanning represented those who denounced all systems of philosophy but were unwittingly captive to one. Richardson identified Fanning as a "philosopher of the school of Locke." Lockean philosophy denigrated the spiritual nature of human beings and made faith a process of human reasoning and cataloguing facts.[23]

Fanning was infuriated and wrote a long reply to Richardson's accusation. He denied that he was an adherent of any philosophy whatsoever. Anyone who truly respected the Bible would reject all philosophical systems in existence. John Locke had not created any system of philosophy; he had simply described how to think correctly.[24]

At some point, Fanning arrived in Bethany unannounced to talk to Alexander Campbell about how to stop what he saw as Richardson's destructive ideas. According to Fanning, Campbell was in such a state of mental decline when he arrived that his wife, Selina, would not allow him to be with Campbell alone but stayed with them and coached Campbell on what to say. Fanning concluded that people who did not hold to the principles Campbell had always advocated had influenced him negatively in his state of mental frailty.[25] Richardson would soon presume the same thing—but saw the influence on Campbell from a very different source.

The wedge between Richardson and Campbell became public in September 1857. Campbell published an article sharply criticizing his coeditor, stating that he did not approve of philosophical debates being published in his magazine. Furthermore, he rejected the idea that faith and philosophy should be set against each other—a clear reference to Richardson's "Faith versus Philosophy" series. There was no need to dip our buckets into the

22. Robert Richardson, "Faith versus Philosophy—No. I," *Millennial Harbinger*, March 1857, 137.

23. Robert Richardson, "Faith versus Philosophy—No. 3," *Millennial Harbinger*, May 1857, 258–59; "Faith versus Philosophy—No. 4," *Millennial Harbinger*, May 1857, 273–75.

24. Tolbert Fanning, "Reply to Professor Robert Richardson," *Millennial Harbinger*, August 1857, 434–48. Richardson printed Fanning's article with his responses interspersed throughout.

25. Tolbert Fanning, "Personal," *Gospel Advocate* 4 (July 1858): 219.

Alexander Campbell's constant clashes in defense of his reformation, growing fear over the tensions in the nation, and the burning
of Bethany College's main building took a tremendous toll on him.
His stern, almost angry expression in this photograph from the
late 1850s reflects the constant stress. Used with permission from
the Disciples of Christ Historical Society, Bethany, West Virginia.

empty well of philosophical systems, Campbell contended. We have taken
the Bible alone as it reveals the person, mission, and character of Christ.
"Why desecrate the '*Faithful and true witness*'?"[26]

Campbell admitted that there was a legitimate use of the word "philoso-

26. Alexander Campbell, "Christianity the True Philosophy. No. 1," *Millennial Harbinger,* September 1857, 481–82.

phy," in the sense of one's seeking to know the reason why things are as they are—the pursuit of wisdom. But no true philosophy could ever contradict anything in the Bible. Christians must test every philosophy by the Bible—the reason and wisdom of God. Then he lowered the boom. Faith, while not identical to reason, was reasonable and therefore in that sense philosophical. It was dangerous to write about "*faith versus philosophy*" or to speak of religion and philosophy as conflicting. Only "sectarians, bigots, enthusiasts, and philosophists" would do so. "I cannot but regret that any enlightened writer amongst us should regard them as necessarily antagonistic to one another."[27]

At one level, Campbell's rebuke could be seen as a reprimand of both Fanning and Richardson. Yet both Fanning and Richardson understood it as aimed at Richardson, and Fanning triumphantly republished Campbell's article in the next issue of the *Gospel Advocate*.

In the very issue of the *Millennial Harbinger* that Campbell's scathing critique had appeared, Richardson tried to clarify some statements he feared had been misunderstood. First, he wanted to make it clear that he did not question the doctrinal teachings of the "leading brethren of the Reformation." He was afraid, however, that many of them had arrived at those teachings by using a dangerous human philosophy. By insisting that facts alone were the basis of faith, they were using a philosophy *about* faith that in reality took the *place* of faith! They had substituted a theory about faith for the real thing. Richardson insisted that he was against using *human* philosophy to define faith, but not the divine philosophy that permeated the gospel. "*It is Christ crucified that is God's philosophy,*" Richardson exclaimed, and he insisted that his understanding was exactly what Campbell was advocating in his critical article a few pages earlier.[28]

As already stated, the human philosophy Richardson was condemning was John Locke's notion that all knowledge came through the human senses. While spiritual truths came only through Scripture, faith was the intellectual acceptance of the facts of Scripture. Richardson believed that to teach that faith was simply intellectual assent to a set of facts, rather than trust in the person of Christ, stripped the spiritual power from Christianity. The focus was on human intellectual achievement rather than the work of God. Facts about Christ were substituted for Christ.[29]

27. Campbell, "Christianity the True Philosophy. No. 1," 482–84.

28. Robert Richardson, "Faith versus Philosophy," *Millennial Harbinger*, September 1857, 491–95.

29. Campbell defined "fact" as something done—an event or saying.

Robert Richardson (1806–1876) was Campbell's personal physician, coeditor of the *Millennial Harbinger*, and professor of
chemistry and chair of the sciences at Bethany College. After
Alexander Campbell's death, the family asked Richardson to
write Campbell's biography. Used with permission from the
Disciples of Christ Historical Society, Bethany, West Virginia.

Richardson's explanation did not stop Campbell's criticism. Deeply hurt,
Richardson resigned from his position as associate editor of the *Millennial
Harbinger* in December. This humiliation was on top of another laid on him
by the Bethany College Board of Trustees the previous July. The Trustees
passed a resolution that all professors at the school had to live in the village of
Bethany or its immediate vicinity, mentioning Richardson specifically. Richardson's home, nicknamed Bethphage after the New Testament village next
to Bethany, was two miles away, across Buffalo Creek. Richardson had tried
to move to Bethany several times, but Campbell and his son-in-law W. K.
Pendleton owned all the desirable property in the village and would not sell.

In response to the board's demand, he resigned from his teaching position at Bethany. In an embarrassing set of events, the board accepted his
resignation, then immediately reappointed him. At first he refused, but when
a friend urged him to stay because of the harm his departure would do to
the school and the movement, he relented. Campbell never came to the
defense of his faithful coworker but allowed the affair to continue with his

tacit approval even as he began his personal attack on Richardson. When the new Kentucky University in Harrodsburg offered Richardson the positions of chair of physical science and vice president of the university in February 1858, he accepted.[30]

But then a curious set of events occurred. On Friday, December 11, 1857, the main classroom and administrative building of Bethany College burned to the ground. The mental cloud that from all accounts Campbell had been in for some time seemed to be blown away by this tragic event that threatened the survival of the school. Campbell immediately began to make plans for rebuilding and set off with W. K. Pendleton on an extensive fund-raising trip. Richardson had to teach Campbell's and Pendleton's classes and do Campbell's administrative work for several months without any additional compensation. He received and accepted the offer from Kentucky University while Campbell was away.

But when Campbell returned in April, he urged Richardson to stay, expressing how much Bethany needed him and that he doubted Kentucky University could survive. Richardson was surprised, to say the least. When he reminded Campbell of his hostility toward him and his articles on faith versus philosophy, Campbell acted as if he did not remember anything about it. Campbell promised that he would set things right, and true to his word, he published a conciliatory article in May 1858. While he did not apologize to Richardson, he clarified that despite a statement suggesting that Richardson taught the "Spirit only" theory, he did not actually believe it at all.[31] He quoted from Richardson's article from the previous June that the spirit and the word should never be separated and affirmed that he and Richardson believed the same thing. In another odd move, Campbell said that he didn't know how he could have made such a misstatement about Richardson, unless he had written it while traveling and without Richardson's article in front of him. He must have been thinking about some misquotation of Richardson that someone had published.[32]

Then Campbell turned his attention toward Fanning. In the next issue, he lashed out at Fanning's labeling of Richardson as a teacher of "unmixed and unblushing infidelity." The *Gospel Advocate*'s editor had committed an outrage on editorial and Christian courtesy as well as the rules of church order and

30. Cloyd Goodnight and Dwight E. Stevenson, *Home to Bethphage: A Biography of Robert Richardson* (St. Louis: Christian Board of Publication, 1949), 174–85, 188–92.

31. The "Spirit only" theory referred to the idea that humans could not understand Scripture or the gospel unless a supernatural act of the Holy Spirit enabled them to do so.

32. Alexander Campbell, "A Correction," *Millennial Harbinger*, May 1858, 289–90.

discipline, Campbell exclaimed. Fanning was totally wrong when he asserted that Richardson had abandoned the principles Campbell believed and taught. And as far as he was concerned, Campbell stated, that was the end of the matter.[33] Campbell reappointed Richardson to the editorial staff of the *Millennial Harbinger*, and though Richardson did move to Harrodsburg, Kentucky, to fulfill his obligations at Kentucky University, he continued to show his support for Bethany College and Alexander Campbell. Perhaps not surprisingly, in his *Memoirs of Alexander Campbell*, Richardson never even alluded to the rift.

What is the point of this story? In the course of the controversy with Ferguson, Richardson, and Fanning, Campbell managed to attack and denounce all three. Ferguson left the movement, Fanning became permanently estranged from Campbell, and Richardson was exonerated, becoming again one of Campbell's closest colleagues. Was Campbell's mental decline behind his erratic behavior, as both Fanning and Richardson believed? Was it Campbell's sense that Richardson's attacks on Lockean philosophy were secretly aimed at him? Was it his realization that Richardson's support and friendship were more important for saving Bethany College than the blessing of his rival editor and school president Fanning?

Whatever the explanation, this was another instance of Campbell's posture of aggressive defense of anything that would in his estimation damage or hinder the progress and advancement of the ancient gospel and order of things and the hastening of the millennium. Was he suffering the early stages of dementia? Likely so. Hints of Campbell's decline came from numerous observers. In a letter to his friend Phillip Fall, Richardson remarked, "Brother C. is getting old. He has been a faithful laborer and perseveres still even when his work is done. . . . Still . . . he ought not to stop others from doing their portion of the work, or put viewpoints into the hands of such a man as Fanning, against his true friend."[34]

In his biography of Campbell, Richardson described how Campbell, unable to continue his teaching and administrative duties, often continued to show up to teach his morning class until reminded it was no longer his class. Whenever no one else was scheduled to preach at the Bethany church, Campbell felt obligated to deliver a message. Richardson described his sermons as rambling and "marred by occasional repetitions."[35] Bethany student Charles Chilton Moore, grandson of Barton Stone, who would later edit the

33. Alexander Campbell, "President Fanning," *Millennial Harbinger*, June 1858, 353.
34. Richardson to Fall, cited in Goodnight and Stevenson, *Home to Bethphage*, 174.
35. Richardson, *Memoirs of Alexander Campbell*, 2:644–45.

atheist paper *Blue Grass Blade,* was a close friend of Campbell's daughter Virginia at the time of the Richardson controversy. Moore recounted in his autobiography how he and Virginia would secretly make fun of how "long and exceedingly dry" Campbell's sermons had become in his old age.[36]

Campbell's conflict with Richardson was not unlike earlier clashes with close colleagues of the reformation. However, his strange move from support of Fanning and denunciation of Richardson to exactly the opposite position symbolized the transition—as uneven as it was—from confident advocate of his millennial vision to surrender to a future known only to God. The outbreak of the long-dreaded war over slavery compelled him to set aside his self-assurance and certainty of the rapid triumph of his reformation.

36. Charles Chilton Moore, *Behind the Bars; 31498* (Lexington, KY: Bluegrass Printing Co., 1899), 65.

Surrender

We claim . . . no prophetic infallibility, but yet, we are sure that we have looked long and steadfastly at the interests of the church, and weighed with an anxious if not often heavy heart the signs of the times, and the shadows of the coming struggles and fortunes, which of late have been thrown thick and dark upon the horizon. We are not ready, the great Master knows, nor willing to see these gloomy portents. We would rather see only the rosy dawn of a peaceful and triumphant procession of a golden age for the church—to imagine her going forth in her bridal adornments to meet the coming of her Espoused in the garments of joy. But it may not be.

—Alexander Campbell, "Preface," 1864

CHAPTER 18

Slavery—the Movement's Greatest Threat

From their first encounters with American slavery, it was deeply disturbing to both Thomas and Alexander Campbell. In 1819 Thomas had gathered a group of slaves in Burlington, Kentucky, where he was then teaching, to read Scripture and sing hymns on a Sunday afternoon. Afterward a friend informed Thomas that he had violated a state law against addressing blacks without one or more white witnesses. Thomas immediately left the state in disgust.[1]

A decade later, in 1829, Brooke County voters elected Alexander Campbell as a delegate to the Virginia state constitutional convention. He came to Richmond with a proposal for the gradual abolition of slavery in the state, and despite resistance from elite Tidewater plantation owners, he found considerable support. In the end, however, he gave in to the consensus that the issue was simply too contentious to deal with. The one concession Campbell and his fellow backcountry citizens achieved was that slavery would not be mentioned in the Virginia Constitution at all, making it possible for future state legislatures to deal with it by law rather than by constitutional amendment.[2]

Clearly, Campbell did not see the plight of enslaved Africans as a major concern for himself or his movement. He assumed, as did virtually all whites, the myth of white supremacy. He opposed slavery, like Thomas Jefferson, because it was unhealthy for the nation and for the white citizenry. Furthermore, controversy over the issue threatened to destroy the republic itself! "Much as I may sympathize with a black man, I love the white man

---

1. Robert Richardson, *Memoirs of Alexander Campbell*, 2 vols. (Philadelphia: J. B. Lippincott & Co., 1868–1870), 1:494–96.
2. William M. Moorhouse, "Alexander Campbell and the Virginia Constitutional Convention of 1829–1830," *Virginia Cavalcade* 24 (Spring 1975): 184–91.

Alexander Campbell served as a delegate from Brooke County in the Virginia Constitutional Convention of 1829–1830. He represented the western "progressives" who pushed for a gradual ending of slavery in the state, as well as public education. Here he met former presidents James Madison and James Monroe, Supreme Court Justice John Marshall, and future president John Tyler. Campbell is seventh from the right in the back row. Used with permission from the Disciples of Christ Historical Society, Bethany, West Virginia.

more," he wrote. "As a political economist, and as a philanthropist, I have many reasons for preferring the prospects and conditions of the Free to the Slave states; but especially as a Christian, I sympathize much more with the owners of slaves, their heirs, and successors, than the slaves which they possess and bequeath."[3]

Yet slavery's potential destruction of the nation was not itself Campbell's main fear. Both Campbells were absolutely convinced that God had prepared America as the chosen nation for restoring the ancient gospel and order and thereby restoring Christian unity. As the nation divided into increasingly strident pro- and antislavery camps, the separation of the Methodist and Baptist churches into Northern and Southern factions frightened Campbell more than anything that had happened before. He had to face the probability that if slavery wrecked the nation, it would wreck his reform movement too.

The only way to avoid this disaster, he believed, was to take a "moder-

3. Alexander Campbell, "Our Position to American Slavery—No. V," *Millennial Harbinger*, May 1845, 234.

ate" position. Even as he denounced American slavery as inconsistent with the "spirit of the age," he insisted that the Bible never condemned slavery as inherently evil. He wrote, "To preserve unity of spirit among Christians of the South and of the North is my grand object, and for that purpose I am endeavoring to show that the New Testament does not authorize any interference or legislation upon the relation of master and slave, nor does it in either letter or spirit authorize Christians to make it a term of communion."[4] He came to believe that the logical plan for preserving the nation and his reform was a gradual process of freeing and educating the enslaved people—as far as they were capable of being educated. This would slowly eliminate slavery and soften the economic and cultural blow to the white slaveholding population. By the 1840s, however, "moderate" or gradualist positions garnered less and less support.

Campbell wrote and published much on slavery as editor of the *Christian Baptist* and *Millennial Harbinger*. In his earliest statements he seems to be making a moral argument against slavery. His first editorial for the *Christian Baptist* in 1823 was a sweeping depiction of "the Christian religion." Quoting Psalm 72, Campbell described the work of Christ as delivering the needy and redeeming their souls. The apostasy of the church was clear, he asserted, in elaborate systems of worship, hierarchical power structures, wars conducted in the name of Christ, and "those Christians, who are daily extolling the blessings of civil and religious liberty, and at the same time, by a system of the most cruel oppression, separating the wife from the embraces of her husband, and the mother from her tender offspring; violating every principle, and rending every tie that endears life and reconciles man to his lot; and that forsooth, because might gives right, and a man is held guilty because his skin is a shade darker than the standard color of the times."[5]

Seven years later when he began the *Millennial Harbinger*, he predicted that among the magazine's major themes would be the injustice in America's political system that hindered the millennium, and "the treatment of African slaves," with a view to their emancipation and "exaltation from their present degraded condition."[6]

By 1835, however, with the significant growth of his reform following the union with many Stone churches, Campbell backed away from extensive treatments of slavery to avoid any semblance of politics. National crises

---

4. Campbell, "Our Position to American Slavery—No. V," 195.

5. Alexander Campbell, "The Christian Religion," *Christian Baptist* 1 (August 1, 1823): 25.

6. Alexander Campbell, "Prospectus," *Millennial Harbinger* 1 (January 1830): 1.

beginning in the 1840s, however, increasingly foreshadowed a coming war and drove him to change his editorial policy. The divisions of the Baptist and Methodist churches in the mid-1840s, the Fugitive Slave Act of 1850, and a student revolt at his own Bethany College in 1855 forced him to return to the issue. In his writing Campbell struggled desperately to stop the increasingly devastating effects of the issue of slavery on his reformation.

Division in the Baptist and Methodist Churches

For both the Baptist "Triennial Convention" and the Methodist Episcopal Church, the battle over the sinfulness or acceptability of slavery for Christians reached the boiling point in 1844. These denominations, along with the Presbyterian Church, had long dominated the American religious landscape. With a significant presence in all parts of the nation, they mirrored the widening split in the country as a whole.[7] Campbell knew that any division of those churches would inevitably influence his movement, potentially emboldening extremists on both sides of the slavery divide to call for separation. The crisis in the Baptist fold especially alarmed Campbell, and he followed its progress closely.[8]

The Baptist General Convention (the foreign missionary society known popularly as the "Triennial Convention" because it met every three years) declared itself neutral on slavery in April 1844. By November, however, Alabama Baptists pressed the issue and asked the Acting Board to rule on whether they would appoint a slaveholder as a missionary or other agent of the Convention. The Acting Board responded that it was a hypothetical question, since no slaveholder had applied, but if one did and insisted on keeping slaves, they could not appoint such a person. Proslavery Baptists met the following May in Augusta, Georgia, and organized the Southern Baptist Convention.[9]

The immediate cause for Methodist separation into Northern and Southern denominations surrounded Bishop James O. Andrew of Georgia. Andrew's wife had inherited two slaves from her deceased first husband's estate, slaves that by law became Andrew's property. The matter of church

---

7. C. C. Goen, *Broken Churches, Broken Nation: Denominational Schisms and the Coming of the Civil War* (Macon, GA: Mercer University Press, 1985), 51–54.

8. He especially drew from the arguments of Baptist antislavery advocate (though not abolitionist) Francis Wayland and South Carolinian Richard Fuller as exemplary positions on the issue. Alexander Campbell, "Our Position to American Slavery," *Millennial Harbinger*, February 1845, 52, and subsequent articles in the series.

9. Goen, *Broken Churches*, 95–96.

leaders owning slaves had been a topic of sharp dispute among Methodists for many years; the Methodist *Discipline* had carried a resolution condemning slavery from the very first edition.

Bishop Andrew was personally opposed to slavery, but Georgia law prohibited emancipation of slaves in the state. By the May 1844 General Conference in New York, the situation had become a major cause for both sides. After a long and grueling debate, a majority of delegates approved a resolution requiring Andrew to step down as bishop until he could divest himself of the slaves. Southern delegates immediately began planning for separation. They formally constituted the Methodist Episcopal Church, South, later that month in Louisville, Kentucky.[10]

Campbell must have felt like Thomas Jefferson in his 1820 letter to John Holmes concerning the spread of slavery to Missouri: "This momentous question, like a fire bell in the night, awakened and filled me with terror. I considered it at once as the knell of the Union."[11] Campbell believed that the divisions of the Methodist and Baptist denominations had terrifying implications for his movement. He seemed to think that he, through his own personal reputation, could do what the "moderates" in those bodies had been unable to do—keep his movement united. A united movement was absolutely crucial to complete his vision—the Lord's vision—of restoring the ancient gospel and order, bringing the unity of all Christians, which would result in the conversion of the world and the beginning of the millennium.

"Our Position to American Slavery"

Alarmed by the division of the Baptist and Methodist churches, Campbell began a series of articles in February 1845 to spell out his views on American slavery and why it must never become a source of division among the Disciples. "We are the only religious community in the civilized world whose principles (unless we abandon them) can preserve us from such an unfortunate predicament. This I feel able to demonstrate to the entire satisfaction of every intelligent brother and candid citizen at the South or at the North."[12]

Between February and June, Campbell published eight articles exam-

10. Goen, *Broken Churches*, 81–83.
11. Jefferson to Holmes, April 22, 1820, Library of Congress, http://www.loc.gov/exhibits/jefferson/159.html.
12. Alexander Campbell, "Our Position to American Slavery," *Millennial Harbinger*, February 1845, 51.

ining the nature of slavery and its relation to Scripture, the church, and the individual Christian. In the eighth and final installment, he summarized his points and rested his case. First, based on abundant Scripture testimony, the relation of master and slave was not in itself sinful or immoral. Second, American slavery was not beneficial to the nation. It was out of step with the spirit of the age, unfavorable to individual and national prosperity, and it made it difficult for Christian masters and their families to develop "that refined and elevated personal and domestic happiness so desirable to any Christian household." Finally, based on what he believed to be clear scriptural premises, he insisted that while the churches should insist that masters treat their slaves with kindness and preserve slave families, the simple relation of slave to master could never be made "a term of Christian fellowship or a subject of discipline" if they were truly governed by the Bible.[13]

These three propositions, backed by extensive discussion in the previous essays, would, he insisted, be sufficient for all who truly loved the peace and prosperity of Christ's kingdom to maintain the unity of the reform. He knew that not everyone in his reform would agree with his assessment. He asked only for a hearing, maintaining the hope that his reasoning would convince the majority and avert a division like the ones occurring in other Christian groups. He was to be greatly disappointed.[14]

Jailed in Scotland

One of the most bizarre incidents concerning slavery in Campbell's life took place not in America but in Scotland, two years after his 1845 *Millennial Harbinger* series on slavery. In May Campbell embarked on a trip to the United Kingdom to raise support for Bethany College and to encourage churches there that were affiliated with his reformation. He spoke in a number of cities before arriving in Edinburgh in early August.

Frederick Douglass, the abolitionist speaker who had escaped from slavery, had lectured across Great Britain the previous year, returning to America less than a month before Campbell started his journey. Douglass's graphic descriptions of the treatment of enslaved persons in America cou-

---

13. Alexander Campbell, "Our Position to American Slavery—No. VIII," *Millennial Harbinger*, June 1845, 263.

14. Campbell, "Our Position to American Slavery—No. VIII," 263–64.

CITIZENS OF EDINBURGH,
Beware! Beware!

THE REV. ALEX. CAMPBELL,
Of VIRGINIA, UNITED STATES, AMERICA.

This Gentleman stated at his Meeting in the Waterloo-Rooms, last night, that a placard, containing what professes to be Extracts from Mr CAMPBELL'S writings, WAS FALSE.

What is the Fact?

Those Extracts were solemnly read over to Mr Campbell, on Tuesday the 10th inst., and Mr Campbell admitted, that he was the Author of said Extracts.

To the truth of this statement, the three Gentlemen, who waited upon MR CAMPBELL, are ready solemnly to depone. —Mr Campbell, is hereby dared to meet these Gentlemen, before a public meeting, where they shall have liberty of speech. Again, it is asserted, that the Rev. Alexander Campbell, was once a SLAVE-HOLDER HIMSELF, and is still the ALLY and DEFENDER of MAN-STEALERS. Besides, Mr Campbell *has admitted*, that the *NEGRO PEW*, is rigidly adhered to in the Churches, with which he is connected—and he himself declares, that he would *not on any account,*

SIT AT MEAT WITH A COLOURED PERSON.

The truth of this will be established, when Mr Campbell accepts of the **PUBLIC CHALLENGE**, given to him, by the Rev. JAMES ROBERTSON.   PRINTED BY ANDERSON & BRYCE.

EDINBURGH, 12th August, 1847.

Campbell's "moderate" position toward slavery was in effect a defense of it. During his trip to Scotland, opponents constantly assailed his position in newspapers and in posters such as this one that challenged him to a public debate. Courtesy of the Center for Restoration Studies, Abilene Christian University, Abilene, Texas.

pled with his appeals to hearers to do everything they could to pressure the United States to abolish slavery had enflamed Scottish passions.[15]

Douglass's antislavery speeches were still very much on the minds of many Scots when Campbell arrived in Edinburgh. The Scottish Anti-Slavery Society had anticipated his coming and immediately started a campaign against him, labeling him a slaveholder and "defender of manstealers"— language Douglass had used earlier. The secretary of the Anti-Slavery Soci-

15. Nikki Brown, "'Send Back the Money!' Frederick Douglass's Anti-Slavery Speeches in Scotland and the Emergence of African American Internationalism," STAR (Scotland's Transatlantic Relations) Project Archive, April 2004; Frederick Douglass, "The Free Church of Scotland and American Slavery: An Address Delivered in Dundee, Scotland, on January 30, 1846," published in the *Dundee Courier*, February 3, 1846, available at http://glc.yale .edu/free-church-scotland-and-american-slavery.

ety, Rev. James Robertson, an ordained minister in the United Presbyterian synod formed earlier that year, issued a challenge to Campbell to debate the sinfulness of slavery.

While Campbell tried to ignore the posters and the challenge, the attacks followed him from Edinburgh to all his other speaking engagements. One poster charged Campbell with being in fellowship with slaveholders, whom it labeled "inhuman tyrants." It urged the people of Scotland to avoid all connections with Campbell and his traveling companion James Henshall "until they go home and urge upon their Slaveholding brethren *to cease to do evil, to learn to do well, to seek judgment, and to* EMANCIPATE ALL THEIR SLAVES."[16]

After three weeks of hounding, Campbell, under the advice of his Scottish friends, published a letter in the *Edinburgh Journal* saying he would debate Robertson, if he were not the James Robertson who had been put out of the Baptist church in Dundee for abusing his mother. This was the first shot by Campbell's supporters of a personal counterattack on Robertson. They also implied that he might not actually be a legitimate minister despite his self-identification as "Rev. James Robertson."

Robertson and his allies came back with a vengeance, formally charging Campbell with libel for the insinuation that Robertson had mistreated his mother. The warrant accompanying the libel charge prohibited Campbell from leaving Scotland until the case was closed. Though Campbell's friends appealed, the local courts judged the warrant to be valid and set a trial date for the following week.

While certainly a nuisance, Campbell thought the charge might actually provide him an opportunity to publicize his cause of Christian unity in the face of what he regarded as abolitionist fanaticism. He rejected the offer from his friends to post bail and was taken into custody. The accounts of those who visited and ministered to him in jail reflect his savoring of the incident. It did indeed generate publicity and some sympathy. After ten days of imprisonment, the judge dismissed the libel charge and ordered Campbell's release.[17]

Throughout the incident, Campbell consistently maintained the "moderate" position expressed in the "Our Position" articles. He repeatedly explained that he did not support American slavery. His equally consistent refusal to

16. "People of Scotland, Beware!!," poster dated August 17, 1847, Campbell Collection, Disciples of Christ Historical Society, Bethany, West Virginia.

17. Richardson, *Memoirs of Alexander Campbell*, 2:552–66; Thomas Chalmers, *Alexander Campbell's Tour in Scotland* (Louisville: Guide Printing and Publishing Co., 1892).

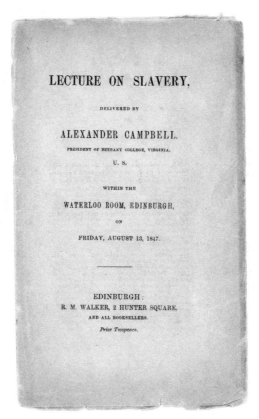

Front page of the speech on slavery delivered by Alexander Campbell in the Waterloo Rooms, Edinburgh, Scotland. Used with permission from the Disciples of Christ Historical Society, Bethany, West Virginia.

condemn slavery as evil, however, cast him as an advocate of slavery to Christian abolitionists and therefore an enemy of truth and virtue. For those in the increasingly polarized camps, there was no such thing as a moderate position.

While accounts of the incident report that Campbell weathered this storm confidently and emerged relatively unscathed, it took a toll on his mental and physical health. Even more devastating, however, was the news he received upon his return to the United States that his eleven-year-old son Wickliffe had drowned in a swimming accident. Wickliffe had been the one of all his children in whom he saw real potential for taking the mantle of the movement's leadership. The child's death was a massive blow to Campbell. Precisely in the midst of dealing with his own crushing sorrow

Wickliffe Campbell (1837–1847) was the son Alexander had hoped would continue his work. His drowning while Campbell was away in Scotland was devastating to both Alexander and Selina. Contemporary accounts indicate Selina may have come close to a nervous breakdown. Used with permission from Bethany College, T. W. Phillips Memorial Library, Archives and Special Collections, Bethany, West Virginia.

and his wife Selina's depression, the threat of slavery confronted Campbell as never before.

In 1850 the crisis reached another boiling point with the passage of the Fugitive Slave Act. This was not the first such law in United States history. In fact, Article IV of the Constitution had stipulated that "No Person held to Service or Labour in one State, under the Laws thereof, escaping into another, shall, in Consequence of any Law or Regulation therein, be discharged from such Service or Labour, but shall be delivered up on Claim of the Party to whom such Service or Labour may be due." The first Fugitive

Slave Act, passed by Congress in 1793, spelled out procedures for capturing and returning fugitive slaves to their masters. But many in Northern states where slavery was abolished resisted enforcement of the law.

The Fugitive Slave Act of 1850 was part of a larger deal known as the Compromise of 1850. The acquisition of a huge tract of land from Mexico in 1848 after the Mexican War had heightened tension over slavery—would new states formed from the land be slave or free? The compromise included five laws designed to keep a balance of power between free and slave states. California was admitted as a free state; New Mexico and Utah territories were created with provisions for a popular vote to decide their status when applying for statehood; and Congress passed a greatly strengthened Fugitive Slave Act.

These measures were intended to give something to both Northern and Southern lawmakers and get the Southerners to back off their threat of secession. Conventions in Mississippi in 1849 and in Nashville in 1850 had raised the real possibility of secession if slavery were kept out of the newly acquired lands. In fact, the Fugitive Slave Act enraged Northerners and Southerners alike, even though its provisions called into question the reality of any state actually being "free."

The firestorm of response in the national media upon passage of the act in September made it impossible for Campbell to be silent. His first article appeared in January 1851, prompted partly by a letter from Ohio Disciple John Kirk. Kirk bluntly accused Campbell of having fellowship with slaveholders, "the vilest thieves and hypocrites that ever lived." Any slaveholder in the churches who refused after being admonished "to let the captive go free" should be treated as "a horse thief, or any other notorious villain." He said he assumed that Campbell approved of the Fugitive Slave Act by his silence and therefore accused Campbell of heresy.[18]

Campbell's reply was short and severe. He accused Kirk of acting as a tyrannical miniature pope, willing to destroy the constitutions of both the United States and the kingdom of Christ "under the frenzied impulse of a perverted mind." "I don't care at all whether I have your frown or smile," Campbell concluded. "I will think for myself and speak as I see things on this matter." He then advised Kirk to read his extensive article on the subject earlier in the same issue.[19]

---

18. Kirk to Campbell, December 12, 1850, in Alexander Campbell, "Our Position to American Slavery," *Millennial Harbinger*, January 1851, 49–50.

19. Kirk to Campbell, in "Our Position to American Slavery," *Millennial Harbinger*, January 1851, 50.

The article to which Campbell referred set the stage for a series on the
Fugitive Slave Act that appeared between January and November 1851 and
provided a comprehensive statement of Campbell's understandings on the
Christian and slavery. As he had expressed in 1845, Campbell insisted that
he hated slavery as a blight on the country—because it was a terrible burden
and evil influence on "the master and his children [more] than to the servant
and his children."[20] However, he continued, far from condemning slavery or
returning runaway slaves, the New Testament consistently sanctioned slavery
and, specifically in the book of Philemon, directed a runaway slave to return
to his master. Furthermore, Campbell continued, the Fugitive Slave Act was
clearly constitutional. Since Christian citizens were sworn to support the Constitution and obey the laws of the United States, they must obey this law too.[21]

Campbell's deeply held notions of white supremacy emerged in the articles in many ways. This was not simply a matter concerning a problematic
political or social institution, he insisted. It was about the complete inconceiv-
ability that blacks and whites could ever live together in a relationship of equality. Campbell attacked abolitionists for having a philosophy completely out of
harmony with the genius of human nature. "There may be black States and
white States, as there are red men and white men. But there shall never be, *on
Abolition principles*, an abolition of slavery in the midst of a white population."[22]

Slavery could be abolished, Campbell insisted, only in one of two ways:
by an amalgamation of the races (an idea he knew would be abhorrent to his
readers) or by complete and permanent separation of blacks and whites by
sending blacks somewhere outside the country or to a place in the country
set aside exclusively for them. He concluded that of these options, the only
feasible choice was that of the American Colonization Society, which proposed to send blacks "back to Africa, with our language, our civilization,
and our religion."[23]

In a long and detailed argument drawn from biblical examples supposedly upholding the legitimacy of owning human beings for life, Campbell
sarcastically accused abolitionists of creating a biblical text to justify their
agenda. "All men are born free and equal," Campbell asserted, comes not

20. Alexander Campbell, "Queries on Masters' Duties," *Millennial Harbinger*, September 1951, 529.
21. Alexander Campbell, "Slavery and the Fugitive Slave Law—No. IV," *Millennial Harbinger*, July 1851, 386–88.
22. Campbell, "Queries on Masters' Duties," 530.
23. Alexander Campbell. "The Fugitive Slave Law—Once More," *Millennial Harbinger*,
November 1851, 632.

from Scripture but from "Saint Voltaire, and baptized by Thomas Jefferson."[24] In other words, such notions of the essential equality of all people came from infidel sources, not God!

Dred Scott Decision

On March 6, 1857, the day the US Supreme Court issued the *Dred Scott* decision, Campbell and his twenty-five-year-old son, Alexander Campbell Jr., were on a steamer headed from Cairo, Illinois, to New Orleans. Just a week before, the two had set out on a ten-week trip to raise funds for Bethany College, through parts of Indiana, Illinois, Louisiana, Alabama, and Georgia. In striking contrast to the extensive treatment of the Fugitive Slave Act in 1850, Campbell never mentioned this massively significant and inflammatory document—a document central to the final events leading to the Civil War. In fact, the only mention of slavery for the whole year was a reprint of an article from a Presbyterian magazine urging Negro evangelism.[25]

It does not seem possible that the *Dred Scott* decision and its implications could have been absent from the pair's conversation during the trip. The multiple articles dealing with the denominational divisions of the mid-1840s and the passage of the Fugitive Slave Act in 1850 attested to Campbell's determination to defuse the divisive potential of slavery in his reformation. Yet his published reports of the trip contained absolutely no hint of the issue. Apparently the terrifying volatility of the decision led Campbell to avoid any printed mention whatsoever.

The *Dred Scott* decision (*Dred Scott v. Sanford*) articulated in no uncertain terms the absolute commitment to white supremacy as a fundamental doctrine of the nation.

> [The negro African race] had for more than a century before [the Declaration of Independence] been regarded as beings of an inferior order, and altogether unfit to associate with the white race, either in social or political relations; and so far inferior, that they had no rights which the white man was bound to respect; and that the negro might justly and lawfully be reduced to slavery for his benefit.

24. Alexander Campbell, "Slavery and the Fugitive Slave Law—No. II," *Millennial Harbinger*, May 1851, 252.

25. "The American Gibeonites—No. IV," *Millennial Harbinger*, March 1857, 161–64.

... the men who framed [the] [D]eclaration [of Independence] were great men—high in literary acquirements—high in their sense of honor. . . . They perfectly understood the meaning of the language they used (i.e., "All men are created equal"), and how it would be understood by others; and they knew that it would not in any part of the civilized world be supposed to embrace the negro race, which by common consent, had been excluded from civilized Governments and the family of nations, and doomed to slavery.

The *Dred Scott* decision declared that a slave brought into a "free state" remained a slave. The clear political implication was that there was no such thing as a "free state." The more long-lasting and destructive parts of the document were the pervasive statements of the inherent inferiority of blacks—whether slave or free—and the unabashed declaration that blacks were unfit to associate on an equal footing with the white race. These ideas had long been an accepted assumption among white Americans, and virtually no white citizen—whether pro- or antislavery—would have disputed them. They were certainly part of Campbell's assumptions. But the explicit articulation of them in a document issued by the nation's highest court codified them as the definitive law of the nation. And Campbell remained silent.

Incident at Bethany College

Campbell's decision to remain completely silent on the *Dred Scott* decision was fueled by an incident at Bethany College in the fall of 1855—an incident that became a spectacle to the entire movement. While the majority of Bethany students were from Southern states, a significant number came from Northern free states. No college rule forbade the discussion of slavery, but a de facto understanding between students and administration was that the topic was off-limits. According to Campbell's account in January 1856, a small number of Northern students had entered the school the previous year with the express goal of agitating the matter of slavery. In a handful of incidents in college literary societies and in Sunday evening sermons at the Bethany church, student speakers had both strongly defended and vehemently attacked slavery.

The incident, which led to the dismissal of five students and the voluntary departure of five others, happened in November. Phillip Burns, a Scottish student from Canada with proabolitionist convictions, preached a Sunday evening sermon in which he indirectly condemned American slavery and the morality of a church that would support it. At some point, twenty or thirty members of the congregation noisily left the building, and someone later pushed open a window from the outside, causing the glass to break. Other disruptive behavior (hitting the windows with sticks, banging on the floor of the building from underneath, loud talking outside) by those who had left continued until the end of the service.

While Burns and those who sympathized with him later recounted receiving verbal threats when leaving the building, and Burns received an anonymous note threatening "consequences which it would be hard to escape and harder to bear," Campbell later downplayed both as common college pranks merely designed to frighten. The next day a large group of students passed resolutions that articulated what had been the unstated rule: "We most heartily condemn all discussions of said question (slavery) either for or against, believing that the agitation of said question will prove disadvantageous to the vital interests of Bethany College." In response, a number of Northern students drew up their own resolutions, including a demand for "the right to discuss, in public debate or in the pulpit, the merits of American slavery."[26]

According to Campbell, though the twenty or so dissident Northern students refused to attend class until the administration had passed their resolution, members of the faculty were still willing to be lenient. If the students would go back to class and stop any further disruptive efforts, no action would be taken against them. Five who refused to return to class were expelled from the college, and five others left with them. Campbell insisted the matter was strictly an internal disciplinary action that any responsible school administration would have taken. He reported that after the departure of the offending students, things returned to normal and no further tensions were evident.[27]

Yet the incident was one more painful thorn in Campbell's side. The expelled students gave accounts of persecution by fellow students and the administration—reports Campbell categorically denied. Such lies, he asserted, were further indication of the unfitness of those students to attend any reputable institution. But to add further injury, Northwestern Christian University in Indianapolis, the "free soil" school founded a decade earlier by abolitionists—including Ovid Butler, after whom the school would eventually be named—accepted several of the expelled students without consulting administrators at Bethany. Campbell was outraged. How could any reputable

26. Alexander Campbell, "Disturbance in Bethany College," *Millennial Harbinger*, January 1856, 59.
27. Campbell, "Disturbance in Bethany College," 60.

school act in such a manner? "If an institution is designed to be a school of refuge for self-willed and self-conceited young adventurers, insubordinate to rational and moral discipline, and whose certificate for admission is to be found in a public or private certificate of dismission or expulsion from a college of fair and honorable standing, . . . then it should be . . . [advertised as] for the accommodation of such young GENTLEMEN."[28]

Campbell regarded the expelled students' stories of being harassed by mobs, threatened with chains, and pelted with eggs as "original creations of their own superexcited imaginations," fabricated to enhance fantasies of a noble quest. Their slander of the Bethany church and community had done great damage.[29] Campbell admonished all the papers that had published accounts based on the students' distortions of the incident to publish his true accounts, and with that, Campbell resumed the virtual ban on any mention of slavery at Bethany and in the pages of his journal.[30]

Evaluation

Campbell's self-perceived moderate position on slavery reflected both his desire to avoid division in his reform and his white supremacist ideology. From an early conviction that American slavery was not good for the country (based on the idea of the inherent inferiority of blacks, who should not be here), Campbell came to focus almost entirely on defending slavery as in harmony with Scripture. He simply could not see slavery as a moral evil because of his literal view of the Bible and his need to maintain the support of a national constituency for the success of the reform. The outbreak of the Civil War in 1861 would largely dash all hope that his strategy could succeed.

28. Alexander Campbell, "Reported Troubles in Bethany College," *Millennial Harbinger*, February 1856, 113.

29. Campbell, "Reported Troubles in Bethany College," 115.

30. After the extensive treatments of slavery in 1851 in response to the Fugitive Slave Act, only eight mentions of the topic—including the two articles dealing with the incident at Bethany College—appeared in the remainder of the journal's existence.

CHAPTER 19

The Civil War and the Millennium

In early April 1861, seventy-two-year-old Alexander Campbell was headed east from his home in Bethany, Virginia. Despite his age and evidence of diminished capacities, he showed little inclination to curtail the extensive travel he had undertaken for decades, making him one of the most widely traveled and famous men of nineteenth-century America.[1]

Campbell, his wife, Selina, and Isaac Errett, a rising leader in Campbell's religious reform, were on their way to collect funds from Christians in eastern Virginia for Bethany College. The devastating fire of December 1857 had destroyed the classroom and administrative building and threatened to shut down the school entirely. Seemingly energized by the tragedy, Campbell had immediately begun an aggressive fund-raising campaign and secured enough contributions and pledges to begin rebuilding within six months. Yet the lingering effects of the economic Panic of 1857 and the North-South tensions that were at the breaking point resulted in a significant decrease in contributions. Campbell and his son-in-law W. K. Pendleton had issued a strong plea for supporters to make good on their pledges in the February issue of the *Millennial Harbinger*, and now he was coming to collect.[2]

Bethany College was a key piece of Campbell's vision for the restoration of the ancient gospel and order of things, the essential first step in bringing in the millennium. And while Campbell truly believed that America had a unique place in God's plan for humanity, his understanding of the precise

---

1. Disciples of Christ Historical Society, "The Tours of Alexander Campbell as Reported by Him in the *Millennial Harbinger* December 1830–October 1862," 1957, Campbell Collection, Disciples of Christ Historical Society, Bethany, West Virginia.

2. A. Campbell and W. K. Pendleton, "An Appeal for Help," *Millennial Harbinger*, February 1861, 117.

Isaac Errett (1820–1888) was considered by some to be Campbell's successor. He wrote frequently for the *Millennial Harbinger* until leaving to become the first editor of the *Christian Standard* in 1866. The front page of the first issue of the new journal carried a long obituary of Campbell written by Errett. Used with permission from the Disciples of Christ Historical Society, Bethany, West Virginia.

nature of the millennium and the role the United States would play in bringing it in had fluctuated during his career.

As early as 1825 Campbell expressed frustration with those who dismissed his efforts to restore the unity of Christians by saying that such problems would all be remedied when the millennium arrived. He believed that such an attitude produced only apathy and inaction. "I reply that it will be by the correction of these errors that the millennial day will be ushered in," he retorted.[3]

In 1830 the church in Pittsburgh asked Campbell to speak at a special service commemorating the Fourth of July. The service was held on Monday

3. Alexander Campbell, "Christian Union, No. II," *Christian Baptist* 3 (August 1825): 10.

the fifth, perhaps to avoid conflicting with Sunday worship the day before. Campbell defended the observation as good and right for Christians. In contrast to the "noisy mirth" of the citizens of this world who celebrated a political event, Christians had every right to make the occasion an opportunity to give thanks to God for their salvation and for making them free citizens—of the United States and the kingdom of heaven.[4]

After giving his audience a grand sweep of divine history, he turned his attention to the American Revolution, praising the United States for emancipating its people from the political and religious tyranny of Europe. But that, he said, was only a precursor to a far greater revolution. This generation had been given a much more glorious task than that of 1776—emancipating the human mind from the chains of superstition and sectarian tyrannies. This work was far greater than substituting representative democracy for oppressive monarchy. Only the "true gospel" could free humanity and bring the final revolution.

> To introduce the last and most beneficial change in society, it is only necessary to let the gospel, in its own plainness, simplicity, and force, speak to men. Divest it of all the appendages of human philosophy, falsely so called, and of all the traditions and dogmas of men; and in its power it will pass from heart to heart, from house to house, from city to city, until it bless the whole earth. See how contagious it is. Since it began to be proclaimed, and sustained by the ancient order of things, see what changes it has made, and what effects it has produced, and with what rapidity it has spread over the country. More new churches have been formed within twelve months, where the primitive gospel has been proclaimed with clearness and power, than the twelve preceding years can count under the humanized gospel of the sects.[5]

He was convinced that the primitive gospel and the ancient order of things were key to what God had in store. Still, he admitted that it was not exactly clear how things would develop in the present chapter of history.

While Campbell's optimistic assessment of the progress of the ancient gospel and order in 1830 seemed consistent with his generally positive view of America's place in bringing in the millennium, the uncertainty he hinted

---

4. Alexander Campbell, "The Fourth of July," *Millennial Harbinger*, July 1830, 299–300.

5. Alexander Campbell, "An Oration in Honor of the Fourth of July," *Millennial Harbinger*, July 1830, 309.

at in his Fourth of July oration became more explicit in 1833. In February he began publishing a series by Samuel M. McCorkle titled "Signs of the Times" that was decidedly pessimistic in tone. In his introduction to Mc-Corkle's articles, Campbell admitted that he had remained relatively silent on "the prophecies and millennial matters" for five or six years because of uncertainty about which system to believe. Though he had leaned toward the optimistic notion that human moral action would bring in the millennium (though "supported by the vials of God's wrath upon an apostate church"), he conceded he had almost been drawn involuntarily into a more pessimistic understanding and was still not sure about where to land. And while Campbell stated that he might not agree with all of McCorkle's propositions, it was clear that he was "destined for the same port" and deserved a hearing.[6]

McCorkle began by arguing that it was a mistake to believe that humans could restore a dispensation that had become corrupted from its primitive purity. God always dealt with corrupt institutions in the same way—he destroyed them and brought something different into existence. The church had become adulterated, therefore God was going to destroy it and end the "church dispensation." Attempts "to restore the ancient order" to a corrupt church that Christ would destroy at his coming reflected a refusal to believe God's word. McCorkle insisted that the error-ridden and divided church's failure to evangelize the world and submit to God's Spirit was proof that truth by itself could not reverse apostasy. Only direct action by God could effect real change.[7]

In response, Campbell pointed out that the biblical record showed vigorous preaching of reform before the end of the patriarchal and Jewish dispensations to persuade and save as many as possible. His own movement's effort to restore the ancient order—an effort McCorkle had attacked—was simply doing what those ancient preachers of the truth had done. Still, Campbell admitted that despite the obligation to preach "the immediate and indispensable necessity of a return to the primitive faith and practice" to prepare as many as possible for the day of the Lord, he knew not all would be persuaded.[8]

In the same issue, Campbell began a four-part series titled "Everlasting Gospel." He contrasted "the gospel of remission," which was what he

---

6. Alexander Campbell, "The Prophecies," *Millennial Harbinger*, February 1833, 49.

7. S. M. McCorkle, "Signs of the Times: Christ's Second Coming Considered, With the Relative Events," *Millennial Harbinger*, February 1833, 50–54.

8. Alexander Campbell, [Comments on] "Signs of the Times: Christ's Second Coming Considered, With the Relative Events," 53–54.

and his allies were preaching, to what McCorkle had called the "Everlasting Gospel" that would be proclaimed by an angel when the corrupt church was destroyed.[9] Campbell began with a strong critique of human governments. All nations, he asserted, were founded in blood by the sword and doomed to suffer the vials of God's vengeance.

Then he turned his focus to the United States. Were we exempt from suffering the same fate as all who live by the sword? Definitely not. "The injustice, cupidity, ambition, oppression, which are found in our political institutions, will doom this nation to the vials of vengeance, and cause it to go the way of all the earth, before the triumphant day of the Lord come."[10] He stated in the next article that the United States was not a kingdom of Jesus Christ but was in rebellion against Christ and an oppressor of those who truly follow Jesus. The only way the kingdoms of this world could truly become kingdoms under Christ was by the direct action of Christ at his return.[11]

Campbell certainly reflected a much more positive role for the United States at times. Yet his lifelong trust in God's absolute sovereignty always operated in the background of his thought and served as a counterbalance to exuberant views of the nation as God's providential agent. This more-chastened posture showed up again a decade later in response to the war with Mexico from 1846 to 1848.

Soon after the war ended, Campbell delivered a widely publicized "Address on War" to the Wheeling, Virginia, Lyceum. In the lecture he repeated and made more explicit an idea he had expressed many times before. "The American nation, as a nation, is no more in spirit Christian than were Greece and Rome when the Apostles planted churches in Corinth, Athens, or in the metropolis of the empire, with Cesar's [*sic*] household in it."[12]

Remorseful that he had failed to speak out against the Mexican War when it began, he exclaimed, "War is not now, nor was it ever, a process of justice. It never was a test of truth—a criterion of right. It is either a mere game of chance or a violent outrage of the strong upon the weak." He ridi-

---

9. Alexander Campbell, "Everlasting Gospel—No. 1," *Millennial Harbinger*, February 1833, 70–71.

10. Alexander Campbell, "Everlasting Gospel—No. 2," *Millennial Harbinger*, March 1833, 119–22.

11. Alexander Campbell, "Everlasting Gospel—No. 3," *Millennial Harbinger*, May 1833, 224–26. See also Alexander Campbell, "Everlasting Gospel—No. 4," *Millennial Harbinger*, July 1833, 318–21.

12. Alexander Campbell, "An Address on War," *Millennial Harbinger*, July 1848, 366.

culed "vain and pompous" volunteers who zealously supported their country "right or wrong" but in reality were using war to get praise and glory for their own self-promotion.[13]

He blamed his hesitation to condemn the war at its beginning partly on his utter surprise that the United States had entered yet another military action—swiftly and with gusto. The conflict was so enmeshed in partisan politics that he had decided to remain silent to maintain his political neutrality. Yet now that the war was over, he confessed that he was "sorry to think—very sorry indeed . . . that probably even this much published by me some three years or even two years ago, might have saved some lives."[14]

His disappointment in America and in himself was real. Events such as the Mexican War constantly challenged his sense of and longing for America's positive role in bringing in the millennium. Within little more than a decade, the pessimistic and skeptical tendency would completely overwhelm the positive. Nevertheless, he ended the address with the assumption that the disease could be remedied by focus and hard work. "Let every one, then, who fears God and loves man, put his hand to the work; and the time is not far distant, when—

No longer hosts encount'ring hosts
Shall crowds of slain deplore;
They'll hang the trumpet in the hall,
And study war no more.[15]

Campbell's deep disappointment in America and in himself for lacking the courage to speak out against the Mexican War seemed largely forgotten, however, when four years later he delivered one of his most striking affirmations of God's glorious intentions for America. Asked to speak to the student Philo-Literary Society at Jefferson College in Canonsburg, Pennsylvania, about thirty miles from Bethany, he chose as his title for the August 1852 lecture "The Destiny of Our Country." In this remarkable statement, Campbell unambiguously depicted white America as God's prepared instrument for ushering in the millennium.

13. Campbell, "An Address on War," 377, 380.
14. Campbell, "An Address on War," 385.
15. Campbell, "An Address on War," 386. From a hymn in the Scottish Psalter based on Isa. 2.

In our country's destiny is involved the destiny of Protestantism, and in its destiny that of all the nations of the world. God has given, in awful charge, to Protestant England and Protestant America—the Anglo-Saxon race—the fortunes, not of Christendom only, but of all the world. For this purpose he has given to them all the great discoveries and improvements in the arts and sciences that have made the wilderness and the solitary places glad, and that have caused the deserts to rejoice and blossom as the rose.

To us, especially, he has given the new world and all its hidden treasures, with all the arts and sciences of the old. Europe, Asia and Africa look to Protestant America as the wonder of the age, and as exerting a preponderating influence on the destinies of the world. We have, then, a fearful and a glorious responsibility. Let us cherish in our individual bosoms this feeling of personal as well as national responsibility; and not only enter upon, but prosecute, the duties which we owe to ourselves, our country and the human race.[16]

This speech seemed to reconfirm his optimistic postmillennial tendency that believed humans—white Westerners—had the God-given ability and responsibility to carry out their "duties" for the blessed age to arrive. He always saw as the core of these duties, whether explicit or not, the restoration of the true gospel—the ancient gospel and order of things. The 1852 Jefferson College speech may have been more an attempt to will his optimistic description into being in the face of increasing signs of the nation's disintegration. As the decade progressed, however, the ambiguity of his millennial vision continued, reflecting the complex interplay of optimism and pessimism seen throughout his career.

In 1858 Campbell printed a refutation of the view many then held that a spiritual awakening that heralded the coming of the millennium was growing throughout America. Too many biblical prophecies had yet to be fulfilled, he claimed, including the return of the Jews to their homeland, the spread of peace throughout the world, and the civilization of the untold numbers of "wild, untaught, and unchristianized barbarians." He could have added that his own country was again preparing for war—this time with itself.[17] The following year he published a report on the Franco-Austrian War in Europe,

16. Alexander Campbell, "The Destiny of Our Country," in *Popular Lectures and Addresses* (Philadelphia: James Challen & Son, 1864), 179.

17. "The Millennium," *Millennial Harbinger*, 1858, 335.

The outbreak of the Civil War was crushing to Campbell and his
vision for his reformation and the millennium. In his last years he
wore an unkempt beard, and his face showed great weariness. Used
with permission from Bethany College, T. W. Phillips Memorial
Library, Archives and Special Collections, Bethany, West Virginia.

expressing his deep pessimism at any "speedy commencement of that long
wished for and prayed for era."[18]

Still, he believed in that "prayed for era." Though his ideas had shifted
over a lifetime of reform, he held doggedly to the conviction that America
had some unique role in God's plan for the end of time. Furthermore, he
had dedicated his life to playing a major role in that plan—a harbinger and
agent of the approaching millennium. The alienation within the nation that
had grown relentlessly for decades between pro- and antislavery advocates

18. Alexander Campbell, "The Great Battle," *Millennial Harbinger*, 1859, 519.

deeply distressed him, primarily because of its potential to derail the progress of his reformation. Yet even as sectional hostility grew, he held out hope that his God-chosen nation would reverse its course toward self-destruction and live out its cosmic destiny. That fragile hope was about to be dashed.

As Campbell and his traveling companions made their way across the beautiful countryside toward Charlottesville, Virginia, they were unaware that five hundred miles to the south, Confederate forces in South Carolina had attacked and taken Fort Sumter, the US military fortification guarding Charleston harbor. After leaving Charlottesville on Thursday, April 18, the little group headed to Washington, DC. It was there that they learned that Fort Sumter had fallen to Confederate forces the previous Sunday, and that Virginia had just voted to secede from the Union. Fund-raising forgotten, the group's only goal was to get back to Bethany as quickly as possible. Taking the road from Washington northeast to Baltimore, then west to Pittsburgh, the three arrived home on Saturday, April 20.

For Campbell, this was the culmination of a nightmare that had grown increasingly intense since his arrival in America. From his first encounters with American slavery, its effect on the nation's unity and progress had troubled him. He wrote extensively on America's slavery controversy in the mid-1840s when the Baptist and Methodist churches divided, and during the crisis provoked by the 1850 Fugitive Slave Act. He saw himself as a "moderate," insisting that while American slavery should be ended because it was harmful to the welfare and progress of the nation and its white citizens, Scripture never condemned holding slaves as sin.

He had always insisted that Christians obey all national laws that did not violate God's laws—including laws that protected slavery and slaveholders. He was confident that God had a plan for Anglo-Saxon America and that its wise leaders would assure slavery's gradual end. His millennial vision, however, depended on a united reform movement based on a united nation, both of which now seemed virtually impossible.

After Campbell's return home in mid-April, seizures of federal property and the arrest of US military officials in the new Confederacy increased. In May, Arkansas, Tennessee, and North Carolina joined the other eight states that had seceded, and Union and Confederate forces clashed in two naval battles in eastern Virginia. As the events of the previous month and the progress of hostilities weighed heavily on his mind, Campbell published an article titled "Wars and Rumors of Wars." He announced that this would be the first of many such editorials, though he was not sure how many or the exact nature of them. It was actually the only article that appeared in the announced series.

He opened by stating the stark reality that now everything was different—neither he nor his readers had ever experienced such a set of momentous events. He still believed America was somehow part of God's will, and that Christians could comprehend God's will if they would just listen to God's voice in faith. Yet he sorrowfully admitted that he could not figure out what God's will was in these circumstances. The only thing he knew to do was to maintain faith that God was still in charge.

As he moved toward the end of the article, however, the tone became more intense. War, he exclaimed, was one of the ways God exercised divine judgment on sinful people and nations, and civil war was the worst kind of all. In his closing paragraphs he literally shouted with despair. "Of all the monstrosities on which our sun has ever shone, that of professedly *Christian* nations, glutting their wrath and vengeance on one another, with all the instruments of murder and slaughter, caps the climax of human folly and gratuitous wickedness. . . . Civilized America! Civilized United States . . . gluttonously satiating your furious appetites for fraternal blood, caps the climax of all human inconsistencies inscribed on the blurred and moth-eaten pages of time in all its records."[19]

The war drastically curtailed the extensive travel that had always seemed to energize him. He continued to make the 250-mile trek to Cincinnati each October for the meeting of the American Christian Missionary Society, which he officially served as president. However, the war completely halted his preaching and fund-raising trips through the South. The suspension of US mail service to the Confederate States and a shortage of paper forced a drastic reduction of the size of the *Millennial Harbinger* and cut him off from most of his supporters and their churches in that region.[20] And though he was still revered in the North, his de facto defense of slavery had alienated many Northern supporters as well.

Yet in the prospectus for the 1862 *Millennial Harbinger*, Campbell urged his readers that though these were difficult days for the church, there was no less need now for Christians to continue energetic and zealous work for the Lord. "Let not the questions of a day part us in the path of eternal life!" he urged.[21]

19. Alexander Campbell, "Wars and Rumors of Wars," *Millennial Harbinger*, June 1861, 344–48.

20. Alexander Campbell, "To Our Subscribers," *Millennial Harbinger*, June 1861, 357. In this note he announced he would not be sending the magazine to subscribers in the South until he could be assured they would receive it.

21. Alexander Campbell, "The Millennial Harbinger for 1862," *Millennial Harbinger*, November 1861, 656.

Even as Campbell urged his readers not to allow the questions of slavery, secession, and war to divide them, Campbell's own family was sharply divided over those very issues. His pro-Union nephew Archibald Campbell was editor of the *Wheeling Daily Intelligencer*, which strongly opposed Virginia's secession. When the state did secede, Archibald became a major leader in the movement to create West Virginia in opposition to the Confederate state of Virginia.[22] Campbell's younger sister Jane and her husband, Matthew McKeever, operated an important station on the Underground Railroad that aided runaway slaves to escape to the North or out of the country.[23]

On the other hand, most members of Campbell's family were strongly prosecession and proslavery. His secessionist son-in-law W. K. Pendleton became the de facto editor of the *Millennial Harbinger*, though Campbell continued to hold the title until 1865. His wife and children were all "bitter Secessionists," in Archibald Campbell's words, and his oldest son, Alexander Campbell Jr., was "the bitterest of all little rebels I have no doubt." Archibald compiled a list of all of Campbell's family members who had damaged his reputation by their disloyalty to the Union, in a defense of his uncle's silence.[24] According to Eva Jean Wrather, when Campbell's two living daughters and his youngest son learned that Campbell had voted against Virginia secession in the statewide referendum on May 23, 1861, they angrily accused him of "terrible duplicity" in betraying the Southern cause.[25]

The terrible disappointment of the dissolution of the Union, the violence of the war, the internal tensions in his family, and concern for his oldest son, Alex Jr.—who lived at his Louisiana plantation during the war and served as a colonel in the Third Louisiana Cavalry—wore heavily on Campbell. His active public role steadily decreased. He contributed a few articles to the *Millennial Harbinger* and preached occasionally at the Bethany church and other congregations in the area. He officially retained his position as president of Bethany College, but his teaching and administrative roles shrank

22. Archibald W. Campbell papers, in the West Virginia Collection, West Virginia University Library, Morgantown, West Virginia; Linda L. Lockhart, "Writing West Virginia: A. W. Campbell Jr., A Biography" (PhD diss., Ohio University, 2016), especially chaps. 4–8.

23. Ethelene Bruce White, "Jane Campbell McKeever (1800–1871): A Brief Biography with Comparison to Her Brother Alexander Campbell on the Issue of Slavery and Abolition," *Stone-Campbell Journal* 13 (Spring 2010): 3–16.

24. Archibald W. Campbell, *Wheeling Daily Intelligencer*, quoted in Eva Jean Wrather, *Alexander Campbell: Adventurer in Freedom; A Literary Biography*, 3 vols. (Fort Worth: Texas Christian University Press, 2005–2009), 3:246–47.

25. Wrather, *Alexander Campbell*, 3:237–38.

Archibald Campbell (1833–1899) was Alexander Campbell's nephew and the abolitionist editor of the *Wheeling Daily Intelligencer* during the Civil War. He was a leader in the movement to form West Virginia. Shown here, standing, with John Frew, who became co-owner of the newspaper in 1866. Courtesy of the Ohio County Public Library Archives, Wheeling, West Virginia.

to nearly nothing—basically to presiding over and handing out diplomas at the annual Fourth of July graduation ceremonies.

The war formally ended with the surrender of Confederate leader Robert E. Lee to Union general Ulysses S. Grant at Appomattox Court House, Virginia, on April 9, 1865. But there was one more ordeal Alexander Campbell would be forced to endure. As mentioned, his son Alexander Jr. had

Alexander Campbell Jr. (1831–1906) supported slavery and Southern secession. Though he lived in Louisiana on a plantation near his wife's family during the Civil War, he returned to Bethany with his family after the war. He inherited much of his father's property in and around Bethany. This photo was taken in 1902. Used with permission from the Disciples of Christ Historical Society, Bethany, West Virginia.

lived on his plantation in Louisiana during the war. Although the village of Bethany itself was mostly pro-Confederate, Brooke County had a pro-Union majority. Voters in the county had rejected the resolution for Virginia to secede from the Union by a margin of seven to one and voted in favor of forming the "Restored State" of West Virginia in October 1861.[26]

When the war ended, Union troops occupied Alex Jr.'s Louisiana plantation.[27] He and his family made their way up the Mississippi and Ohio Rivers to Louisville, Kentucky, where on June 7 he signed an oath of loyalty to the United States and petitioned President Johnson "for a pardon under your proclamation offering amnesty to those lately in rebellion against the United States." In the appeal he asserted that he had never held any office in the Confederate government nor been in the military service of the Confederate States of America.

---

26. "The Vote for Secession in Virginia," *New York Times*, June 1, 1861, 8; Richard Orr Curry, *A House Divided: A Study of Statehood Politics and the Copperhead Movement in West Virginia* (Pittsburgh: University of Pittsburgh Press, 1964), 147–49.

27. Selina Huntington Campbell, *Home Life and Reminiscences of Alexander Campbell* (St. Louis: John Burns, 1882), 476–77.

He admitted that during the first two years of the war he had served as an officer in a Louisiana state militia unit, but that during the last two years he had been completely free of any civil or military service to the Confederacy.[28]

Despite the petition, when Alex Jr. returned to Bethany in July, he was charged with treason against West Virginia. The West Virginia legislature had passed a law the previous November that the property of enemies of the state was to be forfeited and seized. That very month Union loyalist Dr. G. W. Caldwell notified the prosecuting attorney of Brooke County, James Hervey, that he intended to begin proceedings in circuit court to seize Alex Jr.'s property. Caldwell filed an affidavit that Campbell had aided and abetted the Confederate States in hostile action against West Virginia, and that he was an officer in the Confederate army.[29]

One of the attorneys representing Campbell, James S. Wheat, moved to have the case dismissed on several technicalities. First, no grand jury had indicted Campbell. Furthermore, the law for immediate seizure of property applied only to residents of Virginia, and since Campbell lived in Louisiana and was not notified about the proceedings, due process had not been followed. Furthermore, there was no actual evidence that Campbell was an enemy of the state—just Caldwell's assertion that he was. The whole affair, Wheat charged, violated the United States Constitution and was contrary to "the spirit of our republican institutions."[30]

The state's attorney general replied that when people turn on their own government and try to destroy it, they should lose all claim to the immunities and privileges of that government. The law violated no constitutional provisions. Campbell's lawyer again insisted that there was no proof that he was an enemy of the state. Besides, the state constitution provided that only a grand jury could indict a person for treason, and if indicted a jury must try the case. In the end the judge agreed with Campbell's lawyer. He reversed the confiscation order and sent the matter back to the circuit court.[31]

Meanwhile, West Virginia governor Arthur I. Boreman began an inquiry into Alex Jr.'s reputation in Brooke County and whether or not he

28. Alexander Campbell Jr. to His Excellency Andrew Johnson, President of the United States, July 26, 1865, in "Confederate Applications for Pardon and Amnesty, West Virginia: Campbell, Alexander," National Archives and Records Administration, Record Group 94, available at https://catalog.archives.gov/id/57474173.

29. *Reports of Cases Decided in the Supreme Court of Appeals of West Virginia*, 6 vols. (Morgantown, WV: Morgan and Hoffman Printers, 1866), 1:165–66.

30. *Reports of Cases Decided*, 1:168–70.

31. *Reports of Cases Decided*, 1:173–75.

United States of America.

DEPARTMENT OF STATE.

To all to whom these presents shall come, Greeting:

I Certify, That *Alexander Campbell Jr* of the County of *Brooke*, State of *West Virginia*, has deposited in this Department his original Oath, bearing date the *twenty-second* day of *September*, 1865, being in the form prescribed by the President's Proclamation of May 29th, 1865.

In testimony whereof, I *William H. Seward* Secretary of State of the United States, have hereunto subscribed my name and caused the Seal of the Department of State to be affixed.

Done at the City of Washington, this *twenty-second* day of *September* A. D. 1865 and of the Independence of the United States of America the *Ninetieth.*

William H. Seward

Though Alexander Campbell Jr. signed a loyalty oath in Louisville, Kentucky, before returning to West Virginia, he was indicted for treason upon arrival in Bethany. After traveling to Washington, DC, he repeated the oath and received this certificate from the United States Secretary of State William Seward. Used with permission from the Disciples of Christ Historical Society, Bethany, West Virginia.

would likely be loyal to the United States if he were pardoned. In a letter to US Attorney General James Speed dated September 16, Boreman reported that he had asked a "gentleman of intelligence of Brooke County" to consult with residents who knew Campbell and who had remained loyal to the Union, for information about him. The gentleman's informants reported that Campbell had threatened Unionists with violence before the war, that he had persuaded men from Brooke County to go into the rebel army, and that he himself had left with a rebel flag on both shoulders. Furthermore, the gentleman quoted Campbell as saying that "a southern man, who was not a rebel, was a damned fool," and that he had publicly pledged to assassinate President Lincoln. Governor Boreman ended the letter, "I cannot recommend him for pardon."[32]

At the same time Boreman was writing his letter to Attorney General Speed, Alex Jr. was traveling to Washington with his brother-in-law Judson Barclay, former United States consul to Cyprus, to petition the president personally. The sheriff of Brooke County, Samuel George, was a friend of the family and had refused to jail Alex Jr.[33] Through family connections he was able to secure an audience with President Johnson, and despite Governor Boreman's report and negative opinion, Johnson issued Campbell a full pardon on September 19.[34]

Alexander Campbell followed these events with sorrow. The war was over, and his oldest son had escaped a conviction of treason and prison. But the deep wounds within his family, his nation, and his movement were still very much open and painful. He would never recover from the events surrounding the bitter conflict. God was working the divine plan in ways he had not anticipated at all. Within six months of his son's pardon, he would be dead.

32. Boreman to Speed, September 16, 1865, in "Confederate Applications for Pardon and Amnesty, West Virginia: Campbell, Alexander."

33. Alexander Campbell Jr., *Reminiscences*, Campbell Collection, T. W. Phillips Memorial Library, Bethany College, Bethany, West Virginia, cited in R. Edwin Groover, *The Well-Ordered Home: Alexander Campbell and the Family* (Joplin, MO: College Press, 1988), 144; A. T. DeGroot to Eva Jean Wrather, November 26, 1946, Eva Jean Wrather file 158, Disciples of Christ Historical Society, Bethany, West Virginia.

34. The cover of Campbell's case file 2190 recorded the charge as "Rebellion Governor reports adversely Filed Sept 19th Pardoned Sept 19, '65," with the notation across the bottom written in another hand, "Indicted for Treason."

CHAPTER 20

The Death of a Reformer

In January 1863, in the middle of the Civil War, Alexander Campbell penned his last preface to a volume of the *Millennial Harbinger*. The rumors were widespread, he acknowledged, that both the *Harbinger* and Bethany College had ceased operation. He reassured his remaining readers to the contrary and asked them to spread the word that such was definitely not the case.

> Despite of all the draw-backs and hindrances of these gloomy and heart-sickening times, which have fallen so heavily upon all the enterprises of Christian benevolence and hope, we are still, though cast down, not utterly forsaken, but laboring on, without, it is true, the encouragement and support of many who in former years of toil and trial stood so nobly by us, yet with the sustaining power of an unfaltering faith in the help and blessing of Him whose Spirit has so long been our comforter and support, and whose service still calls us to the duties of the foremost ranks in the army of *His* kingdom.[1]

Things were hard—financially, socially, politically, and religiously. Yet Campbell declared that he was determined to do his duty as a soldier in *God's* kingdom—in pointed contrast to the worldly kingdom of his now-divided country.

Campbell was the living icon of the movement to restore the ancient gospel and order of things. His editorial was intended to reassure the churches that he was still at the helm of the reform and that the *Millennial Harbinger* and Bethany College—his two most potent instruments—were "still in vigor-

---

1. Alexander Campbell, "Preface," *Millennial Harbinger*, January 1863, 3.

ous life and activity." Yet the confident tone of the article masked the reality that Campbell himself was far from vigorous life and activity.

Though Robert Richardson in his biography minimized the importance of Campbell's decline and insisted that the significant lapses of memory and strength were simply small, normal signs of aging, even Richardson could not ignore the evidence. At the close of his biography of Campbell, Richardson related that soon after the war began Campbell had become unable to continue teaching his morning class. While other faculty assumed that duty, Campbell continued to come to campus prepared to deliver his morning lecture until reminded he was no longer the teacher.

In 1863 his daughter Decima married John Judson Barclay, United States consul to Cyprus from 1859 to 1865. Decima wrote her parents frequently with engaging and detailed descriptions of the sites she and her husband visited throughout the Middle East, including Jerusalem. Campbell became so engrossed in reading and discussing these accounts that he grew confused and believed he was the one who had been there, excitedly relating stories of his imagined trips to friends and visitors. There were increasing incidents of his waking up at night and, thinking he was opening a worship service, praying and delivering rousing exhortations.[2] Selina reported that shortly before his death, her husband had preached a stirring sermon on Christ's second coming entirely in his sleep.[3]

Richardson's description of what would today be labeled age-related dementia was elegant and tortured. "Here the memories, associations and habits of the past seemed to possess for him greater vividness than even present impressions, and his ever-active mind, released from pressing lifelong labors, made for itself imaginary occasions for exertion."[4]

Campbell's final decline began early in 1866. He had developed a serious chest cold in late 1865 that progressively weakened him. He was largely confined to home during January but was able to attend worship at the Bethany church on February 11. He assisted in the ordination of two new elders and presided at the Lord's Supper, but when he stepped into the pulpit to preach, he was so weak that W. K. Pendleton talked him out of trying. This was the last time he was able to attend a public worship service.

---

2. Robert Richardson, *Memoirs of Alexander Campbell*, 2 vols. (Philadelphia: J. B. Lippincott & Co., 1868–1870), 2:644–47.

3. Selina Huntington Campbell, *Home Life and Reminiscences of Alexander Campbell* (St. Louis: John Burns, 1882), 253.

4. Richardson, *Memoirs of Alexander Campbell*, 2:647–48.

Last photo taken of Alexander Campbell. Used with permission from the Disciples of Christ Historical Society, Bethany, West Virginia.

Throughout his illness and confinement to home, friends, colleagues, neighbors, and family came to his bedside to show their respect. His daughter-in-law, Mary Anna Purvis Campbell—wife of Alexander Jr.—waited on Campbell during his last days and kept a detailed diary. Admittedly, much in the diary as well as in the memorials at his funeral and those published afterward reflected the sentimentality typical of Christian deathbed scenes of the time. Nevertheless, the documents are sometimes moving and generally reliable in the narrowly focused details they provide. Mary

Anna's entries described him as cheerful; always kind, polite, and thinking of others; and frequently quoting Scripture.[5]

On Thursday, March 1, Mary Anna recorded that Campbell was much better, even to the point that the family thought he might recover from his chest infection and "live some time yet." She noted, however, that he did not talk much all day. After two days with no change in his state, she recorded that around midnight Sunday morning he had become restless, then slipped into unconsciousness. The day was cold and sunny and many visitors came to see him. Just before midnight that Sunday evening, March 4, 1866, Alexander Campbell died. He was seventy-eight years old.

The *Millennial Harbinger* carried a seventeen-page notice of Campbell's death written by his son-in-law W. K. Pendleton that amounted to a minibiography and history of the movement. In a revealing evaluation of Campbell's significance and of the main thrust of his reformation, Pendleton gave an account of Campbell's debates on baptism with John Walker and William Maccalla. In those two discussions, Pendleton asserted, Campbell had said everything there was to be said about this all-important subject. Furthermore, "If Alexander Campbell had done nothing else than this single work of restoring the scriptural authority of immersion and exposing the human origin of infant Baptism—his name would deserve to stand among the brightest on the roll of public benefactors."[6]

Believers' immersion for the remission of sins was in fact the hub of Campbell's reform. It was key to the restored gospel, the basis for his doctrine of the church, the hope for the unity of all Christians, and therefore the means to the conversion of the world and the ushering in of the millennium. The events of the previous decade had forced him to question and even abandon his more optimistic visions of God's plan for America. Yet this core doctrine had remained the same.

Pendleton's lavish description of Campbell's death was characteristic of other evaluations of Campbell by other members of his movement. "He went to his rest through fitful gleamings of a sublime intellect, but with a faith that never faltered. He suffered as the strong only *can* suffer. . . . The pulse quivered and stopped—a sudden and convulsive drawing back of the breath

---

5. Two accounts of his death by those closest to him are Richardson, *Memoirs of Alexander Campbell*, 2:677–78, and Selina Huntington Campbell, *Home Life and Reminiscences of Alexander Campbell*, 476–77.

6. W. K. Pendleton, "Death of Alexander Campbell," *Millennial Harbinger*, March 1866, 129.

W. K. Pendleton (1817–1899) was Alexander Campbell's son-in-law twice—first marrying Lavinia (1818–1846) in 1840, then Clarinda (1822–1851) in 1848. He became a key assistant to Campbell at Bethany College and the *Millennial Harbinger*. Pendleton tried unsuccessfully to persuade Campbell to divide his estate equally between his children by Margaret and those by Selina. Used with permission from the Disciples of Christ Historical Society, Bethany, West Virginia.

startled us—and in a few moments the voice of lamentation rose over the lifeless form of him, whom distant generations will rank among the greatest of the many God-given that have blessed our earth."[7]

The April issue of the *Millennial Harbinger* carried resolutions of respect

7. Pendleton, "Death of Alexander Campbell," 136–38.

from the faculty and students at Bethany College, the citizens of Bethany, and the board of the American Christian Missionary Society. To avoid taking up too much space with the large number of tribute letters and articles received and which Pendleton had promised in March to "do justice to," the April issue carried Robert Richardson's announcement that he had been asked by the family to write a memoir of Alexander Campbell as soon as possible that would give a full account of his life and work.[8] In May the magazine published a long memorial sermon preached by Joseph King, pastor of the Christian Church in Allegheny City, as well as notice of an address by Moses Lard available as a pamphlet—typical of a growing body of literature portraying Campbell as a saint that would expand in parts of his movement for decades to come.[9]

In fact, eulogies and tributes appeared in pulpits and newspapers around the country. Many were extravagant in their praise. In a tribute that took up much of the front page of the *Wheeling Daily Intelligencer* of March 6, his nephew Archibald Campbell stated that tens of thousands regarded Campbell as the "greatest theologian of his day" and that his books were in every bookstore and the libraries of almost every clergyman of the time. The public knew him primarily as "the recognized head of a new religious sect" that then numbered almost half a million adherents. The doctrines he and his father had taught fifty years ago—chiefly the rejection of creeds for the Bible alone, weekly Lord's Supper, and baptism by immersion—brought the Disciples into existence.

Campbell had become, his nephew exclaimed, "one of those pioneers in the world of reform that have appeared at rare intervals in the history of mankind, and have had power by 'the sole lever of thought' to upheave the weights of ancient traditions, long adopted formulas, and consecrated theories, from the mind of society." What "justification by faith" had been to Luther, "Christian union through the destruction of creeds" was to Campbell—his first great distinctive dogma.

Archibald briefly recounted Campbell's major debates and his jailing in Edinburgh in the conflict over his views of slavery. Yet he made no mention of Campbell's constant conflicts with other religious leaders nor the harsh condemnations of him and his teachings. "None knew him but to love him"

8. Robert Richardson, "Memoir of A. Campbell," *Millennial Harbinger*, April 1866, 185–86.

9. Joseph King, "A Memorial Sermon on the Occasion of the Death of Alexander Campbell," *Millennial Harbinger*, May 1866, 193–208; W. K. Pendleton, "Alexander Campbell—an Address by M. E. Lard," *Millennial Harbinger*, May 1866, 238.

was Archibald's evaluation. He closed his uncle's obituary with a verse from Alfred, Lord Tennyson's "Ode on the Death of the Duke of Wellington," the last line of which read, "The long self-sacrifice is o'er."[10]

David S. Burnet, in his widely reprinted memorial address, described Campbell's speaking as having "flowed from his lips like water from the rock smitten by the prophet, and the people felt like famished Israel as they drank the cooling draught, that a hand of power had relieved their thirst." Later Burnet went even further. The day of Campbell's death, he exclaimed, was "The first vernal Lord's Day—the astronomical opening of 1866, the year of the greatest conjunction of planets since the creation, the year to which the expectant eye and ear of Christendom have long been turned as the probable dawning of a brighter day for the church; this was the time, the temple of Janus being shut, selected by the Lord for his servant to come higher."[11]

Except for Burnet's allusion to the closing of the temple of Janus, no mention of the Civil War or the massive disappointment and disorientation it had brought Campbell appeared in the lengthy obituary in the *Millennial Harbinger*—or in any contemporary obituary or biography. It is as if there had been no Civil War or division over slavery and sectionalization. These memorials reflected the aura that Campbell had already achieved before his death among many of his followers, an aura that would be augmented and set in stone over the next few decades. But there was one more event that began immediately after his death that would highlight the complexity of Campbell's reality.

The rancorous events surrounding Campbell's last will and testament revealed a long-running, though not always obvious, hostility between Selina Campbell and the descendants of Campbell's first wife, Margaret. When Margaret had died and asked her husband to marry her close friend Selina Bakewell, Campbell had obeyed her wishes nine months later. Yet several things surely contributed to Selina's discomfort connected with the marriage, despite her genuine love and affection for Alexander.

Suddenly Selina was expected to raise Campbell's five daughters by Margaret. She also had to learn to run his extensive farming and printing operations while he was away on extended travels for much of each year. In what seems like a very odd custom, every March 12 Campbell celebrated the

10. Archibald Campbell, "Alexander Campbell. A Brief Sketch of His Life and Public Career," *Wheeling Daily Intelligencer*, March 6, 1866, 1.

11. David S. Burnet, "The Late Alexander Campbell," *Wheeling Daily Intelligencer*, August 1, 1866, 2. In ancient Rome, the doors of the Temple of Janus were open during times of war and closed when there was peace.

Selina Huntington Bakewell Campbell (1802–1897), second wife of Alexander Campbell, was an extremely capable manager of his farm and printing operations while he was away on frequent preaching and fund-raising trips. She lived over thirty years after Campbell's death and contributed to the veneration of Campbell's life and work among Disciples. Used with permission from Bethany College, T. W. Phillips Memorial Library, Archives and Special Collections, Bethany, West Virginia.

anniversary of his marriage to Margaret, and if he were away from home, he wrote Selina about the significance of the day. On March 12, 1861, the fiftieth anniversary of his marriage to Margaret, he gave Selina a ring with a lock of his hair. He announced that the ring represented the full transfer of his affections from his first wife to his second wife—almost thirty-three years after their wedding![12] In addition, he had named his first child by Selina, Margaret Brown Campbell.

According to William F. Arny, Alexander Campbell's clerk between 1835 and 1850 and a close observer of the Campbell household, Selina always favored her children over Margaret's. Arny reported that Selina's treatment of Margaret's daughters often caused them to cry. While perhaps not the proverbial wicked stepmother, she did apparently have an underlying resentment toward the first set of children.[13] For whatever reason, when Campbell wrote his will in 1862, he effectively marginalized his family from his first marriage and distributed most of his wealth to Selina's children.

Campbell had become very affluent during his life. His estate had started with the acquisition of a 300-acre farm and a house deeded to him in 1815 by Margaret's father, John Brown, valued at the time at about $10,000. Campbell intentionally and aggressively added to his property and wealth over the next four decades, holding an estate valued at $228,545 by the time of the 1860 census—nearly $7 million in 2018 values.[14] He owned almost all the property in and around Bethany, including hundreds of acres of choice farmland. He imported merino sheep from Ireland and began a large wool operation. Through the years he also acquired property in Ohio and Illinois, either by outright purchase or from having loaned money to friends who could not pay him back. Robert Richardson stated that while Campbell was sympathetic toward the poor and unfortunate, he was "cautious in his distributions" and usually loaned rather than gave money to friends who were in need so he could maintain control of his wealth, using their property as collateral.[15]

Campbell's will of 1862 said that he had already given his grandchildren by Margaret (all his children having died) $18,000, and that upon his death an additional $14,000 was to be distributed equally among the six living grandchildren—provided they did not sue for possession of the homestead and farm their great-grandfather had given Campbell in 1815. He then bequeathed hundreds of acres of land as well as cash to his four surviving children by Selina. A codicil added to the will in 1864 seemed to reflect a fear that

12. Selina Huntington Campbell, *Home Life and Reminiscences of Alexander Campbell*, 350–53.

13. Cited in Eva Jean Wrather, *Alexander Campbell: Adventurer in Freedom; A Literary Biography*, 3 vols. (Fort Worth: Texas Christian University Press, 2005–2009), 3:190–91.

14. "Inflation Calculator," U.S. Official Inflation Data, Alioth Finance, September 14, 2018, https://www.officialdata.org/1860-dollars-in-2018?amount=228545.

15. Richardson, *Memoirs of Alexander Campbell*, 2:658.

Margaret's grandchildren would contest the will. It stipulated that if they did, they would forfeit what had been left to them and would get nothing from his estate. Campbell also replaced James A. Campbell with lawyer William R. Thompson as an executor of the will. Thompson was his daughter Virginia's husband, who stood to receive a considerable inheritance through his wife.[16]

Within three weeks of Campbell's death, the grandchildren from the first marriage delivered notice through their attorney, J. H. Pendleton, that they were indeed contesting the will. Pendleton was the husband of Margaret Ewing, Campbell's granddaughter through his first daughter, Jane. Pendleton anticipated his wife would inherit a substantial amount if the will were successfully challenged.

Pendleton said the main reason they were challenging the will was that it was written when Campbell was not "of sound mind and disposing memory," and that it was written under undue pressure from others when he was not capable of acting for himself. Pendleton related a proposition that Campbell had made to him in 1860 to pay $14,000 to Margaret's descendants as their portion of his estate, but that he had refused to accept it because he knew Campbell was not competent to transact his own business. All of Campbell's wealth, Pendleton asserted, had come ultimately from Margaret's father's estate, and that even if the original $10,000 value of the property were to be paid back at compound interest, it would exceed the then-current value of Campbell's entire estate. He could not believe that the striking difference between the inheritance of the first and second set of heirs was Campbell's intention. It was unnatural to cut off half of his family for no apparent reason. Pendleton ended by stating that he could only conclude that other parties had influenced Campbell to take this unjust action.

Things dragged on for two years. Selina became convinced that her step-grandchildren were trying to wear them down to get a better settlement and urged Alex Jr. to consult with their lawyers—Judge Jeremiah Black, attorney general and secretary of state under President James Buchanan, and James A. Garfield, former Union general and future US president—about how to proceed. Selina insisted that her husband was perfectly sound of mind when the will and codicil had been written and denied exerting any influence whatsoever on Campbell with the intention to slight anyone.

Selina added an interesting piece to the case in a letter written to her

16. The text of the 1862 will, the 1864 codicil, the notice of contest, and the decision of the referees can be found in several locations. One is the *Cincinnati Daily Enquirer*, March 5, 1868, 1.

Future president James A. Garfield (1831–1881) attended Western Reserve Eclectic Institute (today Hiram College), founded in 1850 by members of Disciples of Christ. He later taught at Hiram and preached in Disciples churches before entering the Union Army and serving in the US Congress. He studied law on his own and passed the Ohio Bar in 1861. Photo courtesy of Mac Ice, Abilene, Texas.

daughter Virginia in 1867. She explained that W. K. Pendleton—who had been husband to two of Campbell's daughters by Margaret as well as vice president of Bethany College and coeditor of the *Millennial Harbinger*—advised Campbell that if he did not divide his estate equally between Selina's and Margaret's offspring, Margaret's grandchildren would contest the will. According to Selina, Campbell had regarded the statement as a threat and refused to change anything.[17]

The case finally came to trial in February 1868. Two prominent lawyers,

17. Selina Campbell to Virginia Thompson, January 25, 1867, Campbell Family Papers, T. W. Phillips Memorial Library, Bethany College, Bethany, West Virginia.

W. H. Lowrie of Pennsylvania and William J. Robertson of Virginia, served as referees to decide the validity of the will. The hearings lasted for ten days and involved over forty witnesses. Margaret's grandchildren had a solid case in their challenge of the validity of the will. Benjamin Stanton, one of their lawyers who was a former Ohio congressman and lieutenant governor, read the accepted legal definition of mental competence to each witness. Most responded that Campbell did not meet the requirements. Though Garfield introduced a few witnesses who vouched for Campbell's soundness of mind, it seemed certain the will would be set aside.[18]

The referees were to make the decision the next day. During the night Garfield reviewed his extensive research on the case from a couple of years earlier when he had first been asked to represent Selina's children. He found a decision that overruled the one Stanton had used for the legal standard of competence for making a valid will—the New York case of Alice Lispenard. That ruling and the expansion of its principles stated that simple memory loss did not constitute proof that a person had reached a "degree of senility which would incapacitate [the person] from making a valid will."[19] Garfield confirmed that the will was in Campbell's own handwriting and that it recorded what he had said for some time about having already conveyed to Margaret's descendants all he intended to. He argued that based on those facts and in conformity with the Lispenard decision, the will should be sustained. He convinced the referees. They ruled that the will and codicil were valid.[20]

In one sense the incident had little to do with his legacy and the continued development of his religious reformation. One eulogist exclaimed that with his death, Campbell's movement would flourish as never before. Yet in another sense, the fight over Campbell's will had implications for the very nature of that movement. Somehow Campbell's deepest convictions about "the image of Christ" being the true measure of a Christian did not capture the minds of his own family.

For many of Campbell's followers over the next century and a half, the test of genuine Christianity was dogged adherence to what he had formulated as the ancient gospel and order of things—and that is exactly what

18. A. G. Riddle, *The Life, Character, and Public Services of Jas. A. Garfield* (Cleveland: W. W. Williams, 1881), 368–69.

19. Quoted in Thomas Jarman, *A Treatise on Wills*, vol. 1 (Jersey City, NJ: Frederick D. Linn & Co., 1880), 95.

20. Riddle, *The Life, Character, and Public Services*, 369–71; "Interesting Report of the Campbell Will Case," *Cincinnati Daily Enquirer*, March 5, 1868, 1.

Campbell had always insisted. Campbell knew that those doctrines and practices were not themselves the point. They were means to the Spirit's transformation of submissive hearts more into the image of Christ. He knew it, but the sheer volume of his activity—preaching, traveling, writing, debating, running a school, publishing a paper, operating an extensive farm, managing substantial property and wealth—seems often to have simply overwhelmed it. When he felt his teaching threatened, he struck out to defend it. Robert Semple's caution to Campbell in 1826 continued to be relevant. Though brilliant and convincing in your arguments, Semple observed, the bitterness of your approach to your opponents "blind[s] their minds with resentment, so as to stop up the entrance of truth."[21]

Nevertheless, Campbell's legacy, though often unknown by those who inherited it, led to the development of his reformation into a global religious communion. This is the subject of the final chapter.

21. R. B. S., "Brother Campbell," *Christian Baptist* 3 (April 1826): 199.

SECTION FIVE

Legacy

The return to the Bible and the Bible alone, and the laying aside of creeds, traditions and doctrines of men, with all sectarian parties and divisions amongst Christians, with the plea for the observance of the "Ancient Gospel" in our religious practice and worship, can only be accredited to the labors and teachings of Alexander Campbell, as drawn from the fountain of Divine Truth, one of the humblest and grandest of men. A short time previous to his departure, he was sitting calmly and thoughtfully, I being alone beside him, when looking up into my face, he said, "well I had a work to do and I did it." He no doubt felt that he was the Lord's servant and had a work to do.

— Selina Huntington Campbell, *Home Life and Reminiscences of Alexander Campbell*, 1882

CHAPTER 21

The Shadow of Alexander Campbell

The tributes and obituary notices that appeared after Campbell's death attested to his fame both in North America and in the British Empire. While not all were as profuse in their praise as the ones cited in the previous chapter, he was clearly one of the most widely known religious leaders of his day. The language of extravagant tributes like David S. Burnet's that elevated Campbell almost to immortality, while not uncommon for the day, set a precedent for idolizing Campbell that would continue far into the future.

The quintessential example of this idolization was Robert Richardson's *Memoirs of Alexander Campbell*. Richardson had been for almost four decades one of Campbell's closest colleagues and friends. Not only did he serve as Campbell's personal physician, but he also taught chemistry at Bethany College and served in the school's administration, and was a coeditor of the *Millennial Harbinger* and frequent contributor. The only break in Richardson's relationship with Campbell occurred in 1857 and 1858 when Campbell harshly criticized him in the incident with Tolbert Fanning. Yet Campbell suddenly swept the conflict aside as if he had forgotten the whole thing, attributing it to a mysterious misunderstanding. The episode apparently did not diminish the affection Campbell and his family had for Richardson. He attended Campbell in his last days, preached his funeral service, and was commissioned by Campbell's family to write the "definitive" biography of the great man.

The first volume of Richardson's *Memoirs of Alexander Campbell* appeared in 1868, with the second published two years later. Richardson's work was extremely valuable for insights into Campbell's life only an insider could know. Inevitably, Richardson was selective in his telling of Campbell's life. He omitted the "bad parts," like the censure Campbell had dealt him over his articles on philosophy and the rancorous contesting of Campbell's will. He consistently depicted Campbell as the winner in conflicts with opponents and friends. Yet he also provided ample clues that Campbell's personality and character were more complex than they might seem at first. Richardson's treatment was not a bald-faced hagiography. Yet the biography functioned as a powerful component in the creation of Campbell as a saint—a hero who became the greatest religious reformer in the history of reform.[1]

Over the next decades insider publications added to the reverence shown Campbell and his work. Chief among these was Selina's *Home Life and Reminiscences of Alexander Campbell*, published first in 1882. Even earlier than Richardson's *Memoirs* and Selina's *Reminiscences*, in 1867 one of Campbell's students, Charles V. Segar, published notes from Campbell's 1859–1860 morning lectures on the Pentateuch. Two books by William H. Whitsett and G. W. Longan appeared in 1888 and 1889—the centennial of Campbell's birth—on his all-important role in the origin of the Disciples of Christ. And in 1892 Thomas Chalmers published an account of Campbell's 1847 trip to Scotland, recounting highly complimentary oral history interviews with two Scotsmen who had seen and heard Campbell on that trip.

In 1896 W. A. Morris published a compilation of Campbell's writings from the *Millennial Harbinger*; this was followed by two biographies by Thomas W. Grafton in 1897 and 1899. The first truly scholarly examination of Campbell's thought came in 1900 from Winfred Ernest Garrison in the form of his revised PhD dissertation from the University of Chicago that examined the sources and historical setting of Campbell's theology. Garrison was the first person in the Stone-Campbell Movement to receive a PhD in church history.

When Disciples leaders began to contemplate a celebration of the beginning of the movement, they chose the 1809 publication of Thomas Campbell's *Declaration and Address* as the date of its birth. As part of the centennial observance, several histories of the movement appeared, all of which rightly gave Alexander Campbell the chief place in the formation of the beliefs and commitments of the reformation. Then, in the first half of the twentieth century, scores of studies by Disciples scholars examined, among other things, Campbell's philosophy, political ethics, views of natural religion, preaching, and translation work—many based on theses and dissertations in church history and theology. The centennial of Campbell's death in 1966 and the bicentennial of his birth in 1988 inspired conferences and publications by

---

1. See Cloyd Goodnight and Dwight E. Stevenson, *Home to Bethphage: A Biography of Robert Richardson* (St. Louis: Christian Board of Publication, 1949), 214–24.

Winfred Ernest Garrison (1874–1969) became the most prominent historian of Stone-Campbell history among Disciples, beginning with his 1900 study of Alexander Campbell's theology. He would later write with Alfred T. DeGroot the classic history of the movement, *The Disciples of Christ: A History*. Used with permission from the Disciples of Christ Historical Society, Bethany, West Virginia.

scholars from all parts of the now-fractured movement and beyond who joined to commemorate the work and thought of the person who had shaped the churches in profound but largely unknown ways.

In addition to books, public knowledge of Campbell was expanded through articles in scholarly journals and denominational periodicals. These often focused on specific parts of his work—like his service in the Virginia Constitutional Convention of 1829, his views on education, or his attitudes on race and slavery. In addition, publishers from all segments of the movement kept his major writings in print, including his five debates; *The Christian System*; his masterpiece, *Christian Baptism: With Its Antecedents and Consequents*; and of course, Richardson's *Memoirs*. The point is, no part of Campbell's reformation ever totally forgot him.

As the 1966 anniversary of Campbell's death approached, leading Disciples took action to gain national recognition for Campbell. In 1960, a group made up primarily of prominent Disciples, including then-senator from Texas Lyndon Baines Johnson, petitioned that Campbell be added to the Hall of Fame of Great Americans at New York University, today Bronx Community College of the City University of New York. The same year the officers of the Disciples of Christ Historical Society applied to the United States Post Office Department to have a commemorative postage stamp issued with Campbell's likeness.[2] Neither petition succeeded.

Despite the efforts to keep Campbell's fame alive and explain his continuing significance for the movement and American Christianity, most historians and theological heirs knew little or nothing about him. While church leaders and scholars generally recognized something of his significance, rank-and-file members had no memory of him. Most had no idea why their religious neighbors sometimes called them "Campbellites." Most histories of American Christianity, and even many general histories of the church, at least mentioned Campbell as a founding leader of the Disciples, often identified as the largest indigenous religious body in America.[3]

Internally, the widespread indifference toward Campbell was partly due to the iconoclasm that Campbell himself had promoted. He attacked Lutherans and Calvinists for using human names rather than the name of Christ. He regarded the label "Campbellism" an insult, however appropriate it might have been. Eva Jean Wrather described it this way: "Campbell's insistence that each guard the sovereignty of mind against the dominion of others was successful."[4] A minister in Churches of Christ expressed the

2. "Alexander Campbell May Get Place in National Hall of Fame," *Wellsburg Daily Herald*, May 22, 1960, 1; copy of petition to Post Office Department, Campbell Collection, Disciples of Christ Historical Society, Bethany, West Virginia.

3. The majority treated the story as a part of early nineteenth-century unrest in the American Presbyterian and Baptist churches, and sometimes linked it to the ideas of the Scottish Independents, especially the Sandemanians. See, for example, Kenneth Scott Latourette, *A History of Christianity* (New York: Harper & Brothers, 1953), 1022.

4. Eva Jean Wrather, *Alexander Campbell: Adventurer in Freedom; A Literary Biography*, 3 vols. (Fort Worth: Texas Christian University Press, 2005–2009), 268.

ahistorical attitude that developed in some parts of the movement when he wrote: "I stand fully committed to the view that we can have a New Testament church today without ever having heard of the Stone-Campbell movement. I appreciate what those men did, but my roots are not in that movement. My roots are in the New Testament itself."[5] In other words, Campbell was in his view irrelevant to anything the churches believed and practiced.

Perhaps the theological and social tensions that divided the churches of his movement twice by the middle of the twentieth century also contributed to their ignorance of Campbell. By 1906 Churches of Christ would be listed as a new denomination separate from the Disciples in the *United States Census of Religious Bodies*, and the body known as "The Undenominational Fellowship of Christian Churches and Churches of Christ" would receive a separate entry in the 1971 *Yearbook of American and Canadian Churches*. When Campbell was invoked at all, partisans on all sides claimed him to bolster their positions as the authentic bearers of the ideals of the movement. This was almost always done without a deep knowledge of Campbell's long and complex career. Yet overall, many in all streams of Campbell's movement rejected the relevance of church history and the significance of any individual for shaping their beliefs and attitudes. That attitude has been responsible for a lack of historical consciousness among many members of the churches of the Stone-Campbell tradition then and today.

But there was another part of Campbell's persona that figured into the formation of attitudes toward him and his legacy. Though largely buried underneath the saintly image created by the literature after his death, Campbell exhibited a clearly elitist attitude toward all those he viewed as beneath him intellectually, socially, and economically. William Cooper Howells, who was later active in Ohio politics and became US consul to Quebec City and Toronto, Canada, worked for Campbell as a typesetter in the late 1820s. In his autobiography Howells recalled the general impression people in Bethany and the surrounding area had of Campbell.

> Whatever opinion the people with whom Mr. Campbell came in contact away from home may have had of him, at home and among his neighbors he was regarded as greatly disposed to lord it over his poor and dependent friends. He was pretty hard in dealing, as I found out, and had little natural

5. Lewis G. Hale, "Spirit of Exclusivism, Isolation May Seem Judgmental to Some but Doctrinally Sound," *Christian Chronicle* 59 (January 2002): 31.

sympathy with those who had not or could not acquire a worldly competence. Still his manner was amiable, and socially he was always accessible
to the man who understood the conversational art of listening, especially if
that man liked to hear Mr. Campbell talked of.[6]

Even W. K. Pendleton, in his memorial article following Campbell's
death, alluded to his domination of any conversation he was in. Though
meant to be a compliment to Campbell's brilliance, it clearly reflects his
self-absorption and arrogance.

> Wherever he might sojourn for the night, and during intervals of public
> speaking, throngs would collect to hear him talk; and between these fireside
> and public preachings, his tours would be almost an endless monologue.
> Nobody wished to talk in his presence. His themes were so much out of
> the range of ordinary conversation, that but few people could sustain a
> part in their discussion. A question would sometimes set him agoing, but
> very soon his vast learning, especially in the department of Biblical lore,
> would lead him into wide fields of discourse, all familiar and easy to him,
> but strange and unknown to his hearers; and it was their pleasure to sit in
> silence and learn.[7]

In Campbell's funeral sermon at the Bethany Church of Christ delivered
by Robert Richardson, his friend acknowledged Campbell's attitude of condescension toward his "inferiors," though depicting a much kinder version
than some others.

> There is . . . one trait in his personal character which I must briefly mention
> as one truly worthy of admiration. I mean his condescension to his inferiors.
> Possessed himself of the most splendid abilities; the peer of earth's high-
> est and noblest ones, he was ever wont to receive and address the lowest
> and most ignorant in a manner most courteous and respectful. Realizing
> as he did the innate dignity of that human nature of which the Son of God
> took part, he slighted and repulsed no one, however humble his sphere in

---

6. William Cooper Howells, *Recollections of Life in Ohio, From 1813 to 1840* (Cincinnati:
Robert Clarke Co., 1895), 165.

7. W. K. Pendleton, "Death of Alexander Campbell," *Millennial Harbinger*, March 1866,
134–35.

life, however rude and uncultivated his mind or manners. He had for all a pleasing word; a kindly greeting; and in all a sincere and heart-felt interest.[8]

Richardson added in the *Memoirs*, however, that though Campbell had "great sympathy for the poor and unfortunate, he was cautious in his distributions, and, preferring to retain control of his means, sought, in most cases, to aid his friends by lending rather than by giving." This was one of the ways that Campbell had expanded his property holdings in Ohio and Illinois, taking possession of his friends' land when they were unable to repay the loans he had made them.[9]

Yet despite the arrogance and elitism Campbell showed toward religious enemies and friends, poorer neighbors and employees, it is also clear that when not in the heat of combat, Campbell's spirituality showed forth and demonstrated that he knew what the bottom line of Christianity really was.

I do not substitute obedience to one commandment, for universal or even for general obedience. And should I see a sectarian Baptist or a Pedobaptist more spiritually-minded, more generally conformed to the requisitions of the Messiah, than one who precisely acquiesces with me in the theory or practice of immersion as I teach, doubtless the former rather than the latter, would have my cordial approbation and love as a Christian. So I judge, and so I feel. It is the image of Christ the Christian looks for and loves; and this does not consist in being exact in a few items, but in general devotion to the whole truth as far as known.[10]

There is no company like that with God in private prayer. It elevates and transforms the soul and assimilates it to God. As the natural face of Moses shone when forty days alone in the mount with God, so the moral face and character of every saint brightens as he long communes with God in private prayer and praise.

Next to the beatific vision of God in his own glorious heaven, there is nothing on earth to compare with the pleasures of a soul-absorbing pro-

8. Robert Richardson, "Address at the Funeral Services of A. Campbell," *Millennial Harbinger*, March 1866, 143.

9. Robert Richardson, *Memoirs of Alexander Campbell*, 2 vols. (Philadelphia: J. B. Lippincott & Co., 1868–1870), 1:657–58.

10. Alexander Campbell, "Any Christians among Protestant Parties," *Millennial Harbinger*, September 1837, 412.

tracted interview in prayer with God; or in the celebration of the Lord's supper in the solemn silence of a sincerely pious and well informed Christian community, while in abstract devotion all unite, each in his own bosom, in adoring him who so loved us, "dead in trespasses and sins," as to send his Son, his only begotten and dearly beloved Son, to expiate our sins and to redeem us to himself by the sacrifice of himself, symbolized and set forth in this hallowed institution.[11]

Upon the loaf and upon the cup of the Lord, in letters which speak not to the eye, but to the heart of every disciple, is inscribed, "*When this you see, remember me.*" Indeed, the Lord says to each disciple, when he receives the symbols into his hand, "This is my body broken for *you.* This is my blood shed for *you.*" The loaf is thus constituted a representation of his body—first whole, then wounded for our sins. The cup is thus instituted a representation of his blood—once his life, but now poured out to cleanse us from our sins. To every disciple he says, "For you my body was wounded; for you my life was taken." In receiving it the disciple says, "Lord, I believe it. My life sprung from thy suffering; my joy from thy sorrows; and my hope of glory everlasting from thy humiliation and abasement even to death." Each disciple, in handing the symbols to his fellow-disciple, says, in effect, "You, my brother, once an alien, are now a citizen of heaven; once a stranger, are now brought home to the family of God. You have owned my Lord as your Lord, my people as your people. Under Jesus the Messiah we are one. Mutually embraced in the Everlasting arms, I embrace you in mine: thy sorrows shall be my sorrows, and thy joys my joys. Joint debtors to the favor of God and the love of Jesus, we shall jointly suffer with him, that we may jointly reign with him. Let us, then, renew our strength, remember our King, and hold fast our boasted hope unshaken to the end."[12]

Campbell's nearly six decades of vigorous public leadership played a major role in creating and shaping a significant part of American Christianity during a crucial time in the nation's history. He left a movement with a zeal for Scripture—for restoring the ancient gospel, order, and unity of the prim-

11. Alexander Campbell, "Tracts for the People—No. XXXI. Prayer," *Millennial Harbinger*, January 1849, 9–10.

12. Alexander Campbell, *The Christian System, In Reference to the Union of Christians, and a Restoration of Primitive Christianity, as Plead in the Current Reformation*, 2nd ed. (Pittsburgh: Forrester & Campbell, 1839), 310.

itive church. He left a body committed to intellectual excellence and simple participatory worship, and to evangelism and international missions that would take his cause to most nations of the world by the twenty-first century.

However, he also left behind a movement that embraced, as did he, the myth of white supremacy embedded in the ethos of the United States yet so contrary to the message of Christ. His North American descendants, with few exceptions, defended segregation and subordination of persons of color during the nineteenth and twentieth centuries, and the churches today remain predominately white.[13] The number of majority black congregations overall is fewer than 10 percent, and creating truly multiracial congregations has been a struggle.[14]

Even at the time of Campbell's death, the churches of his legacy had begun to separate and interpret his theological commitments in significantly different ways. After the American Civil War, the economic, social, psychological, and theological differences between Northern and Southern churches, between urban and rural churches, and between American intellectual and anti-intellectual impulses would lead in the twentieth century to two major divisions and dozens of smaller ones. The movement would also continue adapting to new social and cultural contexts as it moved from North America and Great Britain to nations around the world.[15] In the early twenty-first century, the religious movement Alexander Campbell began numbers over three million members in the United States, with estimates of eight million globally.[16]

13. For statistical data, see Carl H. Royster, *Churches of Christ in the United States* (Nashville: 21st Century Christian, 2018); *2018 Yearbook and Directory, Christian Church (Disciples of Christ)* (Indianapolis: General Office of the Christian Church [Disciples of Christ], 2018); *Directory of the Ministry: A Yearbook of Christian Churches and Churches of Christ* (Springfield, IL: Directory of the Ministry, 2018).

14. Multiracial is defined as having less than 80 percent of any single racial group. Michael O. Emerson, "A New Day for Multiracial Congregations," *Reflections: A Magazine of Theological and Ethical Inquiry from Yale Divinity School*, 2013, https://reflections.yale.edu /article/future-race/new-day-multiracial-congregations.

15. D. Newell Williams, Douglas A. Foster, and Paul M. Blowers, *The Stone-Campbell Movement: A Global History* (St. Louis: Chalice, 2013); Gary Holloway and Douglas A. Foster, *Renewing the World: A Concise History of the Stone-Campbell Movement* (Abilene, TX: Abilene Christian University Press, 2015).

16. For statistics, see *2015 Yearbook and Directory of the Christian Church (Disciples of Christ) in the United States and Canada* (Indianapolis: General Office of the Christian Church [Disciples of Christ], 2015); Carl H. Royster, *Churches of Christ in the United States* (Nashville: 21st Century Christian, 2015); *Directory of the Ministry: A Yearbook of Christian Churches and Churches of Christ* (Springfield, IL: Directory of the Ministry, 2014); for international data, see the website of the World Convention of Churches of Christ, http://www

Some who interacted with Campbell in his own day and afterward viewed him as a bad theologian who had stripped the gospel of grace and quenched the work of the Spirit. On the other hand, some revered him as the savior of Christianity, having set right what was amiss in the church. The striking statement of evangelist Samuel Robert Cassius in 1898 reflected the attitude: "Alexander Campbell, that great man of God—for if there has ever been a man in America sent of God, he was one; sent not to start a new religion, but to show men that they were going slowly but surely away from God and heaven, . . . the influence of that man's voice in the wilderness of sin and sectarianism was so loud and far-reaching that it arrested the attention of every denomination and brought them back to the Bible and God."[17]

The fact is, at times Campbell was exasperatingly inconsistent. Members of his movement who appealed to his spiritual authority picked the statements they agreed with and ignored the others. Sectarians and ecumenists alike can find plenty in Campbell's vast writings to inspire and create support for their positions. Those who focused on his rigorous baptismal theology became ultrasectarians—exclusivists who saw the bounds of Christ's church and kingdom as circumscribed and narrow. Others latched on to his open and inclusive statements, especially in the Lunenburg letter articles, and became open and inclusive in their views of the church. Some have even become "evangelical" in the historical sense of those who in the last few centuries detached baptism from salvation as an essential requirement.

Campbell seems to hold together pieces of a paradox—propositions that cannot, according to human reason, be true at the same time—yet they are. He insisted that immersion in water of those with faith in Jesus as the Son of God is the absolutely essential act that brings one out of the kingdom of darkness into the kingdom of light, that saves one from sin, that places one into the saving grace of Christ. Yet he also preached the absolute sufficiency of Christ's sacrifice as the only requirement for the salvation of humankind.

Campbell's complexity in holding together these ideas is exacerbated by his arrogance and his tendency to fall into some of the worst features of the rough-and-tumble religious strife of his day. The point is not that Campbell was uncommonly vitriolic and hateful in his religious controversies. The point is that he conformed completely to the vicious style of religious con-

.worldconvention.org/resources/profiles/59-countries-nations-and-dependencies-with-no-s-c-presence-out-of-254-in-the-world/.

17. Samuel Robert Cassius, *Negro Evangelization and the Tohee Industrial School* (Cincinnati: Christian Leader Print, 1898), 10.

Photo showing Alexander Campbell with three of his children: Virginia (1834–1908), Decima (1840–1920), and William, known as Willie (1843–1917). It was likely taken shortly after his return from Scotland and the tragic drowning of his son Wickliffe in 1847. Used with permission from Bethany College, T. W. Phillips Memorial Library, Archives and Special Collections, Bethany, West Virginia.

flict characteristic of battles between Christians since Athanasius and Tertullian in the early church, the Protestant Reformation, and in the cutthroat free and open marketplace of America.

Alexander Campbell was a complex, brilliant, indefatigable, arrogant, racist, aggressive, prolific leader who made a lasting impact on the Christian world. He was a man whom God used and whom God chastened. His spiritual descendants have inherited every one of his characteristics. They have been passionate for the truth of Scripture and the will of God. They have been tempted and have often succumbed to the arrogance of believing they alone were legitimately struggling to follow God (a belief, however, not unique to Campbell's heirs). A dominantly rationalistic approach to truth resulted in internal divisions within the movement whose name he now shares, ironically, with Barton W. Stone.

Campbell's incessant and remarkable record of evangelistic travel was duplicated in his descendants' relentless longing to take the ancient gospel and order to the world. They sometimes became focused on getting other followers of Christ "right." But the drive also resulted in taking the message of Jesus to millions who were not Christians. Their focus on intellectual rightness sometimes robbed them of the joy of freedom in Christ—yet the power of the gospel Campbell loved and promulgated often broke through the arrogance, to produce some of the loveliest human beings imaginable.

Though he resisted experiential religion because of reliance on the gift of reason and rejection of what he saw as irrational excesses, he did in fact have a rich Christian experience, from his seldom-mentioned "conversion experience" in Ireland to his moments of expressing the love of God and the beauty of community as clearly as anyone has ever done. Such moments of clarity and wisdom are moving and transformative.

People who write biographies are often tempted to begin with a preconceived notion of the ideas they want to promote and then proceed to look for a "usable history" to promote them. I am not free from that tendency. Yet I hope that this treatment of Campbell provides readers with a picture of a gifted yet flawed man driven to discover and follow the will of God and to teach it as he saw it to as many people as he could. That is not a bad desire.

NOTES ON SOURCES

In 1955, the Gospel Advocate Company of Nashville, Tennessee, reprinted the seven volumes of Campbell's first journal, the *Christian Baptist*, resetting the text so that page numbers did not correspond to the originals. I have used page numbers from the original printing from 1823 to 1830 that is available in digital form at http://www.librarything.com/work/1834543 /details/98607620.

Most volumes of the *Millennial Harbinger* are also available in digital form at http://www.librarything.com/work/2254407/details/98607771.

While the *Chicago Manual of Style* requires volume numbers in footnotes for journal articles, the idiosyncratic numbering system Campbell used for his second journal, the *Millennial Harbinger*, has led Campbell scholars to omit volume numbers, using simply the full date. After the first seven volumes, Campbell started over with series 2, volume 1. Every seven years he began a new series starting with volume 1. After Campbell relinquished the journal in 1865, the new editors simply numbered the volumes from the year of the journal's beginning in 1830. The *Millennial Harbinger* ceased publication in 1870.

Many of the nineteenth-century works cited in this study are available online in digital format. Those wishing to examine these original sources should insert the title and date from the footnotes for the desired work into a search engine.

Parts of chapters 1, 2, and 3 are adapted from chapters 1 and 2 of *The Stone-Campbell Movement: A Global History* (St. Louis: Chalice, 2013), by permission of Chalice Press.

INDEX

Titles published in the

LIBRARY OF RELIGIOUS BIOGRAPHY SERIES

*The Religious Life of **Robert E. Lee***
by R. David Cox

***Abraham Lincoln**: Redeemer President*
by Allen C. Guelzo

*The First American Evangelical: A Short Life of **Cotton Mather***
by Rick Kennedy

***Aimee Semple McPherson**: Everybody's Sister*
by Edith L. Blumhofer

*Damning Words: The Life and Religious Times of **H. L. Mencken***
by D. G. Hart

***Thomas Merton** and the Monastic Vision*
by Lawrence S. Cunningham

*God's Strange Work: **William Miller** and the End of the World*
by David L. Rowe

***Blaise Pascal**: Reasons of the Heart*
by Marvin R. O'Connell

*Occupy Until I Come: **A. T. Pierson** and the Evangelization of the World*
by Dana L. Robert

*The Kingdom Is Always but Coming: A Life of **Walter Rauschenbusch***
by Christopher H. Evans

*A Christian and a Democrat: A Religious Life of **Franklin D. Roosevelt***
by John F. Woolverton with James D. Bratt

***Francis Schaeffer** and the Shaping of Evangelical America*
by Barry Hankins

***Harriet Beecher Stowe**: A Spiritual Life*
by Nancy Koester

***Billy Sunday** and the Redemption of Urban America*
by Lyle W. Dorsett

*Assist Me to Proclaim: The Life and Hymns of **Charles Wesley***
by John R. Tyson

*Prophetess of Health: A Study of **Ellen G. White***
by Ronald L. Numbers

***George Whitefield**: Evangelist for God and Empire*
by Peter Y. Choi

*The Divine Dramatist: **George Whitefield**
and the Rise of Modern Evangelicalism* by Harry S. Stout

*Liberty of Conscience: **Roger Williams** in America*
by Edwin S. Gaustad